I0095904

The formidable and prolific journalist and author Linda Goudsmit warns Americans that our beloved country is being sacrificed on the altar of left-wing political correctness, bogus racial theories, and toxic leftism in order to *fundamentally transform* our nation into a socialist/communist welfare state. With scrupulous research and irrefutable documentation, Goudsmit convinces the reader that the *New Normal* is totalitarianism, diametrically opposed to the America our Founding Fathers gave us nearly 250 years ago. Combatting this sinister globalist plot is imperative, she says, by aggressively opposing it with knowledge, vigilance, and preparation. Goudsmit advises that America's freedom clock is ticking down toward zero. I advise every freedom-loving American to read this amazingly prescient and important book.

—**Joan Swirsky, R.N.,** former longtime journalist for the *New York Times* and author/co-author of 12 books, www.joanswirsky.com

Having written extensively on the globalist agenda, I find *Space Is No Longer the Final Frontier—Reality Is* to be an essential contribution to the 'field.' Here, Linda Goudsmit connects many dots that have hitherto remained unconnected—including transgenderism, transhumanism, and the infiltration and takeover of the educational system. Goudsmit's focus on the assault on childhood by the globalist 'elites' is particularly alarming and necessary to recognize. We are under siege. At stake is the foundation of civilization itself, beginning with the human mind. Be forewarned and forearmed.

—**Michael Rectenwald, Ph.D.,** author; public speaker; former Distinguished Fellow, Hillsdale College; former Professor of Liberal Studies and Global Studies, NYU, www.michaelrectenwald.com

This new book by Linda Goudsmit hits the nail on the head. Her focus on what is happening to our children in government schools is especially critical, as the situation will continue to deteriorate unless and until Americans deal with this existential threat. *Space Is No Longer the Final Frontier—Reality Is* should be mandatory reading for anyone who wants to understand what is happening to America—and how to fix it!

—**Alex Newman,** award-winning international journalist, educator, education reformer, author, speaker, consultant, radio host, CEO Liberty Sentinel Media, www.libertysentinel.org

Linda Goudsmit's latest work gives timely warning to all who value their freedom and want to make sense of seemingly unconnected events—events that, nevertheless, lead to a recognizable goal. She has identified the enemies—many of whom some of us read about and forgot over decades of recent history. It will be up to the rest of us to reject the Globalist and Transhumanist Manifesto(s) out of hand. When Nuremberg-style tribunals convene to try those who attempted a soft conquest of humanity, Linda Goudsmit will be the star witness for the prosecution.

—**Terry A. Hurlbut,** editor and publisher, *Conservative News and Views*, host, Declarations of Truth podcast, author, *The Terra Prime Series* (*Matthew's Run, Matthew's War,* and *The Admiral's Choice)*, www.cnav.news

In this powerful book, Linda Goudsmit unravels the Globalist plot to take down the West. With meticulous research, she exposes how the primary target of the globalist predators is America's children and how generations of teachers trained in Marxist methods have become ideological soldiers for progressive education. This treasonous scheme to weaponize education could never have succeeded without the partnership of the U.S. government. The realization that the planned demolition of America has been in effect for over 100 years is overwhelming.

Linda explains how globalism is a replacement ideology that seeks to reorder the world into one singular, planetary Unistate, ruled by the globalist elite themselves, and believes that the Great Reset is the greatest humanitarian hoax ever conceived. This book is essential reading.

—**Valerie Price,** Founder of ACT! For Canada, www.actforcanada.ca

Linda Goudsmit's latest book, *Space Is No Longer the Final Frontier—Reality Is*, is possibly her most brilliant. Each chapter takes you on a stunning journey, unveiling elements of a coordinated, comprehensive, well-planned, well-funded, globalist War on America that is targeting the nation's children and collapsing the U.S. from within. You think you know a lot about globalism until you read this insightful, piercing exposé. Goudsmit explains how we are being led into a planetary managerial Unistate by the globalist elites who want you to believe there is no objective reality, only extreme solipsism. You will want to see how this turns out, and how to change the course of events.

—**Maureen Dowling,** owner/editor, Independent Sentinel, www.independentsentinel.com

From Linda Goudsmit you can expect relentless research and compelling clarity. She's always a pro.

—**Bruce Deitrick Price,** author, artist, poet, education reformer, www.Lit4u.com

Linda Goudsmit is a prolific and astute writer who thoroughly understands the plight of the United States. Her prior books, *Dear America: Who's Driving the Bus?*, *The Book of Humanitarian Hoaxes: Killing America with 'Kindness'*, and *The Collapsing American Family: From Bonding to Bondage*, clearly demonstrate her knowledge of why and how our great nation is losing its competitive edge in the world. She "pulls back the curtain" for her readers by spelling out very clearly the unpleasant truths about our society. When we destroy the family, babies, education, and morality, a society collapses from within. I really enjoy how Linda dispels the myths and illusions permeating our society, and provides her readers with the unvarnished truths about solving the nation's problems.

—**Brian Massie,** A Watchman on the Wall, publisher, *Lobbyists for Citizens*, a 501(c)(4) Non-Profit, www.lobbyistsforcitizens.com

With her unique ability to observe, analyze, and reduce to simple terms complex events unfolding in our world today, in *Space is No Longer the Final Frontier—Reality Is*, author Linda Goudsmit delves into the origins of the transformation of American education from one emphasizing individualism, personal accomplishment, and meritocracy, to deep investment in the Marxist idea of collectivism, groupthink, and unreality.

An author with a rapidly growing number of books to her credit, including the 14-volume children's book series *Mimi's Strategy*, Goudsmit illustrates the means by which the political left has captured the American educational apparatus and, over time, conducted a psychological battle for children's minds with the goal of creating compliant societal imbeciles who will be easily controlled by a burgeoning globalist cabal with an unquenchable thirst for power.

In the introduction, Linda outlines precisely why she wrote the book and what she hopes to accomplish in the chapters that follow. Dealing with a different contributing factor to the educational metamorphosis currently manifesting itself, Goudsmit deftly exposes the "globalist" agenda which seeks to eradicate national borders, national sovereignty, and individual identity to achieve its goal of "*one singular, planetary Unistate, ruled by the globalist elite.*"

This book is a must-read for all concerned about America's future and that of her children, who will become tomorrow's leaders. As Goudsmit contends, "The radical leftist/Marxist War on America is a sinister effort to shatter objective reality and destroy critical-thinking skills. When critical thinking is destroyed and a society is reduced to childish emotional thinking, that society is easily exploited."

—**Sharon Rondeau**, editor, *The Post & Email*, www.thepostemail.com

Linda Goudsmit has been releasing chapters of her upcoming new book, *Space Is No Longer the Final Frontier—Reality Is.* This is a tremendous undertaking and should be required reading in every college and university in America. It should also be translated into Spanish, French, German, Italian, and RUSSIAN, the latter to make its way into the population by underground operations that have been in place since the Soviet era.

Linda Goudsmit should be offered a place in our State Department once Donald Trump wins his second term this coming November. All of her articles are "professional grade," and each one is a learning experience.

—**Charlotte Ann Baker,** conservative editor, aggregator-distributor, and commentator

Linda Goudsmit has masterfully outdone herself. In a world unable to recognize reality, or embrace principle, evil despots are now inflicting *"psychological, informational, asymmetric warfare to destabilize Americans and drive society out of objective reality into the madness of subjective reality."* In grand artistry, Linda has created a clear-cut Chiaroscuro, sprouting forth great clarity in a dark Marxist Hegelian quagmire of dialectical manipulation. The Western world needs to wake up quickly…or perish into oblivion. This book is a significant *countermeasure* in the arsenal required to understand and eradicate the *synthesis of threats* that the West and our nation now confront internally and externally. Bravo, Linda!

—**Dr. Scott Keller (DSS),** President, Strategic Synergies Inc.–Europe (SSI–E)–Fighter-Town LLC

.

SPACE
IS NO LONGER
THE FINAL FRONTIER

REALITY IS

LINDA GOUDSMIT

CONTRAPOINT PUBLISHING
ST. PETE BEACH, FL

Copyright ©2023 by Linda Goudsmit

Publication date 2024

Contrapoint Publishing
St. Pete Beach, FL
contrapointpublishing.com

All rights reserved. Published in the United States of America by Contrapoint Publishing. No part of this publication may be reproduced, stored in a retrieval system, or transmitted in any form or by any means, electronic, mechanical, photocopying, recording, scanning, or otherwise, without the prior written permission of the author.

Limit of Liability/Disclaimer of Warranty: This publication is designed for entertainment purposes only. It is sold with the understanding that neither the author nor the publisher is engaged in rendering legal, investment, accounting or other professional services. While the publisher and author have used their best efforts in preparing this book, they make no representations or warranties with respect to the accuracy or completeness of the contents of this book and specifically disclaim any implied warranties of merchantability or fitness for a particular purpose. No warranty may be created or extended by sales representatives or written sales materials. Neither publisher nor author shall be liable for any loss of profit or any other commercial damages, including but not limited to special, incidental, consequential, personal, or other damages.

Space Is No Longer the Final Frontier–Reality Is

ISBN: 978-1-953255-27-3 Paperback
ISBN: 978-1-953255-29-7 Hardcover
ISBN: 978-1-953255-28-0 ePub

Library of Congress Control Number: 2023915836
Printed in the United States of America

FIRST EDITION

Designer: Baris Celik

To my beloved husband, Rob

you are the sun in my morning,

the moon at night,

and every moment in between.

CONTENTS

ACKNOWLEDGMENTS

To Rita Samols, whose gifts extend far beyond her extraordinary professional editing skills. I am deeply grateful for her friendship and steadfast personal commitment to the content of this book.

To Baris Celik, my gifted designer, with heartfelt appreciation for his exceptional talents and unwavering patience.

With profound gratitude to the men and women whose work I have quoted within these pages. Their couragous search for truth has informed me, inspired me, and given me hope that freedom can prevail. Knowledge is power, and truth is the most powerful knowledge of all.

We are fast approaching the stage of the ultimate inversion:

the stage where the government is free to do anything it pleases,

while the citizens may act only by permission;

which is the stage of the darkest periods of human history,

the stage of rule by brute force.

—Ayn Rand, *Capitalism: The Unknown Ideal*

xx

PREFACE

Space Is No Longer the Final Frontier—Reality Is

Dear America,

I am writing with a sense of urgency, because the political timer that measures our country's lifespan as a sovereign nation is ticking toward zero. In 1776 our Founding Fathers declared our independence from Great Britain and proposed establishing the United States of America as an independent federation of states. This particular form of government was carefully chosen to repudiate Great Britain's binary, monarchical sociopolitical infrastructure of rulers and ruled. Our forefathers decisively and categorically rejected the supremacist mindset of the British aristocracy and its monarchy.

The Declaration of Independence states unequivocally:

> We hold these truths to be self-evident, that all men are created equal, that they are endowed by their Creator with certain unalienable Rights, that among these are Life, Liberty and the pursuit of Happiness—That to secure these rights, Governments are instituted among Men, deriving their just powers from the consent of the governed—That whenever any Form of Government becomes destructive of these ends, it is the Right of the People to alter or to abolish it, and to institute new Government.

Almost one hundred years later, in 1863, Lincoln's Gettysburg Address affirmed our founding principles:

> Four score and seven years ago our fathers brought forth on this continent, a new nation, conceived in Liberty, and dedicated to the proposition that all men are created equal.
>
> Now we are engaged in a great civil war, testing whether that nation, or any nation so conceived and so dedicated, can long endure. We are met on a great battlefield of that war. We have come to dedicate

a portion of that field, as a final resting place for those who here gave their lives that, that nation might live. It is altogether fitting and proper that we should do this.

But, in a larger sense, we cannot dedicate—we cannot consecrate—we cannot hallow—this ground. The brave men, living and dead, who struggled here, have consecrated it, far above our poor power to add or detract. The world will little note, nor long remember what we say here, but it can never forget what they did here. It is for us the living, rather, to be dedicated here to the unfinished work which they who fought here have thus far so nobly advanced. It is rather for us to be here dedicated to the great task remaining before us—that from these honored dead we take increased devotion to that cause for which they gave the last full measure of devotion—that we here highly resolve that these dead shall not have died in vain—that this nation, under God, shall have a new birth of freedom—and that government of the people, by the people, for the people, shall not perish from the earth.

Today, 248 years after its founding, our nation faces the greatest challenge to its existence as a sovereign nation of the people, by the people, and for the people. American history records many catastrophic events in seismic terms. The United States of America survived the Great War, 1914–1918; the Great Depression, 1929–1939; the Great Drought, 1930–1940; and the global conflict of World War II, 1939–1945. Today, in 2024, We the People must stand for freedom once again, or we may not survive the Great Reset—globalism's War on America. This book focuses on the American experience, but the Great Reset is an existential threat to the entire world order and world population. It is a global war on humanity and on individual sovereignty.

Globalism is NOT to be confused with global trade, the import and export of goods and services across international boundaries. Globalism is a political ideology that seeks to *replace* the existing world order of sovereign nations with a supranational, planetary "Unistate" and a one-world government. The globalist elite advancing this ideology are the Western financial behemoths who already control most of the production and distribution of the world's resources, its goods and services, monetary systems, and political systems.

The globalist war on the world's nation-states cannot succeed without collapsing the United States of America. The long-term *strategic* attack plan moves America incrementally from constitutional republic to socialism to globalism to feudalism. The *tactical* attack plan uses asymmetric psychological and informational warfare to destabilize Americans and drive society out of the objective world of FACTS into the madness of the subjective world of FEELINGS.

Asymmetric warfare is commonly understood to mean small rebel forces or insurgents against a standing army. In the 21st century, however, it is the globalist elite who are waging asymmetric warfare against nation-states and their civilian populations. A small band of unelected megalomaniacs are warring *openly* against nation-states to destroy their national sovereignty, and *surreptitiously* against the sovereignty of individuals to destroy their psychological ability to test reality. The primary target of these globalist predators is America's children, because children are the future of the world.

In an information war, data is the weapon, and the globalist elite already control the content of both the mainstream media and the educational curriculum. This disproportionate advantage is a consequence of the staggering economic power and excessive influence of globalism's leadership.

Globalists recognize neither individual nor national sovereignty. Globalism's planetary Unistate is one-world population, one-world nation, one-world government, one-world language, one-world currency, one-world bank, one-world education, one-world culture, one-world customs, one-world ethic, one-world morality, one-world norm, one-world health organization, one-world court, one-world law, and one-world military police enforcing one-world compliance.

The globalist campaign for one-world government is facilitated by the United Nations and its extensive network of international institutions, entities, special agencies, and organizations; the World Economic Forum, a global platform for public-private cooperation, and its thousands of public-private partnerships; and non-governmental organizations worldwide. The globalist leaders are the managerial elite who control trillions of dollars in assets, the world's elite industrialists, and the world's elite bankers. Together, they have formed an international alliance to merge the world's sovereign nation-states into one planetary nation—ruled by themselves.

The Great Reset is the globalists' seismic scheme to fundamentally transform America from a constitutional republic to a system of feudalism. We live in the digital era of computers, and people understand the word *reset* in computing terms to mean removing all data from a device and restoring it to its original manufacturer settings, represented by the numeral 0. The Great Reset proposed by the globalist enemies of sovereign states cancels all individual financial debts and financial assets, and resets the existing balance sheet to zero.

In practical terms, what this means is that all personal and business debts are canceled. Home loans, personal loans, business loans, student loans, car loans, mortgages, credit card debt, any and every purchase made on credit in any form is canceled. WOW! That sounds great! The problem, of course, is that financial *assets* are also canceled. Americans bedazzled by the enticement of a debt-free life do not realize they forfeit their freedom when they have no financial assets. The shift from capitalism to "managerialism" is the shift from personal independence to perpetual dependence on the state. Freedom is not free.

Managerialism is an entirely foreign concept to most people. It is not capitalism and it is not communism; it is not any *ism* most people have ever heard of. It is 21st-century feudalism. American philosopher and political theorist James Burnham presented the theory of managerialism in his 1941 classic, *The Managerial Revolution: What Is Happening in the World.*[1] Burnham, a former Marxist, rejected Marxism as the inevitable future of capitalism, and theorized that an unaccountable managerial class of technological elites would replace the existing class of capitalist elites.

Globalism is a political ideology rooted in managerialism, and its feudal manifestation is the planetary Unistate. There are no political parties in managerialism, and no alternate political ideologies or philosophies are permitted. The world is reorganized as a planetary corporation—the managerial Unistate.

So, why does the Great Reset cancel personal and business debts? Because cancellation of debt abolishes private property, which is the foundation of personal freedom, personal agency, and individual sovereignty. Resetting the financial ledger to zero cancels capitalism and awards the globalists absolute control over every aspect of human life. It transforms America into a binary sociopolitical structure of rulers and ruled—feudalism. All goods and services are owned and managed by the globalists and distributed according to your compliance with globalism's new currency: Environmental, Social, and Governance (ESG) scores, determined by the globalist elite. The *New Normal* is a cashless, digital, totalitarian, planetary managerial Unistate.

What this means is that government bureaucrats have the power to allot to you all the goods and services they deem necessary, in the amounts they deem necessary. They tell you where you can live, what you can buy, if you can be educated, where you will go to school, and what you will study. Everything you now decide for yourself will be decided for you by the centralized government, because it owns everything and you own nothing.

Like children, Americans are being seduced into the car of a stranger with political candy. The stranger is globalism, and the deceitful slogan describing its *New Normal* is one of the biggest lies of the 21st century: *You will own nothing and be happy.* The Great Reset totally and completely regresses adult life back to a nightmarish existence of infantile dependence for survival upon the government and governmental dictates. The world's people are indentured serfs, all serving the corporation in exchange for food, water, shelter, clothing, medicines, etc., etc., etc., every material and physical need. They own nothing but, contrary to globalist promises, they are definitely NOT happy. It is a *managed* economy and a *managed* life on a planetary scale. The word *managerialism* is the "soft" word for absolute totalitarianism, just as socialism is the soft word for communism. Managerialism is totalitarianism on steroids.

The megalomaniacs intent on imposing the Great Reset are sociopaths who have no respect or regard for any human lives other than their own. Anyone who is actually foolish enough to believe globalism's promise of "happiness" might want to consider whether medieval serfs were happy in their servitude.

Our forefathers fought and died to give Americans the most precious of all gifts: freedom. Americans today must gather their courage and defeat the globalists' War on America, understanding that our children are their primary target, because children are the future of our nation and every nation on Earth. I write to fight for the children because the children cannot fight for themselves.

America's freedom clock is ticking. The imperious, supremacist mindset that created the Great Reset is the same aristocratic mindset that our Founding Fathers rejected in 1776. Once again, Americans must stand together against tyranny in defense of freedom. To save our constitutional republic, we must reject globalism and the Great Reset. We the People must defeat the enemies of freedom in order to preserve individual and national sovereignty for our nation's children. They are the spoils of this war.

Most sincerely,

Linda Goudsmit

USA 2024

INTRODUCTION

Freedom Is an Adult Enterprise

The purpose of this book is the defense of America's children.

The globalist War on America is a war of attrition. I am 76 years old. My generation of American patriots is dying. My children's generation of indoctrinated millennials is transitional. My grandchildren's generation is the targeted prey for the globalist predators. Everyone else is just in the way.

Children are the future of every society on Earth, and the youngest children are globalism's primary target. The battlefronts for children's minds are education, medicine, and the media. This axis of collaboration seeks to separate children from the protection of their parents and psychologically groom them to become compliant citizens in globalism's New World Order, without their parents' knowledge or consent. Psychological warfare is attempting to change the way children think and process information, while simultaneously eliminating parental authority. It is an attempt to change the hearts and minds of America's children.

My goal is to raise public awareness about globalism's asymmetric psychological and informational War on America, on the American family, and most specifically, on America's precious children. Globalists have already infiltrated America's education industry and weaponized education in order to shatter families, destroy children's individual identities, including their sexual identities, and replace parental authority with governmental authority. Schools are the combat zones and teachers the vanguard for indoctrinating America's children.

The future of America lies in the ability of our nation's children to become rational, autonomous, psychological adults with the critical-thinking skills required to preserve our constitutional republic. For this reason I wrote a children's book series, *Mimi's Strategy*.[2] The books are my personal commitment and patriotic effort to teach young children the critical-thinking skills that will protect them, empower them, and ensure American freedom for generations to come.

As I look back over the last several years, it is clear to me that Dr. Anthony Fauci's COVID-19 political medicine protocols and the Biden regime's lawless anti-American policies are both orchestrated, coordinated tactical operations in globalism's War on America. Their interrelated domestic policies have been instrumental in weakening the national economy, national security, national defense, public health, and military readiness, while simultaneously strengthening America's commitment to globalism's internationalized mandates that comport with the United Nations' 17 Sustainable Goals and Agenda 2030, and the World Health Organization's centralized international control.

Political medicine protocols and the Biden regime's policies both utilize the tactical methodology of fear-based psychological regression. Why fear-based? Because fear is arguably the most mobilizing and destabilizing human emotion. If you frighten people enough, you can get them to believe and do almost anything.

Consider Voltaire's famous remark, "Those who can make you believe absurdities can make you commit atrocities." Now consider some of the absurdities Americans accepted as facts during the COVID-19 madness: the necessity for lockdowns, masking, social distancing, school closures, business closures, church closures, social isolation, and especially acceptance of the COVID-19 *vaccines that are not vaccines*. In fact, COVID-19 jabs are experimental gene-altering mRNA treatments that were never properly tested for safety, require continuous boosters, and are now being given to babies!

When politicized medical absurdities are accepted as medical science, atrocities are committed in the name of science. So, when parents surrender their authority and common sense to the "experts" and are convinced of the efficacy of these medical absurdities, the parents commit atrocities against their own children with the help of their doctors and therapists, who are actually ideologues, not doctors and therapists. Parents force their young children to be jabbed and wear masks that restrict oxygen and are entirely useless against viruses. Why? Because parents are frightened.

I discussed the psychodynamics of fear and regression in the philosophy book I wrote years ago, *Dear America: Who's Driving the Bus?*,[3] but at the time I didn't recognize its political implications or applications. Now I do. My last book, *The Collapsing American Family: From Bonding to Bondage*,[4] exposes the relentless attacks on nuclear families as the primary tactical strategy in globalism's War on America. The family must be destroyed in order to collapse America from within and impose the Great Reset. The *New Normal* replaces family bonding with feudal bondage in globalism's managerial Unistate, and promises "you will own nothing and be happy." The closing line in *The Collapsing American Family* warns the nation: "Space is no longer the final frontier—reality is."

Using the last line for its title, my current book explores the dynamics, dimensions, destructiveness, and methodology being used to advance globalism's War on America. Freedom is an adult enterprise. A nation of children and childish adults cannot sustain itself. Globalism's War on America is psychological warfare. I apply the universal behavior paradigm introduced in *Dear America: Who's Driving the Bus?* and present the argument that the success of globalism's War on America depends on its ability to regress chronological adults back to childish psychological functioning, and to prevent America's children from acquiring psychological adulthood.

I will explain why space is no longer the final frontier by explaining how globalism's objective is beyond the colonization of space; it is the colonization of the human mind on Earth in order to establish absolute totalitarian control over the world's population. The entire globalist war effort is an unconscionable attempt to disconnect people from objective reality and drive them to madness in subjective reality, where they can be easily controlled.

Objective and subjective reality are opposing prisms through which we perceive and process information. The traditional metric for sanity and mental health is the degree to which an individual is in touch with objective reality, the world of facts. Someone who is delusional, insisting that he is a purple octopus, lives in subjective reality and is considered mentally ill.

The globalists' psychological warfare embraces subjective reality and its supporting theory of relativism, which deems every perception a matter of opinion, not facts. The War on America replaces America's standard of objective reality with Woke (American Marxism discussed at length in Chapter 11) and its myriad narratives, all of which support relativism.

Historically, the term "woke" meant to be "aware" of discrimination, disenfranchisement, and mistreatment of blacks, particularly in America. The term became associated with Black Lives Matter and the 'Social Justice' movement after the 2014 Michael Brown police shooting in Missouri. Woke has since evolved into a binary subjective prism of oppressor and oppressed used to view, measure, and effect social change. Wokeness has been weaponized.

Its most recent iteration and absurdity is *Sanism*, defined by Woke as "unjust privileging" of sanity over insanity. In the madness of woke subjective reality, sanity and insanity are equivalent.

Education, medicine, and media are working collaboratively, using misinformation, disinformation, and censorship to fundamentally transform America. The psychological objective of all three is to replace the prism for reality-testing from objective to subjective reality.

Understanding fear and regression is essential for effectively opposing globalism's War on America. Fear is an essential human survival mechanism that causes us to withdraw from threatening situations. Fear is also a psychological defense mechanism that can be exploited. On one end of the fear continuum is a person so frightened that he or she curls up in a fetal position screaming, and on the other end is a Navy SEAL. SEALs are not superhuman; they are rational adults trained to resist psychological regression under the most dire and extreme circumstances.

Let's consider the hysteria that surrounded the COVID-19 coronavirus and its political purpose. First, over 99 percent of people who got COVID-19 recovered, so prolonging mandated face masks, social distancing, school closures, business closures, church closures, social isolation, and acceptance of the COVID-19 *vaccines that are not vaccines* made no sense whatsoever. The COVID-19 policies were not appropriate responses to the threat of COVID-19 based on the facts.

When things don't make sense, something else is going on. A useful tool for understanding the motive is looking at the result. Who benefited from the ongoing and extreme COVID-19 restrictions? The globalists, of course! Globalists command the War on America, finance the radical leftist Democrats, own the mainstream media, and support the 'Republicans in Name Only' (RINOS), all of whom are attempting to collapse America from within. Follow the money and the entire strategy becomes clear.

For clarity, let's also consider the state of mind of childhood. Young children live exclusively in the NOW, in the present tense, in the immediate moment, driven by immediate gratification without a concept of past or future.

Why is this important? Because the radical leftist Democrats and their globalist handlers are attempting to regress chronological adults back to childish thinking, where they can be easily manipulated and controlled. It is a sinister and intentional exploitation of the NOW-time thinking of childhood. It is a psychological operation, a PSYOP.

The NOW-time lens of childhood has political implications. Consider the unconscionable political medicine advanced by the corrupt Centers for Disease Control and Prevention (CDC) and the equally corrupt World Health Organization (WHO). Their directives made sense only to psychologically regressed adults. Instead of rejecting the nonsensical politicized medicine of these two organizations, the regressed public submitted. They obediently wore their masks, observed social distancing, accepted business, school, and church closures, got jabbed, got their children jabbed, and got boosted… some of them repeatedly. They naively trusted that the CDC/WHO protocols were necessary to protect themselves, their children, and the nation.

Living in the NOW-time of childhood requires immediacy. Needs must be immediately gratified. Children cannot wait. Fear, whether real or manufactured, must be quelled immediately. Critical-thinking skills are needed to inform adult decisions. Instead, the regressed population accepts what it is told unquestioningly and, metaphorically, hides under the bed. In this instance, they hide behind masks and social distancing, hoping the threat will disappear. Their compliance is rewarded with repetitive virtue-signaling assurances that *we are all in this together*, a particularly manipulative phrase that exploits children's fears of abandonment.

The deliberate disinformation and wildly exaggerated mortality projections spread by the CDC and WHO were orchestrated by the globalist elite who run both organizations. Their coordinated narratives were political medicine disguised as medical science.

If Americans understand how and why we have been misled, we can discipline ourselves to reject the manipulative fearmongering. We can remain rational adults and defy the regression-PSYOP seeking to return us to childhood compliance. We must aspire to be Navy SEALs and reject the sinister attempts to reduce us to the mental state of small children. How do we accomplish this?

Knowledge is power. Our ability to defeat globalism requires an understanding of the basic psychodynamics of behavior. The more we understand the motivations for our behavior, the more we are empowered to control our behavior, improve our lives, and defeat the psychological warfare that seeks to destabilize and destroy us. I will elaborate.

Close your eyes and imagine a big yellow school bus. Now imagine the seats filled with passengers. The question is "Who's driving the bus?" Would you let a toddler drive the bus? Would you let a five-year-old? What about an angry teenager? Or would you insist that a rational adult be at the wheel? As you picture the bus in your mind, remember that the common goals of political medicine, the Biden regime, and the overarching globalist War on America require a frightened child at the wheel. Psychological regression is the war's strategy, and fear is its tactical weapon.

The human growth process has both physical and psychological components. We all grow up physically; it takes no effort and is outside our control. Chronological age is an uncontested biological accomplishment. *Psychological* growth is another matter entirely. The demands of responsible adults trying to draw us out of our state of infantile self-absorption (narcissism) rage against our regressive desire to remain children. We resist psychological growth. We struggle with the wish to become powerful, independent adults and the longing to remain powerless, dependent children. We demand the freedom that belongs to responsible adults, yet we are nostalgic for a time of complete dependence when we were nurtured entirely.

Growing up psychologically is the universal challenge of childhood. The psychological growth process is a difficult struggle, but it always involves a choice. It is impossible to become a responsible adult without choosing to relinquish the irresponsibility of childhood.

If we understand the growth process and the complexities of the human mind, we can be more effective in meeting the challenge. A state of mind is not fixed. It is constantly shifting along the growth continuum, from total infantile narcissism to responsible adulthood, depending upon the level and stability of the individual's inner development and the strength of the external pressures challenging it.

We are each the whole of our life experiences. The children we once were continue to exist inside our minds. So, the narcissistic infant; the demanding two-year-old; the insecure adolescent; the rebel; the adventurer; the happy child; the angry, frightened, timid, or lonely child we once were all persist as states of mind. Each inner child is an accessible entity that seeks to be in control of the individual's mind. The inner child's struggle for power continues to challenge the individual's rational adult state of mind throughout his or her lifetime.

Let's return to the big yellow school bus and understand that the bus is a metaphor for our psychological selves. The bus travels along the timeline that is our lifetime. It picks up new passengers as we grow and develop, each new feeling and each new experience adding another rider. The driver of the bus is always selected from the passengers aboard, and the passengers are constantly competing to determine who will drive the bus. To understand how one person can perceive us in a completely different way from how another sees us, we must ask ourselves the seminal question, "Who's driving the bus?"

When the seats are occupied by the different roles that compose our adult lives, the answer is not too challenging. The driver is mother, father, husband, wife, boss, sister, cousin, friend, employee, or employer. The list is as long as the varying roles we each have in daily life. The complication and challenge come because also riding on the bus are all the inner children of our past, each vying for control.

Sustaining our most rational adult state of mind is the challenge for preserving our constitutional republic, because freedom is an adult enterprise. So, what is the best strategy for sustaining psychological adulthood?

Children universally begin life in a natural state of total narcissism, and they do not give up this state of being without a struggle. That is why growing up psychologically is so difficult and painful. Each individual grapples with his or her own competing desires for growth and regression, and also with society's demands for growth.

Historically, the three supporting pillars of American life—family, faith, and flag—cooperated to encourage emotional growth and the development of independent, autonomous, rational adults, psychologically equipped to preserve our precious American freedoms. Not anymore. The globalist War on America seeks to collapse America from within by encouraging regression.

The education industry obstructs the development of critical-thinking skills in children by teaching them *what* to think, not *how* to think. The media's ceaseless fearmongering narrative is destabilizing and regresses chronological adults back to emotional childhood and a more primitive state of mind before critical-thinking skills were developed.

Thought precedes behavior. If the responsible adult relinquishes his rational state of mind to any one of his young inner children, he will behave in the regressive, self-absorbed pattern that characterizes early childhood. He will be living in childhood's NOW-time. It is a dangerous mindset because his young inner child has not yet developed the critical-thinking skills required to evaluate information rationally and assess consequences. In this circumstance, it is imperative that the individual recognize that he has surrendered to the regressive demands of an inner child. If he can discipline himself to ask himself "Who's driving the bus?" he can visualize his growth continuum, identify his inner child, and respond appropriately. He can shift his state of mind from regressive, narcissistic child to responsible adult. It is an act of volition. It is a choice, and it is a learned skill.

The responsible adult knows that it is imperative to keep his most developed state of mind operative. We have established in our imaginary exercise that no rational adult would permit a toddler or young child to make the decisions required to drive the bus. Likewise, only the psychological adult is able to repel the globalist efforts to regress him to a childish state of being where he can be easily controlled. The globalists are fighting an asymmetric psychological war, and our strategic defense is to arm ourselves with the required knowledge to fend them off. Knowledge really is power.

It is very difficult for the civilized mind to comprehend the absolute malevolence of globalism's War on America. My hope is that this book helps people accept the reality that we are a world at war. Acceptance is the first and most essential step in opposing globalism's objectives and tactical strategies.

Please note: the repeating opening paragraph of each chapter in this book is a reminder for the reader to process the content of every chapter within the context of asymmetric psychological and informational warfare. Remembering that we are a world at war makes sense of the nonsensical and reduces the cognitive dissonance that psychological warfare is designed to produce. We must discipline ourselves to remain psychological adults in our everyday lives. Parents, in particular, must be psychological adults in order to protect their children, who cannot protect themselves.

CHAPTER 1

What Is Reality?

Globalism is a replacement ideology that seeks to reorder the world into one singular, planetary Unistate, ruled by the globalist elite. The globalist war on nation-states cannot succeed without collapsing the United States of America. The long-term strategic attack plan moves America incrementally from constitutional republic to socialism to globalism to feudalism. The tactical attack plan uses asymmetric psychological and informational warfare to destabilize Americans and drive society out of objective reality into the madness of subjective reality. America's children are the primary target of the globalist predators.

What is reality? *Objective* reality is the world of facts. *Subjective* reality is the world of feelings. Objective reality is the fulcrum of human sanity, the foundation of ordered liberty in our constitutional republic. Senator Daniel Patrick Moynihan famously remarked, "Everyone is entitled to his own opinion, but not to his own facts." Opinions are based on feelings; facts are based on actuality. Feelings are not facts.

The ideological moorings of ordered liberty require consensus on what is real. This is no small matter. Language is based on such consensus. Laws are based on such consensus. Without agreement on what is real, there is no societal order; there can be only chaos. It is for this reason that globalists support the leftist Culture War on America and its attack strategy to replace factual, objective reality with subjective multiple realities based on feelings.

Canadian biological psychologist Dr. David Nussbaum captures the multi-dimensional destructiveness of the attack on reality in his precise, unambiguous, succinct definition of *Woke*:

> Woke is a Culturally Acquired Psychotic Disorder denying reality in any fashion that will undermine traditional Western societies, values, and positive identity to help destroy them from within. (David Nussbaum, personal communication, July 2023)

There are iatrogenic diseases in medicine, and Dr. Nussbaum has explicitly described the politically motivated culturally acquired psychosis that is convulsing America. Woke is a *psychoweapon* that is driving sane people out of objective reality into the madness of subjective reality. Woke is a humanitarian hoax.

I discuss what I call humanitarian hoaxes in my 2020 release, *The Book of Humanitarian Hoaxes: Killing America with 'Kindness'*.[5] A humanitarian hoax is the deceitful tactic of presenting a destructive policy as altruistic. The humanitarian huckster presents himself as a compassionate advocate when in fact he is the disguised enemy. Hoax 23 in my book discusses "The Humanitarian Hoax of Multiple Realities":

> The leftist Culture War on America is attacking the ideological strivings and ideological moorings of ordered liberty by attacking its most basic requirement—consensus on what is real. My article "Birdman and the Reality Revolution" exposes the leftist attack strategy seeking to replace factual, objective reality with subjective multiple realities based on feelings. This is how it works.
>
> Tom, a thirty-year-old, 6'2" white male, FEELS like a fifty-year-old, 5' Asian woman named Tuyen. Shall society accept Tom's self-identification as Tuyen? Existing laws in society are based on a consensus of what is real. Conservatives insist that Tom is a thirty-year-old, 6'2" white male no matter how Tom feels. The Left demands that society accept Tom as the fifty-year-old, 5' Asian woman Tuyen—Tom *is* Tuyen because Tom *feels* as if he is Tuyen.
>
> The Left is demanding that Tom's feelings be accepted as fact. What if Tom self-identifies as George Soros? Would über-leftist George Soros accept Tom's self-identification and allow Tom to live as the actual George Soros? I think not. What is instantly apparent is that the leftist demand for society to accept self-identification as fact has serious limitations and convenient self-serving exclusions.
>
> The hypocrisy of the self-serving exclusions is obvious. If Tom can be Tuyen in a ladies' bathroom, why can't Tom be George Soros at the bank? If self-identifying is not universally applicable, why is the Left so insistent that it become normative? If you want to know the motive, look at the result.

The goal of the radical leftist campaign to have feelings accepted as facts is the Humanitarian Hoax of Multiple Realities designed to disrupt our ordered liberty. As described in my article "The Mathematics of the Culture War on America,"[6] if the Left can shatter the reality-based foundation of language and laws, then it has succeeded in shattering our ordered liberty and the morality that supports it. The laws that govern Western society by mutual consent reflect a reality-based consensus on what is right and what is wrong. In America it is both illegal and morally wrong to impersonate another human being. That is because in our ordered society each individual owns his selfness and the rights to his own property.

Our Founding Fathers dreamed a society consistent with psychiatrist Lyle Rossiter's notion of the innate bipolar nature of man—his individualism and his need for mutual consent. Dr. Rossiter's theory on the nature of man, discussed in Hoax 21, "The Humanitarian Hoax of Collectivism," affirms that unless a man is living on a desert island by himself, his survival requires mutual consent for living with others on the island. So it is in modern society. Harmonious living requires both individualism and mutual consent. The most basic requirement for both is ownership of one's self and one's property.

Collectivism denies ownership of one's self and one's property and is, therefore, inconsistent with the fundamental nature of man. Collectivism awards all ownership to the state. The collectivism being sold to America by humanitarian hucksters avoids this inconvenient truth. It disingenuously promises egalitarian social justice and income equality, but without individualism and mutual consent there are only masters and slaves....

The globalist dream of a one-world government cannot come true without first destroying America's consensus on what is real. English aristocrat Lord Bertrand Russell, member of the globalist political elite, detailed the shameless strategy in his shocking 1952 classic, *The Impact of Science on Society*:[7]

> Education should aim at destroying free will so that pupils thus schooled, will be incapable throughout the rest of their

lives of thinking or acting otherwise than as their school-masters would have wished.... Influences of the home are obstructive; and in order to condition students, verses set to music and repeatedly intoned are very effective.... It is for a future scientist to make these maxims precise and to discover exactly how much it costs per head to make chil-dren believe that snow is black. When the technique has been perfected, every government that has been in charge of education for more than one generation will be able to control its subjects securely without the need of armies or policemen. (pp. 27–28, Routledge Classics, 2016 edition)

The first step in the sinister effort to make people believe that snow is black is the acceptance of multiple realities—the acceptance as real that Tom is really Tuyen. Multiple opinions, multiple experi-ences, and multiple perspectives can be debated in a free society. But without an accurate reference to test reality, there is only madness, chaos, and disorder. America is split between those still insisting upon a standard of objective reality and those demanding subjective reality. Freedom and ordered liberty require the infra-structure of objective reality. (*The Book of Humanitarian Hoaxes: Killing America with 'Kindness'*, pp. 87–90)

The Great Reset is the greatest humanitarian hoax ever conceived. It is glo-balism's stupefying War on Humanity that requires psychological regression in order to succeed.

Psychological warfare subdues the enemy without destroying the physical infrastructure of society. It replaces brute force with mind control, shat-tering consensus on what is real by denying the existence of objective reality.

CHAPTER 2

The Art of Psychological Warfare

Globalism is a replacement ideology that seeks to reorder the world into one singular, planetary Unistate, ruled by the globalist elite. The globalist war on nation-states cannot succeed without collapsing the United States of America. The long-term strategic attack plan moves America incrementally from constitutional republic to socialism to globalism to feudalism. The tactical attack plan uses asymmetric psychological and informational warfare to destabilize Americans and drive society out of objective reality into the madness of subjective reality. America's children are the primary target of the globalist predators.

Parents must adopt a wartime mentality in order to understand and challenge the dangerous government policies affecting their children. Globalist strategists base their tactical plans and operational goals for their War on America on Chinese military strategist Sun Tzu's *The Art of War*.[8] The differences between Sun Tzu's strategies of the 6th century BC and 21st-century globalist psychological/informational warfare are the advances in science and technology available to implement the weapons of mass social engineering and mass psychological destruction today.

Modern psychological warfare (PSYWAR) and psychological operations (PSYOPS) utilize the 21st-century digital environment and its integrated communications landscape to communicate and coordinate censorship, disinformation, and misinformation. The hearts and minds of unsuspecting viewers are being manipulated with websites, cloud servers, search engines, social media outlets, mobile apps, audio, video, podcasts, webinars, and even immersive digital environments using artificial, interactive, computer-generated scenes. Information wars are 21st-century propaganda wars, foundational to PSYWAR and PSYOPS because the information presented is socially engineered to produce a desired political effect.

The following quotations from Sun Tzu's *The Art of War* can be interpreted today to show that COVID-19 was a medical PSYOP, with real and lethal consequences.

> *Engage people with what they expect; it is what they are able to discern and confirms their projections. It settles them into predictable patterns of response, occupying their minds while you wait for the extraordinary moment—that which they cannot anticipate.*

Americans have always trusted their doctors, expecting them to honor the Hippocratic Oath that protects every patient. In late fall 2019 when the Wuhan virus first appeared, it was simply inconceivable to the American public that their trusted doctors, and the government medical institutions doctors rely upon for information, would deliberately participate in political medicine, which is not and never was about public health. The public expected honesty and protection.

As more and more information came out about the misinformation, disinformation, and wildly exaggerated projections of the dangers of COVID-19, Americans clung to the fiction that their doctors, the Centers for Disease Control and Prevention (CDC), National Institutes of Health (NIH), National Institute of Allergy and Infectious Diseases (NIAID), and World Health Organization (WHO) were honest medical practitioners and agencies.

On March 11, 2020, the WHO declared COVID-19 a pandemic. That was the extraordinary moment when Americans, including then-President Donald J. Trump, were fooled into believing that political medicine was honest medical science. President Trump initiated Operation Warp Speed, and under the influence of Drs. Anthony Fauci, Deborah Birx, and Robert Redfield, Trump made the catastrophic decision to shut down America's booming economy. Americans continued to believe political medicine's biggest lie, that experimental mRNA jabs were vaccines that would provide immunity to COVID-19 and prevent transmission of the virus. Americans stood in line for jabs for themselves and their children, wore masks, stayed home, and remained convinced that these policies were designed and essential for public health.

The lies began to unravel early in 2021, but the public remained compliant. Honest doctors and scientists around the world tried to warn the people that the COVID-19 policies and protocols were political medicine, not honest medical science. They warned of the dangers of mRNA jabs and were publicly disparaged, fired, and sometimes jailed. Eventually they were vindicated when it became clear that the mRNA injections were not vaccines because they neither provided immunity nor prevented transmission. In fact, the jabs compromised the immune systems of the people they were promised to protect, but political medicine's damage had already been done.

As the catastrophic effects of the policies and protocols were slowly revealed, many people were understandably furious. Yet many more clung to the illusion that masking, social distancing, and more mRNA jabs would protect them. People were dying in hospitals after getting the jabs. Young, healthy athletes were dropping dead after getting the jabs. Still, people clung to subjective reality and the lies the CDC, NIH, NIAID, and their own doctors continued to spew. The COVID-19 propaganda war was extraordinarily effective. It duped an entire nation.

The supreme art of war is to subdue the enemy without fighting.

The whole COVID-19 debacle, its restrictions, protocols, and relentless, coordinated fearmongering campaign, was psychological warfare designed to create public demand for a vaccine. The globalist strategists knew the public would never willingly allow themselves and their children to be jabbed with untested, experimental, gene-altering mRNA injections. They needed to be forced into subjective reality, where they would stand quietly in line for the jabs they believed would protect them and their families from the dreaded coronavirus. And so it was that a terrorized civilian population was *subdued without fighting.*

The CDC approval of experimental mRNA jabs for babies and young children was the ultimate malfeasance of political medicine's participation in globalism's war on children. On July 5, 2022, Medicare.gov sent an email addressed to seniors saying, "Talk with your family about getting the little ones vaccinated. In case you missed it, CDC now recommends COVID-19 vaccines for everyone 6 months and older, and boosters for everyone 5 years and older. COVID-19 vaccines are safe and effective at preventing children from getting seriously sick." Medicare and the CDC knowingly and deliberately misrepresented the known facts and advised seniors to persuade their adult children to have their grandchildren jabbed!

The untested, lethal jabs continued to be endorsed, boosters were recommended, annual jabs were discussed, and then Sun Tzu's *that which they cannot anticipate* happened. On October 21, 2022, the CDC Advisory Committee on Immunization Practices (ACIP) voted unanimously to add the Pfizer and Moderna mRNA COVID-19 jabs to the already bloated immunization schedules for children and adolescents who attend public schools. This action effectively mandated COVID-19 jabs for virtually every child in America.

The primary responsibility of parents is to protect their children and ensure their survival. In the 21st century, parents must protect their children from the malevolence of deceitful globalists who intend to physically destroy them.

> *All warfare is based on deception.*

The Biden regime is a globalist enemy of the state, seeking to shatter American sovereignty and replace our constitutional republic with globalism's planetary managerial Unistate. This enemy within is the most dangerous enemy because so much of the general public lives in subjective reality, unable or unwilling to believe that our own government is deliberately collapsing our American society.

> *The whole secret lies in confusing the enemy, so that he cannot fathom our real intent.*

The public may be confused, but globalist strategists live in *objective* reality and are not confused. Globalism seeks to replace the current system of independent sovereign nations with a one-world Unistate and planetary governance. One-world government, often referred to as the Great Reset and the New World Order, is a totalitarian state that breaches every conceivable boundary. The singularity imagined by globalist technocrats fuses humanity into one nation, one race, one language, one culture, one religion, one digital currency, one digital ID, one educational curriculum, and even one gender.

Parents must fulfill their primary responsibility and protect their children from the grasping globalists. They must reject subjective reality and embrace objective reality in order to recognize globalism's threat to their children. Grandparents must stand up proudly for freedom and ordered liberty in our constitutional republic. If parents and grandparents do not rigorously oppose the globalist takeover, our nation's children will become 21st-century serfs in globalism's planetary feudal order of rulers and ruled. Remember, the globalists live in objective reality, and in life, objective reality always prevails.

CHAPTER 3

Birdman and the Reality Revolution

Globalism is a replacement ideology that seeks to reorder the world into one singular, planetary Unistate, ruled by the globalist elite. The globalist war on nation-states cannot succeed without collapsing the United States of America. The long-term strategic attack plan moves America incrementally from constitutional republic to socialism to globalism to feudalism. The tactical attack plan uses asymmetric psychological and informational warfare to destabilize Americans and drive society out of objective reality into the madness of subjective reality. America's children are the primary target of the globalist predators.

The ability to distinguish between fact and fantasy is an essential survival skill. If a man believes he can fly and jumps off a twenty-story ledge, he falls to his death because gravity is a fact, an objective truth. Birdman's fantasy, a subjective reality, cannot compete with the objective reality of gravity.

Let's break down the process of thinking and doing. Thinking is a private matter and human beings are free to think their thoughts at any time in any place. Birdman is free to *think* he can fly, without consequence to himself or others. It is the moment he steps off the ledge that his subjective reality collides with objective reality.

Adults and children are evaluated differently in society. The fantasies of children are an accepted part of the growth process. In a sane society, adults out of touch with reality are deemed insane. In our example, Birdman would be considered insane.

Civil society and the laws that govern it are based on the acceptance of objective reality by that society's citizens. What would happen if there was a movement that deliberately rejected the teaching of objective reality and taught subjective reality instead? What would be the purpose of driving a society insane?

Remember, the ability to distinguish between fact and fantasy is a survival skill, because thought precedes action. Birdman *thought* he could fly and jumped to his death. Critical thinking is the objective analysis of facts in order to form a judgment. It is the foundation of rational thought and essential in an adult society.

Society's acceptance of objective reality is what made America great, powerful, and undefeatable in World War II. At the end of the war, however, America's enemies did not go quietly into the night. They reconstituted themselves to fight another day, in another way.

America's enemies simply put down their guns, picked up their books, and concentrated on the future. They studied the human mind and decided to exploit the existence of the unconscious to defeat America psychologically. The strategic goal was to infantilize Americans. Children's psychological growth would be paralyzed with educational indoctrination that interrupted their developing critical-thinking skills. Adults would be pressured out of the adult world of objective reality and regressed back into the childish world of feelings.

Vladimir Lenin infamously said, "Give me four years to teach the children and the seed I have sown will never be uprooted."

The leftists have taken a page out of Lenin's communist playbook and indoctrinated two generations of Americans toward collectivism using public/private education, along with mainstream media including television programming and movies. The radical leftist/Marxist War on America is a sinister effort to shatter objective reality and destroy critical-thinking skills. When critical thinking is destroyed and a society is reduced to childish emotional thinking, that society is easily exploited.

In order to stop the radical leftists/Marxists, we need a Reality Revolution. This Revolution would restore objective reality by dismantling the infrastructure of subjective reality that has been established since the end of World War II.

In objective reality, the striving to become an adult, with all its attendant responsibilities, is rewarded with the freedom of adulthood. Children are not free in any society—they are dependent upon their parents/caretakers or the government. The choice between the collectivism offered by socialism/

communism, and the individualism offered by the constitutional republic envisioned by our Founding Fathers, is the choice between childhood dependence and adult independence. It is the difference between servitude and freedom.

What young people in America need to understand is that the *promise* of socialism is never the *reality* of socialism. Cradle-to-grave government care exacts an exorbitant price. When you accept the powerless position of childhood for the rest of your life, the government happily appropriates your freedom and liberty. In socialism/communism you become a permanent ward of the state.

Americans who proudly wear Che Guevara T-shirts display their ignorance. Real people living in actual communist countries risk their lives escaping TO the real freedom of America. No one is trying to escape FROM Miami to Havana. The romanticized version of socialism/communism propagandizing American students is subjective reality.

These young people need to consider the reality of collectivism, but they must be in *objective* reality in order to do so. Otherwise, like Birdman, they will think they can fly. The death of Birdman is the metaphorical death of freedom.

CHAPTER 4

The WHO and the WHAT of Behavior

Globalism is a replacement ideology that seeks to reorder the world into one singular, planetary Unistate, ruled by the globalist elite. The globalist war on nation-states cannot succeed without collapsing the United States of America. The long-term strategic attack plan moves America incrementally from constitutional republic to socialism to globalism to feudalism. The tactical attack plan uses asymmetric psychological and informational warfare to destabilize Americans and drive society out of objective reality into the madness of subjective reality. America's children are the primary target of the globalist predators.

hildren are easily controlled because they live in the world of feelings, subjective reality. They have not yet developed the critical-thinking skills required to survive in the adult world of objective reality.

In a society of ordered liberty, stealing is a crime regardless of who the thief is. Stealing is the WHAT of the crime, the thief is the WHO. Blind justice evaluates behavior according to WHAT was done, not WHO did it, ensuring that no one is above the law. When blindfolds come off and tribal norms of identity politics take over, justice is the casualty.

This distinction is foundational in a constitutional republic and is extremely important for two reasons. First, blind justice is a dramatic departure from the binary sociopolitical infrastructure of rulers and ruled that supports a two-tiered system of justice, one for the rulers and one for the ruled. In a government of the people, by the people, and for the people, the goal is one system of justice for all.

Second, distinguishing between the WHAT and the WHO separates childish feelings, which focus on the WHO, from adult, rational thinking that focuses on the WHAT. Children view authority figures through the unquestioning, trustful eyes of dependence.

If a society can be pressured to remain in or regress to childhood, its citizens remain stalled in an emotional world, accepting what they are told because they never developed the critical-thinking skills needed to question information. A *regressed* society is the unaware, compliant population made famous by the leaked emails of Hillary Clinton's 2016 presidential campaign.

In October 2016, the whistle-blowing website founded by Australian computer programmer Julian Assange, WikiLeaks, released emails that included a March 13, 2016, email written by Democrat strategist Bill Ivey of Global Corporate Strategies to Clinton campaign chief John Podesta. Ivey was worried that Hillary's personality could not compete with political rival Donald Trump's mastery of TV. Ivey worried that Trump could win and disrupt Democrat plans "to produce an unaware and compliant citizenry"! The following are Ivey's own shocking and reprehensible words:

> And as I've mentioned, we've all been quite content to demean government, drop civics *and in general conspire to produce an unaware and compliant citizenry.* The unawareness remains strong but compliance is obviously fading rapidly. This problem demands some serious, serious thinking—and not just poll driven, demographically-inspired messaging.

Identity politics, another name for "progressive" politics, is tribal. Like children, tribalism evaluates behavior according to WHO is doing something, not WHAT is being done. If you are a member of their group, your behavior is defended, no matter how antisocial or criminal. Consider the matter of political medicine—a prime example of identity politics.

On June 11, 2021, in an interview with MSNBC's Chuck Todd, Dr. Anthony S. Fauci, then director of the National Institute of Allergy and Infectious Diseases (NIAID) and head of the COVID-19 response in America, made the outrageous claim that any attack on him was an attack on science. Really? Anthony Fauci is a man who, factually, is *not* science. Science is science. To believe that a man is science is to accept subjective reality as objective reality.

As the lies and malfeasance of Anthony Fauci's political medicine at the

NIAID were revealed, globalism's digital environment and its integrated communications landscape, including search engines (Google) and social media such as Facebook and Twitter with their own "fact checkers," went into action to support subjective reality. The globalists protected Fauci by manipulating the search engines, censoring social media content and closing down oppositional accounts, and declaring any views opposing CDC protocols to be misinformation or disinformation that required censoring.

Political medicine is the vehicle for globalism and its megalomaniacal ambition to rule the world. In a stunning article published by The Gateway Pundit[9] on October 24, 2022, Jim Hoft interviewed whistleblower Dr. Andrew G. Huff. Dr. Huff, former vice president of EcoHealth Alliance, reported directly to Dr. Peter Daszak, president of EcoHealth, a U.S.-based nonprofit, non-governmental organization. Daszak is a British doctor who sent monies approved by Anthony Fauci to fund the Wuhan research labs in Wuhan, China. Dr. Huff came forward with proof in his September 12, 2022, Report[10] to the U.S. Congress in which he stated unequivocally that "the COVID virus that killed millions and resulted in mass starvation and global economic recession was created in a Wuhan laboratory."

Dr. Huff's evidence, submitted under penalty of perjury, completely disproved Fauci's insistence that the coronavirus jumped from bats to humans and therefore was a natural occurrence. During his interview with Jim Hoft, quoting from Hoft's article,

> Dr. Andrew Huff explains how EcoHealth used funding by Dr. Tony Fauci and the NIAID to fund the gain of function research that developed the COVID-19 virus in a Wuhan lab.
>
> Dr. Andrew Huff has the receipts and sent his evidence recently to leaders in Congress.
>
> Dr. Huff told The Gateway Pundit the government then tried to cover this up. They still are covering this up.
>
> Dr. Andrew Huff is a key player in exposing the truth of Dr. Fauci, EcoHealth, Dr. Daszak, and their funding of deadly gain of function projects.

The government then tried to cover this up and are still covering it up. Political medicine is not and never was about public health. Globalism's tribal identity politics shields political medicine and its practitioners from the public scrutiny that would expose WHAT practitioners did, and from the court system that should bring them all to justice. Drs. Anthony Fauci and Peter Daszak belong in prison.

The globalist War on America is an information war that uses the digital environment to manipulate and socially engineer the public to become "unaware and compliant," to quote Bill Ivey in his email to John Podesta, above.

From kindergarten through college, young Americans are encouraged to remain perpetual children. In primary school they are disingenuously told they are all butterflies (subjective reality). Butterflies are a universal metaphor for growth, transformation, and effortless adult competence. The false butterfly narrative denies the reality that the human growth process is twofold, and psychological growth necessarily involves relinquishing the irresponsibility of childhood. The butterfly metaphor ignores individual differences, abilities, and achievements. It discards meritocracy, eliminates competition, discourages individual achievement, and encourages collectivism. Awarding titles and trophies without merit is crippling. By the time they reach college, these butterflies are so fragile they require safe spaces and Play-Doh to hide from opposing ideas. A childish, dependent population is precisely what the globalists need in order to destroy our constitutional republic.

America is at a crossroads, and whoever prevails in globalism's ruthless war on reality will determine our future. The battle for reality is a battle that patriotic Americans must win. Only fully actualized, rational adults, insistent upon transparency and accurate facts, have the power to oppose this attack on America. We must demand psychological growth and a commitment to objective reality in our nascent Reality Revolution. We must embrace the responsibilities of adulthood and encourage critical-thinking skills in our children in order to defeat the malevolent globalist plan to keep Americans paralyzed in eternal childhood.

CHAPTER 5

America Requires an Education Revolution

Globalism is a replacement ideology that seeks to reorder the world into one singular, planetary Unistate, ruled by the globalist elite. The globalist war on nation-states cannot succeed without collapsing the United States of America. The long-term strategic attack plan moves America incrementally from constitutional republic to socialism to globalism to feudalism. The tactical attack plan uses asymmetric psychological and informational warfare to destabilize Americans and drive society out of objective reality into the madness of subjective reality. America's children are the primary target of the globalist predators.

Critical thinking is the objective analysis of facts in order to form a judgment. It is the foundation of rational thought. Critical thinking depends upon accurate information, specifically facts, and therefore relies upon objective reality. The ability to remain in objective reality is threatened when disinformation, misinformation, fiction, and fantasy (all forms of subjective reality) are presented as fact. It is impossible to make an informed decision without an accurate source of information.

Reading is the essential foundational skill individual citizens use to access information and make informed decisions. Together, reading, writing, and arithmetic are the communication tools that equip children with *agency*. Understanding the psychological concept of agency is extremely important to our discussion. Encyclopedia.com[11] defines and discusses agency:

> The concept of *agency* as a psychological dimension refers to the process of behaving with intentionality. Human beings exercise agency when they intentionally influence their own functioning, environments, life circumstances, and destiny. To posit that human beings have agency is to contend that they are self-organizing, proactive, self-regulating, and self-reflecting rather than reactively shaped by environmental forces or driven by concealed inner impulses.

Reading provides agency for learning because textbooks, including math and science textbooks, require the ability to read. Reading provides a sense of independence, accomplishment, and self-sufficiency. Competence is the mother of self-esteem, and learning to read is a seismic shift in a child's perception of self. The child begins to feel his or her power. Encyclopedia. com continues:

> To exercise human agency, people must believe in their capability to attain given ends. These *self-efficacy* beliefs are the foundation of human motivation, well-being, and accomplishment. Whatever other factors serve as guides and motivators, they are rooted in the core belief that one has the power to effect changes by one's actions, that one's locus of control is internal rather than external. This is because unless people believe that their actions can produce the outcomes they desire, they have little incentive to act or to persevere in the face of difficulties.

Truth-in-lending laws exist to provide consumers with informed consent. Surgical consent forms and food labels equip patients with information to make informed decisions about their health. Product labeling, food labeling, Material Safety Data Sheets (MSDS)—all are attempts to provide consumers with the accurate information necessary to make informed decisions. Laws and labels acknowledge the existence of conflicts of interest and are attempts to level the playing field. What happens when Johnny can't read them?

The educational battlefield is grooming children for life without agency in the globalist Unistate. In 2021, education reformers Samuel Blumenfeld and Alex Newman published a stunning book, *Crimes of the Educators: How Utopians Are Using Government Schools to Destroy American Children.*[12] The book describes the intentional exploitation of public education to dumb down American students and condition them for life in a socialist state:

> The plan to dumb down America was launched in 1898 by socialist John Dewey, outlined in an essay titled "The Primary-Education Fetich." In it he showed his fellow progressives how to transform America into a collectivist utopia by taking over the public schools and destroying the literacy of millions of Americans. The plan has

been so successfully implemented that it is now a fact that half of America's adult population are functionally illiterate. They can't read their country's Declaration of Independence. They can't even read their high school diplomas.

The method of achieving this was simply changing the way children are taught to read in their schools. The utopians got rid of the intensive phonics method of instruction and imposed a look-say, sight, or whole-word method that forces children to read English as if it were Chinese. The method is widely used in today's public schools, which is why there are so many failing public schools that cannot teach children the basics. This can only be considered a blatant and evil form of child abuse. (*Crimes of the Educators*, p. xii)

Blumenfeld and Newman explain:

Brain scans now prove beyond a doubt that the sight, or whole-word, method of teaching reading creates dyslexia and functional illiteracy by forcing children to use their right brains to perform functions designed for their left brains. Deliberately impairing a child's brain ought to be a punishable offense. (*Crimes of the Educators*, p. xiv)

Globalist John Dewey (1859–1952), American philosopher, psychologist, and educational reformer, is considered the father of "progressive" education. I put the word *progressive* in quotation marks because the effort to dumb down our nation is entirely *regressive*, precisely the opposite of progressive.

Dewey understood that socialism could not be imposed on America by force, and he advised his followers that change must come slowly. In his infamous 1898 essay, "The Primary-Education Fetich,"[13] Dewey described America's insistence upon high literacy as a "false educational god" that worships "language-study":

This is language-study—the study not of foreign language, but of English; not in higher, but in primary education. It is almost an unquestioned assumption, of educational theory and practice both, that the first three years of a child's school life shall be mainly taken up with learning to read and write his own language.

Blumenfeld and Newman elaborate:

> In America, the greatest, the richest, and freest nation on earth, the imposition had to be subtle, slow, patient, and "democratic." The primary vehicle for this change would be the public schools, where the dumbing-down process could be carried out without parents knowing what was being done to their children. (*Crimes of the Educators*, pp. 2–3)

> The only way to undermine the capitalist system was to get rid of the emphasis primary schools placed on the development of high literacy and independent intelligence. Why? Because both of these sustain individualism. What was needed, they believed, was a new curriculum that emphasized socialization and taught children to read by a whole-word method that would lower the nation's literacy level and make its children more amenable to collectivist values. (*Crimes of the Educators*, pp. 1–2)

> To Dewey, the greatest obstacle to socialism was the private mind that seeks knowledge in order to exercise its own private judgment *agency* and intellectual authority. High literacy gave the individual the means to seek knowledge independently. It gave members of society the means to stand on their own two feet and think for themselves. This was detrimental to the "social spirit" needed to bring about a collectivist society. (*Crimes of the Educators*, p. 5)

Dewey attacked the emphasis on reading, writing, and arithmetic in young children at the time. The "3Rs," the foundational skills that produce highly literate, independent, rational adult individualists, were in conflict with Dewey's collectivism. Dewey advocated a seismic shift in American education that focused on socialization and group interactions to promote a collectivist mentality for life in a socialist America. Dewey's hopes for reconstructing America were resurrected in Barack Obama's collectivist promise to "fundamentally transform America."

John Dewey and his co-conspirators deceitfully presented the shift to teaching reading with sight-words as an advancement in American education. Dewey knew that reading was the foundational skill for acquiring knowledge. He knew his reading program was inferior to the traditional phonics method, but he insisted it was superior. And his deceit was believed by educators for decades.

It wasn't until 1955, when American educator Rudolph Flesch published his stunning exposé, *Why Johnny Can't Read: and what you can do about it*,[14] that the general public had any idea of the disastrous effects of the whole-word teaching method. Even then, it was inconceivable to Americans that whole-word instruction was a deliberate attack on America's children.

According to Sun Tzu, "All warfare is based on deception. Practice dissimulation and you will succeed." The insistence on the benefits of teaching reading with sight-words instead of phonics, disseminated by leftist politicians and embraced by the National Education Association, the largest teachers' union in America, is a weapon of war. Adding insult to injury, it is the U.S. taxpayers who are funding the Department of Education and its inexcusable insistence on whole-word instruction. Deliberately dumbing down children is weaponized, politicized education, and it is an act of war against the United States of America.

Like the chilling success of political medicine, the educational battlefront has been stunningly successful because trusted experts in education continue to promote the lie that whole-word reading instruction promotes literacy.

> Americans cannot believe that our professional and highly respected educators could be involved in a conspiracy to deliberately dumb down the nation. They recognize that we are indeed being dumbed down, but they don't blame the educators. They blame the children and the culture. In short, this conspiracy is protected by incredulity. (*Crimes of the Educators*, p. 29)

The globalist War on America being fought in government schools has made an Education Revolution necessary. Comprehensive education reform is required to finally eliminate *progressivism*'s catastrophic sight-word reading method and its resulting school-induced dyslexia from American schools. Truth in education, like truth in lending, must be demanded in order to provide the American public with accurate information to make decisions about their and their children's future.

Weaponized education has weakened America through illiteracy and individual lack of agency. A life without agency is a life without freedom.

CHAPTER 6

"An Unaware and Compliant Citizenry"

Globalism is a replacement ideology that seeks to reorder the world into one singular, planetary Unistate, ruled by the globalist elite. The globalist war on nation-states cannot succeed without collapsing the United States of America. The long-term strategic attack plan moves America incrementally from constitutional republic to socialism to globalism to feudalism. The tactical attack plan uses asymmetric psychological and informational warfare to destabilize Americans and drive society out of objective reality into the madness of subjective reality. America's children are the primary target of the globalist predators.

W e have discussed the weaponization of education in American schools and its sinister political objective to eliminate high literacy, individual agency, and independent intelligence. Dr. Dennis Cuddy, historian and political analyst, wrote an extraordinary article published on *NewsWithViews*, April 26, 2021, "An Unaware and Compliant Citizenry."[15]

Cuddy documents the seismic shift in public education's mission, from teaching basic skills and foundational knowledge to teachers acting as agents of social change and teaching political activism. The following are excerpts from the article:

> The Clintons' and others' efforts to "produce an unaware and compliant citizenry" began with the National Education Association (NEA), whose President Catherine Barrett wrote in the February 10, 1973 edition of SATURDAY REVIEW OF EDUCATION:
>
> "Dramatic changes in the way we will raise our children in the year 2000 are indicated, particularly in terms of schooling.... We will need to recognize that the so-called 'basic skills,' which currently represent nearly the total effort in elementary schools, will be

taught in one-quarter of the present school day.... When this happens—and it's near—the teacher can rise to his true calling. More
than a dispenser of information, the teacher will be a conveyor of
values, a philosopher.... We will be agents of change."

Via values clarification techniques, the values of students were to
be changed to situation ethics.... In the 1980s, Hillary Clinton
along with David Rockefeller, Jr. and others became Board members of Carnegie's National Center on Education and the Economy
(NCEE), with Mario Cuomo chairman and N.C. Governor Jim Hunt
vice-chairman. The president of the NCEE was Marc Tucker, who
right after Bill Clinton won the presidency in November 1992 wrote
a letter to Hillary Clinton saying this would give them a chance to
implement their "cradle-to-grave" plan for all Americans.

The following year, at the July 2–5, 1993 NEA's national convention,
President Clinton addressed the delegates and thanked the NEA
for "the gift of our assistant secretary," referring to long-time NEA
activist Sharon Robinson, who became U.S. Assistant Secretary of
Education for the Office of Education Research and Improvement
(OERI, where I had worked in the Reagan administration). President Clinton went on to say that he believed his goals for America
closely parallel those of the NEA, further stating: "And I believe that
the president of this organization would say we have had the partnership I promised in the campaign of 1992, and we will continue
to have it.... You and I are joined in a common cause, and I believe
we will succeed." On December 15, 1993, EDUCATION WEEK
reported that "Debra DeLee, the former director of governmental
relations for the NEA, has joined the Democratic National Committee as its executive director." ...

During the 1990s and the Clinton presidency, Outcome-Based Education (OBE) was being emphasized. Its father was William Spady,
who said OBE took three forms: Traditional (not very different
from former educational practices), Transitional (where education
would transition to the final goal of), Transformational Education,
which emphasized changing children's values.

As parents became more aware of what OBE was trying to do, it ran into increasing disfavor, and the planners of our future had to come up with a different tactic. Therefore in 2008, the Hunt Institute (named for formerly mentioned N.C. Governor Jim Hunt) at N.C. State University began to develop what would come to be known as the Common Core (CC) curriculum. It would not take long for parents to realize that CC was not benefiting many students, causing them to not reach proficiency on the National Assessment of Educational Progress. The population would become increasingly "dumbed down" as former Reagan administration OERI member Charlotte Iserbyt called them. This has resulted in "an unaware citizenry," which has become more and more manipulable or "compliant" (giving up some freedoms after the 9/11 attacks, and now taking COVID-19 vaccine shots apparently every year, etc.).

Education is a business, and every business has a business model. When the business of education in America functioned from its original mission of teaching basic skills and foundational knowledge, it had meritocracy as its infrastructure, competency and achievement as primary objectives, and the protection and preservation of our constitutional republic as its goal.

The weaponization of education for political gain is facilitating former president Barack Obama's pledge to fundamentally transform the United States of America. Obama's Marxist business model completed the shift of American education, institutionalizing government schools as the agents of change committed to transforming America from a constitutional republic to a socialist society.

The globalist social engineers in charge of America's education business model will then use socialism's centralized government control to move America from socialism into globalism's totalitarian planetary Unistate, 21st-century feudalism. How will this be accomplished? The answer lies in an extraordinary unclassified report from the Defense Documentation Center for Scientific and Technical Information. The report, written by Don D. Bushnell, submitted on March 27, 1963, is titled "The Effects of Electronic Data Processing in Future Instructional Systems."[16] It is a stunning document and an essential reference. The report is available in its entirety online.

Please keep in mind that Bushnell was reporting on the future capabilities of computer technology for education and its potential application to change attitudes. Bushnell's 1963 report forecast the exploitation and weaponization of American education today.

Of particular interest for our discussion are pages 3 and 4 under the heading "Effortless Learning, Attitude Changing, and Training in Decision Making":

> In 1960, Dr. S. Seshu, Professor of Electrical Engineering at Syracuse University, conceived of the penultimate teaching machine as an electronic transducer or input system which transfers factual information stored on punched cards or magnetic tape directly into human memory. This would be accomplished without preliminary processing of the information by the visual or aural senses. "All that we need to do," suggests Seshu, "is find the input terminals in the human brain and the necessary code—the gadgetry is trivial." His contention is that the basic trouble with the teaching machine or any modern learning method, is that the input is fed in at the wrong place. When the input to the brain arrives visually or aurally, it is often distorted or lost in the transference process. What is needed is a transducer capable of transferring information to the human memory with the same ease and accuracy of data being transferred into the memory of an IBM 7090. Recognizing the major barriers yet to be surmounted by the physiological psychologist, it is conceivable that such a machine may eventually exist. The question arises: should the effortless learning machine teach beyond the limits of factual data? IF the student can assimilate information without error, shouldn't the teacher also steep him in the culture, train him in the proper professional attitudes, and thoroughly ground him in the scientific method as a way of life? It is difficult to know where the responsible instructor would leave off in the use of this effective tool.

Another area of potential development in computer applications is the attitude-changing machine. Dr. Bertram Raven, in the Psychology Department at the University of California at Los Angeles, is in the process of building a computer-based device for changing attitudes. This device will work on the principle that students' attitudes can be effectively changed by using the Socratic method of asking an appropriate series of leading questions logically designed to right the balance between appropriate attitudes and those deemed less acceptable. For instance, after first determining a student's constellation of attitudes through appropriate testing procedures, the machine would calculate which attitudes are out of phase and which of these are amenable to change. If the student was opposed to foreign trade, for example, and a favorable disposition were sought, the machine would select an appropriate series of statements and questions organized to right the imbalance in the student's attitudes. The machine, for instance, would have detected that the student liked President Kennedy and was against the spread of communism; therefore, the student would be shown that JFK favored foreign trade and that foreign trade to underdeveloped countries helped to arrest the communist infiltration of these governments. If the student's attitudes toward Kennedy and against communism were sufficiently strong, Dr. Raven would hypothesize that a positive change in attitude toward foreign trade would be effectively brought about by showing the student the inconsistency of his views. There is considerable evidence that such techniques do effectively change attitudes. The question arises: what is the appropriate subject material, or "attitudes," in this instance, with which to indoctrinate the student?

One further example: At the Catholic University of America in Washington, D.C., a psychological research program is underway to study the problems of training a student in decision-making skills. A special purpose computer and display equipment will present the student with a series of numerical problems designed to test the student's ability to make good decisions at maximum speed.

Admittedly, training in decision-making skills is a legitimate goal of education in this age of automation, but the problem remains— does the educator know what values to attach to the different outcomes of these decisions? What about the students whose values are out of line with the acceptable values of democratic society? Should they be taught to conform to someone else's accepted judgment of proper values? Training in decision making is ultimately compounded with training in value judgment and, as such, becomes a controversial subject that needs to be resolved by educators before the tools can be put to use. Progress must be made not only in data-processing technology, but in our knowledge of educational requirements. Automation requires a clear, operational statement of objectives to be accomplished by the system being automated. The research must be directed toward discovering optimal combinations of instructional techniques to produce these behaviors.

Bushnell documented how computers could be used to propagandize students and teach them *what* to think, rather than *how* to think. That is precisely what is being done in schools across America today, beginning in preschool and extending to advanced degrees in graduate programs.

For sixty years the programs and algorithms have been refined to the precision instruments they are today. The computerized education students receive today is programmed to persuade them to reject Americanism and embrace socialism.

CHAPTER 7

Politicized Education

Globalism is a replacement ideology that seeks to reorder the world into one singular, planetary Unistate, ruled by the globalist elite. The globalist war on nation-states cannot succeed without collapsing the United States of America. The long-term strategic attack plan moves America incrementally from constitutional republic to socialism to globalism to feudalism. The tactical attack plan uses asymmetric psychological and informational warfare to destabilize Americans and drive society out of objective reality into the madness of subjective reality. America's children are the primary target of the globalist predators.

The three pillars of faith, family, and flag were established as the infrastructure of freedom in the United States of America. Our Founding Fathers recognized the importance of an educated citizenry for sustaining ordered liberty in our constitutional republic. The infrastructure and moral tenets in American culture were derived from both the Bible and the Judeo-Christian tradition our Founding Fathers embraced.

> Our Constitution was made only for a moral and religious People. It is wholly inadequate to the government of any other. —John Adams to Massachusetts Militia, 11 October 1798

Our Founding Fathers recognized literacy as the cornerstone of critical thinking and the transfer of information. They knew that an educated, moral, responsible adult citizenry was necessary to sustain and grow our fledgling nation.

> Every child in America should be acquainted with his own country. He should read books that furnish him with ideas that will be useful to him in life and practice. As soon as he opens his lips, he should rehearse the history of his own country. —Noah Webster, *On the Education of Youth in America*, 1788

> A Bible and a newspaper in every house, a good school in every district—all studied and appreciated as they merit—are the principal support of virtue, morality, and civil liberty. —Benjamin Franklin, *Christian Life and Character of the Civil Institutions of the United States* (Benjamin F. Morris, 1864)

> It is an object of vast magnitude that systems of education should be adopted and pursued which may not only diffuse a knowledge of the sciences but may implant in the minds of the American youth the principles of virtue and of liberty and inspire them with just and liberal ideas of government and with an inviolable attachment to their own country. —Noah Webster, *On the Education of Youth in America*, 1788

Reading remains the most fundamental skill required to preserve and protect our constitutional republic. The enemies of freedom targeted American education tactically, to undermine literacy in order to achieve *an unaware and compliant citizenry* decades before that infamous phrase was associated with John Podesta and Hillary Clinton. Children were always the strategic target because they are the future of America.

Industrialists John D. Rockefeller and Andrew Carnegie were major influences in the evolution of American education. Teachers College at Columbia University was endowed with $500,000 from the Rockefeller Foundation in 1902. In that same year John D. Rockefeller created the General Education Board (GEB) with a gift of $1 million. The GEB provided funding and influence to shape American schooling. Rockefeller is quoted as saying, "I don't want a nation of thinkers; I want a nation of workers." Education was being recalibrated to emphasize vocationalism, to produce future factory workers for industrialists' needs. The GEB was subsumed by the Rockefeller Foundation in 1960.

The idea of mandatory education in the United States was embraced and promoted by steel magnate Andrew Carnegie. Carnegie advocated for a teacher certification system, and donated millions of dollars to establish libraries and universities across the country. The Carnegie Foundation for the Advancement of Teaching[17] (CFAT) was originally established as the Carnegie Foundation with a $10 million gift by Andrew Carnegie in 1905, "as an independent policy and research center called to 'do and perform all things necessary to encourage, uphold, and dignify the profession of the teacher and the cause of higher education.'" (Carnegie Foundation History)[18]

Since its inception, CFAT has had a powerful influence on American education, particularly in its efforts at quantifying and standardizing education. In 1906 it introduced the Carnegie Unit, a measurement of education credits required for high school curriculum and graduation requirements. The CFAT pension program, which became an independent nonprofit organization called Teachers Insurance and Annuity Association[19] (TIAA) in 1914, was linked to participation in curriculums using the Carnegie Unit in high schools for graduation, and to colleges and universities for admission.

A 2015 CFAT study authored by Elena Silva, Taylor White, and Thomas Toch, "The Carnegie Unit: A Century-old Standard in a Changing Educational Landscape,"[20] discusses the history and future of the Carnegie Unit. From the report:

The Carnegie Unit and the Credit Hour

The standard Carnegie Unit is defined as 120 hours of contact time with an instructor, which translates into one hour of instruction on a particular subject per day, five days a week, for twenty-four weeks annually. Most public high schools award credit based on this 120-hour standard (one credit for a course that lasts all year; or half a credit for a semester course). And, while state and district coursework requirements for graduation vary, most states require a minimum number of units, typically expressed as "Carnegie Units." A typical high school student earns six to seven credits per year over a four-year program of high school.

In higher education, students receive "credit hours," a metric derived from the Carnegie Unit and based on the number of "contact hours" students spend in class per week in a given semester. A typical three-credit course, for example, meets for three hours per week over a fifteen-week semester. A student, then, might earn fifteen credit hours per semester (fifteen is standard full-time registration for a semester, thirty for an academic year) en route to a four-year bachelor's degree requiring a total of 120 credits. ("The Carnegie Unit," p. 8)

The report recommended replacing the Carnegie Unit with a system of Outcome-Based Education (OBE). Popularized in the 1990s, OBE is an educational theory that rejects traditional content-based learning that emphasizes rote learning and acquisition of foundational knowledge, and bases the educational system instead on personal pre-determined goals called outcomes. It is the quintessential shift from the WHAT of education to the WHO.

Marketed as deeply personalized, empowering, and student-centric, OBE rejects traditional education as old-fashioned, limiting, and educator-centric. In OBE teachers are facilitators, not educators with authority or expertise. The student-centric focus is not on individual academic achievement, but rather on student social interactions and *cooperative* learning experiences.

This seismic shift from traditional to outcome-based education marked the institutional shift of American education from the education our founders envisioned to social activism where outcomes, results, performances, competencies, and standards could all be evaluated with a politicized metric. Outcome-Based Education was the chosen vehicle for social change through education, which was now being used to emphasize political activism and produce anti-American Americans for globalists' needs.

The 2015 study indicated that one of the biggest obstacles to shifting from the Carnegie Unit to Outcome-Based Education (OBE) was federal financing:

> But efforts to further push the boundaries of the design and delivery of higher education face a substantial barrier: the federal government's requirement that most students taking part in the $150 billion federal financial aid program attend colleges or universities using Carnegie Units. ("The Carnegie Unit," p. 25)

The Obama administration was committed to OBE, so it proposed changes to the federal funding model that included other criteria besides the Carnegie Unit:

> To promote competency models in higher education, the Obama administration has endorsed a provision in the federal financial aid regulations that extends eligibility under the program to students

at institutions that use "projects, papers, examinations, presentations, performances, portfolios" and other "direct" measures of learning "in lieu of credit hours or clock hours" to gauge student performance. It initially extended "direct assessment" privileges to two institutions, Capella University, a for-profit online provider, and Southern New Hampshire University's College for America. The University of Wisconsin's Flexible Option, which is led by UW–Extension, received approval for direct assessment in August 2014. ("The Carnegie Unit," p. 25)

The Carnegie Foundation and the Carnegie Foundation for the Advancement of Teaching have politicized American education and abandoned their founding missions. The 2015 CFAT Executive Summary states unequivocally that the Carnegie Unit must be replaced in order to facilitate "solutions" sought by reformers. It is political reform disguised as educational reform:

> The Carnegie Foundation is committed to making American education more effective, more equitable, and more efficient at this critical junction in the nation's history. We share change advocates' goals of bringing greater transparency and flexibility to the design and delivery of K–12 and higher education in pursuit of deeper learning for more students. After studying the Carnegie Unit's relationship to today's reforms, we have concluded that American education's reliance on the Carnegie Unit is an impediment to some of the solutions sought by reformers. Most notably, the federal government's financial aid rules requiring colleges and universities to measure student progress using Carnegie Units are a barrier to the spread of flexible delivery models in higher education. ("The Carnegie Unit," p. 5)

Changing the metrics of education from the Carnegie Unit to OBE weaponized American education, transforming it from its colonial purpose of literacy and support of Americanism to being the political agent for massive social change.

CFAT's current Mission Statement:[21]

> The mission of the Carnegie Foundation is to catalyze transformational change in education so that every student has the

opportunity to live a healthy, dignified, and fulfilling life.

The Carnegie Foundation for the Advancement of Teaching was chartered by an act of Congress in 1906. Since then, it has pioneered a broad range of transformative advancements in K–12 and higher education, including the creation of the Carnegie Unit; TIAA; standards for schools of law, medicine, education, and engineering; Educational Testing Service; the GRE; Pell Grants; the Carnegie Classifications; the U.S. Department of Education; and the use of improvement science to build the field's capacity to improve.

Today, the Carnegie Foundation has set its sights on tackling the nation's most significant educational challenge: achieving educational equity for Black, Latinx, Indigenous, Asian and Pacific Islander, and first-generation students, as well as those from low-income households. Carnegie will leverage its expertise, assets, partnerships, convening power, and social and reputational capital to address longstanding educational inequities that impede economic mobility and exacerbate racial inequality.

Historically, public education supported upward mobility and the middle class through education focused on teaching basic skills and fundamental knowledge. The politicization of American education shifted the ideological focus from meritocracy's equal *opportunity* to socialism's equal *outcome*. It was a seismic shift in both form and content in American education.

We are feeling the aftershocks of this earthquake today. The introduction of racist critical race theory, the staggering increase in functional illiteracy, the profoundly disturbing introduction of pornographic sex education—all are derivatives of the changed purpose of America's education industry.

Journalist and education reformer Alex Newman explores the subject in his September 13, 2023, article, "Lesbian-Marxist US Library Boss: School & Libraries for 'Socialist Organizing'."[22] Newman writes:

> Government schools and local libraries should be used for "socialist organizing," the self-proclaimed "Marxist lesbian" chief of the American Library Association (ALA) proclaimed at a major socialism conference last week. The library boss has also become noto-

rious recently for hating on parents, families, Christians and anyone else who stands in the way of indoctrinating children.

Speaking after a panel at the Socialism 2023 conference in Chicago organized by a coalition of revolutionaries advocating for the "right" of children to engage in prostitution, among other absurdities, ALA chief Emily Drabinski did not hold back. "Public education needs to be a site of socialist organizing," she told attendees.… Among other topics, the panel at which Drabinski spoke out included discussion on how teachers could indoctrinate children with Critical Race Theory propaganda, even in jurisdictions that have banned it. "We need to be on the agenda of socialist organizing," added Drabinski.… The socialism event in Chicago, which featured the Democratic Socialists of America (DSA) as a supporter, featured panels on abolishing the family and replacing it with government, as well as "best practices for developing socialist programming for kids." …

"Ms. Drabinski is a supporter of Critical Race Theory, which Montana rejected as discriminatory, and other far-left-leaning ideologies that have no place in our schools and libraries," said Montana Superintendent of Public Instruction Elsie Arntzen. "By electing a declared Marxist as their President, the ALA has not only turned its back on families, parental rights, and American values—it has turned its back on America itself."

Taxpayer funds are being weaponized to foment a revolution against the very taxpayers coerced into footing the bill for this dangerous extremism. It is time for all library systems to leave the ALA and for government schools turning children into Marxist revolutionaries to be shut down. The future of America is on the line.

Today's American education industry is in direct opposition to our Founding Fathers, who understood that an educated citizenry is required for sustaining ordered liberty in our constitutional republic. The American education industry is now the instrument for anti-American propaganda and Marxist indoctrination. Parents can no longer trust their children's education to it.

CHAPTER 8

Constructivism Impedes Reality-Testing

Globalism is a replacement ideology that seeks to reorder the world into one singular, planetary Unistate, ruled by the globalist elite. The globalist war on nation-states cannot succeed without collapsing the United States of America. The long-term strategic attack plan moves America incrementally from constitutional republic to socialism to globalism to feudalism. The tactical attack plan uses asymmetric psychological and informational warfare to destabilize Americans and drive society out of objective reality into the madness of subjective reality. America's children are the primary target of the globalist predators.

Constructivism is a learning theory that has its beginnings in the educational philosophy of John Dewey (1859–1952) and the work of Swiss developmental psychologist Jean Piaget (1896–1980) and Soviet psychologist Lev Vygotsky (1896–1934).

Piaget believed that human beings pass through four stages of cognitive development based on our brain's growing ability to think in new ways. His theory of cognitive development focuses on childhood and education. In Piaget's view the learner is a unique individual, whose childhood interactions and explorations influence his development. Piaget believed that children act on their environment to learn, and that the function of social interaction is to move the child away from the self-absorption of early childhood. Piaget saw childhood development in universal human terms.

Lev Vygotsky, on the other hand, focused on learning as a social process and developed the sociocultural theory of development called Social Constructivism. Vygotsky considered the learner to be a social being, whose development is influenced by environmental factors. He saw childhood development in culturally determined terms, and believed that children interact socially with their environment in order to learn the cultural values of their specific society. Vygotsky believed that behavior cannot be understood outside its cultural setting, and that culture actually shapes cognition.

The divergent perspectives of Piaget and Vygotsky parallel the differences in educational philosophies and pedagogy that we see in traditional education versus today's politicized education.

An article by educator Chris Drew, PhD, published May 13, 2023, "What Is Constructivism in Education? Piaget's Pros & Cons,"[23] defines Constructivism, describes its key concepts, and compares traditional teachers with constructivist teachers:

> Definition: The constructivist learning theory explains that we learn by "constructing" knowledge in our minds through interaction with our environments. Constructivism argues that learners have an active role in thinking things through, mulling them over, and coming to logical conclusions. We also build on our prior knowledge, like a builder constructing his skyscraper.

> Key Concepts: Learning is a cognitive process; we learn through experiences; we learn through social interactions; we use prior knowledge to make sense of new information; learning occurs in linear stages; students should learn actively rather than passively....

> Central to this theory is the idea that we learn by "mulling over" new ideas in our heads and come to our own conclusions through logic and reasoning. To achieve this sort of learning, students need to engage in active learning, learning by doing, and personal experiences.

Chris Drew's bias toward Constructivism is evident in his description:

> Constructivism in education is the dominant educational theory in the 21st-Century. It helps students to develop 21st-Century skills such as collaboration, cooperation and creativity.

It is also conspicuous in his comparison of teachers' roles:

Traditional Teacher	Teacher as Facilitator
Monologue (teacher talks)	Dialogue (teacher and students discuss)
Tells the answers	Asks questions and guides
Expects one "correct" answer	Lets students come up with their own answers
Believes they know everything	Sees themselves as a co-learner
Teacher-centered classroom	Student-centered classroom
Teaches theories	Links theories to practical experiences
One size fits all lessons	Differentiated lessons to meet students' cognitive needs

Education reformer Bruce Deitrick Price offers a very different view of Constructivism and its catastrophic effects on education. In his *Canada Free Press* article published September 12, 2019, "K–12: How Constructivism constructs confusion,"[24] Price wrote:

> Constructivism is not just another educational gimmick. It can be used in every class, for every subject, and with students of all ages. It is multifaceted, ubiquitous, and grandiose. In fact, the Education Establishment wants you to believe that Constructivism is the King Kong of instructional theories. The educrats want you to take it home for dinner, marry it, and live happily ever after.
>
> We are told that Constructivism adds immensely to the educational experience. On the other hand, students exposed to this thing—*and virtually all American students have been exposed*—seem to become dumber. In some mysterious way, Constructivism is intellectually

befuddling. The acquisition of new knowledge is stymied. WNET, a TV station in Manhattan, prepared a long presentation extolling and explaining Constructivism. **"Constructivism is basically a theory— based on observation and scientific study—about how people learn. It says that people construct their own understanding and knowledge of the world, through experiencing things and reflecting on those experiences."** That's the key claim. You construct your own knowledge. It is not out there somewhere in the world. *You construct it.* Really. Consider an instance of learning. The teacher says, "The capital of France is Paris, a very beautiful city." Does all that verbiage about people constructing their own under-standing and experiencing things, and reflecting on those experi-ences, add anything to the commonsense understanding of what happens when a teacher tells students about Paris?

WNET continues: "The constructivist teacher provides tools such as problem-solving and inquiry-based learning activi-ties with which students formulate and test their ideas, draw conclusions and inferences, and pool and convey their knowl-edge in a collaborative learning environment." Let's imagine a teacher telling students, "Most early settlers in North America came from England or Spain. Crossing the Atlantic Ocean in a small sailing ship is a dangerous adventure." Now look at the WNET spiel. Why do students need to formulate and test ideas? Why do we have to convey the knowledge in a collaborative learning environment? More steps, more clutter. Imagine you're a teacher who wants to teach about the American Revolution, why water freezes, or how the dinosaurs lived. Why do we need the clutter in any of those teaching scenarios? My suspicion is that this clutter is an obstacle, obviously so. We have started to see what may be Constructivism's unavoidable negative. Constructivism adds distractions, like a hyperactive TV series when a child is trying to read his first book. In short, there's too much going on. **WNET continues: "Constructivism trans-forms the student from a passive recipient of information to an active participant in the learning process. Always guided by the teacher, students construct their knowledge actively rather than just mechanically ingesting knowledge from the teacher or the textbook."**

Apparently when somebody tells you something you are passive and that's bad. You are *mechanically ingesting*. But if we label the classroom constructivist, everything changes for the better. Now you are actively constructing knowledge. Do you see any change? **WNET wants us to know: "Students are not blank slates upon which knowledge is etched. They come to learning situations with already formulated knowledge, ideas, and understandings. This previous knowledge is the raw material for the new knowledge they will create."** Really? What does the child know about someone sailing from Spain? Nothing. That's why it's exciting. The conceit in Constructivism is that the speaker or teacher doesn't add very much. You (a student) create the whole experience in your brain, i.e., you construct it. Is this a reasonable expectation? This next passage is so absurd, you might think I wrote it as satire. Not so. **WNET explains: "An elementary school teacher presents a class problem to measure the length of the *Mayflower*. Rather than starting the problem by introducing the ruler, the teacher allows students to reflect and to construct their own methods of measurement. One student offers the knowledge that a doctor said he is four feet tall. Another says she knows horses are measured in 'hands.' The students discuss these and other methods they have heard about, and decide on one to apply to the problem."**

I think this is the paradigm of what is wrong. The obvious next step was to see a picture or a model of the ship, with people nearby for a sense of scale. You could go outside and walk off the basic design of the ship. Children learn about the Mayflower, not about measuring horses. There seems to be a lot of bait-and-switch in Constructivism. You can easily imagine that this elementary school teacher would never reach the heart of any subject. Every comment by every student would be a seductive avenue of distraction. **WNET waxes ever more frenzied: "Students control their own learning process, and they lead the way by reflecting on their experiences. This process makes them experts of their own learning."** *Lead the way? Experts of their own learning?* Wouldn't it be better if they became expert in the subjects being studied? **WNET: "The teacher helps create situations where the students feel safe**

questioning and reflecting on their own processes, either privately or in group discussions. The teacher should also create
activities that lead the student to reflect on his or her prior
knowledge and experiences." Reflecting on their own processes?
Anything, you see, but the new knowledge we want them to learn.
Ironically, Constructivism seems designed to insulate kids from new
knowledge, to keep them busy with extraneous details and tangen-
tial activities. **WNET says: "The main activity in a constructivist
classroom is solving problems."** Maybe. But in a real classroom
the main activity is learning today what you didn't know yesterday.

Constructivism is an educational humanitarian hoax that presents its destructive methodology and relativist perspective as *superior* and *scientific.*
The word *Constructivism* is as misleading as its source: John Dewey and his
educational reform movement he called *progressive education.* Dewey, the
"Father of American Education," believed that "what" students were taught
was not as important as "how" students were taught. His focus was on form,
not content.

As discussed in Chapter 5, Dewey was a globalist, but he was also an elitist
who did not believe in the value of teaching mathematics, geography,
history, science, art, philosophy, archaeology, or any objective truths to the
masses. His 1900 educational manifesto, *The School and Society*,[25] was presented as a three-part lecture series. In Lecture 1, "The School and Social
Progress," Dewey begins:

> We are apt to look at the school from an individualistic standpoint,
> as something between teacher and pupil, or between teacher and
> parent. That which interests us most is naturally the progress made
> by the individual child of our acquaintance, his normal physical
> development, his advance in ability to read, write, and figure, his
> growth in the knowledge of geography and history, improvement
> in manners, habits of promptness, order, and industry— it is from
> such standards as these that we judge the work of the school. And
> rightly so. Yet the range of the outlook needs to be enlarged. What
> the best and wisest parent wants for his own child, that must the
> community want for all of its children. Any other ideal for our
> schools is narrow and unlovely; acted upon, it destroys our democ-
> racy. All that society has accomplished for itself is put, through the

agency of the school, at the disposal of its future members. All its better thoughts of itself it hopes to realize through the new possibilities thus opened to its future self. Here individualism and socialism are at one....

The mere absorption of facts and truths is so exclusively an individual affair that it tends very naturally to pass into selfishness. There is no obvious social motive for the acquirement of mere learning, there is no clear social gain in success thereat.

Words matter—and some words matter more than others. The United States of America was founded as a republic, not a democracy. The distinction is essential and often deliberately obfuscated by the enemies of individualism. The main difference between a republic and a democracy is the degree to which its citizens control the process of making laws. In a republic, the people elect representatives to make laws according to the constraints of a constitution. In a democracy, the majority has almost unlimited power to make laws, and minorities have few protections from the will of the majority. In a republic, the constitution protects the rights of all people from the will of the majority. In a democracy, individual rights can be overridden by the will of the majority. Individualism and socialism are never "at one."

The United States Constitution is the supreme law of the land that protects individualism and individual rights, the hallmarks of Americanism. We are a constitutional republic. It is a grave and consequential error to assume that a collectivist innocently uses the word *democracy* in its colloquial usage as a synonym for *republic*. The enemies of freedom—socialists, communists, and globalists—*exploit* the word in order to confuse the public, collapse our republic, and replace it with the mob rule of pure democracy that our Founding Fathers definitively and categorically rejected.

Collectivist John Dewey believed that experiential learning, social learning, and a basic Constructivist approach to pedagogy could achieve social reconstruction in America. He insisted that education and learning are social and interactive processes, and that schools are the appropriate institutions where social reform should take place. Dewey's manifesto is the bible for the philosophical shift in American education from traditional, foundational learning to *progressive education*. What most Americans have not realized is that "progressive" education is not an advancement in knowledge and skills; to the contrary, it is a pivotal step in the incremental movement toward collectivism, socialism, globalism, and one-world government.

Perhaps the most disturbing of Constructivism's deceitful claims is **"The teacher helps create situations where the students feel safe questioning and reflecting on their own processes, either privately or in group discussions."** Once again, we see the emphasis on *feelings*, subjective reality.

Constructivism is a dangerous, crippling methodology designed to confuse children and deny them the foundational knowledge and skills required for critical thinking and life as a productive citizen in a constitutional republic. Constructivism denies objective reality by making everything a matter of opinion. The subjective reality it embraces intentionally impedes children's developing ability to reality-test. Johnny's feelings are not facts, and Johnny's opinions are not equivalent to his teacher's facts.

Generations of teachers trained in these methods have become ideological soldiers for progressive education. Children are not the only ones who live what they learn; so do indoctrinated teachers. Constructivism is an educational Weapon of Mass Destruction in globalism's attack on America.

CHAPTER 9

Norman Dodd Interview

Globalism is a replacement ideology that seeks to reorder the world into one singular, planetary Unistate, ruled by the globalist elite. The globalist war on nation-states cannot succeed without collapsing the United States of America. The long-term strategic attack plan moves America incrementally from constitutional republic to socialism to globalism to feudalism. The tactical attack plan uses asymmetric psychological and informational warfare to destabilize Americans and drive society out of objective reality into the madness of subjective reality. America's children are the primary target of the globalist predators.

The philosophical rationalization and justification for Barack Obama's shift to Outcome-Based Education (OBE) was presented by John W. Gardner in the 1950s. Gardner served concurrent tenures as president of both the Carnegie Foundation for the Advancement of Teaching (CFAT) and the Carnegie Corporation[26] in the mid-1950s.

In 1961 Gardner published *Excellence: Can We Be Equal and Excellent Too?*[27] The book is a reflection on American excellence that debates the relative merits of focusing on equality and focusing on excellence, and asks if it is possible for society to do both.

Our Founding Fathers advocated meritocracy, a system based on ability, achievement, and equal opportunity. They understood that *equality of opportunity* achieves excellence. Gardner examines an alternative theory that focuses on *equality of outcome*, also known as equity, and argues that the goals of excellence and equity are not incompatible.

In 1965 President Lyndon B. Johnson appointed Gardner secretary of the Department of Health, Education, and Welfare. His appointment institutionalized America's move away from meritocracy, establishing the collaboration of government in the weaponization of American education for political purposes. Meritocracy was replaced with equity as the foundation of American education, and equal outcome became the educational objective. What was the political purpose of this fundamental change?

Equity and Outcome-Based Education (OBE), like every other humanitarian hoax, sounds constructive on the surface. But its destructive political underbelly is that weaponizing education with promises of equity through OBE will destroy America and move her toward collectivism and a globalist one-world government.

In 1953, during the time Gardner was at Carnegie, a New Jersey bank manager, Norman Dodd, was Director of Research for the Reece Committee, the Congressional Special Committee to investigate tax-exempt foundations. Dodd discovered that since 1945 tax-exempt foundations had been operating to promote a hidden globalist agenda.

In 1982, five years before his death in 1987, Norman Dodd was interviewed by G. Edward Griffin.[28] The contents of the interview remain shocking. Griffin introduces the interview:

> The story we are about to hear represents a missing piece in the puzzle of modern history. We are about to hear a man tell us that the major tax-exempt foundations of America, since at least 1945, have been operating to promote a hidden agenda. That agenda has nothing to do with the surface appearance of charity, good works, or philanthropy.

> This man will tell you that the real objective has been to influence American educational institutions and to control foreign policy agencies of the federal government. The purpose of the control has been to condition Americans to accept the creation of world government. That government is to be based on the principle of collectivism, which is another way of saying socialism; and it is to be ruled from behind the scenes by those same interests which control the tax-exempt foundations.

[Transcript: full interview]

G. Edward Griffin: Mr. Dodd, let's begin this interview by a brief statement, for the record, telling us who you are, what your background is, and your qualifications to speak on the subject.

Norman Dodd: Well, Mr. Griffin, as for who I am, I am just as the name implies—an individual born in New Jersey and educated in private schools, eventually in a school called Andover, Massachusetts, and then Yale University.

And, running through my whole period of being brought up, growing up, I have been an indefatigable reader, and I have had one major interest and that was this country, as I was led to believe that it was originally founded.

I entered the world of business knowing absolutely nothing about how that world operated. And I realized that the only way to find out what that world was, and consisted of, would be to become part of it. And I then acquired some experience in the manufacturing world, and in the world of international communications, and finally chose banking as the field I wished to devote my life to.

I was fortunate enough to secure a position in one of the important banks in New York. I lived there. I lived through the conditions which led up to what is known as the crash of 1929. I witnessed what is tantamount to a collapse of the structure of the United States as a whole.

Much to my surprise, my superiors, in the middle of the panic in which they were immersed, confronted me. I was confronted with the question, "Norm, what do we do now?"

I was thirty at the time, and I had no more right to have an answer to that question than the man in the moon. However, I did manage to say to my superiors, "Gentlemen, you take this experience as proof of something that you do not know about banking." And you better go find out what that something is, and act accordingly.

Four days later, I was confronted by these same superiors, with a statement to the effect that "Norm, you go find out." And I really was fool enough to accept that assignment, because it meant that you were going out to search for something, and nobody could tell you what you were looking for. I felt so strongly on the subject that I consented to it.

I was relieved of all normal duties inside the bank and, two and a half years later, I felt that it was possible to report back to those who had given me this assignment. So, I rendered such a report and, as a result of the report I rendered, I was told the following: "Norm, what you are saying is, we should return to sound banking." And I said, "Yes, in essence, that's exactly what it is that I am saying."

Whereupon I got my first shock, which was a statement from them to this effect: "We will never see sound banking in the United States again." And they cited chapter and verse to support that statement.

What they cited was as follows: Since the end of World War I, we have been responsible for what they call the institutionalizing of conflicting interests. And they are so prevalent inside this country that they can never be resolved.

This came to me as an extraordinary shock because the men who made this statement were men who were deemed as the most prominent bankers in the country. The bank of which I was a part was spoken of, a Morgan bank. Coming from men of that caliber, a statement of that kind made a tremendous impression on me.

The type of impression that it made on me was this: I wondered if I, as an individual, as what they call a junior officer of the bank, could with the same enthusiasm foster the progress and the policies of the bank. I spent about a year trying to think this out, and came to the conclusion that I would have to resign.

I did resign. As a consequence of that, I had this experience. When my letter of resignation reached the desk of the president of the bank, he sent for me. I came to visit with him and he stated to me, "Norm, I have your letter, but I do not believe you understand what has happened in the last ten days." I said, "No, Mr. Cochran, I have no idea what's happened."

"Well," he says, "the directors have never been able to get your report to them out of their minds and, as a result, they have decided that you, as an individual, must begin at once, and you must re-organize this bank in keeping with your own ideas." He then said, "Now, can I tear up your letter?"

And inasmuch as what had been said to me, what he was offering me, at the age of (by then) thirty-three, was about as fine an opportunity for service to the country as I could imagine. I said, "Yes." And they said they wished me to begin at once, and I did.

Suddenly, in a span of about six weeks, I was not permitted to do another piece of work. And every time I brought the subject up, I was kind of patted on the back and told, "Stop worrying about it, Norm. Pretty soon you will be a vice president and you will have quite a handsome salary, and ultimately be able to retire on a very worthwhile pension and, in the meantime, you can play golf and tennis to your heart's content on weekends."

Well, Mr. Griffin, I found I could not do it. I spent a year, figuratively, with my feet on the desk, doing nothing. I just couldn't adjust to it. So I did resign. This time my resignation stuck.

Then I got my second shock, which was the discovery that the doors of every bank in the United States were closed to me and I never could get a job, as it were, in a bank. So, I found myself, for the first time since I graduated from college, out of a job.

From then on, I followed various branches of the financial world, ranging from investment counsel to membership in the stock exchange. I finally ended up as an advisor to a few individuals who had capital funds to look after.

In the meantime, my major interest became very specific, which was to endeavor, by some means, to get the educational world to actually, you might say, teach the subject of economics realistically, and move it away from the support of various speculative activities that characterized our country.

I have had that interest and you know how it is, if you generate a specific interest, you find yourself gravitating toward persons with similar interests. Ultimately, I found myself kind of at the center of the world of dissatisfaction with the direction in which this country was headed. And I found myself in contact with many individuals who, on their own, had done a vast amount of studying and research in areas which were part of the problem. Griffin: What point in your career did you become connected with the Reece Committee?Dodd: Nineteen hundred and fifty-three (1953).

Griffin: 1953. And what was that capacity, Sir?

Dodd: That was in the capacity of what they called "Director of Research."

Griffin: Can you tell us what the Reece Committee was attempting to do?

Dodd: Yes, I can tell you. It was operating and carrying out instructions embodied in a Resolution passed by the House of Representatives, which was to investigate the activities of foundations as to whether or not these activities could justifiably be labeled "un-American"—without, I might add, defining what they meant by "un-American." That was the Resolution, and the committee had, then, the task of selecting a counsel, and the counsel, in turn, had the task of selecting a staff; and he had to have somebody who would direct the work of that staff, and that was what they meant by the "Director of Research."

Griffin: What were some of the details, the specifics, of what you told the committee at that time?

Dodd: Well, Mr. Griffin, in that report I specifically—number one—defined what was, to us, meant by the phrase "un-American." And we defined that, in our way, as being a determination to effect changes in the country by un-Constitutional means.

We have plenty of Constitutional procedures, assuming that we wished to effect a change in the form of government, and that sort of thing. And therefore, any effort in that direction which did not avail itself of the procedures authorized by the Constitution could be justifiably called "un-American." That was the start of educating them, up to that particular point. The next thing was to educate them as to the effect on the country, as a whole, of the activities of large endowed foundations over the then past forty years.

Griffin: What was that effect, Sir?

Dodd: That effect was to orient our educational system away from support of the principles embodied in the Declaration of Independence and implemented in the Constitution, and to educate them over to the idea that the task now was to effect an orientation of education away from these briefly stated principles and self-evident truths.

And, that's what had been the effect of the wealth which constituted the endowments of those foundations—foundations that had been in existence over the largest portion of the span of fifty years—and holding them responsible for this change. What we were able to bring forward was— what we had uncovered was—the determination of these large endowed foundations, through their trustees, actually to get control over the content of American education.

Griffin: There is quite a bit of publicity given to your conversation with Rowan Gaither. Will you please tell us who he was, and what was that conversation you had with him?

Dodd: Rowan Gaither was, at that time, President of the Ford Foundation. Mr. Gaither had sent for me when I found it convenient to be in New York. He asked me to call upon him at his office, which I did.

Upon arrival, after a few amenities, Mr. Gaither said, "Mr. Dodd, we have asked you to come up here today because we thought that, possibly, off the record, you would tell us why the Congress is interested in the activities of foundations such as ourselves."

And before I could think of how I would reply to that statement, Mr. Gaither then went on and voluntarily stated, "Mr. Dodd, all of us who have a hand in the making of policies here have had experience either with the OSS [Office of Strategic Services (1942–1945), the intelligence agency of the United States during World War II and precursor to the CIA, established in 1947] *during the war, or with European economic administration after the war. We have had experience operating under directives. The directives emanate, and did emanate, from the White House. Now, we still operate under just such directives. Would you like to know what the substance of these directives is?"*

I said, "Yes, Mr. Gaither, I would like very much to know." Whereupon he made this statement to me: "Mr. Dodd, we are here to operate in response to similar directives, the substance of which is that we shall use our grant-making power so to alter life in the United States that it can be comfortably merged with the Soviet Union."

Well, parenthetically [sic], Mr. Griffin, I nearly fell off the chair. I, of course, didn't, but my response to Mr. Gaither then was, "Oh, Mr. Gaither, I can now answer your first question. You've forced the Congress of the United States to spend a hundred and fifty thousand dollars to find out what you have just told me." I said, "Of course, legally, you're entitled to make grants for this purpose. But I don't think you're entitled to withhold that information from the People of this country, to whom you're indebted for your tax exemption. So why don't you tell the People of the country just what you told me?" And his answer was, "We would not think of doing any such thing." So, then I said, "Well, Mr. Gaither, obviously you forced the Con-

gress to spend this money in order to find out what you just told me."

Griffin: Mr. Dodd, you have spoken before about some interesting things that were discovered by Kathryn Casey at the Carnegie Endowment. Would you tell us that story, please?

Dodd: Sure, glad to, Mr. Griffin. This experience you just referred to came about in response to a letter which I had written to the Carnegie Endowment, asking certain questions and gathering certain information.

On the arrival of that letter, Dr. Johnson, who was then President of the Carnegie Endowment, telephoned me and said, "[Do] you ever come up to New York?" I said, "Yes, I [do], more or less each weekend." And he said, "When you are next here, will you drop in and see us?" Which I did.And again, on arrival at the office of the Endowment, I found myself in the presence of Dr. Joseph Johnson, the President, who was the successor to Alger Hiss; two vice presidents; and their own counsel, a partner in the firm—a fellow by the name of Cromwell. And Dr. Johnson said (again after amenities), "Mr. Dodd, we have your letter. We can answer all those questions, but it would be a great deal of trouble. We have a counter-suggestion. Our counter-suggestion is that, if you can spare a member of your staff for two weeks and send that member up to New York, we will give to that member a room in the library, and the minute books of this Foundation since its inception. And we think that whatever you want to find out, or that the Congress wants to find out, will be obvious from those minutes."

Well, my first reaction was they had lost their minds. I had a pretty good idea of what those minutes would contain, but I realized that Dr. Johnson had only been in office two years, and the vice presidents were relatively young men, and counsel also seemed to be a young man. I guessed that, probably, they had never read the minutes themselves.

And so, I said that I had somebody and I would accept their offer. I went back to Washington, and I selected the member of my staff who had been a practicing attorney in Washington. She was on my staff to ensure I did not break any congressional procedures or rules. In addition to that, she was unsympathetic to the purpose of the investigation. She was a level-headed and very reasonably brilliant, capable lady, and her attitude toward the investigation was this: "What could possibly be wrong with foundations? They do so much good."

[Start of side 2]

Well, in the face of that sincere conviction of Kathryn's, I went out of my way not to prejudice her in any way, but I did explain to her that she couldn't possibly cover fifty years of handwritten minutes in two weeks. So, she would have to do what we call "spot reading." I blocked out certain periods of time to concentrate on. Off she went to New York. She came back at the end of two weeks with the following recorded on Dicta-phone belts.

We are now at the year nineteen hundred and eight, which was the year that the Carnegie Foundation began operations. And in that year, the trustees meeting, for the first time, raised a specific question, which they discussed throughout the balance of the year, in a very learned fashion. And the question is this: Is there any means known more effective than war, assuming you wish to alter the life of an entire people? And they conclude that no more effective means to that end is known to humanity than war. So then, in 1909, they raise the second question and discuss it, namely, how do we involve the United States in a war?

Well, I doubt, at that time, if there was any subject more removed from the thinking of most of the People of this country than its involvement in a war. There were intermittent shows in the Balkans, but I doubt very much if many people even knew where the Balkans were. And finally, they answer that question as follows: we must control the State Depart-ment.

And then, that very naturally raises the question of how do we do that? They answer it by saying we must take over and control the diplomatic machinery of this country and, finally, they resolve to aim at that as an objective. Then, time passes, and we are eventually in a war, which would be World War I. At that time, they record on their minutes a shocking report in which they dispatch to President Wilson a telegram cautioning him to see that the war does not end too quickly. And finally, of course, the war is over.

At that time, their interest shifts over to preventing what they call a "rever-sion of life" in the United States to what it was prior to 1914, when World War I broke out. At that point, they come to the conclusion that, to pre-vent a reversion, we must control education in the United States. And they realize that is a pretty big task. To them it is too big for them alone.

So, they approach the Rockefeller Foundation with a suggestion: that portion of education which could be considered domestic should be handled by the Rockefeller Foundation, and that portion which is international should be handled by the Endowment.

They then decide that the key to the success of these two operations lay in the alteration of the teaching of American History. So, they approach four of the then most prominent teachers of American History in the country— people like Charles and Mary Beard. Their suggestion to them is this: "Will they alter the manner in which they present their subject." And they get turned down flatly.

So, they then decide that it is necessary for them to do as they say, i.e., "build our own stable of historians." Then they approach the Guggenheim Foundation, which specializes in fellowships, and say, "When we find young men in the process of studying for doctorates in the field of American History, and we feel that they are the right caliber, will you grant them fellowships on our say-so? And the answer is "Yes."

So, under that condition, eventually they assemble twenty, and they take these twenty potential teachers of American History to London. There, they are briefed in what is expected of them—when, as, and if they secure appointments in keeping with the doctorates they will have earned.

That group of twenty historians ultimately becomes the nucleus of the American Historical Association. And then, toward the end of the 1920s, the Endowment grants to the American Historical Association four hundred thousand dollars for a study of our history in a manner which points to what this country [can] look forward to, in the future.

That culminates in a seven-volume study, the last volume of which is, of course, in essence, a summary of the contents of the other six. The essence of the last volume is this: the future of this country belongs to collectivism, administered with characteristic American efficiency.

That is the story that ultimately grew out of, and of course was what could have been presented by the members of, this congressional committee, and the Congress as a whole, for just exactly what it said. But they never got to that point!

Griffin: This is the story that emerged from the minutes at the Carnegie Foundation?

Dodd: That's right.

Griffin: And so?

Dodd: It was official to that extent.

Griffin: And Kathryn Casey brought all of these back in the form of dictated notes, or verbatim readings, of the minutes?

Dodd: On Dictaphone belts.

Griffin: Are those in existence today?

Dodd: I don't know. If they are, they're somewhere in the archives, under the control of the Congress, the House of Representatives.

Griffin: How many people actually heard those? Or were they typed up; transcripts made?

Dodd: No.

Griffin: How many people actually heard those recordings?

Dodd: Three, maybe. Myself, my top assistant, and Kathryn. Yeah, I might tell you this experience, as far as its impact on Kathryn Casey is concerned. Well, she was never able to return to her law practice. If it hadn't been for Carroll Reece's ability to tuck her away in a job with the Federal Trade Commission, I don't know what would have happened to Kathryn. Ultimately, she lost her mind as a result of it. It was a terrible shock to her. It was a very rough experience for her to encounter proof of this kind.

Griffin: Mr. Dodd, can you summarize the opposition to the Committee, the Reece Committee, and particularly the efforts to sabotage the Committee?

Dodd: Well, it began right at the start of the week of the operating staff, Mr. Griffin. It began on the day on which the Committee met for the purpose of consenting to, or confirming, my appointment to the position of Director of Research. Thanks to the abstention by the minority members of the Committee from voting, that is, the two Democratic members—that is why, technically, I was unanimously appointed.

Griffin: Wasn't the White House involved in opposition?

Dodd: Not at this particular point, Sir. Mr. Reece ordered Counsel and myself to visit Wayne Hayes. Wayne Hayes was the ranking minority member of the Committee, as a Democrat. So, we—Kathryn and I—had to go down to Mr. Hayes's office, which we did. Mr. Hayes greeted us with the flat statement, directed primarily to me, "I am opposed to this investigation. I regard it as nothing but an effort on the part of Carroll Reece to gain a little prominence. So, I'll do everything I can to see that it fails." Well, I have a strange personality, in the sense that a challenge of that nature interests me.

Our Counsel withdrew. He went over and sat on the couch in Mr. Reece's office and pouted. I, sort of, took up this statement by Mr. Hayes as a challenge and set myself a goal of winning him over to our point of view.

I started by noticing that on his desk there was a book. The book was of the type—and there were many in those days—that would be complaining about the spread of communism, and Hungary. That type of book.

This meant to me that, at least, Hayes had read the book. So, I brought up the subject of the spread of the influence of the Soviet world. For two hours, I discussed this with Hayes and, finally, he ended up by rising from his desk and saying, "Norm, if you will carry this investigation toward the goal that you have outlined to me, I will be your biggest supporter."

I said, "Mr. Hayes, I can assure you, I will not double-cross you. Subsequently, Mr. Hayes sent word to me that he was in Bethesda Naval Hospital, with an attack of ulcers. He asked if would I come and see him. Which I did. He then said, "Norm, the only reason I've asked you to come out here is that I just want to hear you say again you will not double-cross me." I gave him that assurance, and that was the basis of our relationship.

Meanwhile, Counsel took the attitude expressed in these words, "Norm, if you want to waste your time with 'this guy' (as he called him), then you can go ahead and do it, but don't ever ask me to say anything to him, under any conditions, on any subject."

So, in a sense, that created a deck for me to operate, in relation to Hayes, on my own.

As time passed, Hayes offered friendship, which I hesitated to accept because of his vulgarity. I didn't want to get mixed up with him socially, under any conditions.

Well, that was our relationship for about three months. Eventually, I had occasion to add to my staff. As a result of adding to my staff a top-flight intelligence officer, both the Republican National Committee and the White House resorted to stopping me from continuing this investigation in the direction Carroll Reece had personally asked me to go.

Mr. Griffin, that direction was to utilize this investigation to uncover the fact that this country had been the victim of a conspiracy. That was Mr. Reece's conviction. I eventually agreed to carry out that direction.

I explained to Mr. Reece that his own Counsel wouldn't go in that direction. He gave me permission to disregard our own Counsel and to set up an aspect of the investigation outside of our office—more or less secretly. The Republican National Committee got wind of what I was doing, and they did everything they could to stop me. They appealed to Counsel to stop me. Finally, they resorted to the White House.

Griffin: Was their objection because of what you were doing, or because of the fact that you were doing it outside of the official auspices of the Committee?

Dodd: No. The objection was, as they put it, my devotion to what they called "anti-Semitism." That was a cooked-up idea. In other words, it wasn't true at all. But anyway, that's the way they expressed it.

Griffin: Excuse me. Why?

Dodd: Then they made it stick.

Griffin: Why did they do that? How could they say that?

Dodd: Well, they could say it, Mr. Griffin. But they had to have something in the way of a rationalization of their decision to do everything they could to stop completion of this investigation, given the direction that it was moving. That direction would have been exposure of this Carnegie En-

dowment story, and the Ford Foundation, and the Guggenheim, and the Rockefeller Foundation—all working in harmony toward the control of education in the United States.

Well, to secure the help of the White House in the picture, they got the White House to cause the liaison between the White House and the Hill—a major person—to go up to Hayes and try to get him, as it were, actively to oppose what the investigation was engaged in.

Hayes, then, very kindly, would listen to this visit from this major person. Then he would call me and say, "Norm, come up to my office. I have a good deal to tell you."

I would go up. He would tell me he just had a visit from this major person, and he wants me to break up this investigation. So, then I said, "Wayne, what did you do? What did you say to him?" He said, "I just told him to get the hell out." And he did that, three times. I got pretty proud of him, in the sense that he was, as it were, backing me up. We finally embarked upon hearings at Hayes's request. Hayes wanted to get them out of the way before he went abroad in the summer.

Griffin: Why were the hearings finally terminated? What happened to the Committee?

Dodd: What happened to the Committee, or to the hearings?

Griffin: The hearings.

Dodd: The hearings were terminated. Carroll Reece was up against such a furor in Hayes, through the activity of our own Counsel. Hayes became convinced that he was being double-crossed, and he put on a show in the public hearing room, Mr. Griffin, that was an absolute disgrace. He called Carroll Reece publicly every name in the book.

Mr. Reece took this as proof that he couldn't continue the hearings. He actually invited me to accompany him when he went down to Hayes's office and, in my presence, with the tears rolling down his face, Hayes apologized to Carroll Reece for all he'd done, and his conduct. He apologized to me. I thought that would be enough, and Carroll would resume. He never did.

Griffin: This charge of anti-Semitism is kind of intriguing to me. What was the basis of that charge? Was there any basis for it at all?

Dodd: The basis used by the Republican National Committee was that the intelligence officer I had taken on my staff—when I oriented this investigation to the exposure of, and proof of, a conspiracy—was known to have a book, and that book was deemed to be anti-Semitic. It was childish, but it's what the second-in-command at the Republican National Committee said, and he told me I'd have to dismiss this person from my staff.

Griffin: Who was that person?

Dodd: A Colonel Lee Loraine.

Griffin: Lee Loraine. And what was his book? Do you recall?

Dodd: The book they referred to was called Waters Flowing Eastward. It was a very strong castigation of the Jewish influence in the world.

Griffin: What were some of the other charges made by Mr. Hayes against Mr. Reece?

Dodd: Just that Mr. Reece was utilizing this investigation for his own prominence inside the House of Representatives. That was the only charge Hayes could think up.

Griffin: How would you describe the motivation of the people who created the foundations—the big foundations—in the very beginning? What was their motivation?

Dodd: Their motivation was, well, let's take Mr. Carnegie, as an example. His publicly declared and steadfast interest was to counteract the departure of the colonies from Great Britain. He was devoted just to putting the pieces back together again.

Griffin: Would that have required the collectivism to which they were dedicated?

Dodd: No. No. No. These policies are the foundations' allegiance to these un-American concepts; these policies are all traceable to the transfer of the funds over into the hands of trustees, Mr. Griffin. Those trustees were not the men who had a hand in the creation of the wealth that led to the endowment, or the use of that wealth for what we would call public purposes.

Griffin: It was a subversion of the original intent, then?

Dodd: Oh, yes! Completely so. We got into the worlds, traditionally, of bankers and lawyers.

Griffin: How have the purpose and direction of the major foundations changed, over the years, up to the present? What are their purposes and directions today?

Dodd: One hundred percent behind meeting the cost of education, such as it is presented through the schools and colleges of this United States, on the subject of our history—to prove that our original ideas are no longer practical. The future belongs to collectivistic concepts. There is just no disagreement on this.

Griffin: Why do the foundations generously support communist causes in the United States?

Dodd: Well, because, to them, communism represents a means of developing what we call a monopoly—as the organization, we'll say, of large-scale industry into an administrable unit.

Griffin: Do they think that they will?

Dodd: They will be the beneficiary of it, yes.

[End of interview]

The 1954 Dodd Report[29] and the 1982 Dodd Interview[30] document the collaboration of tax-exempt "charitable" foundations with the U.S. government to undermine the founding concepts of our constitutional republic through weaponized education.

I had to read the Dodd Report twice, and listen to the Dodd interview twice, to absorb and process the magnitude of the information. Norman Dodd discovered the conspiracy to move the United States of America from constitutional republic to socialism, perpetrated by "charitable" tax-exempt foundations since 1909. The foundations unapologetically and unambiguously documented their plan to weaponize American education against America in the minutes of their own meetings!

The treasonous scheme to weaponize education could never have succeeded without the partnership of the U.S. government. The realization that the planned demolition of America has been in effect for over 100 years is overwhelming. We have arrived at the tipping point of America's freedom.

CHAPTER 10

Objective Reality Is Required for a Free Society

Globalism is a replacement ideology that seeks to reorder the world into one singular, planetary Unistate, ruled by the globalist elite. The globalist war on nation-states cannot succeed without collapsing the United States of America. The long-term strategic attack plan moves America incrementally from constitutional republic to socialism to globalism to feudalism. The tactical attack plan uses asymmetric psychological and informational warfare to destabilize Americans and drive society out of objective reality into the madness of subjective reality. America's children are the primary target of the globalist predators.

The globalist War on America, documented in the Dodd Report and Dodd Interview (Chapter 9), is a culture war fought without bullets that has targeted America's children for over 100 years. The classroom is the globalists' chosen battlefield, because whoever controls the educational curriculum controls the future. Why is this true?

Because children live what they learn. Education is an industry, and like all industries, it produces a product. The goal of America's enemies is to produce an unaware, compliant citizenry groomed for life in the planned globalist Unistate. The War on America's Children utilizes both informational and psychological warfare to achieve that goal.

The globalist social engineers are skilled strategists applying subversive wartime psychological tactics to "change the hearts and minds" of American children. The strategic goals are to replace parental authority with governmental authority, and to move society from objective reality, the adult world of facts, to subjective reality, the childish world of feelings.

Interfering with a child's developing ability to reality-test is a staggering deceit and a monstrous abuse of power. Education reformer Deborah DeGroff's 2019 handbook *Between the Covers: What's Inside a Children's*

Book?[31] exposes the deceit and documents the sad reality of illiteracy in America today.

In the past, when children were told that every student was a butterfly, the children knew it wasn't true because they could see for themselves that some students were extremely smart and others weren't——no matter what the teacher said. At that time, children were still learning to read with phonics. It was a time before sight-words and whole-word instruction became ubiquitous, and well before "hi-lo" reading even existed.

I had never heard of hi-lo reading before reading Deborah DeGroff's book. Basically, instead of teaching children to actually read, a deceitful system was developed to address and adapt to the alarmingly low reading levels across the country. Hi-lo is a reference to the fact that the book content is considered upper-grade (high school interest), but the actual reading level is lower grade—sometimes as low as second- or third-grade level!!

In a 2012 article directed at the American Library Association, "ALA 2012: What's Up with Hi-Lo?,"[32] *Publishers Weekly* journalist Shannon Maughan wrote:

> Many librarians, teachers, parents—and even students—are aware of the grim, oft-cited statistic: only one-third of eighth-grade students in the U.S. read at or above the proficient level (source: the Nation's Report Card/National Assessment of Educational Progress 2009).[33] While solutions to the problem are always being debated, those who work with struggling and reluctant readers every day want tools they can use right now. Hi-lo books frequently fit the bill....

> Schools, by far, remain the biggest market for hi-lo books, largely because it is the setting where intervention for struggling readers is most likely to occur. In addition to searching for compelling general fiction and nonfiction, publishers are always on the lookout for ways they can create appealing curriculum-related titles. A number of companies offer such ancillary materials as workbooks and teacher guides to support their hi-lo series, as well....

> Most encouraging about the hi-lo market is that librarians, educators, and publishers are seeing the books fill an important

need. Becky Williams, a literacy consultant in Iowa who works with teachers, notes, "It's not a silver bullet, but it's something. They are a wonderful resource for kids that never 'got it.' Having these books has truly made a difference for these kids."

So, instead of improving reading skills by teaching phonics, the education industry dumbed down the books. They moved the goalpost, disingenuously marketing hi-lo in glowing terms as an attempt to encourage "reluctant readers."

In her book, DeGroff quotes Andrew Wooldridge of Orca Book Publishers, one of the largest suppliers of hi-lo books, saying, "We don't use the term hi-lo because it has a bad connotation; we call the books fiction for reluctant readers or struggling readers."

In reality, hi-lo reading is a system that presents great literature as summaries, like Cliffs Notes, or even as comic books deceitfully labeled "graphic novels." Students today who are functionally illiterate because they never learned to read are offered summaries and comic books to read instead of original text.

For me, the horror of hi-lo reading goes far beyond the deliberate illiteracy it supports. The most devastating impact is that students actually BELIEVE they have read great literature. They feel the pride of achievement without the fact of achievement. They have entered the realm of subjective reality, where facts and feelings merge.

Moving the goalpost and changing the name of a thing does not change the objective reality of that thing, but it can change the hearts and minds of individuals responding to that thing. So, telling children they are all butterflies does not change the fact that some students are extremely smart, some are not; some can read, and some cannot. But it can change the children's response to that fact, which means that in subjective reality it no longer matters whether you can read or not, whether you are reading a classic text or a comic book. In subjective reality, literacy and illiteracy are *equivalent*.

The American education industry has replaced meritocracy with educational indoctrination, facilitating deliberate dumbing down of our children. The industry's informational warfare is facilitated by its psychological warfare, because parents and students alike BELIEVE the student has read the novel *Moby-Dick*, not the dumbed-down comic-book version!

Deborah DeGroff's exploration of the content of children's books also exposes the staggering, pervasive, inappropriate, pornographic, and confusing sexual content of books in classrooms K–12 and school libraries. Her research documents how weaponized education targets children's most primary identity, their sexual identity.

The campaign to destabilize and destroy a child's sexual identity is a particularly insidious effort to destroy the child's individual identity. It is catastrophic to the child, and to freedom in a society of ordered liberty.

In every society anywhere in the world, the first words spoken when a baby is born are "It's a boy!" or "It's a girl!"

The globalist social engineers are trying to redefine what it means to be human by attacking the biology of maleness and femaleness, and insisting that gender is a choice—a child's choice. Globalism's War on Children is a long-term, well-planned, well-funded, well-executed mass-casualty campaign. The attack on a child's sexual identity is a catastrophic assault on humanity itself.

In schools, libraries, movies, games, churches, and synagogues, transgender role models are presented as normal human beings. The most bizarre aspect of this particular assault on biology and objective reality is that so many parents actually believe that supporting this false, destructive, and confusing sexual narrative is being inclusive and compassionate!

Our nation's children are being groomed to become compliant, submissive wards of the globalist Unistate, where they will have no individual rights, no freedoms, and no personal or sexual identity. They will be fodder for technocracy and transhumanism without the need of armies or policemen.

America's weaponized education industry is not teaching Johnny to read or to write. It is teaching Johnny that he is a butterfly—and a boy who can become a girl if he so chooses. Take a moment to try to imagine a society of Johnnys, and then you will understand how destroying a child's ability to reality-test is a weapon of mass societal destruction.

Without the ability to reality-test, Johnny remains frozen psychologically in the subjective reality of childhood. He never develops into an independent autonomous psychological adult capable of living in the world of objective reality. Freedom is an adult enterprise, and objective reality is the requirement for a free society.

CHAPTER 11

Critical Race Theory: A Species of the Ideological Thought Genus Marxism

Globalism is a replacement ideology that seeks to reorder the world into one singular, planetary Unistate, ruled by the globalist elite. The globalist war on nation-states cannot succeed without collapsing the United States of America. The long-term strategic attack plan moves America incrementally from constitutional republic to socialism to globalism to feudalism. The tactical attack plan uses asymmetric psychological and informational warfare to destabilize Americans and drive society out of objective reality into the madness of subjective reality. America's children are the primary target of the globalist predators.

D r. James Lindsay, mathematician, cultural critic, political analyst, and prolific anti-Woke/anti-Marxist writer, presents an extraordinary and original analysis of the existential threat facing Western Civilization. He introduces Marxism as a genus of ideological thought, and categorizes classical economic Marxism, Maoism, radical feminism, critical race theory, queer theory, Post-Colonial Theory, and Woke as species in the genus of Marxism. It is a magnificent discourse that identifies Woke as the 21st-century species of Marxism evolved to attack the West, signaling our entry into the transformational stage of education, the final phase of Outcome-Based Education (OBE), discussed in Chapter 6.

Lindsay addressed the European Parliament at its Woke Conference on March 29, 2023[34]. It is a stunning speech in which he states unequivocally, "Woke is Maoism with Western characteristics." The complete transcript follows.

[Transcript]

Woke: A Culture War Against Europe | James Lindsay at the European Parliament

March 29, 2023 [posted May 30, 2023]

Hello. Thank you. I'm glad to be here. I want to address something Tom just said, which is, in fact, that woke is supposed to advance equity in Europe. So, here's the definition of equity and see if it sounds like a definition of anything else you've ever heard of.

The definition of equity comes from the public administration literature. It was written by a man named George Frederickson, and the definition is "an administered political economy in which Shares are adjusted so that citizens are made equal."

Does that sound like anything you've heard of before—like socialism? They're going to administer an economy to make "shares" equal. The only difference between equity and socialism is the type of property that they redistribute—the type of shares. They're going to redistribute social and cultural capital, in addition to economic and material capital.

And so, this is my thesis: When we say, "What is woke?" Woke is Maoism with American characteristics.

If I might borrow from Mao himself, who said that his philosophy was Marxism-Leninism with Chinese characteristics, which means woke is Marxism, and it's a very provocative statement. It's something you will certainly hear. It is not that it is different, and the professors and the philosophers will spend a large amount of time explaining to you why: "No, no, it's about economics when it's Marxism. This is social, this is cultural, this is different." It's not different.

I need you to think biologically for one moment, and I don't mean about your bodies. We could do that—that's a different topic. I want you to think how we organize plants and animals. When we study them, they are species, but above species they are the genus of the animals. So, you think, like the cats, all the cats, but you have tigers, you have lions, you have house cats, you have whatever, leopards, many different kinds of cats.

If we think of Marxism as a genus of ideological thought, then Classical Economic Marxism is a species. Radical feminism is a species in this same genus. Critical race theory is a genus—or, sorry, a species in this genus. Queer Theory is a species in this genus. Post-Colonial Theory that's plaguing Europe is a species in this genus. And they have something that binds them together, called intersectionality, that makes them treated as if they are all one thing. But the logic is Marxist, and I want to convince you of that because Marx had a very simple proposition, but we get lost.

We think that Marx was talking about economics because he often talked about economics. He wrote a book called Das Kapital *[1867–1883]. It's very famous book. We think, well, this is about economic theory, but this isn't true. It is only true on the surface.*

If we go below the surface, what Marx was talking about was something different. We know what Marx's hypothesis was. That we must seize the means of production. If we're going to bring socialism to the nations, to the world, we have to seize the means of production.

So, we have to ask, what does he mean? And if we think that it's about capital, then we miss what he means. If you think it's about the means of production in the factory with a hammer, and it means a production in the field with a sickle, then you miss what it means. Because Marx explained what makes human beings special in his earlier writings. And what makes human beings special is that man is a being that is incomplete, and knows that he is incomplete.

He is a man whose true nature has been forgotten to him, which is a social being. He is a socialist at heart who doesn't realize it, and the reason he doesn't realize it is because of the economic conditions operating as a means of construction or production, not just of the economy, but of him. But of man, of society, and particularly of history. Marx said that he had the first scientific study of history.

How is history produced? By man doing man's activity, and man's key activity was economic activity as he saw it. And so, economic production doesn't just produce the goods and services of the economy, it produces Society itself—and Society, in turn, produces man. He called this the inversion of praxis [practice as distinguished from theory].

And so, when he says we must seize the means of production and he's talking about factories and fields, he's actually talking about how we construct who we are as human beings, so that we might complete ourselves. So that we might complete history, and at the end of history mankind will remember that he is a social being and we will have a socialist society—a perfect communism that transcends private property. That's how he put it. He said, in fact, that communism is the transcendence of private property as human self-estrangement. That's a quote from the economic philosophic manuscripts of 1844.

So, Marx was interested in controlling or understanding and controlling how man produces himself. He writes about this exclusively in the 1840s— very deeply—how do we do this. And he looks at the economic conditions and he says this is where it is, and that's why we get economic Marxism. And that's why we think Marx was an economist, but Marx was never an economist; he was a theologian.

He wanted to produce a religion for mankind that would supersede all of the religions of mankind and bring him back to his true social nature. This is the true fact of Marx, and what the goal was, like I said, was to complete man.

So, what he said is, well, how are we building man currently? All of his economic analysis is about how are we building man at present through what he called material determinism. And he said, well, what we have is a special form of private property in our society. Our society is organized around private property, so all of our thoughts organize around private property. In other words, there's a special kind of property that the bourgeois elite class has access to, and then they organize society to exclude everybody else from access to that property through exploitation, through alienation, through estrangement, through oppression.

And so, what Karl Marx was proposing is the economics becomes a vehicle to separate society into a bourgeois class that has access to a special form of property. The people who have access wish to retain that, so they oppress people and keep other people out of that special form of property. They erect a system of classism to do that; it's enforced by an ideology called capitalism that believes that this is the right way to engage in the world, and what we have to do is awaken the underclass, the proletariat, to the real conditions and the fact that they are historical agents of change, and bring them to do a revolution and transform society so that we would have equity or socialism, whichever word you want. They have the same definition.

Now let's say that we step out—that is, we step back from this species, this economic species, Homo economicus, *and we step back to the genus, and* we look at this idea as a special form of property that segregates society into people who have, the Bourgeois, and the people who do not have, who are in class conflict with an ideology that keeps this in place. And the under-class must awaken with Consciousness to fight back, and to seize the means of production of that form of deterministic property.

And now we say change out class, put in race, and watch—we get critical race theory that falls out of the hat—just like that—very simple. In 1993, Cheryl Harris wrote a long article for the Harvard Law Review called "Whiteness Is Property." She explained that whiteness, or white privilege, constitutes a kind of cultural private property. She says it must be abolished in order to have racial justice, just like Karl Marx said in The Communist Manifesto. He wrote, "Communism can be summarized in a single sentence: The abolition of private property."

Well, this is why critical race theory calls to abolish whiteness, because whiteness is a form of private property. People who have access to this property are whites, or "white adjacent," or they "act white." These are words out of the American lexicon that they've used to describe how people gain access to the private property. People without that are people of color, and they are oppressed by systemic racism. Systemic racism is enforced by an ideology of white supremacy instead of capitalism.

If you think of whiteness as a form of cultural capital, white supremacy, as they define it, is identical to capitalism. It's the belief—it's not believing that white people are superior, it's believing that white people have access to the control of society and should maintain that.

Even if you don't actually believe that, if you merely support that, you have adopted the ideology of white supremacy into your mind. And so, you have the exact same system and the goal is to awaken a racial consciousness in people so that they will band together as a class, and seize the means of cultural production so that white cultural production is no longer the dominant mode.

It's a big mystery in Europe. I know in the UK, throughout Europe, I hear this question again and again. Why on Earth is this very American phenomenon about slavery and so on that doesn't apply to our country, why is it popular here? It's because it's not about history at all, it's not about slavery at all. Those are excuses that they use.

It's about creating a class consciousness that's against this form of property called whiteness. That is against the dominant culture that may just be a matter of fact, say, if you're in Europe. That's why, because it becomes a sight by which people can come together and they can channel resentment and try to claim power. I wrote a book called Race Marxism, *and I defined critical race theory as it really is in that book. On the first page I said that critical race theory is calling everything you want to control racist, until you control it. But couldn't we say the same about Marxism? It's calling everything you want to control bourgeois until you control it.*

But those mean the same thing. They mean exactly the same thing. But what about, say, Queer Theory? How is that Marxist? It's very strange, all this gender and sex and sexuality. Well, Tom said, what is woke attacks the idea of being normal. Well, the Queer Theory thinks that there are certain people who get to set the norms of society. They are privileged. They call themselves normal. They say this is normal—it's normal to consider yourself a man and look like a man and act like a man and dress like a man and eat meat like a man. And then there are women—this should be feminine and pretty and all these things.

And so, they get to define what is normal. They're heterosexuals, so they get to define the heterosexuality as normal, and other sexualities are abnormal. And so, you have a conflict across this cultural property of who gets to be considered normal and who is a pervert or a freak or some other term that gets used in their literature.

But technically, who is a queer? Which sounds like a slur, but they adopted it, and it's a technical academic term now. It means an identity without an essence. By the way, an identity that is strictly oppositional to the concept of the normal, as defined by queer theorist David Halperin in his 1995 book, Saint Foucault: Towards a Gay Hagiography. *I didn't make that up. I'm not extrapolating. So, you see, Queer Theory is just another species of the genus of Marxism.*

What about Post-Colonial Theory, which is plaguing Europe thanks to Franz Fanon and his biggest European fan, Jean-Paul Sartre. What about this? Well, it's the same—you have the West as the oppressor. They have access to the material and cultural wealth of the world because they've decided their culture is the default and have gone and colonized the world to bring culture to the world, as they say. And so, the oppressed natives around the world, the people, have to band together, and their activity is going to be called decolonization.

They have to remove every aspect of Western culture, so when they come to Belgium or they come to France or they come to the United States and they say, we're going to decolonize the curriculum, or they go to the UK and say we're going to decolonize Shakespeare—this is what they mean. We're going to remove the cultural significance of your cultural artifacts because those cultural artifacts themselves are oppressive to us. This is the same system. It's another species and the exact same genus—and that genus is Marxism, which is a way of thinking about the world.

And the goal is always to seize the means of control of the production of man and history and society.

Marx merely believed it was through economic means. Now it's through socio-cultural means. The evolution into this, sometimes called Western Marxism, began in the 1920s. We had a Russian Revolution in 1917 and this did not happen in Europe, and the Marxists in Europe were confused. And so, Antonio Gramsci sat down and wrote out some things, and George Lukács sat down and wrote History and Class Consciousness: Studies in Marxist Dialectics *[1972] after the failure of the revolution in Hungary. And they wrote what became Cultural Marxism—the idea that we have to enter the cultural institutions in order to change them from within, because Western culture has something about it that's repelling socialism.*

So, we have to go inside and change the culture to make it socialist. Now, you aren't allowed to talk about Cultural Marxism now. They've categorized this as a conspiracy theory. They say that it is anti-Semitic—this is not true. Antonio Gramsci wrote books. George Lukács wrote books. You can read those books—they have a philosophy. If they don't like the name Cultural Marxism, we can use the name that other people at the time used, Western Marxism.

So much like, I don't know, a virus adapting to the conditions, it changed. It changed to try to infect a new host. It worked in feudal societies. Marxism took over in Russia, it took over later in China. It took over in all of these kinds of agriculturally driven feudal societies, but it wouldn't work in actual capitalist nations, because Marx was wrong.

Then several Germans from the Frankfurt School started to study this phenomenon in more depth, and they evolved the idea further. They evolved the idea into what's called Critical Marxism, they developed what's called the Critical Theory, and Max Horkheimer, who designed the Critical Theory, explained the Critical Theory. And what did he say?

He said, well, what we came to realize was that Marx was wrong about one thing. Capitalism does not immiserate the worker, it allows him to build a better life. So, I developed the Critical Theory because it is not possible to articulate the vision of a good society on the terms of the existing society. So, Critical Marxism criticizes the entirety of the existing society. Everything is somehow needing to be subjected to Marxist conflict analysis, but how is that to be done?

They sought an answer through the middle part of the 20th century, and World War II breaks out. The Frankfurt School comes to America, which in this metaphor is the Wuhan Institute of Virology, because gain of function began to happen on the Marxist virus very quickly.

In America, American universities adopted these professors from Germany, and Herbert Marcuse, writing in the 1960s, said extremely clearly, this writing in 1969. Not only did he say capitalism delivers the goods, gives people a good life, makes them wealthy and comfortable and happy. He also said that the working class is no longer going to be the base of the Revolution because of these things.

In other words, we don't have to be responsible to the working class any-more, which opens up the ability for Marxists, who are seeking power, to make friends with the corporations. The bosses are no longer the enemy, they're an opportunity, because the working class is irrelevant. He said the energy is somewhere else, he said it's in the racial minorities, the sexual mi-norities, the feminists—the Outsiders. That's who he said have the energy for a Marxist revolution in the West, not the working class. And so, Marxism was able to evolve to abandon the working class.

So, what did they do? Well, all they had studied for thirty years was what they called the culture industry, an industry that commodifies and pack-ages culture and sells it back to people. So, supposedly stripped of what it actually is, empty, abstract now, and so what, of course, did they do? They seized the means of production of the culture industry, because that's what they do, and so they started to transform the culture industry to sell racial, sexual, gender, sexuality-based agitprop, as though that were genuine culture, and so we get concepts like cultural appropriation.

We get concepts like cultural relevance—cultural this, cultural that, cultural everything, and it's all provided in pastiche. It's all provided as a mockery of what's really going on—and this evolved in America's highly racialized context, and we ended up with woke—a form of identity- based Marxism. A constellation of Marxist species that all work with the same operating premise, but locate themselves in different, and I'll use the German term here for this: Volk. LGBTQ is a volk, and they get volkish identity there and become activists.

The black community is a volk. How do I know? That's what W. E. B. DuBois said. It would be when he laid down the foundations that became critical race theory later. They think of themselves as nations. Don't they all have flags? Don't they put them on your buildings like colonizers? Don't they hang them in your streets?

They think of themselves as occupying nations, but they see themselves as bound together, just like the various colonized nations around the world, and seeking liberation from Western Civilization. And so, we end up with Western Marxism taking many forms, but with one overarching approach, and the approach that they use, I started off by saying, is Maoist, not merely Marxist.

Now you know the theory is Marx. It's just evolved into different species to attack the West at its weakest points, through our tolerance, through our acceptance, through our openness, through our generosity, through our best traits—actually, the things that we should be proud of being, the things that we are proud of being. But Mao Zedong knew how to use identity politics.

I don't know how you study in Europe, but in America we have very redwashed education, as we might say. The communists have stripped out all education about communism entirely. You don't learn about it in America at all. So, we don't learn anything about Mao, and maybe you don't know this, but I tell this to American audiences and they're shocked.

Mao used identity politics. He created ten identities in China. Five he labeled red for communist, five he labeled black for fascists, and he cate-

gorized people into these identity categories. What they are doesn't really matter. Of course, they were communists, they were things like landlord and rich farmer, and things like this—right-winger is a bad category in and of itself. By the way, conservatives, all of them bad, bad influences, that's another one; you could be a bad influence for just thinking the wrong thing or saying the wrong thing at any time, or because the government decides it doesn't like you. These are the bad categories, and if you have a bad category, very importantly, your children have a bad category by default.

So, they create a social pressure for your children to identify as revolutionaries, at which point they get a red identity, a communist identity, a good identity, and they get rewarded for it. And the youth led the revolution in China because Mao did this identity politics through the children, in the schools. This should feel very uncomfortable to you because here we have, at least in the United States, we tell our children being white is bad, being white is oppressive.

You automatically hurt people of other races by your very existence, but, by the way, if you become queer, we'll celebrate you, and you can create a radical army of people who identify as gender minorities and sexual minorities at seven years old. You can lead them into paths of puberty blockers in transition, medical transition, which of course Big Pharma profits off of, at seven years old, behind their parents' backs.

There's a reason for this. It's the same program that Mao Zedong used to radicalize the youth in China. The only thing different is the identity categories have shifted. It's Maoist cultural revolution with American characteristics, and it's being exported to Europe. And just like how critical race theory has come to Europe, even though it doesn't make sense, it will come to Europe whether it makes sense or not, and you will have a cultural revolution here too.

You guys even had a kind of offshoot one in 2020. George Floyd dies in Minnesota, which has nothing to do with you, and you guys have statues coming down in Europe. Total nonsense. It doesn't matter, though; the point is to destroy Western Civilization from within, using Maoist techniques.

One last point about Mao to kind of drive that point home. Mao said in 1942 that his formula to transform China was called Unity Criticism Unity.

First you try to create the desire for Unity. Then you criticize people for not living up to that. Then you bring them into Unity under a new standard.

Does that feel like what you're being put through? But the words are different. We use words like inclusion and belonging. We'll have a place where everybody feels like they belong, we just want to have an inclusive space, but unfortunately you have racist ideas, and we have to criticize you for those. You need to criticize yourself for those. You need to go study shuishi, in Mandarin, exactly like Mao said. And then we can bring you into Unity under a new standard, which Mao called socialist discipline, which we in the West would not buy. We call it in the West "inclusion." And so, we have this new program. And within inclusion we have—or above inclusion, actually— we have sustainability. We have a sustainable and inclusive future.

I see the Agenda 2030 here with an X over it. The sustainable and inclusive future is the new socialist standard that we will have freedom under socialist discipline. And Mao said the way that that will work is through what he called Democratic Centralism. We call that Stakeholder Capitalism. And my shot at the World Economic Forum is taken because it's one of the things coordinating this. My shot at the United Nations is taken because it's one of the things that's coordinating this.

So, woke is Marxism, it's advancing through Maoist cultural revolution. It's using Americanized identity categories, and while some of those will not work in Europe, I guarantee you the colonial aspect will. They will find your weakness. They will adapt the theory to fit, because it's like a virus that will evolve to its host, and Europe is at great risk.

The last thing I'll mention is this risk is twofold. When you endure Marx's provocation, Marx's strategy is always of the same type. It's called middle-level violence. They don't come at you with full-blown Bolshevik assault very often. It's middle-level violence they provoke. Which means if you give in, and you do like Jean-Paul Sartre said in his forward to Wretched of the Earth *[1961] by [psychiatrist] Franz Fanon, the post-colonial book.*

He said the violence is coming, so Europe's best bet is to give it away so that they don't kill you. They'll murder you and take it, or maybe you can give it away. Give your culture away, give your countries away, and they'll let you live. They're coming for you, and this is what Europe needs to learn. That's what he says in the forward of Wretched of the Earth, *you can read it for yourself, probably in the original French that I can't read. And I think that's the path Europe has followed.*

So, you can give it away, that's one side because they provoke at the middle, or you can react and overreact. Which, sadly, Europe has had a rough history in the last century with overreactions and if they, if you, overreact, what will they do? They will weaponize your overreaction for a century, forever, and gain moral authority so that you end up having to give it away later anyway.

So, stand firm in your principles. But you have to do so cleverly, you have to do so understanding that you're being provoked. Which means you don't react as the provocateur wants you to react. You have to outsmart them, which is not possible unless you know the diagnosis of your problem.

It's a Polish proverb: Never attempt to cure what you don't understand.

Woke is Marxism evolved to attack the West. If you don't understand that, you will not act correctly. You will not cure it, and it will conquer your countries. It will conquer all of Europe, and we will have a very, very long sustainable and inclusive future with absolutely no freedom, because the goal is to make us into what they call "global citizens." Have you heard this term?

This term is nonsense. There's no global sovereign, so there is no global citizenship. There's no relationship because there's no ruler, and we don't want a ruler of the globe. It's a nonsense term. But they tell you, if you actually read their literature, what is a global citizen. It's somebody, I kid you not, I make no joke, they say this themselves, it's somebody who supports the 17 sustainable development goals of the United Nations Agenda 2030.

That's a global citizen, and they say what are the rights of a global citizen. This is in a book about global citizenship education published two years ago, what are the rights of a global citizen? And the answer one paragraph later is, we're not that interested in rights with global citizenship, it's more about global responsibilities. In other words—slavery.

This is a pivotal moment in the history of the western world. The model that they are pushing us toward using the means and mechanisms of that place is the model we see in China. If you want to know what your future looks like if we don't stop the woke, look at China.

Look at the social credit system. Look at the oppression. Look at people disappearing for having the wrong opinions. One of their greatest billionaires, Jack Ma, said the wrong thing about the government and disappeared. A billionaire.

If you want to know what the future of Europe and America, and the five eyes or whatever the countries, it's China. That's the model. So, we have to fight back against woke, but to fight back against woke we have to understand it, and I will close by restating my thesis:

> *Woke is Marxism evolved to take on the West, and it's been very successful so far because we haven't known our enemy, we cannot name our enemy, and I've come here to name our enemy.*

So, thank you for your time and attention and letting me do that.

[End of speech]

The importance of James Lindsay's speech for Americans is twofold. First, Lindsay names our enemy—Woke. Second, he identifies the enemy's motive—Cultural Revolution. History is repeating itself. Mao Zedong, chairman of the Chinese Communist Party, led the Cultural Revolution in China from 1966–1976. Mao was an ideological supremacist who believed in the superiority of his particular species of ideological Marxism, Maoism.

China had been under dynastic rule for over 3,000 years until its last dynasty, the Qing dynasty (1636–1912). The Boxer Uprising in the summer of 1900, along with the revolutionary ideas of Sun Yat-sen, destabilized the established dynastic order. Mao came to power during the Soviet-Sino split when China and the Soviet Union went their separate ideological ways.

Mao was a pragmatist who realized he could not use the *rich v. poor* Russian model for revolution in China. He decided that, for Chinese communism to succeed, it required a Cultural Revolution, the obliteration of the old China by purging any remnants of traditional Chinese society—old ideas, old values, old artifacts, old habits, old religion, and old customs, including family loyalty and reverence for ancestors. Mao was determined to replace individual Chinese family loyalty with loyalty to the collectivist Chinese Communist state.

Chairman Mao was a supremacist selling a replacement totalitarian ideology, who conveniently failed to mention that Maoism is a binary sociopolitical structure of rulers and ruled. In America, Woke Marxists are selling the same replacement totalitarian ideology, and also failing to mention that American Marxism is that same binary sociopolitical structure.

Every species of ideological Marxism is binary regardless of its name. Socialism, communism, Marxism, Maoism, democratic socialism, all are species of ideological Marxism. References to socialism are particularly misleading because they disguise the binary structure of the incremental stages moving America backward from constitutional republic to medieval feudalism.

The 18th-century Age of Enlightenment inaugurated a period of great tolerance for differing opinions and was the beginning of liberalism as a movement. Freedom of religion, upward mobility, equality of man, all secular ideals of the Enlightenment, were incorporated into the Constitution of the United States. The liberalism of the Enlightenment has morphed into the leftism of today and has replaced Western Judeo-Christian organized religion as the "religion" of Western youth.

Woke is the vanguard of the 21st-century Cultural Revolution in America. Like Chairman Mao, it seeks the obliteration of the old America by purging any remnants of traditional American society. The idea is to rid American society of old ideas, old values, old artifacts, old habits, old Judeo-Christian religion, and old customs including honoring parents and family loyalty. Woke is determined to replace American family loyalty with loyalty to the new American Marxist state.

What ultra-conservatives fail to recognize when they blame atheists for the social chaos in America is that Millennials and Gen Xers are not without religion; they have embraced leftism as their religion. The god of leftism is not an anthropomorphic superpower; it is globalism, and its tenets are Woke. Young people do not seek unity with God, they seek unity with all people of the world. Leftism is a colossal humanitarian hoax that exploits people's desire for Unity to sell the fiction of freedom in globalism's planetary totalitarian Unistate.

CHAPTER 12

Seeding Race Wars

Globalism is a replacement ideology that seeks to reorder the world into one singular, planetary Unistate, ruled by the globalist elite. The globalist war on nation-states cannot succeed without collapsing the United States of America. The long-term strategic attack plan moves America incrementally from constitutional republic to socialism to globalism to feudalism. The tactical attack plan uses asymmetric psychological and informational warfare to destabilize Americans and drive society out of objective reality into the madness of subjective reality. America's children are the primary target of the globalist predators.

James Lindsay's analysis of Woke Marxism (Chapter 11) is supported by the extraordinary Testimony of Dr. Bella Dodd to HUAC in 1953.[35] The U.S. House of Representatives formed the House Un-American Activities Committee (HUAC) in 1938 to look into subversive activity by private citizens. Bella Dodd (1904–1969) was a New York teacher, lawyer, labor union activist, and high-ranking member of the Communist Party USA in the 1930s and 1940s. She speaks candidly about her idealism; her seduction into the Communist Party as a young woman; and her growing disillusionment, disaffection, and final ardent anti-communist stance.

Bella Dodd testifies with an experienced insider's voice, exposing the fundamental deceit of communism in her very personal and powerful sworn statement. She explains how millions of Americans, herself included, were sucked into communism with slogans and generalizations—seduced by feelings, not facts. Excerpts from her testimony are particularly relevant today:

> Take, for instance, the whole question of antifascism. The Communist Party in this country set itself up as the one organization that was fighting fascism. Very few other organizations gave them a battle for that, and so the Americans got to feeling, "These are the anti-Fascists."

We only learn now, after reading documents captured by the American soldiers in Germany, that throughout the time the Communists were calling themselves "anti-Fascists," they were working with the German high brass while Hitler was in power.... Well, they took the anti-Fascist slogan and made themselves the protagonists of antifascism.

They did the same thing with the word "democracy." It became very difficult to oppose them because they posed everything in terms of the word "democracy." ... (pp. 1746–1747)

They divide your loyalty to the "country" from loyalty to the "people." They say, "We are the greatest Americans there are. We believe in supporting the people."

Who are the people? They are for the class society—for the proletariat. They say, "The working class makes up 98 percent of the people. Therefore, we, in our desire to protect the people, are the greatest democrats that there are." But they forget to tell you that as far as they are concerned, before they are through taking power, they will kill off large sections of the working class if it doesn't go along with their program.... (p. 1748)

There is no more depressing problem than the way the party uses the minority groups for the purpose of creating chaos and division among the people, creating fear and hatred among themselves in order that the many Communist organizations may promote the things in which they are interested.... (p. 1755)

You know there is a strategy of the party and tactics of the party. The strategy of the party is world revolution. In a country like the United States which is in preparation, a non-Communist country, this country is being prepared for revolution. The revolution may not be a bloody one, it may be like the one they had in Czechoslovakia where they opened the doors to the Soviet Union.... (p. 1757)

I think there is a responsibility at present in America, the intellectuals, the professional people in America have a special responsibility because they are the ones who have been used.... They are being used in order to divide and to confuse and to create chaos in

American public opinion.... (p. 1765)

The American teachers have to understand that education must have a basic philosophy and they must themselves drink deep of the political genius of America as embodied in the **Declaration of Independence** and the **Bill of Rights**.

They must have a philosophy consonant with the Hebraic-Christian tradition, which has been the basis of western civilization. I think teachers must understand they are the guardians of America's future....

The Communist does not believe in the right of the individual. They believe only in the right of the collective. The individual is only part of a collective group, and whenever he doesn't move according to the collective, he is ousted from the group.... (p. 1772)

There is no doubt in my mind that Czechoslovakia didn't fall before an armed force, but fell because the intellectuals and professional groups in Czechoslovakia came to the conclusion that communism was their salvation. They are the ones who opened the door to the Soviet Union. It is quite possible in the United States to have—it is not a difficult thing for a country to fall. It isn't a question—we must get away from the idea that a country falls by guns alone. A country falls when we adopt Communist ideas and move in the direction of communism. The battle for America is house by house, street by street, city by city.... It is not up to teachers alone, but to each mother and father. Each person within our country has the job of defeating Communist ideas.... (pp. 1773–1774)

Bella Dodd testified before HUAC in 1953, the same year Norman Dodd (Chapter 9) made the stunning discovery that American philanthropic organizations were generously supporting communist causes in the United States. In both cases, education was identified as the chosen vehicle for dismantling the societal infrastructure of the United States.

I could find no connection between Bella Dodd and Norman Dodd outside of their ideological warnings of the existential danger of communism to American freedom and the insidious communist infiltration spreading throughout American life.

Today, communism, philanthrocapitalism (discussed fully in Chapter 25), and education intersect in the prevailing Marxist critical race theory that is battering society and threatening America with societal collapse.

The purpose of all the species of Marxist critical theories is total destruction of the established social norms in the targeted society. To help people understand the destructive seeds of Marxist critical race theory (CRT), investigative journalist Christopher F. Rufo lists nine key concepts in his anti-CRT Parent Guidebook: Fighting Critical Race Theory in K–12 Schools.[36] All of these concepts are being planted in children's fertile minds in American schools. Marxist critical theories are *not* to be confused with critical thinking.

> **Race essentialism:** Critical race theory reduces individuals to the quasi-metaphysical categories of "blackness" and "whiteness" and then loads those categories with value connotations—positive traits are attributed to "blackness" and negative traits are attributed to "whiteness." Although some critical race theorists formally reject race essentialism [the belief that human identity and behavior are genetically race-based], functionally they often use these categories as malicious labels that erase individual identities.

> **Collective guilt:** Critical race theory claims that individuals categorized as "white" are inherently responsible for injustice and oppression committed by white populations in the past. This concept is sometimes framed as "white guilt," "white shame," and "white complicity," which are psychological manifestations of collective guilt.

> **Opposition to equality under the law:** Critical race theorists explicitly reject the principle of equality under the law, including the Fourteenth Amendment and the Civil Rights Act of 1964. They argue that legal equality, nondiscrimination, and colorblindness are mere "camouflages" used to uphold white supremacist structures.

> **Opposition to meritocracy:** Critical race theorists oppose meritocracy, especially standardized testing and competitive admissions in the education system. They claim that meritocracy is a mechanism to uphold racist structures and is derived from "racism, nativism, and eugenics."

Active racial discrimination: Critical race theorists believe that the state must actively discriminate against racial groups that are deemed "privileged," meaning whites and sometimes Asians. Critical race theorists support policies such as racial quotas, race-based benefits, and race-based redistribution of wealth.

Restriction of free speech: Critical race theorists believe that the First Amendment serves to advance the interests of white supremacy and systemic racism under the guise of freedom of speech. They argue that the government should restrict freedom of speech that is "racist" or "hateful."

Abolition of whiteness: Critical race theorists believe that society should work to "abolish the white race." Although they often insist that this means dismantling cultural constructions associated with white identity, this language often adopts tropes associated with race eliminationism.

Neo-segregation: Critical race theorists endorse a new form of racial segregation—often called "racial affinity groups" or "racial caucuses"—with separate meetings, facilities, living quarters, and training programs for whites and racial minorities. The assumption is that whites must "do the work" to address their "internalized racial superiority," and racial minorities must be protected from invasive "whiteness."

Anti-capitalism: Critical race theorists have adopted the core Marxist position of anti-capitalism, arguing that America is an "imperialist white supremacist capitalist patriarchy." They argue that "whiteness, initially constructed as a form of racial identity, evolved into a form of property," allowing whites to extend domination from slavery into the free-market society. The solution is to redistribute private property and dismantle the system of capitalism.

All nine concepts are racist. All nine concepts are rooted in false assumptions that do not comport with objective reality. All nine concepts are anti-American. All nine concepts have their existence only in the subjective reality of radical leftist activism. All nine concepts begin grooming America's children—in kindergarten!—to become anti-American racists. If children are white, they are told they are oppressors, conditioned to feel shame, and groomed to feel inferior. If children are black, they are told they are victims, conditioned to feel anger, and groomed to feel superior. The racist political indoctrination seeded in kindergarten is cultivated all the way through high school and university.

Children graduating from programs designed to create divisiveness and anger are like pit bulls groomed for blood sports. Pit bulls were originally bred for bullbaiting. Now outlawed in most countries, bullbaiting was an extremely cruel sport in which several dogs attacked a tied-up bull until the poor animal collapsed from his injuries. Participating animals were wounded, killed, or eaten. Bullbaiting was done strictly for sport, and only the organizers profited from it.

So it is with critical race theory; only the leadership benefits from this cruel blood sport. Racial discrimination is loathsome and has been outlawed in the United States since the Civil Rights Act of 1964. Racism was malevolent when it was practiced against blacks, and it is equally malevolent as it is being practiced today against whites. It is completely out of touch with reality to claim that only white people can be racist. Racism is racism, no matter who is practicing it. Critical race theory is racist indoctrination and an egregious attack on a child's ability to test reality.

Republican senator Marsha Blackburn of Tennessee is vehemently opposed to critical race theory. On July 12, 2021, Senator Blackburn posted a disturbing column on her website: "Why Is Critical Race Theory Dangerous for Our Kids?"[37]

> For months, parents have raised the alarm about the left's effort to brainwash our children by injecting Critical Race Theory (CRT) into public school curriculum. One Tennessee mom recently warned Williamson County parents that her seven-year-old daughter came home from school saying, "I'm ashamed that I'm White." Her daughter asked, "Is there something wrong with me? Why am I hated so much?" This reaction is reason enough to start asking questions, but those who have yet to investigate the tenets of CRT will be shocked to know that this child's distress was the desired result of her lessons. If left unchecked, this mental and emotional trauma will worm its way into every classroom in America.

> Although promoted as "anti-racist" civil rights education, CRT

actively encourages discrimination. At its core, CRT segregates people into two main categories: oppressors or victims. The calculation is based solely on skin color. The tenets of CRT stretch far beyond the humanities. In some classrooms in Oregon and California, students operate under the understanding that "finding the right answer" in mathematics is racist. "Right" and "wrong" answers are deemed a product of white supremacy. The woke gymnastics required to reach such a conclusion would be amusing if this destructive ideology didn't pose such a danger to education in America.

We can all agree that racism and discrimination are wrong and have no place in the classroom—but neither does racially motivated propaganda. In the U.S. Senate, I've been leading the charge for true equality in the classroom. I led legislation prohibiting federal funding of the "1619 Project," which reframes American history in terms of racial conflict and oppression. I also joined my Senate colleagues in demanding that Critical Race Theory's prejudicial influence be kept out of K–12 classrooms....

Children should not be forced to endure this latest round of revisionist history, but it will take more than letters and legislation to keep CRT out of the classroom. Parents need to keep showing up to school board meetings and reporting discriminatory conduct.

The last thing educators should be doing is encouraging our children to be ashamed of the color of their skin. That same Williamson County mom who warned about the dangers of CRT was left with no choice but to put her seven-year-old in therapy. Why? "She is depressed. She doesn't want to go to school." While parents struggle to help their children manage the mental and emotional damage inflicted by this dangerous ideology, the left will continue to re-write our education system to fit their woke agenda—and they won't stop until CRT is in every classroom in America.

In February 2020, North Carolina's largest school district, the Wake County Public School System, held an equity-themed teachers' conference with over 200 teachers in attendance that launched a campaign against "whiteness in educational spaces." A March 17, 2021, article by Christopher F. Rufo, published in *City Journal*, describes this "Subversive Education."[38] In a stunning demonstration of Marxist equivocation, the district's antiracism narrative is wholly racist.

At the first session, "Whiteness in Ed Spaces," school administrators provided two handouts on the "norms of whiteness." These documents claimed that "(white) cultural values" include "denial," "fear," "blame," "control," "punishment," "scarcity," and "one-dimensional thinking." According to notes from the session, the teachers argued that "whiteness perpetuates the system" of injustice and that the district's "whitewashed curriculum" was "doing real harm to our students and educators." The group encouraged white teachers to "challenge the dominant ideology" of whiteness and "disrupt" white culture in the classroom through a series of "transformational interventions."

Parents, according to the teachers, should be considered an impediment to social justice. When one teacher asked, "How do you deal with parent pushback?" the answer was clear: ignore parental concerns and push the ideology of antiracism directly to students. "You can't let parents deter you from the work," the teachers said. "White parents' children are benefiting from the system" of whiteness and are "not learning at home about diversity (LGBTQ [lesbian, gay, bisexual, transgender, queer/questioning], race, etc.)." Therefore, teachers have an obligation to subvert parental wishes and beliefs. Any "pushback," the teachers explained, is merely because white parents fear "that they are going to lose something" and find it "hard to let go of power [and] privilege."

This isn't an aberration. In fact, the district's official Equity in Action plan encourages teachers to override parents in the pursuit of antiracism. "Equity leaders [should] have the confidence to take risks and make difficult decisions that are rooted in their values," the document reads. "Even in the face of opposition, equity leaders can draw on a heartfelt conviction for what is best for students and families." In other words, the school should displace the family as the ultimate arbiter of political morality.

The reformulation of American education into subversive education is evidence that the final stage of Outcome-Based Education, Transformational

Education, is here. The goal of Transformational Education is to change children's values, and critical race theory is the weapon of choice for American Marxists determined to collapse America from within.

The nuclear family is the societal infrastructure of our constitutional republic. Globalism, a binary sociopolitical system of rulers and ruled, makes no space for the nuclear family because it is a competing ideology. The globalist strategic plan is to destroy the American family in order to destroy America. The tactical plan is to divide and conquer. Subversive education is the weapon, students are the target, and teachers are the foot soldiers.

Subversive education separates children ideologically from their parents and creates family strife. Reformulated educational content replaces American meritocracy with racism, and equal opportunity with equal outcome (equity). It foments family discord and race-based divisiveness. The war effort is facilitated by Marxist publishers of textbooks and teaching materials, and the radical leftist National Education Association of American teachers. The globalist War on America is being fought inside classrooms and inside your child's mind, by a corrupt and politicized anti-American education industry.

Children are being conditioned to reject parental authority and accept the authority of government schools. The destructive seeds of Marxist critical race theory are planted in children's minds to produce activist voters who will embrace anti-American racist ideology, collapse America from within with their votes, and then sustain the globalist Unistate ideologically.

Like pit bulls, your children are being groomed to fight for the benefit of the globalists. But in order to become indoctrinated, anti-American, activist voters, they must be deprived of the basic foundational educational skills of reading, writing, and arithmetic. They must become illiterate tools of the revolution, dumbed down and bereft of critical-thinking skills.

Children spend hours each day in the world of subjective reality created in their classrooms by activist teachers. Parents living in objective reality will necessarily be in conflict with their indoctrinated children, and with the teachers who are indoctrinating them. The world of objective reality is being attacked by the world of subjective reality on the battlefield of your child's mind.

CHAPTER 13

Fomenting Race Wars Begins in Kindergarten

Globalism is a replacement ideology that seeks to reorder the world into one singular, planetary Unistate, ruled by the globalist elite. The globalist war on nation-states cannot succeed without collapsing the United States of America. The long-term strategic attack plan moves America incrementally from constitutional republic to socialism to globalism to feudalism. The tactical attack plan uses asymmetric psychological and informational warfare to destabilize Americans and drive society out of objective reality into the madness of subjective reality. America's children are the primary target of the globalist predators.

National sovereignty is to a country what individual sovereignty is to a human being. In *The Collapsing American Family: From Bonding to Bondage*,[39] I describe the globalist strategy of using reformulated Marxism in American schools in order to replace American individualism with collectivism. The goal is to persuade the individual to stop being an individual:

> The Left had a new marketing, lobbying, and advertising strategy that targeted first American universities and then K–12. American education was chosen as the vulnerable soft target for revolution— no bullets required. The long-term strategy was that two generations of leftist educational indoctrination would transform America from a capitalist constitutional republic into the socialist state required for internationalized one-world government.

> The radical leftists on campus in the '60s did not go quietly into the night after Woodstock. They graduated and became the teachers, professors, textbook writers, psychologists, sociologists, politicians, doctors, lawyers, and decision makers in charge of public education, including curriculum content, that reflected their anti-American bias and globalist views. Gradually the individualism

and critical-thinking skills that had created the vibrant, independent, upwardly mobile middle class and supported the American dream were deliberately dumbed down to encourage dependence, collectivism, groupthink, and a victim mentality.

In a sweeping effort that eventually transformed public education, collectivism was repackaged, marketed, lobbied, advertised, and sold to an unsuspecting American public. The former pro-American curricula that proudly promoted individualism, meritocracy, capitalism, and the middle class was replaced. The revised curricula teach American students to be anti-American, self-loathing, dependent, fragile collectivists, unapologetically preaching global citizenship in a New World Order. (*The Collapsing American Family: From Bonding to Bondage*, pp. 123–124)

Collectivism is the core of John Dewey's infamous *progressive education*, discussed in Chapter 8. Progressivist instructional methods focus on group work and group projects, and promote the experience-centered focus of the progressive philosophy. Progressivism defines itself as a contrast to Perennialism. Perennialism,[40] the foundation of American education established in Colonial America, emphasizes objective reality, universal truths, and an educational curriculum that cultivates students' individual intellectual skills with the "three R's"—reading, writing, and arithmetic.

Education reformer Dr. Samuel Blumenfeld (Chapter 5) describes the destructive ideological foundation of progressive education in his damning analysis of Dewey's 1898 article, "The Primary-Education Fetich." Blumenfeld titled his essay "Preface to John Dewey's Plan to Dumb-Down America,"[41] and both were posted April 30, 2013, by Camp Constitution,[42] an association of Constitutionalists who support the Samuel L. Blumenfeld Literacy Foundation.[43] Blumenfeld writes:

> The dumbing-down of America is no accident. It is not the result of uncontrollable natural forces floating in the air we breathe or the water we drink. It is the result of a planned scheme launched in 1898 by Progressive-in-Chief John Dewey outlined in an article titled "The Primary-Education Fetich" [*sic*]. Dewey was a diehard socialist with a deep hatred of capitalism, individualism, and orthodox Christianity. He, and his small army of academic followers, were

determined to turn America into a humanist collectivist society and he figured out that the best way to separate Americans from their constitutional freedoms and individualism was to dumb them down.

And the easiest way to do this was to change the way children were taught to read in their primary schools. Get rid of intensive phonics, the foundation of language mastery and independent intelligence, and put in its place a "sight" or "look-say" method that teaches children to read English as if it were Chinese. Have them memorize a sight vocabulary so that they develop a whole-word reflex and cannot see the phonetic structure of our alphabetic words. Thus, they will become reading disabled, dyslexic, or simply low-level readers....

We are reprinting Dewey's article because it is important for Americans to understand how they've been deceived by their so-called educators. The plan to deliberately dumb down the nation has been hidden from the public for almost 100 years. Reading it today is to become finally aware of the deceit and treachery behind this treasonous conspiracy to destroy the intellect of millions of Americans behind the benign façade of Progressive education....

Dewey, of course, is long dead, but his disciples control American public education, and whether they know it or not they are continuing to implement Dewey's plan. And we see the results every day. In 2007, the National Endowment for the Arts released its report on the decline of American literacy. Its chairman, Dana Gioia, stated:

> This is a massive social problem. We are losing the majority of the new generation. They will not achieve anything close to their potential because of poor reading.

The only way to reverse this situation is to make sure that every child in every American school is taught to read with intensive, systematic phonics. We know how to restore high literacy to America. But is there the will to do it? Many parents are doing it by homeschooling their own children. But will it be done in the schools? It will be done only if there is enough of an outcry from concerned parents and citizens. That is why we urge readers of this article to distribute copies of it to as many people as possible. If this article is read by millions of Americans, it will have an impact that the educators and politicians will not be able to ignore.

Blumenfeld's Preface was a warning to parents not to be seduced by the humanitarian hoax of progressivism and the deceit of its hucksters. Undeterred, progressive education marched ahead to create an illiteracy epidemic, along with new levels of societal destruction through its anti-American ideological content. Following the precepts outlined in Dewey's plan and the rationalizations it provided for compliance, America's education industry embraced socialism; disguised it as *progressive* education; and marketed it as the modern, *scientific* approach to education. In Dewey's own words:

> To educate on the basis of past surroundings is like adapting an organism to an environment which no longer exists. The individual is stultified, if not disintegrated; and the course of progress is blocked....

> The existing status [perennialism] was developed in a period when ability to read was practically the sole avenue to knowledge, when it was the only tool which insured control over the accumulated spiritual resources of civilization.

> Scientific methods of observation, experimentation, and testing were either unknown or confined to a few specialists at the upper end of the educational ladder.... We often fail to see that the dominant position occupied by book-learning in school education is simply a corollary and relic of this epoch of intellectual development....

> When ability to read and write marked the distinction between the educated and the uneducated man, not simply in the scholastic sense, but in the sense of one who is enslaved by his environment and one who is able to take advantage of and rise above it, corresponding importance attached to acquiring these capacities.

> Reading and writing were obviously what they are still so often called—the open doors to learning and to success in life. All the meaning that belongs to these ends naturally transferred itself to

the means through which alone they could be realized. The intensity and ardor with which our forefathers set themselves to master reading and writing, the difficulties overcome, the interest attached in the ordinary routine of school-life to what now seems barren— the curriculum of the three R's—all testify to the motive-power these studies possessed. To learn to read and write was an interesting, even exciting, thing: it made such a difference in life....

Methods for learning to read come and go across the educational arena, like the march of supernumeraries upon the stage. Each is heralded as the final solution of the problem of learning to read; but each in turn gives way to some later discovery. The simple fact is—that they all lack the essential of any well-grounded method, namely, relevancy to the child's mental needs. No scheme for learning to read can supply this want. Only a new motive—putting the child into a vital relation to the materials to be read—can be of service here. It is evident that this condition cannot be met, unless learning to read be postponed to a period when the child's intellectual appetite is more consciously active, and when he is mature enough to deal more rapidly and effectively with the formal and mechanical difficulties....

All this amounts to saying that school reform is dependent upon a collateral wider change in the public opinion which controls school board, superintendent, and teachers. There are certain minor changes; reforms in detail, which can be effected directly within the school system itself. But the school is not an isolated institution: it is one of an organism of social forces. To secure more scientific principles of work in the school means, accordingly, clearer vision and wiser standards of thought and action in the community at large....

Let the community once realize that it is educating upon the basis of a life which it has left behind, and it will turn, with adequate intellectual and material resources, to meet the needs of the present hour.

American education was the vehicle for seismic social change, and Dewey's dream for the politicization of America's education has been wildly successful. The American education industry continues to perpetuate his progressive education, and has shifted its mission from teaching children fundamental knowledge and *how* to think, to indoctrinating children in *what* to think. Teachers have become agents to effect radical social change, students are the unsuspecting target, and parents are the enemy.

The anti-American social engineers understood that the earlier educational indoctrination begins, the more effective it is. The decision was made to introduce divisive critical race theory to the youngest children. Fomenting race wars now begins in kindergarten.

On June 30, 2021, the National Education Association (NEA), the largest teachers' union in America, voted to approve a plan to promote critical race theory in all 50 states. Investigative journalist Christopher F. Rufo describes the shocking decision in his July 15, 2021, article, "Going All In: The NEA pledges to bring critical race theory to a public school near you."[44]

> Union delegates representing 3 million public school employees approved funding for three separate items related to "increasing the implementation" of "critical race theory" in K–12 curricula; promoting critical race theory in 14,000 local school districts; and attacking opponents of critical race theory, including parent organizations and conservative research centers.
>
> In the resolution, the union agreed publicly to "convey its support" for critical race theory, oppose restrictions in state legislatures, and use schools to promote political activism. The delegates pledged to "join with Black Lives Matter at School and the Zinn Education Project" to hold a "national day of action" on George Floyd's birthday, recruiting teachers to hold political demonstrations and "teach lessons about structural racism and oppression."
>
> The resolution also promised to develop a study to critique "empire, white supremacy, anti-Blackness, anti-Indigeneity, racism, patriarchy, cisheteropatriarchy, capitalism, ableism, [and] anthropocentrism [human exceptionalism]"—that is, adapting the most fashionable and intellectually bankrupt ideas from the universities for use in grade school classrooms.
>
> Finally, the NEA passed a resolution to "research the organizations" that oppose critical race theory—including grassroots parent

> organizations—and provide resources to groups and individuals targeting them. The national teachers' union will use union dues, collected from public employees paid by taxpayers, to attack parents who oppose the racial indoctrination of their children.... The teachers' union has nationalized critical race theory and committed to the full range of left-wing radicalism, including opposition to "capitalism" and "anthropocentrism."

Parents of students, regardless of race, must stand up to oppose racism, regardless of race. Parents cannot allow themselves to be intimidated, and their power usurped, by the corrupt, politicized, anti-American education industry.

Christopher F. Rufo's Parent Guidebook: Fighting Critical Race Theory in K–12 Schools[45] (Chapter 12) is an essential tool. He begins with its definition:

> Critical race theory is an academic discipline that holds the United States is a nation founded on white supremacy and oppression, and that these forces are still at the root of our society. Critical race theorists believe that American institutions such as the U.S. Constitution and the legal system preach freedom and equality but are mere "camouflages" for naked racial domination. They believe that racism is a constant, universal condition that simply becomes more subtle, sophisticated, and insidious over the course of history. In simple terms, critical race theory reformulates the old Marxist dichotomy of oppressor and oppressed, replacing the class categories of bourgeoisie and proletariat with the identity categories of White and Black. But the basic conclusion is the same: in order to liberate man, society must be fundamentally transformed through moral, economic, and political revolution.

All Marxist species, variations of the "genus" of ideological Marxism described in Chapter 11, plan to fundamentally transform society by using the familiar divide-and-conquer strategy. Divisiveness is deliberately exacerbated and then exploited in order to destroy the existing political infrastructure. Societal collapse is followed by replacement with the desired variation of collectivism.

Critical race theory serves the needs of any and all enemies of the state whose political goal is destruction of our constitutional republic. Black supremacists dream of a black-supremacist America. Radical leftists, including Antifa and the loathsome National Education Association, dream of a socialist America.

The problem for all domestic enemies of America is that they all share the same globalist funding sources. They have not yet realized that there is no place for agitators in globalism's planned totalitarian Unistate. Like Vladimir Lenin's "useful idiots" throughout history, they will all be eliminated once their usefulness expires. The anarchy and toxic racism convulsing America today has only one long-term beneficiary: the globalist elite.

CHAPTER 14

Changing Hearts and Minds

Globalism is a replacement ideology that seeks to reorder the world into one singular, planetary Unistate, ruled by the globalist elite. The globalist war on nation-states cannot succeed without collapsing the United States of America. The long-term strategic attack plan moves America incrementally from constitutional republic to socialism to globalism to feudalism. The tactical attack plan uses asymmetric psychological and informational warfare to destabilize Americans and drive society out of objective reality into the madness of subjective reality. America's children are the primary target of the globalist predators.

On October 30, 2008, in Columbia, Missouri, candidate Barack Hussein Obama declared to an unsuspecting public, "We are five days away from fundamentally transforming America." It was the promise of a radical leftist to change the culture of America and move the nation from constitutional republic to socialism. John Dewey's destruction of American minds through progressive education had a partner in president Obama and the Culture War Obama unleashed on America.

To move our constitutional republic to socialism and beyond, globalism's leftist progressive movement adopted the binary victim/oppressor social structure of cultural Marxism. Classical Marxism identifies the oppressors as the bourgeoisie (owners of production) who exploit the proletariat (workers). The metric of classical Marxism is economics. Cultural Marxism re-labels the participants and defines culture, not economics, as the metric of exploitation. It is one *species* of the genus Marxism as described by James Lindsay in Chapter 11. In cultural Marxism, white males are the identified oppressors and everyone else is their victim.

Both classical and cultural Marxism seek to replace the existing order with collectivism, each selling its own idealized form of a secular heaven on Earth. Today's social justice warriors who sign onto this leftist lunacy are ignorant of history, arrogant, and too childish to examine the objective reality of the offer. Leftist ideologues actually believe the fantasy of a Marxist Utopia, and don't realize that the paradise they advocate is the powerless state of infantile dependence, the opposite of individual freedom. When infantile dependence is advanced into adulthood, it awards the state total control.

Cultural Marxism dominates today's far left Democrat Party. Author and political analyst David Horowitz provides important historical context to the radicalization of the Democrat Party in America on his website Discover the Networks: Democratic Socialists of America (DSA):[46]

> At the height of the Cold War and the Vietnam War era, the Socialist Party USA of Eugene Debs and Norman Thomas split in two over the issue of whether or not to criticize the Soviet Union, its allies, and Communism: One faction rejected and denounced the USSR and its allies.... The other faction, however, refused to reject Marxism, refused to criticize or denounce the USSR and its allies, and continued to support Soviet-backed policies.... This faction, whose leading figure was Michael Harrington, in 1973 took the name Democratic Socialist Organizing Committee (DSOC); its membership included many former Students for a Democratic Society activists.

> DSOC operated not as a separate political party but as an explicitly socialist force within the Democratic Party and the labor movement. As such, it attracted many young activists who sought to push the Democratic Party further leftward politically. Among the notables who joined DSOC were Machinists' Union leader William Winpisinger, feminist Gloria Steinem, gay rights activist Harry Britt, actor Ed Asner, and California Congressman (and avowed socialist) Ron Dellums.

> By 1979 DSOC had made major inroads into the Democratic Party and claimed a national membership of some 3,000 people. In 1982, DSOC, under Michael Harrington's leadership, merged with the New American Movement to form the Democratic Socialists of America (DSA).

> Harrington's strategy was to force a "realignment" of the two major

political parties by pulling the Democrats emphatically to the left and polarizing the parties along class lines. He expected that this would drive business interests away from the Democrats and into the Republican Party, but that those losses would be more than offset by an influx of newly energized minority and union voters to the Democratic Party, and that over time the Democrats would embrace socialism as their preferred ideology.…

Harrington sought to establish DSA as a force that worked within, and not outside of, the existing American political system. DSA draws heavily from the ideas of the late Italian Communist Party theoretician Antonio Gramsci. As the Orange County (California) DSA stated in its February 1984 newsletter, Gramsci's writings "have… formed a vital part of the ideas that brought about the formation of today's DSA." …

In 2008, most DSA members actively supported Barack Obama for U.S. President. Said the organization: "DSA believes that the possible election of Senator Obama to the presidency in November represents a potential opening for social and labor movements to generate the critical political momentum necessary to implement a progressive political agenda." …

In 2018, 28-year-old DSA member Alexandria Ocasio-Cortez rose to prominence when, with no prior political experience, she was elected to the U.S. House of Representatives. Another newcomer to Congress in 2018 was DSA member Rashida Tlaib. That same year, DSA member Julia Salazar won a seat in the New York State Senate.

Using the term *Democratic socialism* is a deceptive marketing technique designed to put lipstick on an abhorrent political pig, disguising collectivism's tyrannical core. It advocates a gradual and peaceful transition from capitalism to socialism by purportedly "democratic" means, and is presented with mystical reverence as deliverance of social justice and income equality. Duped millennials argue that old attempts at socialism were not the "real" socialism—democratic socialism is, and this time, they argue, it will succeed.

Barack Obama sold Democratic socialism to America by calling it *hope and change*. Today's radical leftist Democrats, still led by Obama, are the "resistance" movement destabilizing the foundations of America.

The Biden regime's domestic policies are a continuation and escalation of Obama's destructive socialist policies shattering the established Judeo-Christian values of American culture. Faith, family, flag, meritocracy, and traditional definitions of race, gender, and sexual identity—all are now deemed oppressive. Traditional American norms are being dismantled and replaced with romanticized notions of a globalized world without territorial borders, cultural borders, sexual borders, or any other defined boundary. The nation is being fundamentally transformed, just as Obama promised, and the indoctrination is happening in schools across the country. As I stated earlier, America's children are globalism's primary target; everyone else is just in the way.

Freedom in a constitutional republic requires a common denominator for its citizens. Being American is that common denominator. Membership in the American family is not hyphenated. There are no black-Americans, white-Americans, Hispanic-Americans, or Asian-Americans. There are only Americans who are white, black, Hispanic, and Asian.

The same racism that was used against blacks in America is now being used against whites in America. It is being used to turn young children against each other, against their parents, and against themselves in government schools. Critical race theory, discussed in Chapter 12, is the leftists' divide-and-conquer weapon of choice to create social chaos in America.

The goal of critical race theory devotees and their cancel-culture campaign is to foment race riots and a race war in the United States. This is such a shocking yet critical concept that I will repeat it: *The goal of CRT devotees and their cancel-culture campaign is to foment race riots and a race war in the United States of America.* How are CRT and its racist white-privilege narrative designed to foment a race war?? Socialist Saul Alinsky provides the answer in his infamous tactical primer, *Rules for Radicals: A Pragmatic Primer for Realistic Radicals.*[47] Alinsky instructs radicals to "Rub raw the resentments of the people…all issues must be polarized if action is to follow." (pp. 116/133, Vintage)

Race is the simplest division to exploit because it is visible. Fomenting racial hostility is a very effective strategy for dividing and conquering a nation. Rule 13 from Alinsky's primer continues to guide the leftist Democrat War on America:

Rule 13: *Pick the target, freeze it, personalize it, polarize it. Don't try to attack abstract corporations or bureaucracies. Identify a responsible individual. Ignore attempts to shift or spread the blame.* (p. 130)

The relentless ad hominem attacks against former President Donald Trump were, and continue to be, targeted, personal, and polarizing. Rule 13 is the quintessential example of focusing attention on the WHO instead of the WHAT, in order to manipulate public opinion.

Truth is entirely irrelevant for Alinsky and his radical leftist followers. Alinsky writes, "The real and only question regarding the ethics of means and ends is, and always has been, 'Does this *particular* end justify this *particular* means?'" (p. 24) According to Alinsky, "*The third rule of the ethics of means and ends is that in war the end justifies almost any means.*" (p. 29)

Changing hearts and minds is a term used in warfare to indicate an emotional and intellectual method of bringing a subjugated population to the side of the conqueror. Alinsky's Rule 13 is a weapon of war. The ad hominem attacks on Donald Trump are attempts to change the hearts and minds of Americans—Alinsky style.

It does not matter that Trump is not and never was a racist, or that Trump's policies were extremely beneficial to the black, Hispanic, and Asian communities in America. Trump and his entire conservative/populist movement must be portrayed as racist in order to foment race riots. Even President Trump's support of law enforcement and ordered liberty has been perverted by the radical leftists into justification for their own racist attacks on white police officers.

The Democrat outrage over the so-called Capitol "insurrection" by Trump supporters—assisted by embedded plainclothes law enforcement—on January 6, 2021, is pure Alinsky-style political theater. An excellent article on political theater published in *Frontpage Magazine,* July 15, 2020, by John Perazzo, was titled "Why BLM Yawns at Police-Shooting Statistics."[48] Perazzo quotes Alinsky as tutoring his followers to "present themselves as the noble defenders of high moral principles and to react dramatically with greatly exaggerated displays of 'shock, horror, and moral outrage' whenever their targeted enemy erred or could be depicted as having erred."

Congressional Representative Nancy Pelosi (D-CA) is the queen of Democrat hypocrisy and Alinsky-style outrage. Her insistence upon an extended military presence in Washington, DC, after January 6, 2021, was designed to validate her own fabricated fearmongering narrative, and to "protect" politicians from white Trump supporters. On March 4, 2021, Jamaal Bowman (D-NY) said on MSNBC, "We must do everything we can to protect ourselves." Our southern border, under President Joe Biden and Vice President Kamala Harris, is open and unguarded. The racist messaging is that open borders to unvetted migrants of color from hostile foreign countries are less of a threat to the nation than white Trump supporters.

Consider the sequence:

Identify Trump as the target → attack him as a white supremacist → continue the attacks on Trump even after he is out of office → spread the attacks to his supporters → support reverse racism → target white police officers → support violent black supremacist/Marxist movement (BLM) → involve corporate America in the attacks and the support for BLM → indoctrinate adults to support reverse racism with the mainstream media echo chamber of CRT → support defunding the police → indoctrinate children in CRT with educational curricula that support reverse racism → foment CRT with governmental policies that create intolerable cognitive dissonance until the fury breaks out into the streets → incite violence → blame the violence on white supremacists → quell the Democrat CRT-incited violence with government violence (military or National Guard) → present Democrats as saving the country from Trump's white supremacists.

The sinister political purpose of fomenting race wars in America is the elimination of our constitutional republic and the eventual imposition of one-world government. This colossal humanitarian hoax is being sold to a regressed and frightened American public as deliverance. Billionaire globalists finance politicians, who fund the radical leftist Democrats, who support CRT, who foment racial divisiveness and the coming race wars. Follow the money. Always follow the money.

CHAPTER 15

Conflict Theory and the Hegelian Dialectic

Globalism is a replacement ideology that seeks to reorder the world into one singular, planetary Unistate, ruled by the globalist elite. The globalist war on nation-states cannot succeed without collapsing the United States of America. The long-term strategic attack plan moves America incrementally from constitutional republic to socialism to globalism to feudalism. The tactical attack plan uses asymmetric psychological and informational warfare to destabilize Americans and drive society out of objective reality into the madness of subjective reality. America's children are the primary target of the globalist predators.

In order to fully understand the synergistic and catastrophic effects of race wars and Outcome-Based Education's third stage, Transformational Education (Chapter 12), it is necessary to understand that conflict theory is both the fulcrum and the facilitator of Marxism and its various species.

Conflict theory is a derivative of Malthusianism. Thomas Malthus (1766–1834), English economist and demographer, published his famous theory on population in 1798, *An Essay on the Principle of Population*. Malthus applied supply-and-demand economic theory to food-population ratios and ultimately to societal conflict. Malthus theorized that population grows exponentially and food supplies grow arithmetically; therefore, population would necessarily outstrip food resources and eventually result in conflict.

German philosopher Karl Marx (1818–1883) had a broader view of conflict. Marx believed that society exists in a perpetual state of conflict over competition for all resources, not just food. He focused on the conflict between social classes over those resources. Marx identified the wealthy bourgeoisie as oppressors, and the working-class poor as oppressed. Marxist conflict theory assumes that human beings act in their own self-interest, that the resources they seek are limited, and that the pursuit of limited resources necessarily leads to societal conflict.

Marx was also influenced by German philosopher Georg Hegel (1770–1831), whose philosophy rejects objective reality and disdains the individual. Instead, Hegel posits that

> society evolved and progressed in accordance with the laws of "dialectic," a cyclical pattern in which one prevailing idea/worldview (thesis) comes into conflict with an opposing idea/worldview (antithesis), and by means of that conflict causes a new, more meritorious creation (synthesis) to emerge. Marx believed that through this process, society would eventually move past capitalist economics—as it had previously moved past feudalism—and embrace socialism and communism. (David Horowitz, Discover the Networks: Karl Marx)[49]

Dialectic is a confusing term because it is a process of conflict for resolving conflicting ideas. An article by financial analyst Jeff Carlson, CFA, posted on *themarketswork*, February 11, 2017, "Gramsci, Alinsky & the Left,"[50] helps clarify the philosophy and the process.

> The Dialectic Process was created by Georg Hegel. The Dialectic Process was used as *a process to describe change.* Hegel, a social philosopher, used the Dialectic Process to describe how societies could come to a state of more rational, elevated thinking.

> Karl Marx took Hegel's idea of the Dialectic Process and changed it subtly. Marx used it as a process to describe *social* change. There are three key parts to the Dialectic Process:

> The first is the Thesis—or Starting Point. A better term might be the Status Quo—where we are today.

> Marx believed that in order for things to change there would have to be some form of opposition to the Status Quo. This opposition is the second part—the Antithesis—or the mechanism for change. It is the people and ideas that do not support the status quo—the opposing group.

> When the Thesis and the Antithesis meet—or clash—you have the third component—Synthesis. Another word for Synthesis might be Revolution. Marx believed that Synthesis was Progress—a necessary confrontation that would allow for society to emerge as a better

place for most people involved.

Marx believed the Dialectic Process to be a true process—an important distinction—as a true Process does not end—it is ongoing. In other words, once we reach Synthesis the process will start again. Synthesis will now become the Thesis—the Status Quo. And new Opposition will arise.

And that—in very simplistic terms—is how Marx perceived society progressing over time.

Karl Marx applied Hegel's dialectical process for change to his own assumptions about society, and developed Marxist conflict theory. Its political applications continue today to move radical leftist domestic policies from theory to practice.

Consider Herbert Marcuse (1898–1979), the German-born American political philosopher and prominent member of the Frankfurt School, dedicated to moving America gradually to the left following Antonio Gramsci's *long march through the institutions*. The ideological goal of the Frankfurt School and its Marxist theoreticians was to erase the existing social structures and replace them with Marxist notions of Utopia, where distinctions between state and civil society would cease to exist, resulting in universal egalitarianism.

For me, the fatal flaw in Marx's ideological pursuit of a Utopian collectivist society is that neither Marxism nor any of its myriad species acknowledges that there is always a ruling elite that controls the production and distribution of the limited resources that Marxist conflict theory claims exist. So, even if society's resources were *owned* by the masses, their production and distribution are not *controlled* by the masses. Whoever controls the resources rules the ruled.

Marcuse's particular contribution to the Frankfurt School's effort was establishing the *New Left*, which differed from earlier leftist movements by shifting the focus from labor activism to social activism. Marcuse brought his Marxist theories to college campuses, and the 1960s radical leftist student movement advocated anarchy, anti-war protests, second-wave feminism, sexual liberation, and countercultural norms.

Marcuse developed the radical concept of the *Great Refusal*, which is *the protest against that which is.* Basically, it means the total rejection of what exists, in preparation for what is to come. In globalist terms, it is the precursor to the Great Reset, the metaphorical return to zero in order to *build back better.* Both are classic replacement ideologies.

According to German philosopher Max Horkheimer (1895–1973), Marcuse's equally radical Marxist friend and colleague at the Frankfurt School:

> The Revolution won't happen with guns, rather it will happen incrementally, year by year, generation by generation. We will gradually infiltrate their educational institutions and their political offices, transforming them slowly into Marxist entities as we move towards universal egalitarianism.

The 1969 Woodstock Festival in upstate New York focused the Culture War on sex, drugs, and rock and roll. The hedonism of the Me Generation in the 1970s continued to destabilize American society. Wikipedia describes the Me Generation[51] as transitional: "The 1970s have been described as a transitional era when the self-help of the 1960s became self-gratification, and eventually devolved into the selfishness of the 1980s."

As Marxist species continued to undermine the fabric of American life, their ideologies of collectivism and radical activism began shifting toward social justice, identity politics, and alternative lifestyles. The country was primed to elect its first black president, Barack Hussein Obama, in 2008. Obama's particular forte is obfuscating language. Beginning with his infamous speech promising to "fundamentally transform America," Obama seduced a nation with cultural Marxism and its Marxist doublespeak.

Americans were unprepared for the transformation that our nation's first community-organizer-in-chief had planned. They didn't recognize the obvious warning sign that Obama's career as a community organizer was with an Alinsky-inspired group in Chicago, the Gamaliel Foundation. It was simply inconceivable that a president of the United States would govern in accordance with Alinsky's rules:

> *The first step in community organization is community disorganization.* The disruption of the present organization is the first step toward community organization. Present arrangements must be disorganized if they are to be displaced by new patterns that provide

the opportunities and means for citizen participation. *All change means disorganization of the old and organization of the new.* (Rules for Radicals, p. 116)

Under Obama's watch, American education shifted from traditional classical learning to Common Core standards, and teachers became agents of social change rather than educational authority figures and stable cultural role models. Obama facilitated the entry into Outcome-Based Education's third phase, Transformational Education, when the educational emphasis shifts to changing children's actual values.

Barack Obama's radicalism, euphemistically labeled progressivism, is the continuation of Herbert Marcuse's New Left, which resurrected political correctness in order to restrict free speech in America and ultimately criminalize oppositional political speech.

An interesting follow-up article by Jeff Carlson published on February 16, 2017, "The Goal of Political Correctness,"[52] discusses political correctness, Herbert Marcuse, and his contributions to the War on America:

> Political Correctness is the forceful application of whatever belief furthers a political agenda. It is the words themselves. Any ideology that advances the cause *is Politically Correct—because it works.* There is no search for factual correctness—there is only the search for what achieves the goal. In this way, truth has been pulled from itself and is no longer a vehicle for honest discourse. It is a vehicle for control....
>
> As I wrote in "Gramsci, Alinsky & the Left," Critical Theory—a theory used to criticize every traditional social institution—provided the origin of Political Correctness. As noted by Raymond V. Raehn, "Political Correctness seeks to impose a uniformity of thought and behavior on all Americans and is therefore totalitarian in nature". Political Correctness is Cultural Marxism—also known as multiculturalism. Multiculturalism views traditional culture as the true source of oppression in the world. *It is the translation of Marxism from economic to cultural terms....*
>
> Marcuse also embraced the idea of feminism—he saw in it the potential for radical social change. The process of rethinking

femininity and masculinity—gender identity—could lead to a replacement of masculine traits with feminine ones (Marcuse has been credited with advocating and advancing androgyny). Marcuse noted in 1974 that "I believe the women's liberation movement today is, perhaps, the most important and potentially the most radical political movement that we have. Feminism is a revolt against decaying capitalism". Marcuse recognized in Feminism the impact that could be had on the traditional family.

So, consider our backdrop. Gramsci promoted an overturn of societal institutions, values and morals as a means to promote change—to promote Cultural Marxism. The Frankfurt School took Gramsci's ideas and began the process of implementing them—introducing them into American Society. The Theory of Critical Thinking was employed to launch criticisms and attacks on every traditional social institution—oriented toward critiquing and changing society as a whole. Theodor W. Adorno focused this view and narrowed in on Culture as the primary factor in perpetuating Capitalism. His goal—a "genuine liberal" free of all groups, including race, family and institutions. His target—the traditional family model. His premise—the traditional family produced a society defined by racism and inequality and was therefore deserving of overthrow. Marcuse utilized timing and events to engage in a reshaping of morality—engaging and promoting the student uprisings of the 1960s—through his "Great Refusal"—his embrace of feminism—and gender identity. And the process continues today.

Critical thinking is the ability to analyze information effectively and then form a judgment. In Marxist Critical Theory the word *critical* is used to mean criticism. So, Critical Theory is actually Criticism Theory. The goal is to criticize, demean, and destabilize the existing culture in order to create social chaos. Criticism Theory is a tool for conflict, and conflict theory is at the heart of the racism, black supremacism, and the current war on maleness and femaleness that is convulsing America today.

Fomenting race wars and sex wars, based on the two simplest divisions in society to identify, is part of globalism's war on nation-states. Using the tactical divide-and-conquer strategy to create social chaos, the globalist scheme is to make society ungovernable, and then sweep in with its planned Unistate to restore order. What globalists cannot achieve through lawful constitutional means they seek to achieve using Hegel's dialectic for social change:

$$Thesis + Antithesis = Synthesis$$

Thesis: The United States of America exists as a constitutional republic and sovereign nation.

Antithesis: Leftism's march through American institutions creates overwhelming chaos and conflict, including race wars and wars between the sexes, that make the country ungovernable and collapse the economy into socialism.

Synthesis: The globalist elite replace socialism's centralized government with globalism's planetary Unistate.

Globalism insists that in its Utopian managerial Unistate, "You will own nothing and be happy." The reality is that globalism is far more ambitious than any known species of flawed Marxist ideology—the globalist Unistate is 21st-century feudalism on a planetary scale. The ideological genus *Marxism* only works *theoretically* in society. In practice, universal egalitarianism can never be achieved, neither in Marxism nor in any of its myriad species, because its operating infrastructure is a binary system of ruling elites and ruled masses. Globalism regresses humanity back much farther than Marxist fantasies of egalitarianism. The supremacist managerial Unistate unapologetically reverts humanity back to a future of permanent feudal servitude.

CHAPTER 16

Ideological Invasion

Globalism is a replacement ideology that seeks to reorder the world into one singular, planetary Unistate, ruled by the globalist elite. The globalist war on nation-states cannot succeed without collapsing the United States of America. The long-term strategic attack plan moves America incrementally from constitutional republic to socialism to globalism to feudalism. The tactical attack plan uses asymmetric psychological and informational warfare to destabilize Americans and drive society out of objective reality into the madness of subjective reality. America's children are the primary target of the globalist predators.

The Frankfurt School (Chapters 11 and 15) is best understood as a philosophical and sociological movement that spread through Western universities around the world. Instead of embracing individualism and the separation of powers that distinguish our constitutional republic, Frankfurt School émigrés continued to advance their collectivist ideology with religious fanaticism, missionary zeal, and the hubris characteristic of supremacist ideologues.

The movement began with Hungarian Marxist philosopher George Lukács (1885–1971), minister of culture in Bolshevik Hungary in 1919. Before the Bolsheviks came to power, Hungary was a Catholic nation. Lukács recognized the necessity of collapsing the traditional nuclear family in Marxist revolutions, following Lenin's dictum, "Destroy the family, you destroy the country."

As deputy commissar for education and culture, Lukács targeted Hungary's family unit and its traditional sexual morals. He implemented a program called *cultural terrorism*, which had two tactical objectives. First, target children's minds through lectures that encouraged them to ridicule and reject Christian ethics. Second, groom them with graphic sexual content and instruction in free love and sexual intercourse. People in Hungary were so enraged, it forced Lukács to flee the country.

Lukács met Felix Weil, a wealthy German Marxist, at a Marxist study week in Frankfurt in 1923. Together, they set up the Institute for Social Research at the Goethe University in Frankfurt, Germany. Weil's doctoral thesis explored the practical problems of implementing socialism, and he was very interested in Lukács's new cultural approach to Marxism.

Under the direction of radical German philosopher Max Horkheimer, the psychological theories of Sigmund Freud and sociological theories of Karl Marx were integrated, and the Institute for Social Research gave birth to a new species of Marxism. Cultural Marxism presented the novel theory that society was psychologically oppressed by the institutions of Western culture. This new type of Marxism required a new methodology for implementation.

Jeff Carlson, some of whose articles are discussed in Chapter 15, described the method and the methodology in his February 2017 article "Gramsci, Alinsky & the Left":[53]

> The Frankfurt School employed a technique invented by Horkheimer called Critical Theory—a social theory oriented toward critiquing and changing society as a whole. The point of the theory is to criticize every traditional social institution—and to specifically avoid offering any alternatives—as a means to breaking down Western Culture. A better, alternative way is never to be offered—only criticism. While at Columbia, the Frankfurt School shifted [its] focus from Critical Theory directed at German society to Critical Theory directed at American society.

Horkheimer defined the difference in method between social/scientific theories and critical social theories. Social/scientific theories rely on objective reality and the distinction between theory and practice. Critical Theory *merges* theory and practice, rejects objective reality (facts), and defines *itself* as a method—a continuous process for change that relies on subjective reality (feelings) and denies any unequivocal knowledge. Critical Theory is a derivative of Hegel's dialectic for social change:

$$\text{Thesis} + \text{Antithesis} = \text{Synthesis}$$

Horkheimer viewed Critical Theory as the operating system for changing society as a whole. It is the "fundamental change" promised by American Marxist president Barack Obama. The idea was to actively criticize every facet of Western civilization, destabilize its infrastructure of objective truth and reality, collapse society from within, and replace the established Judeo-Christian morality and capitalist economic system with socialism.

In 1933 the Nazis closed the Institute, and the Institute moved its operations to the United States. It reopened in New York at Columbia University in 1935, and came to be known as the Frankfurt School, a school of thought synonymous with Critical Theory.

The Frankfurt School and its Marxist theoreticians trained their sights on America, and like a viral infection, their ideas and theories spread throughout the host country. The ideological objective was to erase the existing American social structures and replace them with Marxist notions of Utopia, where universal egalitarianism would be realized. The tactical strategy was Critical Theory.

When the Institute for Social Research reopened in Frankfurt in 1951, its influence and many of its theoreticians remained in America. Over several decades, the Critical Theory methodology has divided and mutated into critical pedagogy, critical legal theory, critical race theory, critical feminist theory, critical gender theory, and on and on and on, in its never-ending goal of fundamental transformation and societal collapse on the way to the ultimate goal of entirely replacing the existing ideology and social structure.

Changing the hearts and minds of a nation's citizens is a daunting, long-term task. Cultural Marxists understood from the beginning that seismic educational reform was required because children live what they learn, and children are the future of every society on Earth. The Culture War is revolution without bullets that began in universities and wended its way all the way down the educational ladder to preschools.

Progressive education remains the weapon of choice for Cultural Marxists. Its hero, another Frankfurt School Marxist, Paulo Freire, was a Brazilian political reformer. Freire's book *Pedagogy of the Oppressed*[54] is a reference manual for radical leftist educators today.

Freire's specialty was applying Marx's oppressor/oppressed divide to education. His theory of critical pedagogy argues that education cannot be separated from politics and that the rightful goal of education is *emancipation from oppression through the awakening of critical consciousness*. Paulo Freire's critical pedagogy is a derivative of Critical Theory, which advocates criticizing and dismantling every aspect of traditional American education in both form and content. Its planned demolition includes rejecting literacy, foundational skills, and foundational knowledge; eliminating meritocracy, fairness, and equal treatment; and replacing traditional education with Outcome-Based Education and anti-American indoctrination through curriculum content. The Hegelian dialectic for social change—Thesis + Antithesis = Synthesis—is clearly evident in critical pedagogy's *unlearning* model for change: Learning + Unlearning = Relearning.

Unlearning, Constructivism, sight-word reading, and Outcome-Based Education are all deconstruction efforts to dumb down students and promote political revolution. The Frankfurt School émigrés successfully politicized education and launched the Culture War in America. Their devotees and descendants effectively created a victim coalition of supposedly oppressed minorities—blacks, women, and homosexuals. And identity politics was born, another species of Cultural Marxism that fomented racial polarization, radical feminism, and the transgender movement in its efforts to collapse America from within.

American schools have become Marxist indoctrination centers where feelings, not facts, define reality. They no longer teach civics and American history; they teach revisionist critical race theory to, as Saul Alinsky said, "rub raw the resentments" and create social chaos. Revisionism is the reinterpretation of history and historical events, including reinterpreting the motivations and decisions of the people involved in those events. The fiction of critical race theory is taught as fact, to actively raise student consciousness of their respective roles as *white oppressor* and *black oppressed*. The political goal is to create racial divisiveness and break down our shared national identity as Americans.

Critical pedagogy supports radical feminism, which views women as an oppressed class and criticizes motherhood, marriage, the nuclear family, and heterosexual sex as evidence of a patriarchal culture. Radical feminism focuses on dismantling gender roles, advocating the total reordering of society as a response to life in a purportedly misogynistic civilization of domination and oppression of women by men.

Radical feminism does not advocate equality and partnership between men and women; it advocates conflict. Like supremacist critical race theory, radical feminism promotes female supremacy. The political goal of radical feminism is the collapse of the traditional American family. As Vladimir Lenin said, "Destroy the family, you destroy the country."

Without factual knowledge of history, students are easily groomed to become political activists in the Culture War on America. Dumbed-down, regressed students, many of whom are functionally illiterate, are extremely easy to exploit. But cultural Marxists have grown impatient; now they are targeting younger and younger children.

Critical pedagogy advocates the madness of LGBTQ biological revisionism, which denies the biological reality of maleness and femaleness, and teaches the fiction that gender is a social construct, a choice—a child's choice. The transgender movement is viral in America, and it is aiming its particular madness at America's children. Schools are no longer safe places. Lessons not only attack children's American identity, racial identity, family identity, and religious identity, they now also attack children's most primary identity—their sexual identity. The American education industry has crossed the Rubicon in 2023.

How did George Lukács's cultural terrorism, which failed in Hungary, take root in the United States of America? The answer is simple: Barack Hussein Obama.

On May 14, 2008, Michelle Obama told the nation:

> Barack knows that we are going to have to make sacrifices; we are going to have to change our conversation; we're going to have to change our traditions, our history; we're going to have to move into a different place as a nation.

Remember that on October 30, 2008, candidate Obama told the nation, "We are five days away from fundamentally transforming America."

Why are Marxists confident that victory is so close at hand? Because the United States government is now in its third term of Marxist president Obama. In his book *Anatomy of a Bolshevik*[55]Alexander G. Markovsky, an American citizen born and educated in the former Soviet Union, holding degrees in economics and political science from the University of Marxism-Leninism, and an engineering degree from Moscow University, describes Obama's progressivism as Marxism in disguise:

> Obama's agenda is not about business, it's about social justice; it's not about wealth creation, it's about wealth redistribution; it's not about the law, it's about fairness; it's not about individualism, it's about collectivism; it's not about self-reliance, it's about dependency; and, finally, it's not about capitalism, it is about socialism. (p. 77)

> For the last 50 years, the progressives have been waging all-out war against American institutions such as education, religion, and family values. Their tireless efforts have paid off. Early on, they realized there is no better way to subvert America than to have a degraded education system.... The American educational system has been a disgrace for many years, producing an illiterate electorate that gravely endangers our democracy. (pp. 217–219)

Barack Obama's education legacy began by his fast-tracking Common Core State Standards, a derivative of the United Nations' Global Education First Initiative (GEFI). Common Core deconstructed American education with its emphasis on global citizenship, a concept antithetical to national sovereignty. Obama's secretary of education, Arne Duncan, praised universal education and the United Nations' World Core Curriculum (WCC), designed by Robert Mueller (1923–2010), a career civil servant with the United Nations.

Mueller was awarded the 1989 UNESCO Prize for Peace Education, and his World Core Curriculum helped establish the Global Education movement that currently affects all 192 UN member nations. The United Nations Education, Science, and Cultural Organization (UNESCO) is the UN institution responsible for internationalizing education and grooming children to become 21st-century citizens in globalism's New World Order.

Preparing children for life in the 21st century, the desired outcome of Outcome-Based Education, is central to understanding globalism's planned Unistate. In the next chapters we will discuss how the various United Nations specialized organizations and agencies, including UNESCO, World

Bank Group, International Monetary Fund, and World Health Organization, collaborate with the World Economic Forum, Deep State functionaries in the United States, and the virulent species of Marxist education in America to promote internationalism and globalist one-world governance.

CHAPTER 17

Cultural Terrorism Comes to America

Globalism is a replacement ideology that seeks to reorder the world into one singular, planetary Unistate, ruled by the globalist elite. The globalist war on nation-states cannot succeed without collapsing the United States of America. The long-term strategic attack plan moves America incrementally from constitutional republic to socialism to globalism to feudalism. The tactical attack plan uses asymmetric psychological and informational warfare to destabilize Americans and drive society out of objective reality into the madness of subjective reality. America's children are the primary target of the globalist predators.

The upward mobility provided by the capitalist system and meritocracy in the United States created a vibrant middle class. In a land of opportunity, working-class people were no longer reliable revolutionaries. Scott S. Powell, Senior Fellow at the Discovery Institute in Seattle and writer for *The American Spectator*, explains the shift in Marxist strategy with a bit of history about Vladimir Lenin. From Powell's August 15, 2015, article, "The Quiet Revolution: How the New Left Took Over the Democratic Party":[56]

> The proletariat never did revolt successfully en masse in any advanced industrialized state. Instead, Marx's political and economic revolution was first staged in the largely agrarian nation of Russia, carried out by Marxist revolutionary leader Vladimir Lenin. Lenin made major contributions to Marx's theories, so much so that Marxism-Leninism became the dominant theoretical paradigm for advancing national liberation movements, communism, and socialism wherever in the world radical revolutionary movements arose.
>
> Among Lenin's contributions was the theory of the vanguard. Since it was apparent that the proletariat masses were unlikely to rise up,

Lenin argued that it was necessary for a relatively small number of vanguard leaders—professional revolutionaries—to advance the revolutionary cause by working themselves into positions of influence. By taking over the commanding heights of labor unions, the press, the universities, and professional and religious organizations, a relatively small number of revolutionaries could multiply their influence and exercise political leverage over their unwitting constituents and society at large.

It was Lenin who introduced the concept of the "popular front" and coined the phrase "useful idiots" in describing the masses who could be manipulated into mob action of marches and protests for an ostensibly narrow cause of the popular front, which the communist vanguard was using as a means for a greater revolutionary political end.

The Marxists needed to identify a new cohort of rebels to collapse American society from within. They chose academia and anointed its graduating student population of useful idiots to be vanguard leaders for changing hearts and minds in America. What Bolshevik George Lukács was unable to impose in Catholic Hungary, cultural terrorism, has been wildly successful in America; it just needed a different strategy in order to succeed.

The 1969 Woodstock Festival was a watershed event for the counterculture movement in music, drugs, and sexual permissiveness. The sexual revolution was a social and cultural movement advocating sexual liberation and acceptance of public nudity, premarital sex, extramarital sex, alternative forms of sexuality, contraception, pornography, homosexuality, masturbation, and abortion. Significantly absent from any discussion of sexual liberation were love, loyalty, commitment, and respect.

The foundation for the sexual revolution that challenged and defied America's traditional Judeo-Christian standards of sexual behavior in the 1960s and 1970s had its roots in Alfred Kinsey's twin books, *Sexual Behavior in the Human Male* (1948)[57] and *Sexual Behavior in the Human Female* (1953).[58] Alfred Kinsey and the Kinsey Institute were supported by the Rockefeller Foundation and protected by the U.S. government. Kinsey's fraudulent research was presented as scientific, factual, and normative. Its catastrophic consequences continue to reverberate in America, advancing

Marxism's intent to collapse from within America's cultural norms and family infrastructure.

The sexual revolution drastically changed attitudes about sexual behavior and freedom of sexual expression. Those changes were animated, echoed, and reflected in literature, films, and legislation. Eventually the counter-culture attitudes of sexual freedom and liberation from traditional Judeo-Christian sexual restrictions touched the children.

Author and researcher Dr. Judith Reisman (1935–2021) was an indefatigable defender of children and society's moral responsibility to protect them. Her work exposed Kinsey's fraudulent research and abhorrent ideology that *children are sexual from birth and have a right to experience sexual pleasure whenever and with whomever they want.* Kinsey insisted that Judeo-Christian principles concerning human sexuality were outdated, unscientific, and repressive. Dr. Reisman's exposé of Kinsey's work implicated its hidden sociopolitical connections to the globalist War on America. She explained how Kinsey's narrative was weaponized for use in the Culture War to support the sexual revolution, collapse societal norms, and change laws regarding the protection of children, globalism's ultimate target.

Dr. Reisman's seminal work, "MKULTRA, KINSEY & ROCKEFELLER: Instruments of the New World Order,"[59] published by the Reisman Institute on January 27, 2021, provides an overview:

> EXECUTIVE SUMMARY
>
> In 1932 communist W. Z. Foster predicted the destruction of America's "education, morality, ethics, science, art, patriotism, religion" was necessary to establish a "New World Order." [1] America's social, economic, and sexual stability rested on Judeo-Christian beliefs and laws—abstinence before and faithfulness during consensual heterosexual marriage. Her national health and wealth testified to the success of this *normal biopsychological sexual model.* From 1941, when America entered WWII, the Rockefeller Foundation (RF) began funding the work of Dr. Alfred Kinsey, who would have been known to RF as a sadomasochistic bi/homosexual. RF backing ensured Kinsey's 1948 book, *Sexual Behavior in the Human Male,*

---

[1]. William Z. Foster. (1932–2016). Toward Soviet America. Hauraki Publishing. Kindle Edition. p. 313.

instant popularity; "the Kinsey scale" codified "fluid sexuality" for the future, ensuring his enduring international fame. RF connected Kinsey with a wider network of RF-funded scientists. From c. 1946 Kinsey partnered with RF's *Columbia-Greystone Brain Project* at New York's "Snake Pit," *Rockland Mental Hospital.* The results of Kinsey's studies of sexual responses of lobotomized patients are sanitized in Kinsey's 1953 book, *Sexual Behavior in the Human Female.*

This paper provides new evidence that the ~2,034 infants and children sexually violated for Kinsey's globe-changing "scientific proof" of infant/child orgasm were sourced from these and similar entities. 82% of Kinsey's child sex experiments are a match with the "Enhanced Interrogation Techniques" used on terrorism suspects at Guantanamo Bay. Since Kinsey's definition of "orgasm" involves symptomatology indistinguishable from epileptic fit, terror/distress and/or electric shock treatment, the physiological responses he declared as child "orgasm" were true trauma responses. This is a newly uncovered Kinsey fraud represented as "science" by his RF funders. Very far from the organic "shock" of a scientific break-through advertised, this paper argues that Kinsey's sex work served as part of a broader psyops[1] as rationale for thorough social change.

As recently as 2020, RF claimed credit for "funding a sexual revolution" via the "Kinsey Reports." From 1954 Congressional efforts to investigate Kinsey's sex work and the causal connection between pornography and ever-rising levels of child sexual abuse have been successfully blocked. Those acting in Rockefeller interests have prevented Kinsey's exposure while promoting his conclusions. From 1953, Hefner, "Kinsey's pamphleteer," marketed RF/Kinsey's lies to young college men via *Playboy.* The sexual restraint of previous generations—responsible for building America—were reframed as a web of hypocritical lies; premarital, extramarital, meaningless, love-free sex glamorized; and a generation, with Hefner its guru, embraced cynicism

[1]. Psychological operations...to convey selected information and indicators to audiences to influence their emotions, motives, and objective reasoning, and...behavior of governments, organizations, groups, and individuals.

about human relationships, nihilism and rejection of all received wisdom.

The 1955 RF-funded Model Penal Code (MPC), drafted by RF's approved team, citing Kinsey, would over-turn prior sex laws, including obscenity laws by 1957, and trivialized sexual abuse. In 1964, the Sexuality Information and Education Council of the United States (SIECUS), funded by *Playboy*, and based at the Kinsey Institute, taught schools to disparage chastity, heterosexuality and monogamy. Soon, with "obscenity exemptions" allowed for "education," K–12 instructed in exotic sexual behaviors. Ever-greater upticks in child rape, pornography and deadly STDs have, predictably, followed. In 2014, the Kinsey Institute (KI) won United Nations consultative status for "educational" materials which aimed at over-riding the most basic instinct for self-preservation in children of all ages, effectively preparing them to co-operate with RF's social change agenda.

Since 2019 the KI's App., the "Kinsey Reporter", solicited "citizen scientists" (of any age) to record/report all sex acts/crimes *anonymously*.

Congressional investigation of a criminal nexus of RF, KI, Big Pharma, Big Porn, Big Abort and "sexual health" providers and educators, past and present, is critically needed to halt the damage these entities inflicted on three successive generations in their obsession for a New World Order.

THE THESIS

For over seven decades, powerful entities prevented official investigation of Dr. Alfred Kinsey and promoted his conclusions as "truth". The result is that public policy, education, and law have been guided by

> the lies of a psychopathic[1] pedosadist.[2] Instead of protecting children and scaffolding the family, government policy has facilitated the agenda of allied interest groups which benefit personally, financially, and/or politically from sexual exploitation of the vulnerable and the destruction of the nuclear family. Notable among these beneficiaries are the very elites who, wishing to establish a New World Order, initiated and funded Kinsey's work, sold his lies to the public, and obstructed investigation of Kinsey and the Institute that bears his name and continues his work to this day. Official investigation of Kinsey—and the cultural transformation he set in motion—is long overdue.

The leaders of the counterculture on campuses in the '60s and '70s graduated and became vanguard leaders, professional revolutionaries who advance the revolutionary cause by working themselves into positions of influence. They are the labor leaders, the press, and leaders of universities, professional organizations, and religious organizations. They have multi-

[1]. The use of such a term "psychopath" is not simply hyperbole. It is used in the clinical sense of the word. Academic researchers, such as Robert Hare, Ph.D, (1) and James Fallon, Ph.D. (2), and forensic clinicians who have spent years working with incarcerated psychopaths in long-term solitary and in general population, such as Jon K. Uhler, LPC (3), each concur that the clinical definition of a psychopath can be boiled down to someone lacking conscience, empathy, and remorse:
(1) http://www.psychology-criminalbehavior-law.com/2015/01/hare-psychopath/
(2) https://www.crimetraveller.org/2015/07/inside-mind-of-psychopath-psychopathic-killer
(3) https://www.quora.com/Why-do-certain-psychologists-mix-up-cluster-B-traits-and-deem-the-combination-a- sociopath/answer/Jon-K-Uhler
Given that Kinsey elected to sexually abuse children, allow other deviant adults to sexually abuse them under the guise of scientific experiments, and the fact that he would do so to so many children, and never experience any signs of remorse or contrition, would clearly categorize him well within the realm of psychopathy. In fact, given that he would then take such "results" from such diabolically abusive "treatment" of children, which would no doubt have profound life-altering and life-long consequences on those children, and use that in such a brazen manner so as to appear as having done legitimate research (as opposed to having perpetrated and sanctioned the perpetration of children), for the purpose of creating a belief about the supposed sexuality of children, in order to craft public opinion, public policy, judicial decisions, and impact state and federal legislation reveals a profoundly psychopathic agenda-driven mind, intent upon shifting the culture toward a greater acceptance of child sexuality and the narrative of mutual love and sexual expression between persons, regardless of age. After all, we're now told that "Love is Love", "Love knows no boundaries", and "Love knows no age." https://www.growingbolder.com/love-has-no-age-3020496/
[2]. While "pedophile" and "pederast" have been used to describe those who desire to, or who do, sexually violate, exploit children, the term means "child-lover" ("philia" the Greek for love or more recently, "friendly feeling toward," https://www.merriam- webster.com/dictionary/-philia).

plied their influence and exercise political leverage over their unwitting constituents and society at large, exactly as Scott S. Powell described.

Today's vanguard leaders are called "influencers," and they are manipulating today's masses of useful idiots into mob action just as their predecessors did. The difference between the nascent counterculture of the '60s and '70s and the radical leftist Democrats of the 2024 Democrat party is in both form and content. Today's influencers reach a worldwide audience using the Internet, and their new corps of chosen rebels are young American parents—indoctrinated millennials.

The communist vanguard and influencers use the "popular front" of parents as "useful idiots" for the revolutionary end of grooming American children to become the newest counterculture generation of anti-American socialist citizens. Today's American parents, the second generation of useful idiots, are low-information voters who surrender their authority and common sense to the influencers. Rather than protect their precious children, they accept the horrific sexualization of them as harmless and embrace the insanity of cultural terrorism as normal.

Let's take a look at sex education in American schools in 2024. Any school, public or private, that receives government funding is subject to the overt sexualization of children. Political analyst Karen McKay, LTC USAR (Ret.), offers a helpful overview in her *American Thinker* article published November 5, 2022, "Weaponizing Children."[60] She writes:

> To achieve an American Marxist utopia, it would be necessary to dismantle the Judeo-Christian values that have undergirded America since the founding. Adult Americans being incorrigibly patriotic and religious, it was necessary to capture their kids.
>
> In 1928, Fabian Socialist George Bernard Shaw [1856–1950] boasted in his *The Intelligent Woman's Guide to Socialism, Capitalism, Sovietism and Fascism*:
>
> > In the case of young children, we have gone far in our interference with the old Roman rights of parents. For nine mortal years the child is taken out of its parents' hands for most of the day, and thus made a State-school child instead of a private family child....

> The social creed must be imposed on us when we are children; for it is like riding, or reading music at sight: it can never become a second nature to those who try to learn it as adults; and the social creed, to be really effective, must be a second nature to us. It is quite easy to give people a second nature, however unnatural, if you catch them early enough. There is no belief, however grotesque and even villainous, that cannot be made a part of human nature if it is inculcated in childhood and not contradicted in the child's hearing.

Marxists are confident that victory is now at hand. The tactics to achieve that victory are societal chaos and confusion. Their weapons include disinformation and propaganda, language distortion, violence, moral degradation, and sexual perversion.

Sex education, once presented in high school as clinical biology, became graphic and presented in elementary schools. Without parents' knowledge, children are encouraged to "discover" that they are homosexual. Drag queen story hours target toddlers in libraries and kindergartens—even on military bases.

Books like *Gender Queer* and *It's Perfectly Normal* are included among the reading material for young kids. Curricula include gems like the film *Pornography Literacy: An intersectional focus on mainstream porn. Heather Has Two Mommies* and *Daddy, Papa, and Me* undermine the concept of traditional families. Teachers promote gender dysphoria. Comprehensive Sexuality Education (CSE) instills an early obsession with sex in small children. "Sexual diversity" in children's entertainment is also key to grooming them. When the fruit of explicit sex education is pregnancy, schools arrange abortions without parents' knowledge.

The United Nations Population Fund stresses that CSE needs to start very young, in preschool. But the Center for Family and Human Rights [a conservative advocacy organization founded in 1997 to challenge UN policies] warns that CSE teaches "very young children about sexual pleasure, sexual orientation, gender identity, and access to and use of contraceptives, abortion, and other drugs and medical procedures." ...

United Families International [a nonprofit organization founded in 1978 working internationally to advocate maintaining and strengthening the family] is even more explicit in its warning: CSE teaches "children how to have sexual pleasures; whether…to themselves or with a partner…. At a United Nations conference, a moderator said, 'If we can just get this…program into every school and fully implemented around the globe…it would solve all our problems!'… Its main purposes are to elevate such things as masturbation, oral and anal sex, and techniques for achieving an orgasm. And basically, teaching our children to be gender and sexual rights activists."

Controlling the minds of our kids is the ultimate strategic terrain. Without the complete programming of America's children—weaponizing them—Marxism cannot win in America.

There cannot be an armistice in this war. There can be only one victor.

Karen McKay speaks with objective military precision and a seasoned military voice. Her dire warning echoes ancient military strategist Sun Tzu, *The Art of War:*

> *If you know the enemy and know yourself, you need not fear the result of a hundred battles. If you know yourself but not the enemy, for every victory gained you will also suffer a defeat. If you know neither the enemy nor yourself, you will succumb in every battle.*

CHAPTER 18

American Marxism: The Biden Regime—Obama's Third Term

Globalism is a replacement ideology that seeks to reorder the world into one singular, planetary Unistate, ruled by the globalist elite. The globalist war on nation-states cannot succeed without collapsing the United States of America. The long-term strategic attack plan moves America incrementally from constitutional republic to socialism to globalism to feudalism. The tactical attack plan uses asymmetric psychological and informational warfare to destabilize Americans and drive society out of objective reality into the madness of subjective reality. America's children are the primary target of the globalist predators.

Karen McKay (Chapter 17) described with precision the cultural terrorism Marxist George Lukács brought to Hungary as deputy commissar for education and culture in 1919, and Marxist Barack Obama brought to the United States as president in 2008. The ideological motivation for cultural terrorism is purely political, and it is documented in America by W. Cleon Skousen, a former FBI employee, in his 1958 book, *The Naked Communist.*[61] Skousen lists forty-five communist goals that promote social progressivism, internationalism, societal collapse, and imposition of communism worldwide.

On January 10, 1963, the forty-five communist goals were read into the United States Congressional Record to archive them for future generations. The goals that articulated and exposed the thinking and strategies of the political elite sixty years ago are the same goals and policies being implemented collaboratively by today's radical leftist Democrat party, corrupt Republicans (RINOs), the colluding media, and the globalists who pull all of their strings. Some of the familiar names are Barack Obama, Nancy Pelosi, Mitch McConnell, Mike Pence, George Soros, Bill Gates, and Klaus Schwab.

Of particular interest in this chapter are Goals 24, 25, 26, 40, and 41:

24. Eliminate all laws governing obscenity by calling them "censorship" and a violation of free speech and free press.

25. Break down cultural standards of morality by promoting pornography and obscenity in books, magazines, motion pictures, radio, and TV.

26. Present homosexuality, degeneracy, and promiscuity as "normal, natural, and healthy."

40. Discredit the family as an institution. Encourage promiscuity and easy divorce.

41. Emphasize the need to raise children away from the negative influence of parents. Attribute prejudices, mental blocks and retarding of children to suppressive influence of parents.

The first Marxist president of the United States, Barack Hussein Obama, governed in accordance with socialist Saul Alinsky's *Rules for Radicals* (Chapter 14), not the United States Constitution. During his eight-year term, every government institution was politicized to move the country toward socialism.

Obama's vision of internationalism (global integration) at the expense of national sovereignty (territorial borders) was stated unequivocally during his last speech to the United Nations on September 20, 2016:[62]

In order to move forward, though, we do have to acknowledge that the existing path to global integration requires a course correction. As too often, those trumpeting the benefits of globalization have ignored inequality within and among nations; have ignored the enduring appeal of ethnic and sectarian identities; have left international institutions ill-equipped, underfunded, under-resourced, in order to handle transnational challenges.

And as these real problems have been neglected, alternative visions of the world have pressed forward both in the wealthiest countries and in the poorest: religious fundamentalism; the politics of ethnicity, or tribe, or sect; aggressive nationalism; a crude populism—sometimes from the far left, but more often from the far right—

which seeks to restore what they believe was a better, simpler age free of outside contamination.

We cannot dismiss these visions. They are powerful. They reflect dissatisfaction among too many of our citizens. I do not believe those visions can deliver security or prosperity over the long term, but I do believe that these visions fail to recognize, at a very basic level, our common humanity. Moreover, I believe that the acceleration of travel and technology and telecommunications—together with a global economy that depends on a global supply chain—makes it self-defeating ultimately for those who seek to reverse this progress. Today, a nation ringed by walls would only imprison itself....

So, we need new models for the global marketplace, models that are inclusive and sustainable. And in the same way, we need models of governance that are inclusive and accountable to ordinary people.

Obama was not speaking American English. Consistent with his 2008 promise to "fundamentally transform America," Obama's parting 2016 United Nations address was spoken in the Marxist language of deceit.

Words matter. Language is the foundation for community. It is the means by which individuals make themselves understood within groups and why translators are necessary to make them understood outside the group. One of the most powerful weapons of war is the deliberate confusion of the meaning of words within a group. In Islam there is a name for this tactic: *taqiyya*. It means lying in the service of Islam. Radical socialist Saul Alinsky introduced the concept to America in his 1971 book, *Rules for Radicals*. He instructed his students to cut their hair, put on a suit, and blend in so that no one would suspect they were trying to overthrow the government of American capitalism and impose socialism.

There is no equivalent word in the English language for the deliberate deception of *taqiyya*, so I coined the term *Alinskiyya*. Candidate Barack Obama practiced Alinskiyya when he disguised his radical socialist agenda and promised "hope and change" to an unsuspecting American public. President Obama practiced Alinskiyya when he deliberately rebranded terrorism as workplace violence, and scrubbed all mention of Islamic jihad from national security manuals and training.

Shouting "Allahu Akbar," self-proclaimed "Soldier of Allah" Palestinian-American Army psychiatrist Maj. Nidal Hasan went on a killing rampage on November 5, 2009, at the Army base in Killeen, Texas, leaving thirteen American soldiers dead. Obama's immediate response was to caution against "jumping to conclusions" regarding the shooter and his motivations. On August 23, 2013, Hasan's trial concluded and he was unanimously convicted on all forty-five counts of killing thirteen fellow soldiers and wounding thirty-two others at Fort Hood. Yet Obama and his administration refused to recognize Hasan's attack as an act of war, labeling the massacre *workplace violence.*

Obama's contemptible designation of the Fort Hood attack as *workplace violence* instead of *combat related* or terrorism denied Hasan's victims the right to receive Purple Heart medals and other veteran benefits they would be entitled to had the attack been properly labeled. And Obama's deceitful same-day declaration[63] after Muhammad Youssef Abdulazeez opened fire on two military installations in Chattanooga, Tennessee, on July 16, 2015, "We know that what appears to be a lone gunman carried out these attacks," diverted public attention from Islamic terrorism to the absurd, politically motivated, mental health explanation of *lone-wolf* attacks.

It took six years after the Fort Hood attack, and a provision in the 2015 National Defense Authorization Act that expanded eligibility to include an attack by a "foreign terrorist organization" for the U.S. Army to finally approve the medals and benefits to victims of the Fort Hood and Chattanooga jihadi terrorist attacks.

Radical Islamic terrorism is the violent expression of Islam's goal of world dominion, and changing the meaning of words by *taqiyya* is stealth jihad. To an Islamist, the word *peace* means the whole world is Muslim and sharia law, the law of Islam, governs the world. Redefining jihadi terrorism as mental illness is a powerful political tactic used to intentionally confuse the public and engage their humanitarianism to view terrorists as victims who need understanding and refuge, instead of recognizing the existential threat such terrorists pose to a nation.

Why would any civilized Western society deliberately rebrand terrorism as mental illness and become an apologist for the barbarism of terrorists and sharia law? To make sense of the nonsensical, it is necessary to examine the motives of the participants. Leftist leaders across the world in Germany,

Sweden, England, Canada, Australia, and the Democrat party in the U.S. believe in internationalism and one-world government. Their political platforms reject national sovereignty and seek to destroy Western capitalist infrastructures and replace them with socialism—the stepping-stone to one-world government.

Anarchists and terrorists provide leftist politicians here and abroad the social chaos and instability necessary to dupe the unsuspecting public into surrendering their freedoms for promises of government *safety*. Once the government imposes martial law to quell social chaos, it is a very short step to internationalizing the police force and imposing one-world government.

The anarchists, including George Soros's paid political protesters, believe they will realize their Utopian dream of one-world government, social justice, and income equality. The Islamists believe they will realize their dream of a one-world caliphate ruled by religious sharia law. What neither group realizes is that they are Lenin's useful idiots for the globalist elite, who manipulate both groups to create the instability required for the elite to impose their own dystopian one-world government.

Lord Bertrand Russell's 1952 book, *The Impact of Science on Society*,[64] unapologetically describes in chilling detail the intention of globalist elites in England and America, including the Rothschilds and Rockefellers, to impose one-world government to solve the purported Malthusian problem of Earth's resources being unable to sustain population growth. They envision a binary sociopolitical system of masters and slaves where they are the masters served by an enslaved population—everyone else is simply eliminated.

At the 1992 Bilderberg Conference, an annual private meeting of the political elite established in 1954, Henry Kissinger remarked:[65]

> Today Americans would be outraged if U.N. troops entered Los Angeles to restore order; tomorrow they will be grateful. This is especially true if they were told that there were an outside threat from beyond, whether real or promulgated, that threatened our very existence. It is then that all peoples of the world will plead to deliver them from this evil. The one thing every man fears is the unknown. When presented with this scenario, individual rights will be willingly relinquished for the guarantee of their well-being granted to them by their world government.

The social chaos that Henry Kissinger described in 1992 is fomented and financed today by the globalist elite, and implemented by leftist leaders who are too arrogant to realize they are participating in their own destruction. In case anyone doubts the reality of the elitist one-world-government intention, just read David Rockefeller's own words at Bilderberg and in his book *Memoirs* (2002),[66] where he admits he is part of a secret cabal working to destroy the United States and create a New World Order. These claims are not unhinged conspiracy theories—they are the sinister, long-range plans of a determined few to enslave and rule the world.

> Some even believe we [Rockefeller family] are part of a secret cabal working against the best interests of the United States, characterizing my family and me as "internationalists" and of conspiring with others around the world to build a more integrated global political and economic structure—one-world, if you will. If that's the charge, I stand guilty, and I am proud of it. (*Memoirs*, p. 405)

> We are grateful to *The Washington Post, The New York Times, Time* magazine and other great publications whose directors have attended our meetings and respected their promises of discretion for almost forty years. It would have been impossible for us to develop our plan for the world if we had been subject to the bright lights of publicity during those years. But the work is now much more sophisticated and prepared to march towards a World Government. The supranational sovereignty of an intellectual elite and world bankers is surely preferable to the national auto-determination practiced in past centuries. (David Rockefeller, Bilderberg 1991)[67]

Obama's message to the world, delivered at the United Nations a few weeks prior to the 2016 election, was meant to reaffirm his commitment to internationalism in legacy candidate Hillary Clinton's anticipated presidency. The election of President Donald Trump stunned the Democrats, who responded by savaging him with four years of Alinsky's Rule 13:

> Pick the target, freeze it, personalize it, polarize it. Don't try to attack abstract corporations or bureaucracies. Identify a responsible individual. Ignore attempts to shift or spread the blame.

Trump's presidency was a temporary setback in globalism's War on

America. The 2020 election put Joe Biden in the White House, and Obama began serving his third term. The Democrats were back in business, the regime's allegiance to global governance renewed.

The Biden-Obama-Harris regime recommitted the United States to United Nations Agenda 2030 and its 17 Sustainable Goals, designed for international control of "sovereign" governments. Target 7 of Sustainable Development Goal (DG) 4, "Quality Education," stipulates that "all learners acquire the knowledge and skills needed to promote sustainable development, including, among others, through…global citizenship."

The regime also pledged to rejoin UNESCO, the United Nations Educational, Scientific and Cultural Organization, a specialized agency of the United Nations aimed at "promoting world peace and security through international cooperation in education, arts, sciences, and culture." The Trump administration had withdrawn from UNESCO on December 31, 2018, citing the need for sweeping reform of the organization.

The educational reformation that Obama launched and escalated in his first two terms was put into high gear in his third. UNESCO's 2022 report, "Where Do We Stand on Education for Sustainable Development and Global Citizenship Education,"[68] lists two primary outcome-based goals and features an internationalized educational curriculum that indoctrinates students worldwide with belief in the benefits of collectivism, internationalism, and the LGBTQ+ agenda:

> By 2030, ensure all learners acquire the knowledge and skills needed to promote sustainable development, including, among others, through education for sustainable development and sustainable lifestyles, human rights, gender equality, promotion of a culture of peace and non-violence, global citizenship, and appreciation of cultural diversity and of culture's contribution to sustainable development.

> Education should be infused with the aims and purposes set forth in the Charter of the United Nations, the Constitution of UNESCO and the Universal Declaration of Human Rights. "In order to enable every person to contribute actively to the fulfilment of [these] aims…and promote international solidarity and co-operation, the following objectives should be regarded as major guiding principles

of education policy:

- an international dimension and a global perspective in education at all levels and in all its forms;

- understanding and respect for all peoples, their cultures, civilizations, values and ways of life, including domestic ethnic cultures and cultures of other nations;

- awareness of the increasing global interdependence between peoples and nations;

- abilities to communicate with others;

- awareness not only of the rights but also the duties incumbent on individuals, social groups and nations towards each other;

- understanding of the necessity for international solidarity and co-operation;

- readiness on the part of the individual to participate in solving the problems of his community, his country and the world at large."

The influencers in America embraced these goals and objectives with religious zeal, and the National Education Association (NEA), the largest labor union in the United States, representing public school teachers and support personnel from preschool to university graduate programs, joined them. Why?

The answer is found in those communist goals cited above: Goals 24, 25, 26, 40, and 41. Obama's Marxist America required educational indoctrination in schools, away from parental influence. The tactical plan was the seismic shift to Outcome-Based Education in America that aligned with the UN's internationalized OBE curriculum. The plan's success relied on exploiting the difference between univocal and equivocal use of language.

Dr. Dianne N. Irving defines this particular deceit in her March 29, 2019, essay, "'Social Justice' Today Grounded in Marxist Communist 'Liberation Theology'":[69]

A term or phrase used **"univocally"** means that the same term or phrase **has only one meaning**; a term or phrase used **"equivocally"** means that the same term or phrase is used but it has *a different meaning* [e.g., "bank" can mean where you keep your money, or it can mean the earthen side along a river (a river bank), etc.].

Before teaching the History of Philosophy I discovered how the equivocal use of major terms/phrases can be used as a *political tool* without people realizing what is going on. This was made crystal clear in the terrific book I read by historian of philosophy Etienne Gilson, *'Being' And Some Philosophers*, in which he explained how the major term in philosophy—"being" (the subject of metaphysics, from which all other sub-fields of philosophy flow)— was used equivocally over 20 times throughout the entire History of Philosophy. (E.g., for some schools of philosophy, it meant "matter only"; for others it meant "form only"; for others it meant "form and matter"; for others it meant "esse", etc.). *Same term, different meanings*—and thus different consequences.

There is a seismic difference in meaning between the way Americans use and understand the word *democracy* and the term *critical thinking*, and the way Marxists use and understand them. In colloquial usage, Americans often use the word democracy synonymously with our constitutional republic. They are not synonymous. This error has been exploited by Marxists, who use the term democracy as a synonym for socialism or communism, or both. When Marxists, including Obama, talk about their battle for democracy, they are quoting directly from *The Communist Manifesto*.[70] The words of communism's supreme leaders, Karl Marx and Friedrich Engels, are the primary source of Marxist equivocation:

> We have seen above, that the first step in the revolution by the working class is to raise the proletariat to the position of ruling class to win the battle of democracy.

> The proletariat will use its political supremacy to wrest, by degree, all capital from the bourgeoisie, to centralise all instruments of production in the hands of the State, *i.e.*, of the proletariat organised as the ruling class; and to increase the total productive forces as rapidly as possible....

Nevertheless, in most advanced countries, the following will be pretty generally applicable.

1. Abolition of property in land and application of all rents of land to public purposes.

2. A heavy progressive or graduated income tax.

3. Abolition of all rights of inheritance.

4. Confiscation of the property of all emigrants and rebels.

5. Centralisation of credit in the hands of the state, by means of a national bank with State capital and an exclusive monopoly.

6. Centralisation of the means of communication and transport in the hands of the State.

7. Extension of factories and instruments of production owned by the State; the bringing into cultivation of waste-lands, and the improvement of the soil generally in accordance with a common plan.

8. Equal liability of all to work. Establishment of industrial armies, especially for agriculture.

9. Combination of agriculture with manufacturing industries; gradual abolition of all the distinction between town and country by a more equable distribution of the populace over the country.

10. Free education for all children in public schools. Abolition of children's factory labour in its present form. Combination of education with industrial production, etc., etc. (*The Communist Manifesto, Chapter II. Proletarians and Communists*, pp. 54–56).

The phrase *critical thinking* is another example of Marxist linguistic obfuscation. In American colloquial usage, critical thinking is the objective analysis and evaluation of an issue in order to form a judgment. Critical thinking is an essential survival skill for an independent, autonomous, rational adult in a constitutional republic. Marxists use the same phrase to describe the thought process necessary to actively criticize that which exists in service of Marxist Critical Theory, a social theory designed to destabilize and collapse Western society from within, particularly the nuclear family structure. Another quote from *The Communist Manifesto* describes replacing home education with education by the state, to *rescue* children from the *exploitation* of their parents!

> Abolition (*Aufhebung*) of the family! Even the most radical flare up at this infamous proposal of the Communists.
>
> On what foundation is the present family, the bourgeois family, based? On capital, on private gain. In its completely developed form, this family exists only among the bourgeoisie. But this state of things finds its complement in the practical absence of the family among the proletarians, and in public prostitution.
>
> The bourgeois family will vanish as a matter of course when its complement vanishes, and both will vanish with the vanishing of capital.
>
> Do you charge us with wanting to stop the exploitation of children by their parents? To this crime we plead guilty.
>
> But, you say, we destroy the most hallowed of relations when we replace home education by social. (*The Communist Manifesto, Chapter II. Proletarians and Communists*, pp. 47–48).

A third example from *The Communist Manifesto* asserts communism's internationalism.

> The Communists are further reproached with desiring to abolish countries and nationality....
>
> In proportion as the exploitation of one individual by another will also be put an end to, the exploitation of one nation by another will also be put an end to. In proportion as the antagonism between classes within the nation vanishes, the hostility of one nation to another will come to an end. (*The Communist Manifesto, Chapter II. Proletarians and Communists*, pp. 50–51).

The final pages of *The Communist Manifesto* exhort the working classes of the world to unite in proletarian internationalism to defeat capitalism, raise the proletariat to the position of ruling class, and achieve communist Utopia—heaven on Earth:

> In short, the Communists everywhere support every revolutionary movement against the existing social and political order of things.

In all these movements, they bring to the front, as the leading question in each, the property question, no matter what its degree of development at the time.

Finally, they labour everywhere for the union and agreement of the democratic parties of all countries.

The Communists disdain to conceal their views and aims. They openly declare that their ends can be attained only by the forcible overthrow of all existing social conditions. Let the ruling classes tremble at a Communistic revolution. The proletarians have nothing to lose but their chains. They have a world to win. Working men of all countries, unite!

(*The Communist Manifesto, Chapter IV. Position of the Communists in Relation to the Various Existing Opposition Parties*, p. 79).

The heaven on Earth promised by the ideological genus of Marxism, including all of its myriad species, seduces impatient, regressed millennials whose infantile longings make them susceptible to the deceitful promises of their Marxist leaders. Regressed adults lack the developed critical-thinking skills required to question the feasibility of Marxist promises, and to examine the actual outcome in communist countries, like Cuba, where the same Utopian promises were made. Regressed adults don't question why people risk their lives on rafts to escape communism and find freedom in America. They don't ask why the rafts always float *from* Havana to Miami—never in the opposite direction.

American Marxism is lipstick painted on an old feudal pig, marketed worldwide by skilled equivocators. It is collectivist political candy in a shiny new wrapper, dangled in front of psychologically regressed millennials, who forfeit their children's freedom in exchange for deceitful promises of heaven on Earth made by humanitarian hucksters in government, the United Nations, and the World Economic Forum.

On June 12, 2023, UNESCO Director-General Audrey Azoulay formally announced the request of the United States to return to the institution. This means the Biden-Obama-Harris regime plans to return to UNESCO's internationalized educational curriculum and ideological Marxism, marketed as deliverance from capitalist inequality and oppression. Its curriculum promises worldwide "diversity, equity, and inclusion" through what it calls "critical thinking" and "democracy." The *Great Reset* is the *new normal* of feudal enslavement in globalism's planetary Unistate, governed under the auspices of the lethally corrupt United Nations and its specialized organizations and agencies.

CHAPTER 19

From Sex Education to Sexuality Education

Globalism is a replacement ideology that seeks to reorder the world into one singular, planetary Unistate, ruled by the globalist elite. The globalist war on nation-states cannot succeed without collapsing the United States of America. The long-term strategic attack plan moves America incrementally from constitutional republic to socialism to globalism to feudalism. The tactical attack plan uses asymmetric psychological and informational warfare to destabilize Americans and drive society out of objective reality into the madness of subjective reality. America's children are the primary target of the globalist predators.

UNESCO, the United Nations Educational, Scientific, and Cultural Organization, is a specialized agency of the United Nations and a member of the United Nations Sustainable Development Group (UNSDG), a coalition of thirty-six UN funds, programs, specialized agencies, departments, and offices aimed at fulfilling UN Sustainable Development Goals (SDG). The SDG is defined as "a collection of seventeen interlinked objectives designed to serve as a shared blueprint for peace and prosperity for people and the planet, now and into the future."

Let's look at the United Nations Department of Economic and Social Affairs Sustainable Development website and examine the 17 Sustainable Development Goals of the UN planetary 2030 Agenda. The UNSDG mission headline is *Transforming our world: The 2030 Agenda for Sustainable Development*.[71] The 17 Goals are item number 59 on the 91 listed items in the UNSDG Declaration.

Sustainable Development Goals

- Goal 1. End poverty in all its forms everywhere

- Goal 2. End hunger, achieve food security and improved nutrition and promote sustainable agriculture

- Goal 3. Ensure healthy lives and promote well-being for all at all ages

- Goal 4. Ensure inclusive and equitable quality education and promote lifelong learning opportunities for all

- Goal 5. Achieve gender equality and empower all women and girls

- Goal 6. Ensure availability and sustainable management of water and sanitation for all

- Goal 7. Ensure access to affordable, reliable, sustainable and modern energy for all

- Goal 8. Promote sustained, inclusive and sustainable economic growth, full and productive employment and decent work for all

- Goal 9. Build resilient infrastructure, promote inclusive and sustainable industrialization and foster innovation

- Goal 10. Reduce inequality within and among countries

- Goal 11. Make cities and human settlements inclusive, safe, resilient and sustainable

- Goal 12. Ensure sustainable consumption and production patterns

- Goal 13. Take urgent action to combat climate change and its impacts*

- Goal 14. Conserve and sustainably use the oceans, seas and marine resources for sustainable development

- Goal 15. Protect, restore and promote sustainable use of terrestrial ecosystems, sustainably manage forests, combat desertification, and halt and reverse land degradation and halt biodiversity loss

- Goal 16. Promote peaceful and inclusive societies for sustainable development, provide access to justice for all and build effective, accountable and inclusive institutions at all levels

- Goal 17. Strengthen the means of implementation and revitalize the global partnership for sustainable development

* Acknowledging that the United Nations Framework Convention on Climate Change is the primary international, intergovernmental forum for negotiating the global response to climate change.

Item 91, the closing statement of the Declaration, confirms that the United Nations Sustainable Development Group 2030 Agenda is a planetary mission to fundamentally transform the entire world into its own vision of a *better* world. Agenda 2030 is a supremacist replacement ideology on a planetary scale:

> We reaffirm our unwavering commitment to achieving this Agenda and utilizing it to the full to transform our world for the better by 2030.

Agenda 2030's lofty language appeals to emotion, the desire to help people around the world. It is the bait. The next two items after the 17 Sustainable Goals, items 60 and 61, reveal the switch. Full implementation of Agenda 2030 requires "*a revitalized and enhanced Global Partnership*" and "*the means required to realize our collective ambitions.*" The price of full implementation is the surrender of individual agency and national sovereignty to the agencies and authority of the United Nations. Compliance is the universal objective of Agenda 2030.

> 60. We reaffirm our strong commitment to the full implementation of this new Agenda. We recognize that we will not be able to achieve our ambitious Goals and targets without a revitalized and enhanced Global Partnership and comparably ambitious means of implementation. The revitalized Global Partnership will facilitate an intensive global engagement in support of implementation of all the goals and targets, bringing together Governments, civil society, the private sector, the United Nations system and other actors and mobilizing all available resources.

> 61. The Agenda's Goals and targets deal with the means required to realise our collective ambitions. The means of implementation targets under each SDG and Goal 17, which are referred to above, are key to realising our Agenda and are of equal importance with

the other Goals and targets. We shall accord them equal priority in our implementation efforts and in the global indicator framework for monitoring our progress.

Goal 3 is of particular interest to this chapter, especially section 3.7:

> By 2030, ensure universal access to sexual and reproductive health-care services, including for family planning, information and education, and the integration of reproductive health into national strategies and programs.

What, exactly, is the "information and education" young children will receive? Parents around the world will be shocked to learn what the United Nations and its specialty agencies consider appropriate sexual and reproductive information and education.

UNFPA, the United Nations Population Fund (originally United Nations Fund for Population Activities), is the UN's sexual and reproductive health agency. Its motto is *Ensuring rights and choices for all*. The agency's 2014 "Operational Guidance for Comprehensive Sexuality Education (CSE): A Focus on Human Rights and Gender"[72] is extremely enlightening. Its Introduction states authoritatively and unapologetically:

> The Operational Guidance is founded on scientific evidence, international human rights conventions and best technical standards so that a common definition of CSE and associated best practices are promoted by the organization in discussions with counterparts....

> The implementation of this Operational Guidance across UNFPA, and in cooperation with our partners, is designed to help achieve the vision of comprehensive rights-based, transformative sexuality education for young people throughout the world.

UNESDOC, UNESCO's digital library, states unequivocally:

> Sexuality education should start early, be age and developmentally appropriate, and should follow an incremental approach. This helps learners internalize concepts, make informed decisions, understand sexuality and develop critical thinking skills that mature as they grow older. Starting CSE early is important because children and young people need specific knowledge and skills at the appro-

priate time, for example, learning about puberty shortly before they go through it, not after. Moreover, in some countries, many students do not make the transition from primary to secondary school and therefore need access to critical information before leaving formal education.

The foundational assumption in CSE is that schools are the appropriate place for "sexuality education," not the home. This assumption facilitates the Marxist objective of replacing family authority with the authority of the state in order to collapse America from within. So, let's take a look at what the United Nations, the international state in this metaphor, considers "age and developmentally appropriate."

In 2013, the Office of the United Nations High Commissioner for Human Rights (OHCHR) launched UN Free & Equal,[73] a global UN public information campaign to promote equal rights and fair treatment of LGBTIQ+ (lesbian, gay, bisexual, transgender, intersex, queer/queer questioning, plus others) people. Promoted as the United Nations' global campaign against homophobia and transphobia, the UN Free & Equal campaign targets youth with the motto *When #YouthLead, anything is possible!* and tagline: *In a fearless future everyone's an ally. Take a stand with LGBTIQ+ youth!*[74]

The United Nations is calling on the youth of the world to unite in common LGBTIQ+ cause:

> Young people are leading us towards a fearless world. Together, they are standing up and fighting for a world free of poverty, racism, sexism, ableism and all forms of violence, inequality and discrimination.
>
> For LGBTIQ+ youth, this is a fight for survival. LGBTIQ+ youth are more likely to experience family rejection, poverty, discrimination, bullying, violence, exclusion from education—based on their age as well as their sexual orientation, gender identity, gender expression or sex characteristics. As a result, they are at a higher risk of homelessness, poor health outcomes and suicide compared to their peers.
>
> Trans youth are denied recognition of their gender identity and face high levels of hate speech, bullying and exclusion. Intersex

children are often subjected to medically unnecessary interventions that cause lifelong pain and trauma. Lesbian, gay, bi and trans youth are subjected to unethical, harmful and traumatic so-called "conversion therapy". Young LGBTIQ+ people who also face discrimination based on their race, ethnicity, gender, disabilities, religion and migration status are disproportionately affected by exclusion, discrimination and violence.

In a number of countries, LGBTIQ+ youth face censorship both when they seek information and when they speak about their issues, online or offline. In some contexts, discriminatory laws criminalize same-sex relations as well as trans people. Those who speak out and demand equality sometimes face imprisonment, hate speech, violence—even killings.

With great courage and resilience, young LGBTIQ+ people are leading change and standing up for a future that is safe, respectful, empowering and celebrates the beautiful diversity of humankind. A world where each and every one of us is free to be who we are and love whom we choose. Together, all of us can make this future a reality—when #LGBTIQ+ #YouthLead, anything is possible!

UNESCO's International Technical Guidance on Sexuality Education (ITGSE) revised edition (2018)[75] is the United Nations' updated platform for international instruction, and it bills itself as an evidence-informed approach:

> Together with UNAIDS, UNFPA, UNICEF, UN Women, and the WHO, UNESCO completed the extensive technical and political process of updating the "International Technical Guidance on Sexuality Education" in January 2018. As a result, the UN has a unified stance on the justification, supporting data, and recommendations for creating and delivering comprehensive sexuality education (CSE).

> The updated guidance expands upon the original guidance and incorporates updates and enhancements based on fresh research and verified best practices from around the world. The revision process was influenced and steered by user surveys and structured consultations with experts from a wide range of fields and interest groups.

The updated Guidance is a convenient and very important instrument to move closer to a tipping point for the widespread use of high-quality CSE because of its unified voice, forward-thinking attitude, and focus on significant implementation problems....

It examines frameworks and agreements at the global, regional, and local levels that can be utilized to assist CSE implementation at various levels. The updated Guidance also takes into account CSE's role in achieving several SDGs, particularly **Goal 3:** Good Health and Well-Being, **Goal 4:** Quality Education, and **Goal 5:** Gender Equality.

It all sounds good. So, what is the problem?

First, sex education is no longer just about human reproduction. The new label, Comprehensive *Sexuality* Education (CSE), is far more expansive and is defined on the Health and Education[76] section of the UNESCO website:

"**Sexuality**" is defined as "a core dimension of being human which includes: the understanding of, and relationship to, the human body; emotional attachment and love; sex; gender; gender identity; sexual orientation; sexual intimacy; pleasure and reproduction. Sexuality is complex and includes biological, social, psychological, spiritual, religious, political, legal, historic, ethical and cultural dimensions that evolve over a lifespan." (International Technical Guidance on Sexuality Education, p. 17)

Key values of CSE include:

Transformative: CSE impacts whole cultures and communities, not simply individual learners. It can contribute to the development of a fair and compassionate society by empowering individuals and communities, promoting critical thinking skills and strengthening young people's sense of citizenship. It empowers young people to take responsibility for their own decisions and behaviours, and how they may affect others. It builds the skills and attitudes that enable young people to treat others with respect, acceptance, tolerance and empathy, regardless of their ethnicity, race, social, economic or immigration status, religion, disability, sexual orientation, gender identity or expression, or sex characteristics.

CSE is weaponized education on a global level. Its universal curriculum is designed to collapse existing cultures into a singular culture of the planetary Unistate, and indoctrinate students with politicized education according to Marxist collectivist dogma. CSE grooms the children of the world to unite and become activists in preparation for global citizenship in the Unistate.

The deceitful manipulation of language is a weapon of war designed to dupe parents into accepting Comprehensive Sexuality Education as equivalent to the familiar and accepted Sex Education. There is no equivalence. Comprehensive Sexuality Education is a colossal deception that presents lessons in pornography as equal to lessons in human reproduction.

We can no longer trust American schools to teach basic foundational knowledge, or to support American Judeo-Christian values. We are the generation of parents and grandparents who must end the amoral, anti-American, anti-reality indoctrination in American schools. We must read what our children are reading, and see what our children are seeing. We must bring the offensive materials to our local school board meetings and read them into the record.

We the People must exercise our power by recognizing that political power begins locally. It is the foundation of community organizing. Now is the time to organize our community of parents and grandparents across America to oppose existing local school boards. We must run for election to our school boards. We must stand and unapologetically voice our objections at school board meetings, demand accountability, and remove the anti-American ideologues from power. We must protect the children.

CHAPTER 20

In Their Own Words: The Sexual Revolution Begins in Kindergarten

Globalism is a replacement ideology that seeks to reorder the world into one singular, planetary Unistate, ruled by the globalist elite. The globalist war on nation-states cannot succeed without collapsing the United States of America. The long-term strategic attack plan moves America incrementally from constitutional republic to socialism to globalism to feudalism. The tactical attack plan uses asymmetric psychological and informational warfare to destabilize Americans and drive society out of objective reality into the madness of subjective reality. America's children are the primary target of the globalist predators.

Planned Parenthood[77] is the instrument of *transformative sexual change* in the United States. Marketed as *scientific* and *evidence-based*, transformative sexual change advocates changing restrictive laws that hinder the exercise of *reproductive rights*, and transforming social norms that perpetuate *prejudices on reproductive rights*. Over 40 percent of the organization's revenue comes from your tax dollars in the form of government reimbursements and grants. Planned Parenthood (PP) is a political organization that disguises its political agenda as health education. My last book, *The Collapsing American Family: From Bonding to Bondage* (Chapter 10, "The Scheme and the Schemers Determined to Reeducate America"), exposes Planned Parenthood's infiltration of the classroom, and its catastrophic Marxist agenda.

In an August 20, 2020, *Daily Signal* article, "Problematic Women: Planned Parenthood Ideology 'Killing the Family,' Ex-Volunteer Says,"[78] Monica Cline, former volunteer and "comprehensive sex educator" at Planned Parenthood, is quoted. She explains how children were being pressured and deliberately sexualized in school because no adult was offering them the alternative of abstinence.

At one point she asks a group of thirteen- and fourteen-year-olds, "Guys, do you realize you don't have to have sex? You don't have to have oral sex, vaginal sex, or anal sex. And if you don't, you never have to come in contact with someone else's body fluids." A little girl raised her hand and said, "Ma'am, no one has ever told us that." That was the turning point for Monica Cline. She finally and fully understood:

> There is a "huge movement to normalize childhood sex." The sex education program of Planned Parenthood is "encouraging children to dehumanize themselves and each other, making them sexually active at a young age, normalizing every sexual behavior.... By doing that those children become dependent on getting condoms and contraceptives and getting treated, and yes, even getting abortions. And so, once that dependency occurs, and the parent who is purposely left out of the picture, there's no one else who's really guiding those children.... They empathize with them and say, "Oh, yeah. Your mom and dad would probably be really mad to know you are sexually active. But we know it is perfectly normal, and we're here to help you." ... It sounds so positive. But what they are really doing is creating a barrier between a family and their child, the guidance of a parent.

Cline explains that parents have absolutely no input or control over the sex ed content. PP and other comprehensive sex education organizations consider parents a barrier to services. The goal is to mandate their sex education, which is really an ideology, and change the sexual attitudes of our entire nation by influencing our children. PP volunteers are not supposed to be in schools unless invited, but volunteers are sneaked into schools by sympathetic teachers and administrators. Cline describes the radical sexual ideology being taught by teachers and supported by school administrators and local school boards entrusted with educating America's children:

> They believe that children are sexual from birth. And they use a little bit of truth, and then distort it completely. And just because we're born with sexual parts doesn't mean that we should be sexually active.

> According to Planned Parenthood and "The Future of Sex Education"[79] [an initiative based on the National Sex Education Standards (Second Edition)[80]], they believe in the sexual rights of children.

They do believe that children at any age, even infancy, have the right to sexual pleasure. You can read that in their own mission statements. You can go to their websites and learn that. They're not hiding it anymore. And they believe it's normal, and so they're really trying to change the sexual attitudes of a whole nation and across the globe that this is true.

And so, you're going to see that they are now creating programs for parents, to start convincing parents that their children are sexual beings, and that they should be able to learn about their bodies and pleasure themselves, or with other children.… They use a lot of Alfred Kinsey's research, which is incredibly unethical and should have been illegal. But yet, Alfred Kinsey has influenced public health education and has influenced our laws in this nation as well.… Kinsey, they consider him a hero because he loosened the belt of people, of sexual repression, and gave people the spectrum of being from homosexual to straight and everything in between.

And now they are using that same "spectrum" for gender identity as well. So, I think parents need to be very concerned, because even if the curriculum is not in your school, I get phone calls from parents all over the country that progressive teachers are teaching their children this in class, even if it is history, or whatever it may be.…

A big piece of this, which for some people, it's something I think is hard for them to understand, is that there is a huge movement through socialism that really wants to do away with the nuclear family. They want to do away with anything that is of [one's own], whether it's private property, or private family.

And so, they believe that children do not necessarily belong to their parents, but that they can educate the children in the way that they want them to go. And sex education is a big piece of that, because when you teach children to dehumanize themselves, to take intimacy and family and marriage out of sex, even to the point of killing your own children through abortion, you are essentially killing the family. You're destroying the family.

And of all the tactics they are using—you can read any curriculum—not only is it going to be graphic, but they will not ever guide a child to talk to their own parent ever. You won't hear a word about the parent. A parent is completely eliminated from this education.

They want the children dependent on the government, or on public health, whatever it may be, but they do not want the children to be depending on the parent anymore. And so, all of this really is to break down the family. And they're essentially…we're watching it happen…they basically have been given words in school. And they go home and tell their parents, "You're just old fashioned, or you are worshipping a god of hate, or you're very conservative. You don't understand the culture."

And these kids are learning all this at school.

The primary source of school sexuality education is the Sexuality Information and Education Council of the United States (SIECUS). The organization was founded in 1964 by Dr. Mary Calderone, then medical director of Planned Parenthood, to be the national resource for teaching sex education in public schools. In 2019 the organization changed its name from the *Sex* Information and Education Council of the United States, to the *Sexuality* Information and Education Council of the United States, to reflect its expanded perspective.

Wikipedia reports[81] that SIECUS disseminates the SIECUS State Profiles, which monitor sex education in all fifty states, the District of Columbia, Puerto Rico, and the other U.S. territories. Each profile includes an overview of current sex education laws, policies, and guidelines, newly introduced legislation, and relevant action that advocates have taken to advance or defend sex education in their communities. SIECUS funds and manages The Future of Sex Education (FoSE) project, which promotes institutionalizing Comprehensive Sexuality Education in public schools. (Comprehensive Sexuality Education is discussed at length in Chapter 19.)

In 2019, the organization officially rebranded itself and added a tagline to its name, SIECUS: Sex Ed for Social Change,[82] acknowledging that it is no longer a single-issue organization. That same year, it launched the Sex Education Policy Action Council (SEPAC),[83] a movement to have Comprehensive Sexuality Education (CSE) become compulsory in all fifty states. SEPAC began with twenty-four participating states: Alabama, Arizona, California,

Colorado, Georgia, Kansas, Kentucky, Michigan, Minnesota, Mississippi, Missouri, Nevada, New Mexico, New York, North Carolina, North Dakota, Oregon, South Dakota, Tennessee, Texas, Utah, Virginia, Washington, and Wyoming. SEPAC lists Planned Parenthood as an active member in almost all states listed.

SIECUS: Sex Ed for Social Change is part of the international consortium of organizations fomenting seismic social change across the globe. SEICUS is working to fundamentally transform America. How can sexuality education fundamentally transform a society?

James Lindsay provides an extraordinary explanation in his series of podcasts on "groomer schools." The first podcast, "Groomer Schools 1: The Long Cultural Marxist History of Sex Education," *The New Discourses Podcast with James Lindsay*, Episode 54,[84] which aired on November 21, 2021, is introduced with the following:

> Through brand names like "comprehensive sex education" and one of its parent programs, "Social Emotional Learning (SEL)," our government schools have been turned into Groomer Schools, and parents are beginning to notice. What many will not understand, however, is that this isn't just a fluke of our weird and increasingly degenerate times. It is, in fact, a long-purposed Marxist project reaching back into the early 20th century. In this episode of *The New Discourses Podcast*, join James Lindsay as he explains the long history of the sexual grooming that has come into our schools through Critical Gender Theory and queer theory as they have crept into educational programs. If you want an explanation for how sexually explicit materials, gender ideology, pornography, and strippers have made their way into our government schools, including for young children, this is a must-hear.

One of Lindsay's most profound and shocking insights is that sexualization of children through critical theories of identity is purposely designed to dismantle the *innocence* of children. Critical theorists see the innocence of children as a fundamental problem that must be overcome in order to achieve their dreams of sexual liberation, gender liberation, and racial liberation. The woke consider children's innocence evidence of a hegemonic narrative that maintains the existing social order and relations of society.

Their innocence must be destroyed in order to achieve revolution. The woke intentionally destabilize children as early as possible for maximum political gain. It is horrifying.

Being sexualized is extremely damaging to children, and queer activism attacks a child's most primary identity—his or her sexual identity. Yet queer activists see themselves as righteous. Lindsay explains the definition of queer theory as an *identity without essence*. This is an extremely important consideration, because the objective is beyond destroying a child's sexual identity; the goal is to literally dissolve *self*.

Queer theory is by far the most regressive sociopolitical construct imaginable. It advocates the boundaryless existence of infancy as liberation while ignoring the powerlessness and total dependence of infancy. Infantile bliss is appropriate in infancy because the ability to reality-test does not exist in newborns. In adulthood, the inability to reality-test—to perceive reality or experience self, or both—is insanity.

Civilized and sane people have a great deal of difficulty wrapping their minds around such malevolence. Yet in the Orwellian madness of Marxist subjective reality, the justification for the assault on children is that children are being *rescued* from current capitalist *hegemonic normativity*. In the perverse spirit of globalism's *build back better*, the woke are unapologetically destroying children's sexual identities to groom them to become angry Marxist radicals who will destroy capitalist society and its *hegemonic normativity*.

Identity is the universal conundrum of the human experience. We want to know who we are, where we came from, and if our lives have meaning. So, who are we?

We begin with our most basic identity. "It's a boy!" "It's a girl!" After sexual identity comes family identity, national identity, religious identity, educational identity, professional identity, and so on. Our various identities add up to give us one distinguishing identity.

We have identification cards that verify our identity—passports, driver's licenses, diplomas, marriage certificates, etc. We verify our identity because we value our identity personally, and because ordered liberty requires verification that we are who we say we are. We trust that a board-certified surgeon is operating on us. We trust that a licensed pilot is flying our plane. We trust that teachers are teaching our children fundamental skills of reading, writing, arithmetic, and basic knowledge.

Identity is an integral part of the universal human experience because it defines and identifies reality. We either are, or we are not, who we say we are. In politics and international affairs, identity has both domestic and international implications. National identity is predicated on both family identity and individual identity.

Without an identity, children become depressed, anxious, politically malleable, and groomable. Groomer schools are designed to dismantle children's family identity, individual identity, and sexual identity. Because the earlier that grooming begins, the more effective it is, children in kindergarten are targeted for psychological destruction and *build back better* educational reprogramming.

The compulsory sex education that George Lukács brought to Hungary is parallel to the Comprehensive Sexuality Education disseminated throughout the United Nations institutions and taught in American schools, public and private, under the umbrella of Social and Emotional Learning (SEL), specifically the Marxist version of SEL, transformative SEL.

SEL is an educational method marketed to the public as fostering social and emotional skills within school curricula. It is designed to have the same emphasis as classical subjects such as math, science, and reading. It is important to understand that SEL is not equivalent to what was once called *good citizenship* in school, defined as cooperative, respectful, courteous behavior. SEL is ideologically driven, and it focuses on feelings.

The program began in the 1960s as an effort to address the poor academic report cards of low-income African American communities in New Haven, Connecticut. Its approach supported a *whole child* perspective that focused on the social and emotional needs of the children. Over the years the program developed SEL strategies across K–12 classrooms, and its framework was adopted by the New Haven public schools. In 1994, the Collaborative for Academic, Social, and Emotional Learning (CASEL) was founded and three years later published its training manual, *Promoting Social and Emotional Learning: Guidelines for Educators*, which formally defined the field of SEL. The concentric circular framework for applying SEL strategies is called the CASEL wheel.

The CASEL[85] website describes its continued advocacy for expanded systemic implementation of its program through federal policy in the U.S. that supports state-wide and district-wide implementation of social and emotional learning in K–12 schools. CASEL also seeks to expand SEL in support of *workforce preparation* and *career readiness*. The website drop-down menu Systemic Implementation[86] directs users to an overview that explains the approach:

> A systemic approach ensures that SEL is woven into all students' educational experiences. More than a single lesson or activity, SEL is integrated across key settings where students live and learn: classrooms, schools, homes, and communities. It also aligns school district and state policies, resources, and actions to support SEL. Federal policies play a role in creating ripe conditions for supportive environments and rich learning experiences.

The "whole child" approach of Social and Emotional Learning expanded again in 2019 to become Transformative Social and Emotional Learning (TSEL)[87] to "critically examine root causes of inequity, and to develop collaborative solutions that lead to personal, community, and social well-being." You will notice the similarity in the language of transformation that describes TSEL, Marxist critical (criticizing) theories, Obama's promise to "fundamentally transform America," and the United Nations 17 Sustainable Goals. TSEL is the parent program of Comprehensive Sexuality Education (CSE).

CSE is designed to destabilize existing morality, destroy childhood innocence, collapse sexual identity, and tear down the existing culture in the classroom, away from parental oversight. Children are assaulted with graphic sexual literature, including scenes depicting oral sex, anal sex, same-sex sex, and adult-child sex. Monogamous sex is mocked and promiscuous sex promoted as freedom and liberation. It is sexual and psychological grooming to bring about societal destruction. That is what *transformative* education means to the Marxist ideologues in charge of curriculum content. Let's take a look.

Drag Queen Story Hour (DQSH) is the most publicized demonstration of queer theory being foisted on children in schools, public libraries, and bookstores across America. DQSH is the creation of San Francisco author and queer activist Michelle Tea. Started in 2015, it is geared toward children ages three to eleven and is disingenuously marketed as *promoting reading and diversity*. Drag queens, men dressed as glamorous, sexualized women, read children's books featuring LGBTQ characters and themes to the children, and engage in other "learning activities" including nightlife events and sing-alongs.

Wikipedia[88] reports:

> As of February 2020, there are 50+ official chapters of DSH [DQSH], spread internationally, as well as other drag artists holding reading events at libraries, schools, bookstores, and museums. In October 2022, the nonprofit organization officially changed its name to Drag Story Hour, to be more inclusive and "reflect the diverse cast of storytellers."

From the Drag Story Hour[89] website:

> ### What Is Drag Story Hour?
>
> It's just what it sounds like! Storytellers using the art of drag to read books to kids in libraries, schools, and bookstores.
>
> DSH captures the imagination and play of the gender fluidity of childhood and gives kids glamorous, positive, and unabashedly queer role models.
>
> In spaces like this, kids are able to see people who defy rigid gender restrictions and imagine a world where everyone can be their authentic selves!

Clemson University,[90] a public university in South Carolina self-described as a place *where purpose-driven students, faculty, and staff collaborate on projects that impact our state, country and world*, promoted its Drag Storytime with the following invitation:

> Beginning with author and activist Michelle Tea in 2015, Drag Storytime aims to "inspire a love of reading, while teaching deeper lessons on diversity, self-love, and an appreciation of others." Gather your friends and family and join us for Clemson's first Drag Storytime picture book reading! Saturday, April 17, 2021 at 1:00p to 2:00p.

Clemson's invitation reveals both the bait, the love of reading, and also the switch, the sexual politics embedded in DQSH. Investigative journalist Christopher F. Rufo's Autumn 2022 *City Journal* article, "The Real Story Behind Drag Queen Story Hour,"[91] explains:

> Families with children find themselves caught in the middle. Drag Queen Story Hour pitches itself as a family-friendly event to promote reading, tolerance, and inclusion. "In spaces like this," the organization's website reads, "kids are able to see people who defy rigid gender restrictions and imagine a world where everyone can be their authentic selves." But many parents, even if reluctant to say it publicly, have an instinctual distrust of adult men in women's clothing dancing and exploring sexual themes with their children.

> These concerns are justified. But to mount an effective opposition, one must first understand the sexual politics behind the glitter, sequins, and heels. This requires a working knowledge of an extensive history, from the origin of the first "queen of drag" in the late nineteenth century to the development of academic queer theory, which provides the intellectual foundation for the modern drag-for-kids movement.

> The drag queen might appear as a comic figure, but he carries an utterly serious message: the deconstruction of sex, the reconstruction of child sexuality, and the subversion of middle-class family life. The ideology that drives this movement was born in the sex dungeons of San Francisco and incubated in the academy. It is now being transmitted, with official state support, in a number of public libraries and schools across the United States. By excavating the foundations of this ideology and sifting through the literature of its activists, parents and citizens can finally understand the new sexual politics and formulate a strategy for resisting it.

Rufo's article provides a valuable history of queer theory and its stated objective: to destroy that which exists in order to *build back better*. He begins with lesbian writer and activist Gayle S. Rubin, who launched the academic discipline of queer theory with her 1984 seminal essay, "Thinking Sex: Notes for a Radical Theory of the Politics of Sexuality."[92] In the paper,

Rubin compliments Alfred Kinsey's "positive concept of sexual variation," saying, "his scientific detachment gave his work refreshing neutrality." (Kinsey's work is discussed in Chapter 17.)

Rufo quotes Rubin:

> "Modern Western societies appraise sex acts according to a hierarchical system of sexual value," Rubin wrote. "Marital, reproductive heterosexuals are alone at the top erotic pyramid. Clamouring below are unmarried monogamous heterosexuals in couples, followed by most other heterosexuals.… Stable, long-term lesbian and gay male couples are verging on respectability, but bar dykes and promiscuous gay men are hovering just above the groups at the very bottom of the pyramid. The most despised sexual castes currently include transsexuals, transvestites, fetishists, sadomasochists, sex workers such as prostitutes and porn models, and the lowliest of all, those whose eroticism transgresses generational boundaries."…

> For Rubin and later queer theorists, sex and gender were infinitely malleable. There was nothing permanent about human sexuality, which was, after all, "political." Through a revolution of values, they believed, the sexual hierarchy could be torn down and rebuilt in their image.…

> "There [are] historical periods in which sexuality is more sharply contested and more overtly politicized," Rubin wrote. "In such periods, the domain of erotic life is, in effect, renegotiated." And, following the practice of any good negotiator, they laid out their theory of the case and their maximum demands. As Rubin explained: "A radical theory of sex must identify, describe, explain, and denounce erotic injustice and sexual oppression. Such a theory needs refined conceptual tools which can grasp the subject and hold it in view. It must build rich descriptions of sexuality as it exists in society and history. It requires a convincing critical language that can convey the barbarity of sexual persecution." Once the ground is softened and the conventions are demystified, the sexual revolutionaries could do the work of rehabilitating the figures at the bottom of the hierarchy—"transsexuals, transvestites, fetishists, sadomasochists, sex workers."

Where does this process end? At its logical conclusion: the abolition of restrictions on the behavior at the bottom end of the moral spectrum—pedophilia. Though she uses euphemisms such as "boylovers" and "men who love underaged youth," Rubin makes her case clearly and emphatically. In long passages throughout "Thinking Sex," Rubin denounces fears of child sex abuse as "erotic hysteria," rails against anti–child pornography laws, and argues for legalizing and normalizing the behavior of "those whose eroticism transgresses generational boundaries." These men are not deviants, but victims, in Rubin's telling.

Rubin's prism is thoroughly Marxist. She perceives a Marxist oppressor/oppressed infrastructure of capitalism as the hidden politics of modern sexuality, and insists that both must be destroyed in order to fundamentally transform society. From the conclusion of "Thinking Sex":

> Like gender, sexuality is political. It is organized into systems of power, which reward and encourage some individuals and activities, while punishing and suppressing others. Like the capitalist organization of labour and its distribution of rewards and powers, the modern sexual system has been the object of political struggle since it emerged and as it has evolved. But if the disputes between labour and capital are mystified, sexual conflicts are completely camouflaged.

Rufo continues his history of queer theory with quotes from Rubin's collaborator, Pat Califia, a sexually confused individual born female in 1954 who became a lesbian until transitioning into a bisexual trans man. From Califia's essay "The Age of Consent: The Great Kiddy-Porn Panic of '77":[93]

> American society had turned pedophiles into "the new communists, the new niggers, the new witches." For Califia, age-of-consent laws, religious sexual mores, and families who police the sexuality of their children represented a thousand-pound bulwark against sexual freedom.

Quoting from Califia's 1991 article, "Feminism, Pedophilia, and Children's Rights":[94]

> "You can't liberate children and adolescents without disrupting the

entire hierarchy of adult power and coercion and challenging the hegemony of antisex fundamentalist religious values."

Califia is a member of the third wave of feminism launched with Judith Butler's 1990 book, Gender Trouble: Feminism and the Subversion of Identity.[95] *Gender Trouble* presents Butler's theory of social change based on the concept of *performativity*. Performativity claims that gender identity results from enforcing a series of repetitions of verbal and nonverbal acts that generate the "illusion" of a coherent and intelligible gender expression and identity, which otherwise lack any essential property. Basically, Butler is saying that gender is a social construct derived completely from nurture, not nature. Performativity is the foundation for using DQSH and its related interactive drag events to collapse the "social construct" of gender.

Rufo's *City Journal* article beautifully summarizes Rubin and Califia's position, and how TSEL is being used to fundamentally transform America: "All of it—the family, the law, the religion, the culture—was a vector of oppression, and all of it had to go."

Rufo continues his analysis with references to college professor and drag queen performer Harris Kornstein (aka Lil Miss Hot Mess) and queer theorist Harper Keenan. Kornstein and coauthor Keenan published drag pedagogy's manifesto, "Drag Pedagogy: The Playful Practice of Queer Imagination in Early Childhood."[96] Its goal was the application of queer theory to the education system. Rufo continues:

> "The professional vision of educators is often shaped to reproduce the state's normative vision of its ideal citizenry. In effect, schooling functions as a way to *straighten* the child into a kind of captive alignment with the current parameters of that vision," Kornstein and Keenan write. "To state it plainly, within the historical context of the USA and Western Europe, the institutional management of gender has been used as a way of maintaining racist and capitalist modes of (re)production."
>
> To disrupt this dynamic, the authors propose a new teaching method, "drag pedagogy," as a way of stimulating the "queer imagination," teaching kids "how to live queerly," and "bringing queer ways of knowing and being into the education of young children." As Kornstein and Keenan explain, this is an intellectual and polit-

ical project that requires drag queens and activists to work toward undermining traditional notions of sexuality, replacing the biological family with the ideological family, and arousing transgressive sexual desires [those violating socially accepted standards of behavior] in young children. "Building in part from queer theory and trans studies, queer and trans pedagogies seek to actively destabilize the normative function of schooling through transformative education," they write. "This is a fundamentally different orientation than movements towards the inclusion or assimilation of LGBT people into the existing structures of school and society."

Queer theory presents the sexualization of children as a human rights issue—specifically children's human rights. The delivery system is Comprehensive Sexuality Education under the umbrella of Social and Emotional Learning (SEL), specifically transformative SEL, the Marxist version of SEL. Drag Story Hour is Marxist transformative SEL that exploits word obfuscation and deconstruction to advance queer theory in public/private American schools, libraries, and bookstores. It is George Lukács's dream come true in America.

In conclusion, Rufo provides multiple examples of the spread of drag events across America and issues a warning to parents never to forget the purpose of DQSH:

> As the movement behind drag shows for children has gained notoriety and expanded its reach, some drag performers have let the mask slip: in Minneapolis, a drag queen in heels and a pink miniskirt spread his legs open in front of children; in Portland, a large male transvestite allowed toddlers to climb on top of him, grab at his fake breasts, and press themselves against his body; and in England, a drag queen taught a group of preschoolers how to perform a sexually suggestive dance.

> Scenes from drag events hosted across the United States in bars, clubs, and outdoor festivals have been even more shocking and disturbing: in Miami, a man with enormous fake breasts and dollar bills stuffed into his G-string grabs the hand of a preschool-aged girl and struts her in front of the crowd; in Washington, D.C., a drag queen wearing leather and chains teaches a young child how

to dance for cash tips; in Dallas, hulking male figures with makeup smeared across their faces strip down to undergarments, simulate a female orgasm, and perform lap dances on members of a roaring audience of adults and children.

Advocates of Drag Queen Story Hour might reply that these are outlier cases and that many of the child-oriented events feature drag queens reading books and talking about gender, not engaging in sexualized performances. But the spirit of drag is predicated on the transgressive sexual element and the ideology of queer theory, which cannot be erased by switching the context and softening the language. The philosophical and political project of queer theory has always been to dethrone traditional heterosexual culture and elevate what Rubin called the "sexual caste" at the bottom of the hierarchy: the transsexual, the transvestite, the fetishist, the sadomasochist, the prostitute, the porn star, and the pedophile. Drag Queen Story Hour can attempt to sanitize the routines and run criminal background checks on its performers, but the subculture of queer theory will always attract men who want to follow the ideology to its conclusions.

Parents must understand that the attacks on their children's sexual, individual, family, and national identities are weapons of war disguised as *whole child* education. The sexual revolution that begins in kindergarten can be defeated only by parents, grandparents, and other concerned citizens who understand the weaponization of education and oppose its sinister ideological and tactical purpose of *whole child destruction*. We the People must stand up to defy whole child education and prevent whole child destruction by protecting children's innocence.

Our defiance is rooted in education. We fight fire with fire—we protect our children with lessons about secrets. We teach our children that secrets are danger signals. If anyone tells them *don't tell your parents*, it is the signal that they will be hurt. Children must be taught to tell their parents the secret. Just like a red light means STOP and a green light means GO, being asked to keep a secret means TELL.

CHAPTER 21

Montessori and Drag Queen Story Hour

Globalism is a replacement ideology that seeks to reorder the world into one singular, planetary Unistate, ruled by the globalist elite. The globalist war on nation-states cannot succeed without collapsing the United States of America. The long-term strategic attack plan moves America incrementally from constitutional republic to socialism to globalism to feudalism. The tactical attack plan uses asymmetric psychological and informational warfare to destabilize Americans and drive society out of objective reality into the madness of subjective reality. America's children are the primary target of the globalist predators.

For readers who may be under the impression that private schools are exempt from the humanitarian hoax of whole child education and its sociopolitical intent, I have included an informative article written by retired Montessori educator Charlotte Cushman, published online in *American Thinker*[97] and on her website, Authentic Montessori Education,[98] on January 21, 2023.

Charlotte Cushman taught the Montessori Method for over 40 years, and co-owned and operated two Montessori schools. She is appalled by today's woke (Marxist) trend in Montessori, and advocates a return to *authentic* Montessori and its founder's principles:

> *Not in the service of any political or social creed should the teacher work, but in the service of the complete human being, able to exercise in freedom, a self-disciplined will and judgement, unperverted by prejudice and undistorted by fear.*
> —Maria Montessori

The Real Purpose of Drag Queen Story Hour

By Charlotte Cushman

Those who have voiced concerns about the dangers that drag events, such as Drag Queen Story Hour (DQSH), pose for children (namely, sexualization and grooming) have been told that those concerns are baseless, that the events are harmless, that it is all just entertainment and fun, and that attending drag events is a way to understand the gay culture.

On January 25, 2021 an academic paper entitled, Drag pedagogy: The playful practice of queer imagination in early childhood" was published online in *Curriculum Inquiry*, an educational journal. The paper, recently called out by James Lindsay (here) and (here) and also by Christopher F. Rufo (here), was written by Harper Keenen and Lil Miss Hot Mess (a founder of DQSH), who describe themselves as "a gender-queer drag performer/scholar and a trans scholar." (p. 443)

Right off the bat, the abstract tells us the purpose of DQSH:

> Ultimately, the authors propose that "drag pedagogy" pro-
> vides a performative approach to queer pedagogy that is not
> simply about LGBT lives, but *living queerly*. (p. 440)

Then the authors state,

> Through this programme, drag artists…[are] positioning
> queer and trans cultural forms as valuable components of
> early childhood education. We are guided by the following
> question: what might Drag Queen Story Hour offer educators
> as a way of bringing queer ways of knowing and being into the
> education of young children?

The purpose of DQSH is not entertainment, nor to understand gay culture. The purpose is to turn children "queer" through an educational process.

What is queer, you might ask? Queer in this context comes from Queer Theory, the idea that asserts that sexual norms are oppressive, that actually anything normal is a problem. Ronald Pisaturo, author of *Masculine Power, Feminine Beauty*, a book that condemns the LGBT movement, defines a queer as "an activist dedicated to overthrowing capitalism, the system alleged to enforce oppressive sexual norms such as masculinity, femininity, and heterosexuality."

Turning children into Marxist activists is the goal. Because capitalism has not produced a populace motivated to revolt, Herbert Marcuse, the father of the New Left, advocated creating discontented groups, one of which is sexual "queers." This goal is supported by LGBT ideology. Pisaturo explains (p. 113) that, according to LGBT theory,

> Infants are "polymorphously perverse," to use Freud's term. That is, an infant will be sexually excited by anyone and anything anywhere. Freud considered this infantile state an early stage of development. Marcuse and many LGBT activists, in contrast, consider this state the ideal end state for adults. According to Marcuse, people leave this ideal state only because they become repressed, limiting the kinds of sexual responses available to them. The repressed energy of such people becomes channeled into economic production.... That is, productive work is the repressed alternative to blissful, indiscriminate sex. Capitalism, of course the system of greatest economic production, is hence also the system of greatest sexual repression.

Therefore, capitalism must be destroyed.

The "Drag Pedagogy" paper tells us,

> It may be that DQSH is "family friendly," in the sense that it is accessible and inviting to families with children, but it is less a sanitizing force than it is a preparatory introduction to alternate modes of kinship. Here, DQSH is "family friendly" in the sense of "family" as an old-school queer code to identify and connect with other queers on the street. (p. 455)

Pisaturo explains, "The phrase 'preparatory introduction to alternate modes of kinship' means sexual and Marxist grooming. The authors want to eradicate the traditional family by grooming children to join the 'family' of queers."

In her 1984 essay, "Thinking Sex," leading queer theorist Gayle Rubin blamed capitalism for suppressing sexual deviancies and defended child pornography, pedophilia, promiscuity, sadomasochism, and other sexual perversions. One can see these perverse elements when the drag queen struts around like a slut, grooming children by exposing them to explicit sexual acts and/or private body parts. And when the queen invites the child to participate, that is sexual assault of a minor.

Attempting to turn children into queers is bad enough, but there are other alarming elements to DQSH. Drag queens teach the children that reality is fluid:

> Drag similarly breaks boundaries between reality and fantasy in allowing performers to take on new identities and social relationships in material form, just by playing the part. (p. 449)

> At many DQSH events, children ask genuine questions like "are you a boy or a girl?" ... In many cases, drag queens may not respond with answers, but with questions meant to complicate perceptions of gender and society: "Why does it matter if I'm a boy or a girl?" (p. 452)

That response reveals an astonishing ignorance about child development. The answer matters a great deal to the child who is just beginning to learn about reality and form concepts. The first judgment anyone perceives about another person is whether the person is a girl or a boy. Man or woman? To destroy that demarcation and bring in the arbitrary to a child, that a man can be a woman, is to undermine the important, fundamental concept of reality, that reality is stable and cannot be wished away. Serious cognitive damage is done by blurring the child's grasp of reality. For the child, an unstable reality confuses him, frightens him, and sabotages his ability to navigate the world.

Children are also taught to be defiant—not for a valid reason, but for the sake of defiance:

> While drag has some conventions, it ultimately has no rules— its defining quality is often to break as many rules as possible! (p. 448)

An implicit objective of DQSH is acknowledged:

> There is a premium on standing out, on artfully desecrating the sacred. (p. 451)

They do not want to broaden or enrich the sacred (sexuality) through some kind of deeper understanding. They want to desecrate, to vandalize, to destroy.

And this is disturbing:

> She is less interested in focus, discipline, achievement, or objectives than playful self-expression. Her pedagogy is rooted in pleasure and creativity borne, in part, from letting go of control. (p. 451)

The authors are not teaching children how to use their minds. Instead, they are teaching children to be abnormal, to be queer, to be pawns in the movement to tear down the normal.

Do people really think it is harmless to bring children to see sexuality portrayed not as a sacred expression of love for one special individual, but as frivolous "desecrating" for the benefit of any and all strangers? To see sexuality divorced from thought and romance? To see sexuality portrayed as ugly caricature? To see sexuality, which is intensely personal, selective, and meaningful, made voyeuristic, indiscriminate, and meaningless?

The young child learns from observation; he learns from absorbing his environment. Everything that he sees and experiences makes an impression upon his mind before he has the ability to evaluate it. The "desecrating" of sexuality will make a child's mind abnormal regarding sex and all cognition, and that is exactly the goal of the drag queens. The concerns about DQSH aren't baseless, and DQSH isn't harmless. It is precisely child abuse.

If the purpose of DQSH is to turn children "queer" through an educational process, the next questions to ask are: What is the social purpose of turning children queer and destroying their innocence? Why would governments participate in this process of destruction?

The catastrophic psychological damage done to children by destroying childhood innocence is a political goal, and normalizing sexual perversion exploits the perversion for political gain. Woke "culture warriors" are validating their own sexual perversions, and the enemies of freedom are using them as useful idiots to help collapse society from within.

Canadian cultural anthropologist Geoffrey Clarfield offers an interesting perspective on the impact of self-interest in changing social norms. His fascinating article "Nurture not Nature,"[99] published June 19, 2023, in the National Association of Scholars publication *Minding the Campus,* presents a compelling argument that the findings of early American cultural anthropologists were self-serving. The article is subtitled "Wokeism and the Anthropological Origins of Gender Bending."

> American cultural anthropology has a lot to answer for.
>
> Its icons—people like Franz Boas, Margaret Mead, Ruth Benedict, and Edward Sapir—were the indispensable precursors of the woke ideology now so deeply entrenched in our schools and universities, courts, politics, and business.
>
> This is not to say that cultural anthropology is the sole source of wokeism, but that its contribution was seminal. Its mid-twentieth-century practitioners took what began as a simple field method, cultural relativism, and by insensible degrees transformed it into a philosophical movement. What started out as the common-sense proposition that you could only understand a culture from the inside was soon transformed into the rather different notion that every culture was just as good as every other culture, and that there was no ground on which to prefer one over the other....
>
> But what if these early practitioners of cultural anthropology, driven by a desire to "normalize" their own behavior at home, committed the cardinal scientific sin of reading into cultures what they needed to find there, rather than describing those cultures as they found them? If so, subsequent anthropological investigations of those same cultures would not reproduce the pioneers' original findings, and cultural anthropology's contribution to the intellectual foundations of wokeism would be revealed as a sham and a travesty. This article presents the prosecution's case against cultural anthropology's American founders....

Mead and her colleagues succeeded in challenging the darker side of Western civilization (eugenics), but they threw out the baby with the bathwater. Alongside cultural anthropologists, radical feminists, Marxists, and haters of the West have given us a generation of Tenured Radicals, mostly baby boomers, who have indoctrinated Generation Z. They have created a generation that now sees Western civilization as the problem, not the solution, to the question of how one should live life....

When the president of the United States [Joe Biden] endorses the transhumanist agenda and encourages children to change their sex surgically without their parents' permission, one may start to long for the good ol' days of patriarchy. Margaret Mead and her followers clearly have won the culture war.

Early American cultural anthropology's great legacy is the widespread adoption of the idea that nurture trumps nature. According to most of today's mainstream cultural anthropologists, the very concept of an objective nature outside humanity's control is just a propaganda tool of a power structure imposed by morally corrupt oppressors. If you publicly oppose that worldview, expect to be persecuted and prosecuted.

Geoffrey Clarfield's article exposes the very personal underbelly of today's woke ideology and its academic origins in the homosexuality of the American cultural anthropology icons whose self-serving findings provided its foundation. The real purpose of Drag Queen Story Hour is societal destruction—to *build back better.*

CHAPTER 22

What Is Social Justice?

Globalism is a replacement ideology that seeks to reorder the world into one singular, planetary Unistate, ruled by the globalist elite. The globalist war on nation-states cannot succeed without collapsing the United States of America. The long-term strategic attack plan moves America incrementally from constitutional republic to socialism to globalism to feudalism. The tactical attack plan uses asymmetric psychological and informational warfare to destabilize Americans and drive society out of objective reality into the madness of subjective reality. America's children are the primary target of the globalist predators.

The inherent child abuse in Drag Queen Story Hour described by Charlotte Cushman in Chapter 21 is part of the greater Marxist social justice campaign that is attacking America through politicized education in both public and private schools. Cushman defines social justice and explains its political objective in the social justice link[100] on her Authentic Montessori Education[101] website:

What Is Social Justice?

Social justice is grounded in Marxism, the ideology of communism. Marxists seek to destabilize society so that they can take power. They want an unstable population so they create an educational system that keeps the population uneducated and weak. Then they create constant conflict which results in revolutions. The conflict created is over the issue of oppression. Marxists hold that society is divided into two classes, the oppressed and the oppressors, and seek to take from the oppressors to give to the oppressed. They attempt to make the "oppressors" feel riddled with guilt so that they will cooperate more easily when discriminated against.

Social justice claims that certain groups are inherently evil. For example, they claim that all people that are white are racist. It places groups higher than individuals, and holds that all groups should be equal. If there are any disparities in group outcomes, it is attributed to discrimination and group injustice rather than individual choices and actions, and therefore the more successful groups need to be punished. This results in groups constantly fighting with each other. Currently, social justice sees America as inherently racist and it therefore holds that our country must be dismantled (also known as the Great Reset).

The American ideal of individual justice is equality under the law regardless of group affiliation—such as race, sex, religion, etc.—whereas social justice seeks to reward or punish individuals based on their group affiliation. Actual justice means that every individual must be judged for who he/she is and treated accordingly. If individuals work to earn their living, they can keep the fruits of their labor. If individuals violate the rights of others (stealing, murder, etc.), it means the violators go to jail.

Justice applies to everyone. Therefore, to add the concept "social" is an attempt to change the meaning of justice from equality under the law to equity, equity meaning everyone has a right to something whether or not he has earned it. That requires the use of force to take from one person for the benefit of another. This is racist and the very antithesis of justice. The real purpose of social justice in education is to change innocent children into racists. This will assure class (group) struggles and conflict.

Sexualizing children is one of the best ways to destabilize society. This is done with gender fluidity, sex transitioning, inappropriate exposure to and/or participation in sex such as drag queen shows, books showing sex acts such as oral sex, instruction in how to masturbate, pornography, and so on.[1]

The next step is pedophilia, which was openly defended by Gayle Rubin, a neo-Marxist, in her paper "Thinking Sex," a founding

---

[1]. Sex transitioning is pushed because of gender dysphoria, a psychological disorder where a person feels he or she is of the opposite sex. There is no scientific proof that this disorder has a biological source.

document for queer theory.[1] Queer theory includes, but is not limited to, the following:

- Queer means an identity without an essence, or to be outside the norm.

- Queer theory opposes normality and ethics with regards to sex—everything must be opened up or it is oppression.

- In order for the child to develop outside of reality, the adult should eliminate all boundaries.

- Children are oppressed by adults who think that "cross generational encounters" (in other words pedophilia) are horrors.

- Exposure to sexual acts is fine for children (anyone under the legal age of consent).

- Children need to be seen as equal to adults. Therefore, they can consent to sex.

- Child pornography is fine and there should be no laws restricting it.

- It is a "considerable burden" for sadomasochists and pedophiles to maintain absolute secrecy about their real sexual identities.

- There should be no separation between "adult" sexuality and childhood "innocence."

- The child should not be kept racially or sexually innocent or they are privileged.

- Every child should be treated as if they are queer and kept queer so they are an outcast and can be utilized for revolution.

The child finds inappropriate and shocking exposure to sex confusing and frightening. The pornography is so disturbing that there are teens who give up interest in sex permanently. This degrading introduction to sex makes a child feel insecure. It is massively dam-

---

[1]. Parker, Richard, Culture Society and Sexuality, "Thinking Sex: Notes for a Radical Theory of the Politics of Sexuality" by Gayle Rubin, 2006, Chapter 9.

aging when a child is sexually abused, and it leads to serious psychological problems. But that is exactly the goal—for the child to feel insecure. If a child is insecure, he doesn't know who he is, and is more easily manipulated, both morally and politically. Destroying a child's innocence is a part of the plan.

Social justice prepares children for sexualization by teaching them that certain groups are fundamentally bad. It preaches that it is awful to be white because of the "systems" whites put in place to oppress people of color, and then enjoy unearned "privilege." This is having devastating effects. There are white children who are so consumed with guilt for being white, that they claim to be transgender or homosexual. They would rather be accepted as members of a perceived oppressed group because more than anything they do not want to be thought of as vicious oppressors. Being diagnosed with a mental health problem, such as ADHD, multiple-personality disorder, depression, or anxiety, is another consequence of their undeserved oppressor status. Social justice is not only a lie, it creates psychological and emotional damage.

Transitioning to the opposite sex during childhood is messing with fire. There are unknown, long-term effects of puberty blockers and sex-change hormone therapy. There is evidence that transitioned children are at risk for health problems such as bone loss, diabetes, blood clots, stroke and heart disease. The impact that suppressing puberty will have on their brain development is unknown, an aspect that should be determined before treatment. The brain is crucial to human life—what if the growth of the brain is stunted? If these dangers pan out, it is undeniable that the lives of these children will have been permanently negatively impacted.

A person can't change their sex. We are all born with male or female chromosomes that exist in every cell of our bodies, and that doesn't change by taking hormones or by adding or subtracting body parts. It is psychologically damaging to spit at reality by pretending to be something you are not. Transitioning one's body is not only gruesome and horrific, it is also irreversible. It is beyond tragic that children would want to change to the opposite sex in order to escape condemnation for being white (or in order to be accepted by others, or for gender dysphoria). Anyone promoting this mutilation procedure for children should be ashamed of themselves. A friend of mine, Linda Blood, observed:

> It is WRONG and RACIST to claim that anyone is born an oppressor or a victim merely because of the color of their skin. There is no excuse for teaching such irrational rejections of reality to children when it should be obvious to anyone that this will result in unearned guilt, shame, and anxiety. The same goes for the rejection of objective reality that is the "transgender" craze. Those who continue to push these destructive ideologies bear most of the guilt for the damage they are causing and will continue to cause in the future.

Next on the chopping block is the family. Since most parents want to keep their children racially and sexually innocent, they are considered to be oppressors of children, and ultimately pose a threat to the destabilizing of society.[1] Therefore, the family unit must be destroyed by driving a wedge between children and parents. This is already in play. Marxist schools are hiding their criminal deeds from parents such as teaching social justice, teaching gender fluidity, reading pornographic books and administering sexual transitioning medical treatment to children, and so on. This is frequently done without parental knowledge or consent, and the children are even told not to tell their parents what is going on. When parents do find out about it and object, they are subjected to ad hominem attacks, and, in the state of California, they might get a visit from the government.

Marxist schools are also hiding the fact that they are teaching incorrect [revisionist] American history, changing it, or even eliminating it altogether. Many American cultural traditions such as Halloween and Christmas have been eliminated. It is very common for other cultures to be studied, but the American child is denied knowledge about his culture. Why? Because America, the nation founded on the principle of individual rights for everyone, is accused of being repressive. No matter where the child turns, he is given the message

---

[1]. There are other reasons for the destruction of the family, but for the purpose of this discussion, it is not necessary to name them here.

that he is either oppressed or the oppressor because of his race, sex, family, culture, country, and so on.

Within the Marxist philosophy, the populace must be loyal to the state and only to the state. Therefore, the child must be brainwashed to believe that he is determined by group status instead of his own individual thought process. He must be separated from reality. He must be separated from his mind so that he can't think for himself, and only repeats what the state has told him—that he needs to judge others on the basis of skin color, race, genetics, or other irrelevant factors, rather than on the basis of their actions and character. Social justice is helping the government to achieve that goal.

"The Communists' chief purpose is to destroy every form of independence—independent work, independent action, independent property, independent thought, an independent mind, or an independent man. Conformity, alikeness, servility, submission and obedience are necessary to establish a Communist slave-state." (Ayn Rand)

Social justice in Montessori is an embarrassment and a betrayal to the Montessori principles of individualism and independence. If we want to keep our children, culture and country healthy and stable, we must crush Marxism and uphold authentic Montessori education.

Cushman exposes the humanitarian hoax of *social justice* that presents itself as fairness but is actually a disruptive Marxist political strategy designed to destabilize and collapse society. She exposes the pervasive infiltration of Marxism throughout American education. Montessori schools are tuition-based private schools. As more Americans become aware of the Marxist indoctrination in public schools and turn to private schools for their children's education, many do not realize that private schools have also been infiltrated by Marxist philosophy. Even homeschooling is affected because the curriculum materials purchased by unsuspecting parents are also affected.

Any school that accepts government funds is affected. Charlotte Cushman's article is a warning to all parents whose children attend public schools, private schools, or are homeschooled that the American education industry can no longer be trusted to help children become the independent, autonomous, rational adults required to sustain life in our constitutional republic. What parents think schools are teaching their children is not what is actually being taught. Marxism is real, and it is being taught to America's children as a superior ideology to Americanism, without parents' knowledge or consent. Social justice is not American justice.

CHAPTER 23

Legalizing Pedophilia—The Sorensen Report

Globalism is a replacement ideology that seeks to reorder the world into one singular, planetary Unistate, ruled by the globalist elite. The globalist war on nation-states cannot succeed without collapsing the United States of America. The long-term strategic attack plan moves America incrementally from constitutional republic to socialism to globalism to feudalism. The tactical attack plan uses asymmetric psychological and informational warfare to destabilize Americans and drive society out of objective reality into the madness of subjective reality. America's children are the primary target of the globalist predators.

David Sorensen, anti–mainstream media journalist and founder of the website Stop World Control,[102] provides the most comprehensive data on the United Nations' and World Health Organization's criminal efforts to legalize pedophilia in a stunning report, "'Schools must equip children to have sexual partners'—The UN agenda to normalize pedophilia."[103] The September 2022 Sorensen Report is an unflinching exposé of globalism's orchestrated, coordinated effort to destroy children's innocence worldwide in its megalomaniacal campaign for world domination. The report begins with an invitation to download and disseminate the information in order to raise public awareness of the insidious attack on children worldwide:

> This evidence report reveals how the World Health Organization and United Nations are sexualizing little children in primary education worldwide, for the purpose of normalizing pedophilia. This report consists of nothing but solid evidence, with many official documents, videos, books, archives, etc. All PDF documents may be downloaded from the references section at the end of this report [or by using Archive.org][104].

Readers are invited to share the Sorensen Report with the world:

It is critical that this report reaches as many people as possible. Please send it far and wide, using all possible means. You can, for example, copy this short letter and send it to local newspapers, schools, law enforcement, churches, hospitals, politicians, etc. You can find their contact info with a quick search on the Internet.

> To whom it concerns,
>
> The World Health Organization and the United Nations are instructing education authorities worldwide to teach babies, toddlers and young children to masturbate, use pornography, learn different sexual techniques such as oral sex, and engage in same-sex relationships. The WHO and UN instruct educators to encourage children to start with sex as young as possible, and help all children to have sexual partners. Evidence shows how this is part of a worldwide operation to normalize pedophilia. See the following report: https://www.stopworld-control.com/children
>
> We invite you to carefully consider this information.
>
> Sincerely,
>
> Your signature

I was absolutely shocked by the Sorensen Report. I read it and reread it to be sure of what I was reading, because its contents are so sexually explicit, sexually graphic, and sexually inappropriate. The report is horrific and emotionally overwhelming, but essential reading to fully understand how widespread and sinister the campaign to destroy children's innocence actually is. After validating the report's sources, I include excerpts here, but I highly recommend that the reader take a deep breath and read the report in its entirety.

The Sorensen Report is summarized in its opening paragraphs:

> **"Little children are sexual beings who must have sexual partners and begin with sex as soon as possible. For this reason, kindergartens and elementary schools must teach children to develop lust and sexual desire, learn masturbation, build same-sex relationships, use online pornography, and learn**

different sexual techniques such as oral sex."

The above is a paraphrased summary of the official guidelines issued by the World Health Organization and the United Nations to educational authorities worldwide. Meanwhile, judicial organizations are issuing statements that sex between little children and adults should be legalized, while media outlets and political parties are calling for the acceptance of pedophilia as a "normal sexual orientation".

Supporting evidence for the claims being made is provided by primary sources—the United Nations' own documents. It is very difficult and painful reading, but necessary for people to grasp the absolute malevolence of the assault on children's minds, their sexuality, and their developing ability to reality-test.

The 2021 publication of the United Nations Educational, Scientific, and Cultural Organization (UNESCO), "The journey towards comprehensive sexuality education," describes comprehensive sexuality education (CSE), discussed at length in Chapters 17 and 19, as essential information for children:

> Comprehensive sexuality education is central to children and young people's health and well-being, equipping them with the knowledge and skills they need to make healthy, informed, and responsible choices in their lives, including to prevent HIV and promote gender equality.

The first document presented in the Report is the United Nations "International Technical Guidance on Sexual Education,"[105] the official guideline for elementary schools around the world. The actual goals of this document are described on pages 16 and 17. In its own words:

> "It [CSE] aims to equip children...to develop sexual relationships." (p. 16) "These skills can help children and young people form respectful and healthy relationships with family members, peers, friends and romantic or sexual partners." (p. 17)

On page 71, under Key Concept 7: Sexuality and Sexual Behaviour, educators are instructed to teach little kids from the age of five about kissing, hugging, touching, and sexual behaviors. Nine-year-old children are to be taught about masturbation, sexual attraction, and sexual stimulation.

The World Health Organization document "Standards for Sexuality Educa-tion in Europe" contains instruction for preschool children, kindergarten, and elementary schools:

- **Children between 0 and 4 years must learn about mastur-bation and develop an interest in their own and others' bodies.**

- **Children between 4 and 6 years must learn about mastur-bation and be encouraged to express their sexual needs and wishes.**

- **Children between 6 and 9 years must learn about sexual intercourse, online love and self-stimulation.**

- **Children between 9 and 12 years should have their first sexual experience and learn to use online pornography.**

Sorensen includes logos of the most familiar organizations actively involved in advancing CSE. They appear under the heading "Sexualizing kids is part of UN Agenda 2030":

> The logos on the United Nations "International Technical Guid-ance on Sexual Education" document show that this is part of the UN's Agenda 2030 Sustainable Development Goals.
>
> UNESCO, United Nations Educational, Scientific and Cul-tural Organization
>
> United Nations Sustainable Development Goals
>
> UNAIDS
>
> UNFPA
>
> UNICEF
>
> UN WOMEN
>
> World Health Organization
>
> Education 2030

United Nations Agenda 2030 is a plan to transform every aspect of human existence on the earth by the year 2030. In their own words:

> We have adopted a historic decision on a comprehensive, far-reaching and people-centered set of universal and trans-formative goals and targets. We commit ourselves to working tirelessly for the full implementation of this Agenda by 2030.

> As we embark on this collective journey, we pledge that no one will be left behind.

> These are universal goals and targets which involve the entire world, developed and developing countries alike.

The official statements from the United Nations are clear: they want the entire world to be transformed. Making sure that little children have sexual relationships, learn how to masturbate and use online pornography is part of this agenda. In the United States, the Biden administration has released statements confirming plans to implement this agenda throughout the USA as soon as possible, and no later than 2030.

The World Economic Forum (WEF) is an unapologetic supporter of Comprehensive Sexuality Education worldwide. The WEF's *build back better* campaign must first destroy what already exists, including your children's innocence. Echoing UNESCO's Orwellian claims, the WEF posted the article "Comprehensive sexuality education can prevent rapes, unsafe abortions and save lives"[106] on its website on October 16, 2019.

The Sorensen Report examines the Rutgers Foundation,[107] the Dutch equivalent of Planned Parenthood. The importance of the Rutgers Foundation to our discussion is that it is a main source of educational materials internationally, and collaborates with the United Nations and its Agenda 2030. Any nation's commitment to Agenda 2030, including the United States, involves Rutgers Foundation materials.

On its website link About Rutgers,[108] it self-describes as *the Netherlands on Sexuality*, and traces its origins back to founder Dr. Johannes Rutgers (1850–1924) and his wife, both driven by feminism, socialism, and, like Planned Parenthood, the plan to provide contraception to all—particularly poor people. From the Sorensen Report:

Contraception for all

Johannes Rutgers worked in the poorest neighbourhoods of Rotterdam and saw the distressing situations that arose because poor women in particular had no access to contraception. Therefore, from 1892, he gave free consultations on contraception in his practice.

He focused on the fight for free access to contraception and became an active member of the New Malthusian Union in 1898.

Malthusianism was an international movement based on the ideas of English pastor and economist Thomas Malthus. Malthus wrote "An essay on the principles of Population" in 1798, in which he said that population growth and food production would remain unbalanced, resulting in poverty and hunger. Sexual (total) abstinence was the only way to counter this, according to Malthus. In the Netherlands, these ideas led to the New Malthusian Union (NMB, founded in 1881). But unlike its English counterpart, the Dutch Malthusians believed that contraception was also a way to limit population growth, hence the "new" in the name New Malthusian Union.

The start of the Rutgers Foundation

Johannes Rutgers died in 1924, leaving numerous publications and a large network of expert collaborators in the field of contraception. As early as the 1930s, the NMB opened consultancies "on marriage and sex life" in Amsterdam and Rotterdam. In 1946, the union continued under the name Nederlandse Vereniging voor Seksuele Hervorming (NVSH).

The huge demand for the consultancies meant that this branch of the organisation was created [as] a separate foundation in 1969: the Rutgers Foundation (the predecessor of today's Rutgers). Named after Doctor Johannes Rutgers. People that needed help with sexuality could attend these consultancies at so-called Rutgers houses. In 2002, these Rutgers houses became part of the municipal health authorities. The foundation itself continues—to this day—to work for people's sexual and reproductive health and rights.

Rutgers and 'racial improvement'

Johannes Rutgers is often mentioned together with early "eugenics" [eugenicists], people who argued that races could be improved by sterilising poor or mentally disabled people. A theory that was popular in the Netherlands from around 1900 until well into the 1950s. At the time, Johannes Rutgers also put forward the idea that it would be better for some people, such as those living in poverty, not to have children.

The Rutgers Foundation is the worldwide publisher of sexuality education materials[109] chosen by the WHO and UN to implement their CSE agenda in twenty-seven countries around the world. Funded by Bill Gates, Planned Parenthood, and the UN, Rutgers launched its 2023 "Spring Fever" campaign aggressively pushing homosexuality in the Netherlands. A school poster teaching young children of the same sex to "do it" with each other was put up in elementary schools across the Netherlands.

Under the heading "**Teaching 6-year-old children about oral sex**," The Sorensen Report provides a shocking example of what Rutgers deems appropriate sex education material for young children.

> One of the children's books recommended by Rutgers for use in elementary schools is called "What is Sex?" by Channah Zwiep. Here is a page from this book, with an excerpt [translated] below it:

"Blowjob is sex with the mouth. That is why it is called **oral sex.**"

"Have you ever given yourself a kiss on a soft spot of your body? **Try it. How does that feel?**"

"The skin of a dick or vagina is also very sensitive. Because of this, people sometimes like to touch each other there with their mouths. When someone licks or suckles a dick, this is called sucking. Of course, the same is true for a woman. If someone licks a vagina, this is called **pussy eating.**"

Rutgers has published a guide for training teachers how to indoctrinate little children about sex. In the guide they reference the WHO guide, "Standards for Sexuality Education in Europe." The Sorensen Report includes mention of this because it is an international program, and not to be dismissed as a localized program in Europe.

Rutgers instruction advocates sex games in elementary schools in which kids take the genitals of their classmates in their mouths, lick them, and put their fingers in the vaginas of girls. For those who insist this cannot be happening in the United States, please read Alex Newman's article from May 9, 2023, "Girl, 6, Performed Oral Sex in Class with Teacher in Room."110 From that article:

> Critics say government "educators" and the sex-ed fanatics have some serious explaining to do after a 6-year-old girl at a government school in Texas was forced to perform oral sex on a boy in first-grade class. Classmates filmed the monstrous crime on April 19 [2023] even as a teacher was in the room, according to news reports.

> The horrific event at South Elementary first came to the attention of parents after a video of the sex act was found on a district-issued device. From there, despite officials' efforts to cover it up, word spread rapidly as parents and members of the community began protesting and demanding answers from officials online and outside the school....

> The horror comes as the United Nations also remains under scrutiny for peddling the idea that children can and should be allowed to "consent" to sexual activity.

Sorensen explores the real motivation behind the strategic operation to sexualize little children, and presents undeniable evidence that it is part of the agenda to normalize pedophilia in every nation of the world in its push to reduce the world's population.

> This is particularly evident when we consider the publisher who was handpicked by the WHO and UN to execute this agenda in 27 nations: *the Rutgers Foundation.*

> When the Rutgers Foundation was founded in 1969, its main purpose was to reduce population growth through sex education, abor-

tion and contraception. In 1999, Rutgers merged with the NISSO group (Netherlands Institute for Social Sexological Research), whose goal was also to reduce birth rates by encouraging abortion, free sex, and sex education. In 2011, Rutgers merged again with the World Population Foundation, which had the same mission of reducing the world population through abortion and sex education.

The common thread in the history of Rutgers is the agenda to reduce the human population by pushing unbridled sex in society. When people are sexually perverted, they can't form healthy families and are not as likely to produce offspring.

Rutgers always pushed for the normalization of pedophilia

Aside from the agenda to reduce the human population, Rutgers was always heavily involved in the worldwide movement to normalize pedophilia. In 1946, the Netherlands Association for Sexual Reform (NVSH) was founded, once again with the objective of reducing the human population. NVSH organized working groups on pedophilia that were supported by Labour Party Senator **Dr. Edward Brongersma.** This same Brongersma then became the foreman of the pedophilia acceptance movement in the 1970s....

The magazine published by Brongersma featured in its September edition of 1982 a comic [strip] that describes how a pedophile has oral sex with a young girl.... **The mindset propagated through this publication is that being with a pedophile is preferable over being with the family. It is "wrong" that the predator is in prison, while the man who caught him red-handed is free.**

These are the fundamental mindsets of pedophilia: that what they are doing is good, and people who are against it are bad. This mindset is also promoted in the guides of the United Nations, World Health Organization and Rutgers, albeit in more sophisticated wordings. It is nevertheless the same: *promoting sex with little kids is a human right, and opposing it is a violation of human rights.*

In The Netherlands, which appears to be the center for the worldwide agenda to normalize pedophilia, a political party for pedophilia was founded and was supported by the government. This

"Pedo Party" distributed a 1,000-page **Manual for Pedophiles** that teaches adults how to rape babies and toddlers.

The Manual for Pedophiles explains such things as:

• Methods of seducing children, for example by deflating the tires of their bike and then offering to fix it to gain their trust;

• How to use psychological techniques to get children to consent to sex—for example by rewarding them with money or gifts;

• How to stretch the rectum of babies and toddlers for anal sex;

• Where to find children;

• What ages are the safest (babies are safe, as they can't speak yet; 3–4 year olds are dangerous, as they can't keep secrets);

• How to use forensic techniques to hide your DNA, so the police can't track you.

Here are a few quotes from this handbook:

"The pedagogy of secrecy is about educating the child on how to keep secrets. We accomplish this by using special pedagogical methods based on a combination of child psychology and real-life experiences of professional pedophiles."

"You need to learn a lot about evidence and forensics so that you make it as difficult as possible for the police to arrest you. These three important tips ensure that all DNA traces are removed after sexual activity with the child.… It may sound like hassle, but many pedophiles have been sent to jail because they were too lazy to perform these three simple tasks. If they had done so, the police would have no evidence and they would have their freedom."

David Sorensen summarizes:

> It's beyond alarming that this explicit pedophile organization was handpicked by the WHO and UN to execute their agenda for the sexualization of little children all around the world.

Legalizing pedophilia is globalism's nuclear weapon that will vaporize every boundary of a child's selfhood, collapse the child's developing identities, and, finally, destroy the child's ability to reality-test—the primary requirement for living in the world of objective reality. The child's entire sense of self disappears. This monstrous abuse of power is reflected in the linguistic demand for plural pronouns, which I discuss in the next chapter.

CHAPTER 24

The Politics of Pronouns

Globalism is a replacement ideology that seeks to reorder the world into one singular, planetary Unistate, ruled by the globalist elite. The globalist war on nation-states cannot succeed without collapsing the United States of America. The long-term strategic attack plan moves America incrementally from constitutional republic to socialism to globalism to feudalism. The tactical attack plan uses asymmetric psychological and informational warfare to destabilize Americans and drive society out of objective reality into the madness of subjective reality. America's children are the primary target of the globalist predators.

In an information war, fought without bullets or bombs, language is weaponized. The globalist campaign promoting gender fluidity in order to destroy individual selfness manipulates spoken and written language to achieve its goal. Perversion of pronoun usage in the English language has a particularly destructive political purpose. The enemies of national and individual sovereignty are revising language to reflect human existence without the boundaries of self. Words matter. The switch to third-person plural, *gender-neutral* language is a weapon of mass psychological destruction that begins in early childhood.

Consider this: young children who do not learn the first- and second-person individual and possessive pronouns *I, me, mine, you, yours, he, him, his, she, her, hers* do not learn to name or identify themselves or others as individual gendered selves. Without a personal, individual, gendered, identifiable self, children become confused, destabilized, and vulnerable.

Instead of singular pronouns, young children are intentionally being taught to use the third-person plural pronouns *they, them, theirs,* so that they identify themselves in terms of the non-gendered collective. It is linguistic demolition of the individual. Plural pronouns effectively erase the concept of an individual self from the English language, and support the replacement of the individual with the preferred non-gendered collective identity.

Globalism's tactical strategy is to have the Left focus its Marxist ideological values of *diversity, equity, and inclusion* on cultural and educational institutions. The incremental strategic objective is for those values to be accepted as normative, then become social policy, and ultimately become the law of the land.

This is how globalism's linguistic hoax works to change the hearts and minds of America's children in classrooms K–12 and online. Disingenuously presented as *diverse, equitable*, and *inclusive* language to make people feel respected and included, *gender-neutral* substitutions are promoted as empathetic, kind, and caring. Grammarly, the popular cloud-based typing assistant, instructs writers on "How to Use Gender-Neutral Language at Work and in Life"[111] in an article by freelance journalist Devon Delfino, June 17, 2022:

> Gender-neutral language is simply a way of talking about people without assuming their gender. For example, it's referring to someone you don't know as "they" rather than using the pronoun "he" or "she," or addressing a group as "everyone" rather than saying, "Hey, guys."
>
> Luckily, the English language is relatively gender-neutral in many respects. For instance, many nouns (think: "writer," "president," or "acrobat") are gender-neutral. However, that doesn't mean that gendered language is uncommon. In fact, gendered language has been a part of our lexicon for a long time. (The United States' Declaration of Independence even proclaims that "all men are created equal.") So, you may not realize when you're using gendered language, even as it shapes how you see the world.
>
> Using gender-neutral language is an important habit because it demonstrates respect for people of all backgrounds, genders, and beliefs, and it includes everyone in the conversation. This is an especially helpful way to show support for members of LGBTQIA+ communities. And while not everyone finds the language people use about them important, it's best to land on the side of using inclusive and empathetic language....

It can feel awkward or forced when you start implementing gender-neutral language. That's normal. The important thing is to keep at it so that it has a chance to become a part of your everyday communication. That way, you'll not only be able to use inclusive language but also be better able to perceive the world in those terms....

Whether you're just now adopting gender-neutral language, or you've been using it for years, Grammarly's sensitivity suggestions can help your writing be both inclusive and up-to-date.

In January 2021, Bloomberg[112] reported that "Grammarly Is Now the 10th Most Valuable U.S. Startup." Grammarly is valued at $13 billion after new funding; $200 million came from investment firms Baillie Gifford, BlackRock, and others. BlackRock Investment Management Company, ticker symbol BLK, is the world's largest asset manager. In September 2023, global database online platform Statista reported[113] the total assets under BlackRock management at $9.43 trillion.

BlackRock Chairman and CEO Larry Fink also serves on the World Economic Forum Board of Trustees. Fink is often considered the architect of *woke capitalism*, which uses the metrics of globalism's new currency, Environmental, Social, and Governance (ESG), to pressure the companies it controls into compliance with its subjective social goals.

An article by senior news reporter Jekaterina Drozdovica, published on Capital.com[114] April 13, 2023, "BlackRock shareholders: Who owns the most BLK stock?" reports:

> According to the data from *WallStreetZen* as of 13 April [2023] ...61.87% of BLK shares are owned by institutional investors. This means that over half of the BlackRock Inc. shareholders were investment firms and asset managers, similar to BlackRock, which hold shares on behalf of their clients.

BlackRock's largest institutional investors are Vanguard Group, Inc., BlackRock Inc. (the parent company of BlackRock Investment Management), State Street Corporation, Bank of America, Temasek Holdings (Private) Limited, and Charles Schwab Investment Management. This means that the same globalist entities driving Agenda 2030 control the firms they invest in and initiate their political agenda without disclosing the source.

For example, Grammarly pledges its commitment to the *responsible*[115] innovation and development of AI:

> At Grammarly, we're guided by the belief that AI innovations should enhance people's skills while respecting personal autonomy and amplifying the intelligence, strengths, and impact of every user.

Remember that words matter. What Grammarly means by *responsible* innovation is that which comports with globalism's Agenda 2030, which is diametrically opposed to both national sovereignty and sovereignty of the individual.

Grammarly is just one example of how BlackRock, Vanguard, and State Street, the Big Three institutional investors, influence social policy by exerting their enormous financial power through boards of directors and proxy voting outcomes of the businesses they control. It is no secret that outside of small, independent mom-and-pop stores, the American business sector is being centralized, much like the media sector.

Businesses that appear to be competitors are controlled by the same institutional investors, and speak with the same *diversity, equity, and inclusion* voice regarding social policy. For example, BlackRock and Vanguard are in the top three institutional investors in both Coca Cola and Pepsi. Institutional investors currently own 68.75 percent of Coca Cola and 74.33 percent of PepsiCo.

In publishing, Houghton Mifflin Harcourt Books & Media and Harper-Collins are both owned by News Corp. Whether the product is soft drinks, children's books, young adult books, graphic novels, K–12 textbooks, graduate-level textbooks, medical textbooks, movies, videos, or clothing, globalism's *diversity, equity, and inclusion* narrative will be evident throughout in plural pronouns, book content, plot lines, music lyrics, training manuals, or screen prints on T-shirts.

The manufacturing, distribution, and sale of any product or service in the American economy is affected by the administrative choices of globalism's Big Three and the socialist policies of Agenda 2030 they support. Currently, the Big Three control over $22 *trillion* in assets, which represents a 20 percent ownership of America.

Business developer Steve J. Sands published an informative report on his website December 28, 2022, "Who Owns Corporate America":[116]

> Three fund management firms, BlackRock, Vanguard, and State Street, represent 40% of the shareholders of all listed firms and 88% of the S&P 500 index. In addition, they are now the dominant shareholder in 88% of the firms listed on the S&P 500.

> Isaiah McCall from Medium.com states in his blog post:

>> *BlackRock's absurd liquidity means that if you look at just about every major publicly traded company in the world, you'll find that BlackRock is its first, second or third-largest shareholder. Go ahead, try it.*

Globalism's Big Three exert enormous influence on the changing landscape of American culture. The seismic shift in education and the workplace that supports collectivist plural pronouns and blurs boundaries between male and female is another aspect of the coordinated attempt to destabilize Judeo-Christian morality, Judeo-Christian sexuality, and American family norms. It is the politics of pronouns.

CHAPTER 25

Philanthrocapitalism and Collectivism

Globalism is a replacement ideology that seeks to reorder the world into one singular, planetary Unistate, ruled by the globalist elite. The globalist war on nation-states cannot succeed without collapsing the United States of America. The long-term strategic attack plan moves America incrementally from constitutional republic to socialism to globalism to feudalism. The tactical attack plan uses asymmetric psychological and informational warfare to destabilize Americans and drive society out of objective reality into the madness of subjective reality. America's children are the primary target of the globalist predators.

In order to fully comprehend the scope of the planned globalist assault on your children's minds, it is helpful to review Norman Dodd's 1982 interview with G. Edward Griffin, and Dodd's stunning 1954 Report (Chapter 9). You will recall that Norman Dodd was appointed Director of Research of the Reece Committee to investigate tax-exempt foundations and determine if their activities could justifiably be labeled *un-American.* Dodd examined the recorded minutes of the Carnegie Corporation's board meetings and discovered how tax-exempt foundations in America, since at least 1945, had been operating to promote a hidden agenda. The foundations' *real* objectives were to influence American educational institutions and control foreign policy agencies of the federal government in order to condition Americans to accept world government. The government was to be based on the principle of collectivism (socialism) and ruled by the same interests that control tax-exempt foundations.

Twenty years after the Dodd Report, in 1974, Congress passed and President Gerald Ford signed into law the Employee Retirement Income Security Act (ERISA). Steve J. Sands explores its seismic societal consequences and reviews the history of third-party investment management in America in his previously referenced article, "Who Owns Corporate America?"[117]

Prior to 1980, most investments were made directly by each corporation. Sands asks, "What changed around 1980 to make the market shift toward third-party investment management?" The answer is fascinating:

> In 1974 The Employee Retirement Income Security Act (ERISA) was passed. One of the elements of ERISA was that it made it clear that companies could use third-party investment management. Hence the rise of third-party investment management by companies like BlackRock, State Street and Vanguard Group. BlackRock was founded in 1988. Vanguard was founded in 1975. While State Street was founded in 1792 [as Union Bank], it created the Standard & Poor's Depositary Receipt (SPDR) in 1993. State Street's SPDR 500 (SPY) Trust exchange-traded fund (ETF) was the first of its kind, and they are now one of the largest ETF providers worldwide. Trading on SPY began January 29, 1993. ETFs are widely used for mutual fund investments by third-party investment companies. The clear demarcation from direct to third-party investment management was the passage of ERISA.

> It is interesting to note that while ERISA's intent was to fix pension problems [crisis], one of the solutions was to introduce the allowance of third-party investment firms. The report from the WEF states:

>> *With economic and demographic fundamentals promoting ever faster growth in institutional assets since around 1980, the stage was set for the emergence of the modern asset management industry.*

Sands provides an incisive timeline of events chronicling the shift from direct investment to third-party investment management, and its acquisition of controlling interests in America's publicly held companies:

Timeline

- 1965/1967: Vance Hartke introduces and Jacob Javits sponsors Pension Reform bills
- 1971: World Economic Forum founded
- 1972: Documentary *Pensions: The Broken Promises* aired

- 1974: Jacob Javits main architect of ERISA

- 1974: Gerald Ford became President with Nelson Rockefeller as Vice President

- 1974: Ford signs ERISA into law

- 1975: Vanguard founded

- 1988: BlackRock founded

- 1993: State Street created SPDRs

- Today: BlackRock, Vanguard, and State Street together have a 20% ownership in American's S&P 500 and Fortune 1000 companies

Under the heading "Wash, Rinse, Repeat," Sands concludes with a reflection on philanthrocapitalism (discussed just below) and its application of the Hegelian dialectic for social change at work. Philanthrocapitalism manifests the *never let a crisis go to waste* axiom invoked by political figures from Winston Churchill, to Saul Alinsky, to the Obama Administration's Rahm Emanuel.

> As with other crises we have seen in the last 50 years, this [pension] crisis takes on the same formula:
>
> 1). Take advantage of a problem;
>
> 2). Gain public support through the media;
>
> 3). Present a solution through passage of legislation.
>
> 4). The legislation has secondary consequences not known by the public at large. Thereby, another crisis does not go to waste.

The 1954 Dodd Report exposed the hidden agenda of tax-exempt foundations, including the Carnegie Corporation. In 2006 the agenda was given a name by an editor at *The Economist* magazine, Matthew Bishop. He named it *philanthrocapitalism*—capitalism working for the good of mankind. Bishop's ideas were expanded into a book he co-wrote with Executive Director of the Social Progress Imperative, Michael Green, *Philanthropic Capitalism: How the Rich Can Save the World.*[118] The title's deceitful self-description is the marketing strategy for selling the sinister philanthrocapitalism to an unsuspecting public.

An extremely informative analysis of philanthropic capitalism written by University of Essex, UK, sociologists Linsey McGoey, Darren Thiel, and Robin West was published in *Politix*, Volume 121, Issue 1, January 2018, pages 29–54. "Philanthrocapitalism and crimes of the powerful"[119] concludes with an instructive summary of the humanitarian hoax of philanthropic capitalism:

> Sometimes new social practices solidify as tolerable and even admirable so quickly that people forget that, not long before, those same practices were seen as unacceptable or even harmful—and the philanthrocapitalism movement provides one such example. Until recently, the idea that personal profiteering is naturally 'philanthropic' for the wider community and inevitably beneficial to humankind was a laughable proposition. Today this has changed, and the concept of philanthrocapitalism is being hailed across the political spectrum as a laudable way to improve human welfare, and, in just over 10 years, the notion of philanthrocapitalism has evolved from a derided fringe philosophy to a powerful 'gospel' of wealth....

> The novelty of our approach has been to document the role that philanthrocapitalists play in proselytizing a gospel of market munificence. We have shown that what is really new about the 'new' philanthropy is not the comparative magnitude of new giving practices, but the *structure* of giving, and particularly the worrying and likely harmful enlargement of the sphere of entities, public or private, that are deemed as deserving charity. These structural changes have enabled organizations such as the Gates Foundation to use comparatively small 'gifts' in order to command widespread public allegiance and even reverence—smothering demands for corporate accountability and higher taxes. Old metaphors about the 'vampire-like' tendencies of capitalists have missed the most important thing to remember about vampires: they are most dangerous when circulating in disguise among the living, offering a warm smile that conceals their darker being.

The Sands Timeline above reveals how the pension crisis provided public support for passage of ERISA in 1974, and resulted in a seismic economic paradigm shift away from capitalism toward managerialism in America today. The economic shift reflects a wider philosophic shift away from individualism and laissez-faire capitalism based on private ownership, competition, free trade, self-reliance, self-interest, and the principles of supply and demand. The movement toward managerialism is a gargantuan leap toward collectivism, where the ruling managerial elite, not individuals, determine the course of one's life through Environmental, Social, and Governance (ESG) metrics that include *diversity, equity, and inclusion* (DEI).

In response to the deceit of philanthrocapitalism, a new word is finding its way into the lexicon. A *philanthropath* is a psychopath masquerading as a philanthropist. Beware the philanthropath!

CHAPTER 26

Pronouns and Publishing

Globalism is a replacement ideology that seeks to reorder the world into one singular, planetary Unistate, ruled by the globalist elite. The globalist war on nation-states cannot succeed without collapsing the United States of America. The long-term strategic attack plan moves America incrementally from constitutional republic to socialism to globalism to feudalism. The tactical attack plan uses asymmetric psychological and informational warfare to destabilize Americans and drive society out of objective reality into the madness of subjective reality. America's children are the primary target of the globalist predators.

The acceptance of philanthrocapitalism as the munificent foundation for globalism's New World Order provides the philosophical rationalization for social engineering throughout the publishing industry. Over the last twenty-five years, the U.S. trade publishing business has been centralized and reduced to five main players. The Big Five are Simon & Schuster, Penguin Random House, HarperCollins, Hachette Book Group, and MacMillan.

British-owned Pearson Education is the largest publisher of educational books, professional training manuals, and educational assessment services in America. Pearson Education was created when its parent company, Pearson PLC, purchased Simon & Schuster's education division from Viacom and merged it with its own education division in 2011.

In February 2019, Pearson sold its U.S. K–12 business to the private equity firm Nexus Capital Management LP for $250 million. In July 2019 Pearson announced its decision to move to a digital-first strategy, and began phasing out the publishing of printed textbooks.

BlackRock and Vanguard are among Pearson PLC's top ten institutional shareholders, and BlackRock is among the top three institutional shareholders of Cevian Capital, Pearson PLC's largest institutional investor.

The Big Five publishing companies and Pearson publish digital and printed books that follow an ESG/DEI editorial formula. Let's take a look.

Kiri Jorgensen, Publisher and Senior Editor at Chicken Scratch Books, posted an excellent article in *The Federalist* on July 13, 2023, "A Woke Children's Literature Cabal Is Conditioning Your Kid to Be an Obedient Leftist."[120] Jorgensen begins with a warning:

> Children's books are one of the most powerful tools parents have to help teach their kids how to be good human beings. From picture books being read at bedtime to novels being read by flashlight under the blankets, kids flourish in the safety of stories as they develop their belief systems. Resilience, respect, and many other noble traits are portrayed and experienced vicariously through books. What a powerful tool!

> Having been a part of the children's book publishing industry for several decades, and as a passionate participant, I have watched in growing dismay as the children's literature, or "kidlit," world has shifted and changed, and most recently taken a drastic plummet. Parents need to understand the destructive path this industry has taken, or they will discover too late as the damage hits home.

> This shift in kidlit has been happening for a long time. About 25 years ago, novels that portrayed kids as environmental activists began to win awards. About 15 years ago, the award-winning books showed shocking, disturbing scenarios. Ten years ago, books that depicted sexualization and abuse at younger ages began to win awards. Then, five years ago, it shifted a bit more to where books focused on systemic racism and sexual identity won awards. Today, if books don't include any of the above depictions, they are rarely published by medium and large publishing houses.

> And it's the medium and large publishing houses that supply schools, libraries, and bookstores.

During a 2015 writers' conference for children's book authors, a respected editor from a major publishing house admonished a writer over a character in his manuscript struggling with homosexuality. Jorgensen relates the incident:

"No." She explained that in kids' books, we must present the ideal as if it already exists. There can be no "being troubled by" gayness. There can be no "coming to terms with" sexual identity. The characters in our stories must immediately accept with positive responses any representation of modern social constructs. This immediately laudatory reaction to woke ideology is now required in kidlit. If an author doesn't portray it as such, his book will not be published.

This pronouncement by the editor shocked me and many other writers there. The line had now been drawn. As writers, our hope of publication rested on our willingness to positively portray woke ideology.

The deliberate social engineering apparent in the Big Five editorial formula deceitfully presents woke ideology as normative, because familiarity breeds acceptance. Authors with a traditional point of view are not published. It is a form of censorship and distortion of reality that is reinforced at the library.

Jorgensen talks about the complicity of libraries, and how librarians have purged their shelves of classics and replaced them with woke books, from board books for babies to young adult novels. She reports that of 12,000 librarian donors to the 2020 presidential campaign, 93 percent went to Joe Biden.

The distortion of reality in books is reinforced by advertising and the entertainment media. Children are inundated with over-sexualized images of woke ideology on television, in movies, in video games, in school, and in the library. Jorgensen describes it as a *normalization* campaign:

> Woke ideology has shifted from being the make-up of a book's plot lines to the fabric of the setting—the normal backdrop of the story as if it exists that way in real life.

> This normalization leads to acceptance, which leads to embracing. By weaving these social agendas into the "normal" background of a story, a child who feels shocked at a scene or description immediately shifts to feeling shame for being shocked in the first place. Kids will seek to replace their shame with acceptance. This is the power of normalization....

This is what we're up against. The entire children's book publishing industry—from authors to publishers to librarians—believes it should have the power to control your children's minds. And it has systematically and progressively gained that access.

For readers who still doubt the complicity or extensiveness of children's book publishing in woke indoctrination that Jorgensen exposed, I invite you to review a few of the books I found listed on Amazon's July 2023 list of Pronoun Books for Preschoolers:

- *The Pronoun Book*, by Chris Ayala-Kronos and Melita Tirado, April 5, 2023. Ages: Baby–3 years

- *What Are Your Words?: A Book About Pronouns*, by Katherine Locke and Ann Passchier, May 25, 2021. Ages: 4–8 years

- *Being You: A First Conversation About Gender* (First Conversations). Ages: 2–5 years

- *It Feels Good to Be Yourself: A Book About Gender Identity*, by Theresa Thorn and Noah Grigni, June 4, 2019. Ages: 4 and up

Under Amazon's search heading Children's Books, Growing Up & Facts of Life:

- *The Light of You*, by Trystan Reese and Biff Chaplow, March 1, 2022. Ages: 3–5

The book cover illustrates a pregnant man, his male partner, and two children smiling.

Amazon book summary:

A new baby is joining the family, and the whole community joins in to celebrate! Bringing gifts to celebrate the baby with art, music, jokes, cuddles and delicious food, they also bring their love and support for the pregnant transgender dad who will give birth to the baby soon!

- *My Own Way: Celebrating Gender Freedom for Kids*, by Joana Estrela, March 1, 2022. Ages: 3–6

Amazon book summary:

Small children are often asked to choose between a gendered binary—"boy" or "girl", "pink" or "blue". This colorful picture book smashes these stereotypes and encourages the reader to follow their own way!

Amazon editorial reviews:

- "Reminiscent of Todd Parr…this book offers support and acceptance" Angela Leeper, *Booklist*

- "An encouraging, cheerful introduction for younger children" Patricia D. Lothrop, *School Library Journal*

- "An encouraging guide to considering gender identity" *Publishers Weekly*

Marxist cultural terrorism is tearing American families apart, destroying children's ability to reality-test, creating racial tension, and fomenting race wars. Why would the Big Three leviathans of institutional investing, BlackRock, Vanguard, and State Street, join with the Big Five publishing houses and the philanthrocapitalists in supporting cultural Marxism?

This critical question is answered at the end of the Dodd interview in Chapter 9:

> *Griffin: How have the purpose and direction of the major foundations changed, over the years, up to the present? What are their purposes and directions today?*

> *Dodd: One hundred percent behind meeting the cost of education, such as it is presented through the schools and colleges of this United States, on the subject of our history—to prove that our original ideas are no longer practical. The future belongs to collectivistic concepts. There is just no disagreement on this.*

> *Griffin: Why do the foundations generously support communist causes in the United States?*

> *Dodd: Well, because, to them, communism represents a means of developing what we call a monopoly—as the organization, we'll say, of large-scale industry into an administrable unit.*

The "administrable unit" perfectly describes the operations of the globalist managerial Unistate.

CHAPTER 27

Pronouns and Pantheism

Globalism is a replacement ideology that seeks to reorder the world into one singular, planetary Unistate, ruled by the globalist elite. The globalist war on nation-states cannot succeed without collapsing the United States of America. The long-term strategic attack plan moves America incrementally from constitutional republic to socialism to globalism to feudalism. The tactical attack plan uses asymmetric psychological and informational warfare to destabilize Americans and drive society out of objective reality into the madness of subjective reality. America's children are the primary target of the globalist predators.

The weaponization of language is not a new phenomenon. The politics of pronouns has dimensions in both form and content. Gender-neutral plural pronouns, the grammatical form for linguistic deconstruction, were introduced in America almost fifty years ago. The pro-pedophile advocacy group Child Sexuality Circle advocated passage of a Child's Sexual Bill of Rights that included use of "the new unisexual pronoun…co for he/she/him/her and cos for his/hers" in January 1977.

Gender-neutral language that blurs male/female identity with plural pronouns derives its ideological content from the unifying sexual ideal of androgyny. The *new sexuality* that deconstructs traditional Judeo-Christian sexuality and replaces it with total sexual liberation and freedom from all sexual boundaries is an ideological return to ancient pantheism—the belief that God and the universe are one and the same.

Pantheism predates monotheistic Abrahamic religions by thousands of years, but the word *pantheism* was not used until the early 18th century. The word is derived from Greek (*pan* = everything, *theos* = God), and means "All is God, and God is all." There is no distinction between the two; all things are connected and are ultimately of one substance. Pantheism is a *belief system* rather than a religion, comparable to the terms monotheism (belief in a single God) and polytheism (belief in multiple gods).

Pantheism revered the androgyne as the archetype of human beings before the Judeo-Christian recognition of man and woman as two sexes. The globalist wrecking ball is attempting to shatter Judeo-Christian religions with the narrative that they are not "true" religions, that before Judaism and Christianity, the true religions were monistic (the doctrine of oneness that denies duality between man and God, or matter and mind) and revered androgyny.

Infantile fusion, the inability to distinguish self from other, is the psychological equivalent of infantile political narratives seeking to obliterate any and all distinctions and boundaries between self and other, including sexual boundaries. The promise of boundaryless infantile bliss is being resurrected and exploited to seduce psychologically regressed millennials to reject their Judeo-Christian identities, embrace Marxist queer theory in all its iterations, and recast themselves as citizens of globalism's New World Order.

Religious art is usually a reflection of an ideological ideal, and so it is with pantheistic art. In 2017, Dutch sculptor Femmy Otten's life-size bronze hermaphrodite sculpture, *And Life Is Over There*,[121] was unveiled at The Sculpture Gallery in the city center of The Hague. It is a disturbing totem-like statue of a woman with long hair, full breasts, a penis, three arms, and a hybrid creature of a bear head and human body perched atop her head. The sculpture is a rejection of Judeo-Christian duality and a celebration of androgyny in pantheism's singularity.

A press release[122] from Stroom Den Haag art center identifies the title of the sculpture as a stanza from Emily Dickinson's love poem "I Cannot Live without You." The release explains that "the titles of Otten's work often refer to the poetry of Dickinson, in which she recognizes a feeling of loneliness, a longing and disappointment and a desire to be (set) free."

In the press release Otten describes the androgyne as the ideal state of being:

> *The Greek god Hermaphroditus was literally merged with his beloved. Ever since I started drawing and making my work genders have effortlessly merged into each other. For me this feels very*

natural. I can identify with the one or with the other. To me it feels strange to view men and women as separate entities—we are so deeply involved with each other and our lives are so intertwined. I myself feel a deep urge to blend.

In this sculpture I was very much concerned with finding the right posture, it had to be perfectly natural. No shame and no explicit pride—to me that was very important.

It is a shocking statement, and even more shocking as an ideological goal for an adult. Adulthood recognizes separateness as a desired state of physical, emotional, and psychological being. In a free society, the psychological adult has personal agency to decide when and if to blur the physical boundaries of self with another.

The brief blurring of boundaries during the fusion of sexual intercourse does not deny the existence of boundaries. Individual sovereignty embraces both physical separateness and the agency to control the boundaries of one's physical separateness. It is why the violation of physical boundaries during non-consensual sex is a crime. It also explains how the elimination of individual boundaries reflected in unisexual pronouns advocated by the pro-pedophile group Child Sexuality Circle limits personal agency to control the boundaries of self, and why it was used as a tactic in the organization's strategic effort to legalize pedophilia.

In a sane society of ordered liberty, Femmy Otten's goal of infantile fusion would be considered insanity, yet it is exactly what the globalist sociopaths are trying to achieve. Men and women who cannot distinguish boundaries are as dependent and controllable as infants. Describing her work as a statement about freedom is simply Orwellian.

Psychologically regressed adults live in the subjective reality of *feelings*. They lack the adult critical-thinking skills required to examine the facts and consequences of a boundaryless existence in objective reality: that the total dependence of infancy requires either a caretaker family or a caretaker government. The tactical destruction of family awards control of children to the government.

When regressed parents take their children to drag queen story hour events, participate in the destructive convention of plural pronouns, and support their children's demands for transgender transitioning, they are unwittingly participating in the totalitarian destruction of the family and ceding control of their precious children to the state by embracing queer theory.

Queer theory, discussed at length in Chapter 11, one of the species of the genus Marxism, rejects traditional Judeo-Christian heterosexual norms including the idea of childhood innocence. Instead, it promotes the pansexual transformation of society and embraces complete sexual liberation including children's "rights" to sexual liberation, which is the end of childhood innocence. Queer theory supports abrogation of the age of sexual consent, normalization of pedophilia as legally and culturally acceptable, and the teaching of queer theory precepts, including pansexuality, in K–12 schools. Derived from the Greek prefix "pan" meaning "all, every, whole, all-inclusive," pansexuality does not limit sexual choice to biological sex, gender identity, or even being human.

The deliberate effort to reorient children in American schools to reject their Judeo-Christian norms and accept Marxist queer theory is documented in a stunning 2018 research paper written by Judith Reisman, Ph.D., Director of the Child Protection Institute and Research Professor at Liberty University School of Law, and attorney Mary E. McAlister. Published in the *Journal of Law and Social Deviance,* Volume 16, 2018, "Gender Identity, Transgender Issues in Public Schools"[123] explains:

> In school districts throughout the country, the pansexual transformation of society has been stealthily making inroads into the minds of children. The latest manifestation of the decades-long revolution is the concept of gender identity now being integrated into non-discrimination policies, student codes of conduct and curriculum.... (p. 121)

> The reformers have moved from promoting "safe" premarital sexual intercourse to teaching that masturbation, oral and anal sodomy, homosexuality and bisexuality are healthy and normal. Now concepts of "gender identity," "gender fluidity," "transgenderism" and similar terms will become part of the children's lexicon, relegating "girl," "boy," and "man," "woman," much less "maiden," "ladies," and "gentleman," to the dustbin of ancient history. New language is

invading everything from "family life education" to English, social studies, science and math.

The invasion does not stop at classroom instruction. For at least 10 years the federal Department of Education ("DOE") has cautioned school officials that sexual "innuendoes," "graphic pictures" and "language" can create an environment that is detrimental to students. The DOE warns school boards that they can be liable for sexual harassment "when a teacher, school employee, other student, or third party creates a hostile environment that is sufficiently serious to deny or limit a student's ability to participate in or benefit from the school's program." However, during the Obama Administration, the DOE and Department of Justice ("DOJ") pressured school districts to amend their non-discrimination policies to include "gender identity" or lose federal funding. By requiring that schools add "gender identity," which does not have an accepted, objective definition, to school policies, the DOE/DOJ directive introduced "gender uncertainty" into children's lives, as males who "identify" as females regardless of their biologically obvious physical genitalia were to be permitted to use females' private spaces like restrooms and showers, and vice versa. Such policies would cause some students to be confused and distracted, many even frightened, by the appearance of students and staff who externally resemble one sex but say they "identify" as another. This would limit the student's ability to participate in and benefit from the school's program, *i.e.*, create a hostile learning environment. The federal government not only created a Hobson's choice, but was also actually encouraging students whom the American Psychiatric Association defines as "mentally disordered" to continue suffering rather than seeking assistance.

The Trump Administration rescinded the Obama Administration's DOE/DOJ guidance on February 22, 2017. However, many school boards throughout the nation, including in Fairfax County, Virginia, caved to the DOE's pressure and voted to add "gender identity" to their non-discrimination policy and student code of conduct. Those school boards also voted to train and test children in "sexual orientation terms," including heterosexuality, homosexuality, bisexuality—"and the gender identity term transgender," as part of their "sex education" or "Family Life Education" curriculum. Students are trained/indoctrinated in the Kinsey-created theory that "sexuality evolves from infancy to old age." The "FLE/sex education" curricula not only present the experimental construct of "gender identity" as scientific fact, but also hide from students and parents critical information such as that condoms only protect against certain limited sexually transmitted diseases if used properly each time during normal vaginal male-female sexual relations.

Many schools have been advocating training children that oral and anal sodomy are acceptable, even normal, variations of sexual activity and safe if condoms are used properly. In fact, condoms have had a sufficient failure rate when they were tested, so that no condom has ever been approved for the FDA for use in oral or anal sodomy. Now schools are poised to introduce a new gender paradigm comprised of "four parts—biological gender, gender identity (includes transgender), gender role, and sexual orientation (includes heterosexual, bisexual, and homosexual)." This endangers children even further. While those advocating for sex education claimed that it would be the best "step in crime prevention" which states can make, in fact, violent crime has increased exponentially since sex stimuli education programs were launched. For example, in Illinois, violent crime per capita increased by 754 percent between 1965, when proponents touted sex education as the best crime prevention, and 2011. Now, introducing "gender uncertainty" so that boys can be girls and girls can be boys, and allowing private spaces to be open to all (including pedophiles and pederasts of any age), sex crimes will predictably increase, not decrease. Violent crime, especially sexual offenses, based on the empirical data, increases as protection afforded by sex-segregated private spaces are, by edict, removed.

School policies and curricula embracing "gender identity" as an "orientation" protected against "discrimination" are the latest manifestations of the theory, first widely touted by Kinsey, that "children are sexual from birth" and that there should be no boundaries placed upon human sexual behavior. Kinsey's pansexual worldview has become predominant in academia, law, medicine, the media and other cultural institutions. There have been almost 17,000 citations to Kinsey in virtually every scholarly and mainstream publication since 1948. This includes more than 700 law review citations for Kinsey and 4,531 academic journal citations containing "Kinsey" and "gender." Sexually radical scholars began setting the stage for the Kinseyan societal transformation almost immediately [after Kinsey published his research], calling for wholesale reform in laws, medical protocols and public policy to correspond to Kinsey's findings.... (pp. 125–132)

The sexual transformation of society has moved to the public schools where the goal is to train the next generation in "Kinseyan sexology" under multiple stimuli as "education" guises, e.g., "family life," "bullying," "diversity," "sex," and myriad constantly changing politically correct masquerades. In many schools now, that training includes the concept of "gender uncertainty," *i.e.*, that a person's sex is not limited to male and female, but can be one of any number of combinations based upon any number of factors that change throughout one's lifetime, and might not have anything to do with their biological sex.... (p. 134)

Dr. Paul McHugh, the chief psychiatrist at Johns Hopkins Hospital who requested the study, said the research found that adult recipients of "sex reassignment surgery" ... "had much the same problems with relationships, work, and emotions as before. The hope that they would emerge now from their emotional difficulties to flourish psychologically had not been fulfilled."

> We saw the results as demonstrating that just as these men enjoyed cross-dressing as women before the operation so they enjoyed cross-living after it. But they were no better in their psychological integration or any easier to live with. With these facts in hand, I concluded that Hopkins was fundamentally cooperating with a mental illness. We psychiatrists, I thought, would do better to concentrate on trying to fix their minds and not their genitalia. Based upon that study, Johns Hopkins discontinued adult sex re-assignment surgery in 1979.... (pp. 163–164)

Subsequent studies have confirmed the sanity, or wisdom, of Dr. McHugh's actions, finding that just as there is no evidence of a "gay gene," there is also no evidence that "gender identity disorder" is an innate condition justifying drastic medical intervention such as hormonal treatments and genital mutilation. Scientists have determined that "[a] baby is conceived genetically male or female. Prenatal brain development is influenced by the same hormones that trigger the development of the reproductive organs." "The sex of each individual is encoded in the genes—XX if female, XY if male." ...

In fact, scientists now know that the DNA blueprint for a male versus a female brain is established eight weeks after conception. The hormonal changes that create a male versus a female brain are permanently determined at that time, in utero, even though many of the effects will not manifest until puberty. Therefore, contrary to [New Zealand–born sexologist] Dr. [John] Money's theory, still being followed by those seeking to transform the culture, "we're not psychological hermaphrodites at birth, potentially masculine or feminine—we are wired for one or the other in the womb." Consequently, as Dr. McHugh's studies found, those who express a sense of "disquiet" between their biological sex and their "sexual identity" are suffering from a mental disorder, not an innate abnormality, and should be treated with therapy, not with medical, surgical mutilation as intervention. (pp. 168–170)

Challenging boundaries might be exciting for adults who know the boundaries and can process risks associated with the challenge. However, it is traumatic and harmful for children, who have just begun to understand the concepts of "boy" and "girl," and realize that they are one or the other. As Dr. McHugh said, subjecting children to such psychological turmoil is tantamount to child abuse.... (p. 179)

Introducing Gender Uncertainty into the Already Sexualized Classrooms Will Psychologically Traumatize Children.

Asking children to disregard biological reality and embrace a myth of gender uncertainty can be expected to create further dysfunction and even open new channels for acting out. Psychiatrist Keith Ablow has discussed the potentially traumatic consequences of instructing children to deny biological reality. "The mere fact that teachers and administrators will have to explain to kindergarten and first grade students that they might see girls in the boys' restroom, or boys in the girls' locker room, but that those really aren't kids of the gender they appear to be, could do harm to their own developing sense of self by suggesting to them that their gender is fluid, that it well might change for them, too, and that they should be on the lookout for signs that they want to switch." ... (pp. 216–217)

Most importantly, children will explicitly and implicitly be told to question the truths they learn at home regarding their own identities as boys and girls.

Gender Uncertainty Will Further Undermine the Family and Create Cultural Conflicts.

As well as wreaking havoc with children's mental and physical health, the continuing infusion of pansexuality, and particularly introducing the concept of gender confusion into the schools, wreaks havoc with the family, its authority, and culture. Schools will teach doctrine that directly conflicts with the students' personal reality, but also with what they are taught at home and commonly in church regarding what it means to be male and female. Students are taught to disregard their physical and psychological makeup, what their parents tell them, and embrace the idea that gender is an identity that incorporates not only physical appearance, but also an amorphous gender identity, which is a person's internal, deeply felt sense of being either male or female. Children whose cultural background teaches that a person with female genitals is a female and a person with male genitals is male, which comports with biological reality, will be told by their school teachers, librarians, counselors, lecturers, etc., that is not the case. Their parents provide them with the facts as established by medical science, but when they attend school, other trusted, paid, educated, professional adults will tell them that gender is different from sex and that some people look male but are not because they do not "feel" male while some others look female but are not because they do not "feel" female. Children might not have the courage to challenge such fraudulent claims made by those adults, who hold power over them, because they are captive, easily intimidated and manipulated. Students will also be told that there is something known as "gender expression," which is "society's perception of the external characteristics and behaviors that are socially defined as either masculine or feminine," such as the way one dresses, speaks, or interacts socially. (pp. 222–224)

CONCLUSION

Scientific advances have proven the truth of the natural law concept that human beings are created either male or female, and that the sexual differentiation is complete in utero, not "assigned at birth." Societal change agents seeking to further Alfred Kinsey's fraudulent, criminal pseudo-science used rare instances of children born with ambiguous genitalia, or tragically a boy whose genitals were damaged in surgery, to create a new social construct of gender identity and to deconstruct the barriers of gender binaryism.

Despite mounting evidence of the fallacy of their theories, the change agents have persisted in pursuing their agenda through orchestrated efforts to change public opinion, the law, public policy and academia. Now, the agenda is moving into the public schools, which are still reeling from the introduction of "comprehensive sex education" and the sexualization of the entire educational experience. Young students whose brains have not fully developed and cannot undertake the complex reasoning necessary to process sexual messages will be required to abandon biological reality and accept the idea that "gender" is a multi-faceted concept that does not necessarily correspond with a person's physical, emotional and psychological reality. Women are again being driven into compromising positions, and put at risk of harm from the new sexuality that would again relegate them into the position of second-class citizens, exposed to harassment and rape to fit the newest pansexual ideology.

The consequences of this latest manifestation of the pansexual worldview are far-reaching and potentially traumatically devastating to the next generation. (pp. 250–252)

Alfred Kinsey's fraudulent research has been used for seven decades to support the pansexual transformation of American society, the sexual revolution, cultural Marxism, queer theory, queer pedagogy, the destruction of the American family, and the collapse of the Judeo-Christian norms that are our nation's infrastructure.

Globalism's war on national sovereignty targets the American family and its Judeo-Christian foundation as a competing ideology. Pansexual transformation, and the sexual perversions and elimination of sexual distinctions introduced by Marxist George Lukács to deconstruct the family in Hungary, are the same sexual perversions and elimination of sexual distinctions that are convulsing the United States today.

Sex and sexuality have been weaponized, and are being used as instruments of cultural mass destruction. The pro-pedophile Child's Sexual Bill of Rights advocated by the Child Sexuality Circle in 1977 has been revitalized. The current linguistic blurring of male/female identities reflected in gender-neutral unisex pronouns is supported with destructive pornographic educational grooming, and glorified in artwork that idealizes androgyny.

The political campaign to legalize pedophilia is embraced within the woke tenets of diversity, equity, and inclusion. The objective is to reclassify pedophiles as "child-attracted persons," remove the stigma of their perversion, and erase the reality of pedophilia's catastrophic harm to children.

It is very difficult for the civilized mind to process such malevolence. Adults in a civilized society are expected to protect children, but civility is a peacetime attitude, and America is at war. America's enemy within considers childhood innocence to be an impediment to its political objectives. Childhood innocence is a political target, and children are intentional casualties of globalism's war on nation-states.

CHAPTER 28

Pantheism, Gnosticism, and Marxism

Globalism is a replacement ideology that seeks to reorder the world into one singular, planetary Unistate, ruled by the globalist elite. The globalist war on nation-states cannot succeed without collapsing the United States of America. The long-term strategic attack plan moves America incrementally from constitutional republic to socialism to globalism to feudalism. The tactical attack plan uses asymmetric psychological and informational warfare to destabilize Americans and drive society out of objective reality into the madness of subjective reality. America's children are the primary target of the globalist predators.

G*nosis* is the Greek word for knowledge. Gnosticism is an ancient ideological genus with many species, pantheism being one of them. Gnosticism is a paganistic, pantheistic, polytheistic cosmology. A cosmology is an account of the origin of the universe. The tenets of Gnosticism are rooted in dualism, and are diametrically opposed to Judeo-Christian doctrines and morality. Gnostic tenets are the ancient source of modern anti-Semitism, population control, abortion, embryonic/fetal research, eugenics, transhumanism, and New Age ideologies.

Judeo-Christian philosophy and beliefs are consistent with the Aristotelian "principle of non-contradiction." In reference to George Orwell, this means that in the Judeo-Christian tradition, up is not down, black is not white, war is not peace, and ignorance is not strength. Life in the Judeo-Christian world is rooted in objective reality. In Gnosticism, just as in Orwell's *1984*, up *is* down, black is white, war is peace, and ignorance is strength. Such contradictions and dualities are foundational to its beliefs and teachings.

Bioethicist and professor of philosophy Dr. Dianne Irving provides an extraordinary and impassioned analysis of the importance of understanding ancient Gnosticism and its massive influence in contemporary America in her 2006 article, "Gnosticism, the Heretical Gnostic Writings, and 'Judas'." [124] She states:

> It is a moral crime that the on-going spread of Gnosticism—both ancient and post-Christian—is not identified or acknowledged in most "ethical" treatises, religious/secular "teachings" or the media. To not know or understand what Gnosticism is, is to be incapable of putting a name and a face on, questioning, or evaluating one of the most pervasive and influential mythological ideologies in our global society today.

Understanding the fundamentals of Gnosticism will help the reader identify its underlying connections to Marxism. Remember, Karl Marx was never an economist, as Dr. James Lindsay reminded us in Chapter 11; he was a theologian. As Lindsay told the European Parliament on March 29, 2023:

> He [Karl Marx] wanted to produce a religion for mankind that would supersede all of the religions of mankind, and bring him back to his true social nature…and at the end of history mankind will remember that he is a social being and we will have a socialist society—a perfect communism that transcends private property.

It should not surprise us that current species of ideological Marxism are practiced with religious zealotry. The linguistic reversals and dialectical processes being used to destabilize America and collapse its capitalist, Judeo-Christian infrastructure have their roots in ancient Gnosticism.

Gnosticism is the philosophical foundation of the Marxist Cultural Revolution that is destabilizing American society in the 21st century. It is the foundation for the elitist perspective of Wokeism that describes itself as "enlightened," "awakened," and having superior "knowledge" (gnosis). The elitism that is an intrinsic part of Gnosticism is being exploited for political gain by globalist social engineers who fully understand the seduction and political candy of playing the "superiority" card.

Barack Obama brought Marxist dualism to the White House with his infamous campaign slogan of "hope and change." Obama was speaking the dialectical language of Marxist deconstruction, yet Americans heard the *constructive* language of racial unity and national pride.

Obama's deliberate perversion of the English language is a familiar tactical tool of political Marxism, with its roots in Gnosticism. War is deceit, and the culture war is no different. In *The Collapsing American Family: From*

Bonding to Bondage (pp. 115–120),[125] I discuss the weaponized language of leftist deception and provide a short glossary to help readers identify dialectical language. The terms *antiracism* and *woke* are additions to the glossary:

> "Political language…is designed to make lies sound truthful and murder respectable, and to give an appearance of solidarity to pure wind." (George Orwell essay, *Politics and the English Language*, 1946)
>
> Dialectical speech is the political language of doublespeak and double meanings. Doublespeak is language deliberately constructed to disguise or distort its actual meaning. The words used in doublespeak are ambiguous, often have two different meanings, and are spoken to deliberately confuse the listener.…
>
> The word doublespeak derives from two Orwellian words (from his novel *1984*), "doublethink" and "Newspeak." Doublethink is when a person accepts two mutually contradictory thoughts as correct without being aware of or troubled by the glaring contradiction between them. Doublethink eliminates cognitive dissonance—the anxiety ordinarily generated by conflicting thoughts. "War is peace," "freedom is slavery," and "ignorance is strength" are examples of doublethink.
>
> Newspeak controls thought through language. Doublespeak combines doublethink and Newspeak in language that deliberately obscures, distorts, disguises, or reverses the actual meaning of words. It is semantic deception designed to manipulate public opinion in a mass social engineering campaign. Doublespeak is the language of fake news, and the language of the leftist coup against Western democracies and national sovereignty.…
>
> ### GLOSSARY OF LEFTIST DOUBLESPEAK
>
> **1. Antiracism = Anti-white**
>
> **2. Build Back Better = Slogan of the Great Reset**
>
> Build Back Better follows Saul Alinsky's social demolition model: *All change means disorganization of the old and organization of the*

new. The Great Reset requires destruction of the existing economic structure of private property, and rebuilding with a new economic structure in which: "You'll own nothing, and be happy."

3. Comprehensive immigration reform = Open borders

"Comprehensive immigration reform" advocates open borders, sanctuary policies, and mainstreaming illegal aliens into American life at taxpayer expense in order to collapse the economy and surrender American sovereignty to the globalist elite.

4. Consensus = Unanimity of thought

In doublespeak, consensus means unequivocally accepting the leftist narrative in science, economics, social policy, and medicine. There is no consideration of dissenting opinions.

5. Critical thinking = Marxist Critical Theory

Critical thinking is an essential survival skill for an independent, autonomous, rational adult in a constitutional republic. Marxists use the phrase to describe the thought process necessary to actively criticize that which exists in service of Marxist Critical Theory, a social theory designed to destabilize and collapse Western society from within.

6. Diversity = Differences in appearance but not in thought

Diversity means "variety." Leftist diversity includes only appearances; it does not tolerate any variety of opinions. Leftism is tyrannical in its demand for conformity to its politically correct left-wing narrative of moral relativism and historical revisionism.

7. Domestic terrorists = Trump supporters

8. Education = Indoctrination

What was once a traditional American education of core subjects and pride in American exceptionalism has been transformed into an echo chamber of anti-American leftist propaganda promoting globalism, socialism, political correctness, moral relativism, historical revisionism, self-loathing, and critical race theory.

9. Extremist = Trump supporter

Under the Biden-Obama-Harris regime, political opposition has been reclassified as a prosecutable national security threat, and no longer protected by free-speech guarantees.

10. Freedom of speech = Approved speech

Leftists in America are determined to eliminate freedom of speech by enforcing their own code of political correctness, which labels any opposing speech as hate speech. Speakers with conservative points of view are disinvited, censored, or intimidated through organized boycotts and violent protests.

11. Global warming/climate change = Redistribution of wealth

In 1992 UN scientists on the Intergovernmental Panel on Climate Change (IPCC) stated: "It is extremely likely that human influence has been the dominant cause of the observed warming since the mid-20th century." But as Greenpeace founder Patrick Moore testified before the Senate Environment and Public Works Committee on June 24, 2014:

> Extremely likely is not a scientific term but rather a judgment, as in a court of law. The IPCC defines "extremely likely" as a "95–100% probability." But upon further examination it is clear that these numbers are not the result of any mathematical calculation or statistical analysis. They have been "invented" as a construct within the IPCC report to express "expert judgment," as determined by the IPCC contributors.

Man-made climate change, among the greatest hoaxes ever perpetrated on industrialized countries, is designed to transfer their wealth to non-industrialized countries. The United Nations is committed to globalization and one-world government, and is supported worldwide by leftists with the same objective.

12. Globalism = One-world government

Leftists are not using the word globalism to mean global trade. When leftists say globalism, they mean one-world government. Their intention is to eliminate national boundaries and impose one-world rule.

13. Great Reset = New World Order = One World Order

In doublespeak, the Great Reset is the rebranded globalist New World Order of planetary governance. The Great Reset is also a reference to United Nations Agenda 21, United Nations Agenda 2030, and the Fourth Industrial Revolution.

14. Greater good = Collectivism

Government-mandated sacrifice by the individual for the group.

15. Human infrastructure

This is a new term coined by the Biden-Obama-Harris regime so that welfare payments and assistance checks can be included in the infrastructure spending bill.

16. Income equality = Redistribution of wealth

Income equality is achieved through equal *opportunity*—there is no guarantee of equal *outcome*. When leftists speak of income equality, they mean compulsory income redistribution that guarantees equal outcome.

17. Ingsoc = English socialism (*1984*)

The political philosophy of the ruling class in Orwell's *1984* using Newspeak, doublethink, and constant historical revision to make people think they are voluntarily supporting a system that depends on unthinking obedience.

18. Irregular migrant = Illegal alien

19. Literacy = Illiteracy

The goal of "progressive" leftist education is compliant universal human beings prepared for life in the New World Order. Molding requires children who are dumbed down and lacking foundational skills (reading and math) and foundational knowledge.

20. Progressive = Regressive

The word progressive has a positive connotation and is commonly understood to mean something that happens or develops gradually or in stages. Synonyms for progressive include continuing, continuous, increasing, growing, developing, ongoing, accelerating, escalating, gradual, step-by-step, and cumulative. Progress leads to a society of growth and independence, which entails rational adulthood and maturity.

In doublespeak, progressive is synonymous with regressive—the opposite of progressive. In the upside-down world of doublespeak, steps toward socialism's cradle-to-grave dependence are considered progress, including John Dewey's crippling *progressive education.*

21. Resistance = Overthrow of the government

Resistance is the refusal to accept or comply with something. In a democracy there are laws and elections designed for citizens to legally and peacefully express their discontent at the voting booth. When leftists speak of resistance, they are fomenting the overthrow of the government.

22. Science = Scientism

Scientism is an exaggerated trust in the efficacy of the methods of natural science applied to all areas of investigation (as in philosophy, the social sciences, and the humanities). It has replaced traditional religion as the moral and ethical authority for woke members of society.

23. Social justice = Reverse discrimination

Social justice in a democracy is achieved through laws and constitutional protections that guarantee equal rights, equal opportunity, and equal protection under the law. When leftists speak of social justice, they mean reverse discrimination and a two-tier system of justice. White people are openly and institutionally discriminated against, sanctuary cities protecting illegal alien felons are endorsed, and anarchy and violence are fomented to effect social change.

24. Socialism = Communism

The goal of socialism is communism. Socialism is the soft sell.

25. Sustainable = Supports UN Agenda 2030 goals and one-world government

The goal of the man-made climate change/global warming narrative is the redistribution of wealth from industrialized to non-industrialized nations. It is socialism on a planetary scale. In doublespeak, sustainable is the code word for anything supportive of the United Nations movement toward planetary governance.

26. Teacher = Change agent

Leftism views education as the vehicle for social change. Teachers are seen as facilitators who promote social change and student acceptance of planetary governance in the New World Order.

27. Tolerance = Intolerance

Leftism tolerates differences in race, religion, gender, ethnicity, and socio-economic status, but not differences of opinion.

28. Undocumented immigrant = Illegal alien

29. "Vaccine" = experimental mRNA COVID-19 treatments

COVID-19 "vaccines" are distinctly different from legitimate vaccines which provide immunity, prevent transmission, and have been rigorously safety tested on animals. COVID-19 jabs are experimental gene-altering mRNA treatments which neither provide immunity nor prevent transmission. Safety tests on animals were halted due to adverse reactions—humans are the test cohort for COVID-19 jabs.

30. Woke

Woke is a Culturally Acquired Psychotic Disorder denying reality in any fashion that will undermine traditional Western societies, values, and positive identity to help destroy them from within. (David Nussbaum, personal communication, July 2023)

My hope is that the glossary will also help the reader interpret, in practical terms, the dualism presented by Dr. Dianne Irving (Chapter 18). Understanding dualism and being able to recognize its dialectical language is essential for opposing the weaponized language that is assaulting, confusing, and destabilizing America's children.

CHAPTER 29

Gnosticism, the Frankfurt School, and Freirean Education

Globalism is a replacement ideology that seeks to reorder the world into one singular, planetary Unistate, ruled by the globalist elite. The globalist war on nation-states cannot succeed without collapsing the United States of America. The long-term strategic attack plan moves America incrementally from constitutional republic to socialism to globalism to feudalism. The tactical attack plan uses asymmetric psychological and informational warfare to destabilize Americans and drive society out of objective reality into the madness of subjective reality. America's children are the primary target of the globalist predators.

The reader will recognize the unmistakable voice of Gnosticism in ideological Marxism and the myriad Marxist species attacking America and its children in schools today. Political Marxism, which focuses on social agency (an individual's independent capability or ability to act on one's own will) and class conflict, was reconstituted as cultural Marxism by the Frankfurt School (Chapter 15). Its members launched the Marxist Cultural Revolution against America in 1935. To understand the foundations of Frankfurt School tactical maneuvers, particularly social change through education, a 2009 article written by Timothy Matthews is very instructive. "The Frankfurt School: Conspiracy to Corrupt"[126] begins with a prescient quote by English Catholic historian Christopher Dawson:

> *Western civilization at the present day is passing through a crisis which is essentially different from anything that has been previously experienced. Other societies in the past have changed their social institutions or their religious beliefs under the influence of external forces or the slow development of internal growth. But none, like our own, has ever consciously faced the prospect of a fundamental alteration of the beliefs and institutions on which the whole fabric*

*of social life rests…. Civilization is being uprooted from its foun-
dations in nature and tradition and is being reconstituted in a new
organisation which is as artificial and mechanical as a modern
factory.* —Christopher Dawson. *Enquiries into Religion and Culture*
(1936), p. 259.

Basically, the Frankfurt School believed that as long as an individual
had the belief—or even the hope of belief—that his divine gift of
reason could solve the problems facing society, then that society
would never reach the state of hopelessness and alienation that they
considered necessary to provoke socialist revolution. Their task,
therefore, was as swiftly as possible to undermine the Judeo-Christian legacy. To do this they called for the most negative destructive
criticism possible [Marxist Critical Theory] of every sphere of life
which would be designed to destabilize society and bring down what
they saw as the 'oppressive' order. Their policies, they hoped, would
spread like a virus, 'continuing the work of the Western Marxists by
other means' as one of their members noted.

To further the advance of their 'quiet' cultural revolution—but
giving us no idea about their plans for the future—the [Frankfurt]
School recommended (among other things):

1. The creation of racism offences

2. Continual change to create confusion

3. The teaching of sex and homosexuality to children

4. The undermining of schools' and teachers' authority

5. Huge immigration to destroy identity

6. The promotion of excessive drinking

7. Emptying of churches

8. An unreliable legal system with bias against victims of crime

9. Dependency on the state or state benefits

10. Control and dumbing down of media

11. Encouraging the breakdown of the family

One of the main ideas of the Frankfurt School was to exploit Freud's idea of 'pansexualism'—the search for pleasure, the exploitation of the differences between the sexes, the overthrowing of traditional relationships between men and women. To further their aims, they would:

- attack the authority of the father, deny the specific roles of father and mother, and wrest away from families their rights as primary educators of their children

- abolish differences in the education of boys and girls

- abolish all forms of male dominance—hence the presence of women in the armed forces

- declare women to be an 'oppressed class' and men as 'oppressors'

[German communist political activist Willi] Münzenberg summed up the Frankfurt School's long-term operation thus: "We will make the West so corrupt that it stinks."

The [Frankfurt] School believed there were two types of revolution: (a) political and (b) cultural. Cultural revolution demolishes from within. 'Modern forms of subjection are marked by mildness'. They saw it as a long-term project and kept their sights clearly focused on the family, education, media, sex and popular culture.

The *fundamental alteration of the beliefs and institutions upon which the whole fabric of society society rests,* to quote Dawson, is the fundamental transformation of America that Barack Obama promised the nation in 2008. Frankfurt School Marxist Paulo Freire (Chapter 16) is a prime-time player in the transformation of America's education industry. *The Politics of Education: Culture, Power, and Liberation,*[127] published in 1985, is Freire's manual for educational deconstruction. Paulo Freire developed a politicized approach to education called *critical pedagogy* that rejects acquisition of knowledge as the educational objective. Instead, critical pedagogy advocates acquisition of knowledge for the sole purpose of social change.

James Lindsay's 2022 book, *The Marxification of Education: Paulo Freire's*

Critical Marxism and the Theft of American Education,[128] is a powerful indictment of Freire's *critical pedagogy*. Lindsay's conclusion is unequivocal in its condemnation of Freirean education:

> Our kids currently go to Paulo Freire's schools. These schools are unambiguously Marxist (unless we split hairs and call them neo-Marxist or Woke Marxist) in their architecture, pedagogy, methods and goals. They have abandoned the idea of educating American children to grow toward becoming successful and prosperous adults in American society because they want to undermine, destroy, and replace American society. Rather than teaching literacy, numeracy, or other educational basics, Freirean schools use subject matter like reading, writing, mathematics, history, social studies, and science lessons to teach Marxist consciousness of one or more forms at a time. As a result of more than a decade of this practice, American schoolchildren are almost universally failing in basic competency in virtually every subject at virtually every grade level. They are more "politically literate," in the Freirean sense, than ever before, though. There's no other way to put this than their education has been *stolen* from them and what replaces it is meant to be weaponized against the society upon which their futures depend....

> Freirean education is Marxist education, and it has no place in any American public school system. It is also explicitly religious education, for those who have read Freire and understand just how prominently Liberation Theology (fusion of Marxist Theory and Catholic Theology) features not just in Freire's underlying thought but in his explicit framing of education. This, rightly understood, makes its inclusion in the American public-school systems a severe First Amendment violation on multiple counts that, so far, goes unrecognized and uncorrected. Because it steals our children's education from them, it also denies their legally protected right to obtain an education, which is a further potentially actionable violation against them still. Beyond these points, Freirean education is also a *failing* education....

> Freirean education doesn't work *because it cannot work*, if "working" in education means *educating students*. It explicitly and intentionally replaces gaining mastery in any subject with using

that subject as a proxy for generating "political literacy," by which is meant Marxist critical consciousness for engendering a cultural revolution, i.e., Maoist thought reform.

Freirean education is a euphemism for Maoist thought reform, which is a euphemism for brainwashing. To brainwash children is to make them adopt radically different beliefs by using systematic and often forcible pressure. Freirean education is Marxist brainwashing disguised as education. It uses the same mind-altering strategies against America's children that were used against American POWs in the Korean War.

In a stunning address to the officers and supervisors of the San Francisco Naval Shipyard in the Naval Radiological Defense Laboratory on October 4, 1956, Army psychiatrist Major William E. Mayer presented communism's new method of absolute control, achieved without violence, called *brainwashing*. He described the new control technique as "a well-organized educational program." The title of the address, "Brainwashing: The Ultimate Weapon,"[129] reveals the power of educational programming.

Major Mayer studied over 4,000 returning prisoners of war from Korea in an attempt to better understand the new technique, and presented his incisive commentary on the new weapon. In his address, he began by comparing brainwashing to any other weapon. "First, it can be dissected, analyzed, taken apart, laid out on a table, understood. As long as you understand it is a weapon and go about it.… Secondly, once we understand this or any other new weapon, we start contriving defenses."

What puzzled Major Mayer was what distinguished prisoners of war returning from Korea from those returning from previous wars. They were almost totally unable, or unwilling, to communicate with one another:

> They were willing to communicate with us, not with each other. They would sit on the ward in the Tokyo Army Hospital—80 men. Eighty who'd spent three years of community captivity who knew each other intimately. You could walk on the ward any time of the day or night and it was silent. They just weren't talking to one another. And that was a very interesting thing.

> So, we started prying and trying to find out why it was. We found there was no buddy system among these people. None to compare

with previous wars. We found there'd been no organized resistance of any significant kind. We found there'd been no organized escape committees. We found, in general, an abandonment of any system of internal organization or military justice even approaching in any remote way what had occurred among Americans in previous times of captivity. And so, we set to work to analyze how this had been accomplished. (p. 2)

Using intercepted documents written by Communists about Americans, Mayer and his team uncovered three premises from which the Communists approached their American prisoners. First, Americans are materialistic and opportunistic, and will always make a deal—they have a price. Second, Americans are ignorant about America, so you can teach them what you want them to know. Third, Americans are not a loyal people.

The first thing the Communists did was segregate the leaders. Leadership, which is valued in America, is what Communists call "poisonous individualism." Mayer provides an astute explanation:

Once they had the leaders segregated, they invoked the techniques which have become universal throughout the Communist world. These techniques, psychologically, are of tremendous interest for the simple reason that they're all designed with one objective in mind. *All of these things are directed at making members of a group stay with a group and yet feel that they are apart, that they are isolated in a very real emotional, or psychological, way from the other members of the group.* Now that's a very important thing to achieve if you want to run a dictatorship. The Communist bugaboo is the counter revolution—meaning, the revolution. And revolutions begin with a conspiracy between two people. They inevitably have to begin that way. And the conspiracy enlarges and more and more people are enlisted, and finally the dictator is overthrown. And so, if you can prevent the first conspiracy between the first two people, you have a kind of social control which you cannot possibly achieve by machine guns or slave camps or torture or anything else. And that's exactly what these devices are designed to do. Exactly the opposite of what we preach. Exactly the opposite of what we consider to be desirable.

They wanted to separate these men, to put them into solitary confinement cells of their own making, which were psychological in nature rather than steel and concrete. And of course, you can just build and maintain so many steel and concrete solitary confinement cells. But if you can engender this kind of solitary confinement, there is no limit on what you can do. They did this, first of all, by cultivating the typical kind of informing which is absolutely characteristic in every Communist society on earth. I'm sure you've read accounts which you've probably dismissed as being pretty incredible, of even, in the Communist society reporting things that their parents have done and getting them in trouble with the authority. This isn't untrue at all. And it isn't dreamed up as a horror story to make you hate Communism. It is a simple reality of Communist social organization. Informing, in our culture, is the lowest form of human endeavor. The informer meets a horrible end in many cases. Even in childhood informing is looked down upon almost instinctively. The tattletale is the kid who just doesn't get along. But informing in the Communist society is a social and civic responsibility, and it's constantly, repeatedly painted as such.... (pp. 3–4)

The social and civic responsibility of informing provided the opportunity for the second technique in Communist brainwashing: *self-criticism and confession.* If you were a POW who was informed upon, you were not beaten or tortured; instead, you were given the opportunity to confess your transgression:

They simply took you aside into a hut, one man took you, a man not in a military uniform, a young Chinese ordinarily, who was or claimed to be, and evidently was, a graduate of an American university, a man who spoke no Pidgin English, he spoke your kind of English. Maybe he even knew about your home town, he'd been there. And he was a very friendly kind of a guy. And he talked to you in a moderately stern voice and told you that you'd done wrong and they knew it, and they wanted you to confess it. And don't be afraid to confess, he would say, you're not in the hands of capitalists now, you're in the hands of the people. And in our society, when you've made a mistake and you recognize it and confess it, recant, criticize your behavior, analyze it, and assert your determination not to repeat it, that's all we ask. (p. 4)

Mayer describes the process of self-criticism and confession associated with informing. What distinguishes communist self-criticism from introspective American self-criticism is that communist self-criticism is a collective group event, and what is being criticized is an attitude, not an action. This is an extremely important distinction, because attitudes live in the subjective realm of thoughts and feelings.

In America there is a behavioral and legal distinction between thinking and doing. We are constitutionally free to think our thoughts and even speak them, but our actions are legally restricted by laws. In the Communist brainwashing technique, thoughts are treated as behaviors, and thought reform leading to behavior change is clearly the political objective.

Korean POWs were unprepared for this psychological weapon, and so they confessed without understanding its psychological effects. The result was an explosive growth in the informing system, and by the end of the first year in captivity, one in ten Americans were informers. At that point, the prisoners began to distrust each other, and when they were no longer sure who they could trust, they began withdrawing socially and stopped trusting anyone.

During the repatriation process it became painfully clear that the outcomes military analysts had predicted as possible consequences of brainwashing were woefully inaccurate. So, a group of men assembled by President Eisenhower created a military Code of Conduct to be used as a basis for behavior.

Major Mayer moved point-by-point through the six points of the military Code of Conduct, and explained how the lack of application of the Code was directly responsible for the success of the Communist brainwashing technique, and was the source of the puzzling social isolation exhibited by returning Korean POWs.

I have included the original Code of Conduct for Members of the Armed Forces of the United States,[130] passed by Executive Order 10631 of President Dwight D. Eisenhower on August 17, 1955, that Mayer referenced:

CODE OF CONDUCT FOR MEMBERS OF THE UNITED STATES ARMED FORCES

I

I am an American fighting man. I serve in the forces which guard my country and our way of life. I am prepared to give my life in their defense.

II

I will never surrender of my own free will. If in command I will never surrender my men while they still have the means to resist.

III

If I am captured I will continue to resist by all means available. I will make every effort to escape and aid others to escape. I will accept neither parole nor special favors from the enemy.

IV

If I become a prisoner of war, I will keep faith with my fellow prisoners. I will give no information or take part in any action which might be harmful to my comrades. If I am senior, I will take command. If not, I will obey the lawful orders of those appointed over me and will back them up in every way.

V

When questioned, should I become a prisoner of war, I am bound to give only name, rank, service number, and date of birth. I will evade answering further questions to the utmost of my ability. I will make no oral or written statements disloyal to my country and its allies or harmful to their cause.

VI

I will never forget that I am an American fighting man, responsible for my actions, and dedicated to the principles which made my country free. I will trust in my God and in the United States of America.

Dwight D. Eisenhower, Executive Order 10631—Code of Conduct for Members of the Armed Forces of the United States Online by Gerhard

*Peters and John T. Woolley, The American Presidency Project https://
www.presidency.ucsb.edu/node/235515*

---

*The Code of Conduct applies to all members of the U. S. Armed Forces, at
all times.*
There are six (6) articles in the Code of Conduct.
*The original Code of Conduct was established August 17, 1955 by Presi-
dent Eisenhower.*
*The legal authority supporting the Code of Conduct is The Uniform Code
of Military Justice (UCMJ); https://ucmj.us/about-the-ucmj/*

Major Mayer's commentary on the specific points in the Code is instructive,
and his description of the devastating psychological effects of Communist
brainwashing techniques is particularly relevant today.

In closing, Major Mayer returned to the Code of Conduct and reminded
the audience, "The Code is a code of standards of behavior for any fighting
man fighting any kind of a battle." President Eisenhower understood in
1956 that the war was not over because the shooting had stopped. America
was still fighting an ideological battle at home that required strict adherence to the Code of Conduct. Mayer explained how adherence to the Code
is a matter of discipline, and that our national defense begins with teaching
discipline in the family home:

> Discipline, somehow, has become synonymous with abandoning
> your own—your own self-respect. Abandoning your individualism
> and becoming a helpless machine, a part of the military machine.
> And that isn't discipline at all. The only kind of discipline that
> really exists and really works is an internalized system of values, a
> set of standards existing within the individual which characterize
> and guide his behavior whether there's a cop or a shore patrolman
> standing there or not. And it's this kind of discipline we have to
> seek from people. This is the kind of discipline that makes individ-
> uals able to join a team. Individuals able to respond to competent
> leadership. And individuals able to have the intestinal fortitude nec-
> essary to be leaders. To set limits, to award punishment and reward.
> And that includes even to our children. And naturally, of course,
> this is where the problem mainly lies.

Discipline is not taught when a kid is 18 years old. It's taught in homes, and Sunday schools sometimes, in churches. It's taught partly in the military. It's taught mainly in the family. It's taught from the cradle onward or it's not ever adequately taught at all. It's taught at parents' knees, and even possibly across parents' knees. It has to be taught throughout the educational process. And that educational process includes the training and indoctrination of people who work at the San Francisco Naval Shipyard. And who work in every one of our specialized, highly technical, scientific organizations. We even try to teach this to medical officers and dental officers who come into the Army. But it's awfully late at that point. We need a lot of help. We need a lot of thought about how to do this. We don't pretend to have the answers. We know that the Communist is one of the most finely disciplined enemies we have ever encountered. He is not necessarily just blindly disciplined, either. He works at what he's working at with great intensity and sincerity.

And the solution to—at least suggestions about the solutions would seem to be obvious. We found men with a real system of values who were committed in their thinking. Who had roots, who had loyalties, who actively thought about it, who resisted in some small but symbolic way. These were the men who survived in largest number, who came out almost unscathed from the experience. But the opportunist, the guy who's trying to look for the easy way, the person who doesn't believe in the value of work as something in itself, who doesn't believe in service unless there's something in it for me—this guy's a sitting duck. This was demonstrated over and over again. And so, you can solve this problem, you who are parents or school teachers or managers, or supervisors. You can solve it little by little by little. It's the only way it ever will get solved. (pp. 14–15)

Major Mayer's address was an appeal to the civilian sector to recognize and actively do its part for national security by strengthening family bonds of loyalty and raising rational, responsible adults who are loyal to America and capable of preserving and protecting our constitutional republic by actively adhering to the Code of Conduct at home and in military service.

The most stunning observation Mayer made was that *the key to our defense against brainwashing is recognizing the well-organized educational program as an offensive weapon.* Until Freirean education is recognized as an offensive weapon, we cannot mount a defense against the Marxist Cultural Revolution in America today.

Consider the parallels. Students, particularly young children, are basically imprisoned for most of their day in government schools and separated from their leadership—their parents. It is a psychological and emotional vacuum where they are subjected to Freirean critical pedagogy by activist teachers, who have been trained in critical pedagogy and embrace its political objectives of "liberation." The children are told, "We are here to help you and support you. We understand you and won't tell your parents."

Freirean education's favored topic is race essentialism. Essentialism is the philosophical term that means things have a set of characteristics which make them what they are, and the task of science and philosophy is the discovery and expression of these characteristics. It is the doctrine that essence precedes existence, and provides a convenient foundation for Marxist critical race theorists promoting the fiction that the United States is systemically racist. Revisionist history and distortion of facts are foundational for advancing the Marxist Cultural Revolution in America.

Today, Marxist critical race theory, founded upon race essentialism, is brainwashing American children in anti-American racialism that reduces their identity to either blackness or whiteness. Instead of teaching the common denominator of being American that unifies the nation, children are being divided by race and taught to see the world as literally black and white. Critical race theory is often repackaged and disguised as Social and Emotional Learning (Chapter 20).

Christopher F. Rufo's "Parental Guidebook, Fighting Critical Race Theory in K–12 Schools"[131] (Chapter 12) provides a useful definition of critical race theory, and lists nine key concepts to help the reader recognize symptoms of brainwashing in their children.

When your child expresses any variation of the racialist themes below, it is evidence of Marxist brainwashing. Black is used throughout Marxist Critical Theory to include all people of color:

1. Race essentialism = *White is bad and black is good*

2. Collective guilt = *White people are oppressors and black people are oppressed*

3. Opposition to equality under the law = *Legal equality, nondiscrimination, and colorblindness are "camouflages" to uphold white supremacist structures*

4. Opposition to meritocracy = *Meritocracy is a mechanism to uphold racist structures*

5. Active racial discrimination = *The government should actively discriminate against the privileged (white) with racial quotas, race-based benefits, and race-redistribution of wealth*

6. Restriction of free speech = *The First Amendment advances the interests of white supremacy and systemic racism, and the government should restrict speech that is "racist" or "hateful"*

7. Abolition of whiteness = *The white race should be abolished*

8. Neo-segregation = *Races should be segregated with separate graduations, meetings, facilities, living quarters, training programs for whites and blacks*

9. Anti-capitalism = *America is an "imperialist white supremacist capitalist patriarchy" that allowed whites to extend domination from slavery to the free-market society. The solution is redistribution of private property and dismantling the system of capitalism*

We are a world at war. The American education industry is an instrument of globalism's war on the nation-state, specifically targeting our children's minds, because children are the future of every society on Earth. The globalists are exploiting wartime brainwashing techniques to ideologically groom America's children for their future in the planetary globalist Uni-state.

The Marxist enemy is applying the same brainwashing tactics in American schools against children as young as kindergarten that were successfully used by the Communists in Korea against American POWs. If the enemy can brainwash trained soldiers, it can certainly brainwash children.

Only by recognizing *critical pedagogy* as weaponized education, and its anti-American critical race theory as brainwashing, can we defend and protect our children, ourselves, and our nation. Whether used against adults or children, the military objective of brainwashing is reeducation.

The tactical objective is to eliminate the ability to think critically. The strategic objective is to turn Americans against themselves, their families, and their country. Changing the hearts and minds of Americans is Cultural Revolution—revolution without bullets.

Today's American parents and grandparents must adapt the Military Code of Conduct to civilian life and apply the Code's principles. We must stand together and unapologetically defend, preserve, and protect our American way of life in order to overhaul the anti-American education industry.

We must pledge our allegiance to the United States of America, and to the republic for which it stands. We do this by getting actively involved in our children's education. We read what they are reading. We go to their schools and voice our opposition to anti-American lessons. We run for school boards. We attend school board meetings and voice our opposition to anti-American lessons, teachers, principals, and school board members, and we seek their removal when necessary.

The War on America is a war on our children. We must fight on their behalf, because they are helpless to protect themselves.

CHAPTER 30

Marxist Past, Present, and Future

Globalism is a replacement ideology that seeks to reorder the world into one singular, planetary Unistate, ruled by the globalist elite. The globalist war on nation-states cannot succeed without collapsing the United States of America. The long-term strategic attack plan moves America incrementally from constitutional republic to socialism to globalism to feudalism. The tactical attack plan uses asymmetric psychological and informational warfare to destabilize Americans and drive society out of objective reality into the madness of subjective reality. America's children are the primary target of the globalist predators.

The woke leftists advocating Marxist Cultural Revolution in America continue to believe in "real" socialism—Karl Marx's *perfect socialist society, the perfect communism that transcends private property.* Woke young people have yet to discover that they are means, not ends, in globalism's War on America. The woke are useful idiots, Marxist soldiers conscripted into service to collapse America from within, whose lives will be terminated once their usefulness expires. There is no place for agitators in the globalist managerial Unistate.

We all live our lives within a historical context. Understanding history is essential for making sense of the present, and for being able to anticipate the future. James Lindsay's warning, "A Note to Young Woke People," in his May 2, 2023, *New Discourses* article, "Intersectionality Is American Maoism,"[132] provides a compelling description of tomorrow for woke idealists participating in America's Cultural Revolution today:

A Note to Young Woke People

I think you'll find what I have to say to you mostly incomprehensible, but you need to hear it.

This is what you are participating in, whether you know it or not.

This is what your schools and universities and influencers are miseducating you—brainwashing you—into. Western Maoism. Maoism with American characteristics. And this is what you need to know about where it goes. The whole philosophy is based upon the formulations of Georg W. F. Hegel's vision for how to move History to its intended "End" (the right side of history), and what Hegel said about you is this: "History uses people and then discards them."

As a movement Woke believes itself to be the movement of History. History is using you to move itself. It will discard you. You know how everything in Woke philosophy is "temporal," "spatial," and "contingent"? So are you. You are a contingency for the Woke movement. You have your time—until you don't. When you become useless or a hindrance to the movement of History, you will be discarded. Every Marxist and Hegelian movement in history has proceeded this way, and this one will not be different. I wish you luck with that.

What you need to understand about the people you've been trained to see as your "enemies," or "transphobes," "racists," "fascists," "homophobes," or whatever else is that most of the people you think are those things are not those things at all. You have been trained to hate, allegedly in the name of "stopping hate." These people are, by and large, trying to *warn* you, not trying to uphold "oppression."

What you need to know about the people in the movement you're supporting, including your friends in the movement, is that you're less than disposable to them. Contingent barely covers it. The Woke movement pretends to care about you—or, worse, "people who look like you"—but it does not. It is using you so its sociopathic fringe can gain power over society, using you as cannon fodder for their unconventional political warfare apparatus. Instead of living your life, growing, learning, preparing a future, you're doing activism, for them. And they will discard you. *Will.* You are worse than disposable once they get power: you're a problem.

You are being trained by this movement to be a destabilizer. That's what all that "disrupt and dismantle" stuff is about. Their intention is to establish a perfectly stable system with them (not most of you) on top of it, and people trained and brainwashed to be destabilizers are a problem in such a system. Mao said that himself too. He said that the handling of the people is different in the different phases of the revolution. First you encourage and support destabilizers, and then you crack down on them so that there's total stability under the new standard. You are an asset today and will be a liability tomorrow. You will be discarded, coldly and possibly violently.

Make no mistake. This fate has awaited the "change agents" of every red revolution in history. Communist defectors have been trying to tell you for decades, longer than most of you have been alive. It will not be different in anything except method this time. If you, as Wokes, "win," you surely lose—all but the most sociopathic and sycophantic of you, in which case you hollow yourselves out, sell your souls (if you have one left by then), and become a true monster of history.

If you don't believe me, let me ask you: do you see any identity politics in China today? Is China Woke? Will it go Woke? No! They already did that, and that phase of their revolution is over. It is viciously suppressed there, and they laugh at you here in the West and call you *baizuo*, white left. They know what you are and how misinformed and misguided you are. Their operatives attempt to stoke these fires and use you because you are strategically useful to their anti-American aims, which you foolishly might share. In China, however, they're openly encouraging patriarchy and masculinity. They're racially ruthless. They stamp out homosexuality. Why? They did intersectionality already, got what they wanted out of it, and discarded it (and its change agents) in favor of power. That's your future. Look at the screen, scan your face, and smile for the government, and don't dare signal in any way that you think anything you shouldn't be thinking.

You have been falsely convinced that you're the protagonists in a vast morality play called "the arc of History" and that you're "bending it toward justice." You're "on the right side of History," and that feels good—right up until the boot comes crashing down on your face. Then you'll realize it. You are bending the arc of history, of course, if we can even indulge such a metaphor, and you're bending it straight into a twenty-first-century gulag, whatever those will look like in our increasingly Black Mirror [the reflection you see on a device when you turn it off] society. You will be "thought reformed," or you will be discarded.

Do you want to be its guard, Agent Smith? Would you like to be its administrator? Is it worth the sale of your soul? Some of you might aspire to such a demonic station in your lives, but most of you don't. You'll be subjected to it instead, even as a student at an elite university.

This corruption of you and your future is happening in place of your education, which is simultaneously being degraded in every meaningful sense of the word. You're not getting the education you could be or perhaps aren't getting a real education at all. You're not learning to be informed, independent adults who can answer questions about reality and navigate it successfully. You're being taught you have to defer to some kind of expert to answer a question like "what is a woman?"

Meanwhile, you're getting degrees that are increasingly being seen as *liabilities*, not assets, in the working world outside of the most corrupt megacorporate sector that is our new Western Soviet—a council of "stakeholders" that knows "the Science of Right Human Relations" and the keys to "Sustainable Development." Employers are increasingly suspecting you're probably Woke, radically Leftist, entitled, unlikely to work hard, likely to create a hostile working environment, under-skilled, and likely to sue if fired even on perfectly solid grounds. You're a *liability* to them, and many of them are only still hiring you because *they have to*, to keep their place in the corrupt corporate scoring schemes that control the way business is now done in the West. If that gives way, who are you? If it succeeds and you participate in it, what are you?

Make no mistake, if this system loses, you lose because your university tried to make you "change agents" and "global citizens" instead of educated adults. If this system wins, you lose because you know too much and are too big a problem. Your only option will be to sell your soul to it, and how much is that worth to you?

Think I'm kidding? Mao said, "Not to have correct political

opinions is like not having a soul." Think about that and what this is costing you, whether you participate or cower against it. Doesn't that ring true? That's what you're sacrificing.

So, why you? Because you happen to be the age you are at the worst time in Western history to be the age you are, and because many of you come from wealth and status and other resources the System covets and requires to succeed (they're not really against "privilege," they just want to redistribute and repurpose it). They need those resources. They need your enthusiasm and zeal. They need your impressionable minds. They need the future citizens and the future leaders, but History uses people and then discards them. They don't need you for long, and they only need you for specific purposes, then you will be corrected or discarded, unless you choose to come off worse by selling out.

My message to you about intersectionality is simple. You need to know what you're really involved in, stop participating, deprogram yourself and your friends, and start fighting for the blessings of Liberty that allowed you to have the privilege to think this way in the first place. You can and might lose it—the first generation in American history to face the loss of liberty, and you're enslaving yourselves. "Liberation" movements are lies. Mao called his army— the same one he dispatched to destroy your counterparts in the Red Guard—the People's *Liberation* Army for a reason. You need to fight for Liberty. Your chains are forged by frauds and locked only in your heads.

The oldest recorded cautionary tale in human history, the story of the Serpent and Eve in the third chapter of Genesis, warns you about liberation, whether you are religious or not. Liberation is a destructive lie. You are the future. Your choices matter. Choose better.

James Lindsay's impassioned warning to woke Americans is an exposé of the reality of cultural Marxism and a grim warning about the real conspiracy to rob Americans of their precious freedoms.

CHAPTER 31

Marxism, Gnosticism, and Transgenderism

Globalism is a replacement ideology that seeks to reorder the world into one singular, planetary Unistate, ruled by the globalist elite. The globalist war on nation-states cannot succeed without collapsing the United States of America. The long-term strategic attack plan moves America incrementally from constitutional republic to socialism to globalism to feudalism. The tactical attack plan uses asymmetric psychological and informational warfare to destabilize Americans and drive society out of objective reality into the madness of subjective reality. America's children are the primary target of the globalist predators.

If "liberation is a destructive lie," as James Lindsay stated at the end of Chapter 30, what is the truth? Lindsay offers an incisive analysis in this summary of *The New Discourses Podcast*, Ep. 61, The Gnostic Temptation:[133]

> Why are Gnostic cults so tempting? Why do people get sucked into them? It's not because Gnostics go around telling people they're *wrong*. It's because they go around telling people they're *limited*. Your beliefs, maybe in science, spirituality, Christianity, politics, or whatever, aren't *wrong*; they're *low-level*. The Gnostics hold themselves out as people who know more about whatever you're into than you do, and they explain their superiority as being "liberated" from the limitations "THEY" (your teachers, pastors, etc.) are placing upon your knowledge. *They* don't want you to know these secrets, but *we do*. That's the Gnostic temptation.

So, "liberation" is presented as transcending one's mortal limitations, including one's own physical body. Understanding the gnostic roots of transgenderism is essential for understanding Marxist political exploitation and its implications for the modern trans movements. One of Gnosticism's core beliefs is its dualistic worldview. Adam Drakos's January 17, 2022, article on

Thinking West, "The Gnostic Roots of the Trans Movement,"[134] explains the importance of understanding this duality:

> Gnostics viewed the physical world as inherently flawed or even evil and claimed that the material universe was created by a lesser divinity known as the *demiurge*. During creation, bits of divinity were mixed in along with tainted material, and Christ undertook the mission to re-order this chaos. Therefore, the spirit of the supreme God entered into the shell of a man's body to remedy the situation and help believers reach *gnosis*—the revelation of man's true divine nature. In the gnostic view, what defines personhood is not the union of spirit and body (the traditional Christian view), but a divine spirit which merely occupies a physical body....

> Transgender ideology stems from the dualist philosophy of the Gnostics. In transgenderism, a person's feelings and beliefs about their identity reveal their "true" self, while the physical reality of their genitals or hormones can be false. If a person believes themselves to be a female despite having male reproductive organs, the will wins out, not the material reality. Whether the adherents understand or not, they are promoting a dualist interpretation of the cosmos. There is the spiritual "real" (divine) world of the mind which cannot be wrong, and then there is the physical (fallen) world of material, which can be mistaken if it conflicts with the reality created in the mind.

> Like its gnostic roots, transgender ideology is in direct opposition to Christian beliefs, which firmly state that mankind was created by God as a union between spirit and body. Though subordinate to the spirit, the body is intrinsic to a person's identity, hence the importance of the "resurrection of the body" referenced in the Apostle's Creed. The Creed affirms the goodness of God's physical creation and rejects the idea that salvation is *gnosis* or any other merely esoteric transformation or enlightenment.

The notable New Testament theologian N. T. Wright voices a similar observation:

> *The confusion about gender identity is a modern, and now internet-fueled, form of the ancient philosophy of Gnosticism.*

> *The Gnostic, one who "knows", has discovered the secret of "who I really am", behind the deceptive outward appearance.... This involves denying the goodness, or even the ultimate reality, of the natural world. (London Times)*

Denying biological reality is a central tenet of trans movements and, like transgenderism, denying reality has a political purpose. Drakos continues:

> Like transgenderism, much of transhumanist thought is rooted in Gnosticism. Although there are various strains of transhumanist thought, many adherents seek to augment or transcend natural human evolution. Transhumanists believe that our future as a species is dependent on furthering our evolutionary process through the aid of modern science or technology. One common though far-fetched belief is that one day we will be able to upload human consciousness into a computer, freeing humans from the bonds of physicality and allowing people to process information faster and have unlimited access to the "cloud" of information.
>
> In this scenario "consciousness" can be viewed as synonymous with the "divine spirit" central to Gnosticism. Transhumanists assume that *only* consciousness is fundamental to a person's identity, and that the body is merely a receptacle to house consciousness. Once consciousness is uploaded into a machine, *the person* will now be in the machine. This of course suffers from the same fallacy as transgender ideology and Gnosticism: that our bodies are unimportant to our identity and only the spirit/consciousness is of ultimate value.

Transhumanism is no longer a "far-fetched" belief; it is a central feature of globalism's megalomaniacal campaign for world domination. The World Economic Forum (WEF) and its members are unapologetic in their gnostic beliefs and elitist plans for one-world governance in their planetary managerial Unistate.

If transhumanism is the aspiration of life in globalism's Unistate, how will Americans be persuaded to accept it? First, we must remember that globalism's War on America is a war of attrition. The older generation of patriotic seniors is dying. Their children's generation of indoctrinated millennials is transitional. It is the grandchildren and great-grandchildren that are the ultimate target of the globalist predators. Let's review their strategy.

The Marxist Cultural Revolution in America is the philosophical battle between objective reality (facts) and subjective reality (feelings) discussed in Chapter 1. From a tactical point of view, educational brainwashing is begun as early as possible, because the younger the child, the less the necessity for *reeducation.*

Our constitutional republic is rooted in the Western philosophy of realism, the view that there is a reality independent of any beliefs or perceptions. Anti-realism is the belief that reality is a matter of *perception*, that reality exists only in the mind. It is the philosophical foundation for Marxist critical pedagogy, which uses the Hegelian dialectical process to reject objective reality and embrace subjective reality.

Bertrand Russell's infamous quote about weaponizing education to make children believe that snow is black is being implemented in American schools across the country today. It is a weapon of mass cultural destruction, an assault on reality—the final frontier.

When children believe that snow is black, they have rejected objective reality, embraced subjective reality, and are now successfully brainwashed. They are primed for gnostic perceptions of reality that include the vision that the only way to achieve true freedom is to escape from the human body. The gnostic roots of transgenderism are evident in the dualism of the transgender narrative: *people's "feelings" about their identity reveal their "true" self. The physical reality—chromosomes, genitalia, and hormones— is a "false" self.*

Dr. Miriam Grossman is a 21st-century maverick in child psychiatry, attempting to help children cope with the dangerous ideas they are being indoctrinated with. Her extraordinary book, *Lost in Trans Nation: A Child Psychiatrist's Guide Out of the Madness,*[135] was released in July 2023. It is an unflinching look at the madness of the trans movement and the politicization of medicine. Her thesis is straightforward and unapologetic:

> The beliefs that male and female are human inventions; that the sex of a newborn is arbitrarily "assigned"; and that as a result the child requires "affirmation" through medical interventions—these ideas are divorced from reality and therefore hazardous, especially to chil-

dren. The core belief—that biology can and should be denied—is a repudiation of reality and a mockery of what hard science teaches about being male and female.

Dr. Grossman speaks with passion and disgust about the horrific effects of the trans movement, and helps parents hold on to objective reality in order to protect their children's developing ability to reality-test and oppose trans educational indoctrination:

> My profession captured. My colleagues spineless. Educators corrupted. Children sacrificed. Families destroyed. Civilization dismantled. Fighting Gender Ideology for Over a Decade. No child is born in the wrong body, their bodies are just fine; it's their emotional lives that need healing.

Paul McHugh, MD, Distinguished Professor of Psychiatry at Johns Hopkins University School of Medicine (Chapter 27), endorses Dr. Grossman's book on her website. "You've become a household name here at Hopkins psychiatry as the best contemporary example of a good doctor who notices what is happening around her and to her patients and strives to do something about it."

Johns Hopkins University was the first medical facility in the United States to perform sex reassignment surgeries. Dr. McHugh, with colleague statistician Dr. Lawrence Mayer, conducted a study examining the "born this way" claims of the Lesbian/Gay/Bisexual/Transgender (LGBT) community. The 2016 report, "Sexuality and Gender: Findings from the Biological, Psychological, and Social Sciences,"[136] is discussed in an article by Louis DeBroux published in *The Patriot Post* on August 25, 2016, "'Born This Way'? New Study Debunks LGBT Claims":[137]

> Among the political Left, it is an accepted fact ("settled science," you might say) that homosexuals and transgendered people are "born that way", that their sexual attractions or gender identities are not the product of choice, but a matter of genetics. A new report, instantly controversial, torpedoes that understanding of homosexuality and gender dysphoria (the medical term for transgenderism).
>
> The report, entitled "Sexuality and Gender: Findings from the Biological, Psychological, and Social Sciences," is co-authored

by two of the most well respected experts on mental health and human sexuality; Dr. Paul McHugh, described as "arguably the most important American psychiatrist of the last half century", is a professor of psychiatry and behavioral sciences at the prestigious Johns Hopkins University School of Medicine, and served for 25 years as Psychiatrist-in-Chief for Johns Hopkins Hospital; and Dr. Lawrence Mayer, Psychiatry Department scholar-in-residence at Johns Hopkins University, is a professor of statistics and biostatistics at Arizona State University.

While, not surprisingly, many on the Left and in the LGBT "community" immediately raged against the report as anti-LGBT, it should be noted that Johns Hopkins University was the first medical facility in the U.S. to perform sex reassignment surgery, and did so for a period spanning decades until a growing body of peer-reviewed studies, including an analysis of how Hopkins' own transgendered patients fared over time, led the hospital to end those types of surgeries. Furthermore, McHugh is no far right-wing ideologue or Bible-thumper, he is a self-described "politically liberal" Democrat.

Yet it was his long-term experience with patients who suffer from gender dysphoria that led him to his conclusions, summarized in a report which analyzed more than 200 peer-reviewed studies. McHugh and Mayer are also very up front about what the science does and does not show, and freely admit the gaps in the available research, which they argue underscores the need for more research before establishing medical standards, public policy guidelines, and laws, based on "settled science" which is not at all settled....

One of the most shocking findings in the report is that not only do people who suffer from gender dysphoria experience far higher rates of social pathologies (depression, substance abuse, suicide) than the general population, but sex reassignment surgery does not offer the relief that those on the Left claim. One study finds that "compared to [the general population], sex-reassigned individuals were about five times more likely to attempt suicide and about 19 times more likely to die by suicide." The study finds a staggering 41% of transgendered individuals will attempt suicide in their lifetime.

The duo investigated the underlying causes of these tragic statistics, and found that while "stressors like stigma and prejudice account for much of the additional suffering observed in these subpopulations... [this theory] does not seem to offer a complete explanation for the disparities in the outcomes." Even in social environments where transgendered people are accepted, they still suffer from above-normal rates of these social pathologies. McHugh and Mayer encourage additional research be done to study the correlation between childhood sexual abuse and sexual orientation (studies have shown non-heterosexuals to be 2–3X more likely to have experienced childhood sexual abuse as compared to heterosexuals)....

The authors declare they are *"...disturbed and alarmed by the severity and irreversibility of some interventions being publicly discussed and employed for children.... We are concerned by the increasing tendency toward encouraging children with gender identity issues to transition to their preferred gender through medical and then surgical procedures,"* noting *"There is little scientific evidence for the therapeutic value of interventions that delay puberty or modify the secondary sex characteristics of adolescents."*

The Obama administration has used (and abused) its vast power to dismiss the concerns of parents, policymakers, and medical professionals in implementing policy in the furtherance of its ideological goal—forced social acceptance of gender dysphoria as normal, all under the guise of medical science.

Part of that effort was Obama's announcement earlier this year [2016] that schools receiving federal funding were prohibited from requiring students to use the restroom and shower facilities of their birth sex, while threatening a loss of funding for any school that didn't comply with his imperial decree. Essentially, this meant boys who think they are girls would get to shower with female classmates.

Transgenderism is a return to the religion of Gnosticism, in its latest iteration as 21st-century Wokeism. Marxist Critical Theory is a political movement being practiced as a religion in the United States, brainwashing America's children and violating America's constitutional separation of church and state with critical pedagogy and radical gender ideology.

For readers who still doubt the political underbelly of the trans movement, its weaponized sexuality for social change, and its intersection with Woke Marxism, Christopher F. Rufo's, February 13, 2024, article "The Business of Transgenderism"[138] offers stunning confirmation:

> In the late 1980s, a group of academics, including Judith Butler, Gayle Rubin, Sandy Stone, and Susan Stryker, established the disciplines of "queer theory" and "transgender studies." These academics believed gender to be a "social construct" used to oppress racial and sexual minorities, and they denounced the traditional categories of man and woman as a false binary that was conceived to support the system of "heteronormativity"—i.e., the white, male, heterosexual power structure. This system, they argued, had to be ruthlessly deconstructed. And the best way to achieve this, they argued further, was to promote transgenderism. If men can become women, and women men, they believed, the natural structure of Creation could be toppled.

> Susan Stryker, a male-to-female transgender professor currently at the University of Arizona, revealed the general thrust and tone of transgender ideology in his Kessler Award Lecture at the City University of New York in 2008, describing his work as "a secular sermon that unabashedly advocates embracing a disruptive and refigurative genderqueer or transgender power as a spiritual resource for social and environmental transformation." In Stryker's best-known essay, "My Words to Victor Frankenstein above the Village of Chamounix: Performing Transgender Rage," he contends that the "transsexual body" is a "technological construction" that represents a war against Western society. "I am a transsexual, and therefore I am a monster," Stryker writes. And this monster, he continues, is destined to channel its "rage and revenge" against the "naturalized heterosexual order"; against "'traditional family values'"; and against the "hegemonic oppression" of nature itself.

> It is clear from this and from other transgender scholarship that the transgender movement is inherently political. Its reconstruction of personal identity is meant to advance a collective political reconstruction or transformation. Some trans activists even view their movement as the future of Marxism. In a collection of essays titled

Transgender Marxism, activist writer Rosa Lee argues that trans people can serve as the new vanguard of the proletariat, promising to abolish heteronormativity in the same way that orthodox Marxism promised to abolish capitalism.

"In a different era," Lee writes,

> Marxists spoke of the construction of a "new socialist man" as a crucial task in the broader process of socialist construction. Today, in a time of both rising fascism and an emergent socialist movement, our challenge is transsexualising our Marxism. We should think [of] the project of transition to communism in our time—communisation—as including the transition to new communist selves, new ways of being and relating to one another.

This is the great project of the transgender movement: to abolish the distinctions of man and woman, to transcend the limitations established by God and nature, and to connect the personal struggle of trans individuals to the political struggle to transform society in a radical way.

The United States of America, the greatest experiment in individual freedom the world has ever known, is being stripped of its unique insistence upon separation of church and state. If Marxist culture warriors succeed, religion and politics will once again merge and award totalitarian social control to the leadership. This time, the award will go to globalist sociopaths and megalomaniacs who control the science and technology to depopulate the earth, and who dream of moving humanity to asexual transhumanism and immortality in their planetary Unistate.

Transgenderism is the stepping-stone to transhumanism, the deceitful political purpose of the transgender movement. The movement's mutilated, sterile, psychologically devastated victims are collateral damage of globalism's ultimate war on humanity.

CHAPTER 32

Transhumanism, Big Lies, and the Great Reset

Globalism is a replacement ideology that seeks to reorder the world into one singular, planetary Unistate, ruled by the globalist elite. The globalist war on nation-states cannot succeed without collapsing the United States of America. The long-term strategic attack plan moves America incrementally from constitutional republic to socialism to globalism to feudalism. The tactical attack plan uses asymmetric psychological and informational warfare to destabilize Americans and drive society out of objective reality into the madness of subjective reality. America's children are the primary target of the globalist predators.

We begin our discussion of transhumanism with its 2018 description from the World Economic Forum (WEF), "What is transhumanism and how does it affect you?":[139]

> The central premise of transhumanism is that biological evolution will eventually be overtaken by advances in genetic, wearable and implantable technologies that artificially expedite the evolutionary process.... The result is an iteration of Homo sapiens enhanced or augmented, but still fundamentally human....

> Some distinguished scientists, such as Hans Moravec and Raymond Kurzweil, even advocate a posthuman condition: the end of humanity's reliance on our congenital bodies by transforming "our frail version 1.0 human bodies into their far more durable and capable version 2.0 counterparts".

Transhumanism is the political ideology promoted by the globalist elite in their quest for immortality. "Humanity 2.0" is the biological objective of the Fourth Industrial Revolution, and *stakeholder capitalism* is its economic engine.

Klaus Schwab, the premier 21st-century humanitarian huckster, is selling stakeholder capitalism as the central feature of the *Great Reset*, WEF's economic recovery plan in response to the COVID-19 pandemic. Schwab is selling enslavement dressed up as freedom, with the infamous slogan "You will own nothing and be happy." In reality, stakeholder capitalism is a return to the binary sociopolitical system of feudalism, where you will be an indentured serf who owns nothing because the elite own everything, including you.

The reader will remember that *ownership* is an ambivalent word as it relates to private property. Ideological Marxism rejects private property and promises that *the people will own everything*. Of course, the elite leadership deceitfully omit the essential operating principle: that the elite control the production and distribution of everything. So, the Big Lie of Marxism is *public, not private, ownership;* "the people" have no agency over that which they "own." Whoever controls the production and distribution is functionally the *owner*.

On December 1, 2019, Klaus Schwab, founder of the WEF, posted an article on its website under the heading "Corporate Governance": "Why we need the 'Davos Manifesto' for a better kind of capitalism."[140]

> What kind of capitalism do we want? That may be the defining question of our era. If we want to sustain our economic system for future generations, we must answer it correctly.
>
> Generally speaking, we have three models to choose from. The first is "shareholder capitalism," embraced by most Western corporations, which holds that a corporation's primary goal should be to maximize its profits. The second model is "state capitalism," which entrusts the government with setting the direction of the economy and has risen to prominence in many emerging markets, not least China.
>
> But, compared to these two options, the third has the most to recommend it. "Stakeholder capitalism," a model I first proposed a half-century ago, positions private corporations as trustees of society, and is clearly the best response to today's social and environmental challenges.

On December 2, 2019, Klaus Schwab posted a lofty description of stakeholder capitalism and its trustees in "The Davos Manifesto 2020: The Universal Purpose of a Company in the Fourth Industrial Revolution":[141]

A. The purpose of a company is to engage all its stakeholders in shared and sustained value creation. In creating such value, a company serves not only its shareholders, but all its stakeholders—employees, customers, suppliers, local communities and society at large. The best way to understand and harmonize the divergent interests of all stakeholders is through a shared commitment to policies and decisions that strengthen the long-term prosperity of a company.

i. A company serves its customers by providing a value proposition that best meets their needs. It accepts and supports fair competition and a level playing field. It has zero tolerance for corruption. It keeps the digital ecosystem in which it operates reliable and trustworthy. It makes customers fully aware of the functionality of its products and services, including adverse implications or negative externalities.

ii. A company treats its people with dignity and respect. It honours diversity and strives for continuous improvements in working conditions and employee well-being. In a world of rapid change, a company fosters continued employability through ongoing upskilling and reskilling.

iii. A company considers its suppliers as true partners in value creation. It provides a fair chance to new market entrants. It integrates respect for human rights into the entire supply chain.

iv. A company serves society at large through its activities, supports the communities in which it works, and pays its fair share of taxes. It ensures the safe, ethical and efficient use of data. It acts as a steward of the environmental and material universe for future generations. It consciously protects our biosphere and champions a circular, shared and regenerative economy. It continuously expands the frontiers of knowledge, innovation and technology to improve people's well-being.

v. A company provides its shareholders with a return on investment that takes into account the incurred entrepreneurial risks and the need for continuous innovation and sustained investments. It responsibly manages near-term, medium-term and long-term value creation in pursuit of sustainable shareholder returns that do not sacrifice the future for the present.

B. A company is more than an economic unit generating wealth. It fulfils human and societal aspirations as part of the broader social system. Performance must be measured not only on the return to shareholders, but also on how it achieves its environmental, social and good governance objectives. Executive remuneration should reflect stakeholder responsibility.

C. A company that has a multinational scope of activities not only serves all those stakeholders who are directly engaged, but acts itself as a stakeholder—together with governments and civil society—of our global future. Corporate global citizenship requires a company to harness its core competencies, its entrepreneurship, skills and relevant resources in collaborative efforts with other companies and stakeholders to improve the state of the world.

The Davos Manifesto 2020 is an advertorial masterpiece of deceit. It presents the universal purpose of a company in the Fourth Industrial Revolution, but it does not define the Revolution or its global implications. The Fourth Industrial Revolution (4IR) is a way of describing the blurring of boundaries between the physical, digital, and biological spheres. It is a fusion of advances in artificial intelligence (AI), robotics, the Internet of Things (IoT), Web3, blockchain, 3D printing, genetic engineering, quantum computing, and other technologies.

A bit of history is helpful. The steam engine launched the initial Industrial Revolution in the 18th century, moving industry from hand tools to machines. Electricity launched the Second Industrial Revolution, called the Technological Revolution, which brought mass production to industry. The Third Industrial Revolution, called the Digital Revolution, introduced computer technology in the 1950s. Each industrial revolution brought seismic social changes. So, what are and will be the social changes brought by the 4IR?

Klaus Schwab presented his perspective in 2016, "The Fourth Industrial Revolution: what it means, and how to respond":[142]

> We stand on the brink of a technological revolution that will fundamentally alter the way we live, work, and relate to one another. In its scale, scope, and complexity, the transformation will be unlike anything humankind has experienced before. We do not yet know just how it will unfold, but one thing is clear: the response to it must be integrated and comprehensive, involving all stakeholders of the global polity, from the public and private sectors to academia and civil society.

The most notable social change announced by Klaus Schwab is in the size and scope of the 4IR, which requires a unified planetary response provided by the private corporate "trustees of society." Today, in 2024, the WEF describes itself and its mission on its website:[143]

> *The World Economic Forum is the International Organization for Public-Private Cooperation.*
>
> The Forum engages the foremost political, business, cultural and other leaders of society to shape global, regional and industry agendas.
>
> It was established in 1971 as a not-for-profit foundation and is headquartered in Geneva, Switzerland. It is independent, impartial and not tied to any special interests. The Forum strives in all its efforts to demonstrate entrepreneurship in the global public interest while upholding the highest standards of governance. Moral and intellectual integrity is at the heart of everything it does.
>
> Our activities are shaped by a unique institutional culture founded on the stakeholder theory, which asserts that an organization is accountable to all parts of a society. The institution carefully blends and balances the best of many kinds of organizations, from both the public and private sectors, international organizations and academic institutions.
>
> We believe that progress happens by bringing people together from all walks of life who have the drive and the influence to make positive change.

What is the foundational "stakeholder theory" that distinguishes the WEF's plan for positive change, and how does it differ from traditional shareholder capitalism? First, the reader will note the similarity between the word *shareholder* and *stakeholder*. Many people won't notice the difference, and will assume the WEF is supporting an improved capitalist system that includes upward mobility and a robust middle class, rather than the binary feudal replacement ideology the WEF actually supports. This is the same ambiguity that duped voters into assuming Obama's *hope and change* were improvements on our capitalist society, not the Marxist ideology he planned to put in place.

Stakeholder capitalism distinguishes itself from shareholder capitalism in both form and content. The words *stakeholder* and *shareholder*, different by only two letters, are intentionally confusing. They are worlds apart. In shareholder capitalism the investor invests assets in a company by purchasing shares of ownership in that company. The shareholder is a stockholder and understands the risks and rewards of his capital investment.

Stakeholder capitalism is global in form and social in content. The Stakeholder Model is a marketing masterpiece, an emotional appeal to psychological yearnings for purpose, recognition, and union. It identifies *people* and *planet* as the central stakeholders. The planet is the center of the interconnected global economic system, and all decisions made must support the health of the planet. The well-being of both people and the planet is the interconnected center of business.

The Davos Agenda 2021,[144] presented by the WEF, includes an article posted on the WEF website, "What is stakeholder capitalism?"[145] It identifies four main stakeholders, with a stunningly sophomoric assumption that since the four main stakeholders consist of people who make use of the planet, they will necessarily seek to optimize the well-being of everyone and also the well-being of the environment:

> Stakeholder capitalism is a form of capitalism in which companies do not only optimize short-term profits for shareholders, but seek long-term value creation, by taking into account the needs of all their stakeholders, and society at large....
>
> To ensure that both people and the planet prosper, four key stakeholders play a crucial role. They are: **governments** (of countries,

states, and local communities); **civil-society** (from unions to NGOs, from schools and universities to action groups); **companies** (constituting the private sector, whether freelancers or large multinational companies); and the **international community** (consisting of international organizations such as the UN as well as regional organizations such as the European Union or ASEAN).

All these stakeholders crucially consist of people and make use of the planet. It is no surprise, then, that they should want to optimize the well-being of all of us as well as that of the environment. But equally, it should be clear they have specific objectives that make them distinct organisms in the first place.

- Governments focus on creating the greatest possibly ***prosperity*** for the greatest number of people.

- Civil society exists to advance the interest of its constituents and to give a meaning or ***purpose*** to its members.

- Companies aim to generate an economic surplus, measurable in ***profits*** in the short run, and **long-term value creation** in the long run.

- And the overarching goal for the international community is to preserve ***peace***....

The model is simple, but it immediately reveals why shareholder primacy and state capitalism lead to suboptimal outcomes: They focus on the more granular and exclusive objectives of profits or prosperity in a particular company or country rather than the well-being of all people and the planet as a whole.

American scholar Dr. Michael Rectenwald provides a brilliant analysis of the humanitarian hoax of the *Great Reset* in his November 7, 2021, article, "What Is the Great Reset?"[146] Excerpts from the article expose the Big Lies, word obfuscation, and disguised intent of Schwab's Stakeholder Theory:

The WEF is the source for the stakeholder and public-private partnership rhetoric and policies embraced by governments, corporations, non-governmental organizations (NGOs), civil society organizations, and international governance bodies worldwide.

Public-private partnerships have played a key role in the response to the covid crisis and are instrumental in the response to the supposed climate change crisis....

On June 13, 2019, the WEF signed a Memorandum of Understanding with the United Nations (UN) to form a partnership centered on advancing the UN "2030 Agenda for Sustainable Development." The WEF published the "United Nations–World Economic Forum Strategic Partnership Framework for the 2030 Agenda" shortly thereafter. The WEF promised to help "finance" the UN's climate change agenda. The framework also commits the WEF to helping the UN "meet the needs of the Fourth Industrial Revolution," including providing assets and expertise for "digital governance." Agenda 2030 appears to have been tailor-made to accommodate the UN-WEF partnership. It adopts the stakeholder concept introduced by Schwab decades before. The word "stakeholders" is used no less than thirteen times in the 2030 resolution. The Great Reset, then, may be understood, in part, as the WEF's contribution to Agenda 2030....

While approved corporate stakeholders are not *necessarily* monopolies, the tendency of the Great Reset is toward monopolization—vesting as much control over production and distribution in these favored corporations as possible, while eliminating industries and producers deemed either unnecessary or inimical. To bring this reset about, "every country, from the United States to China, must participate, and every industry, from oil and gas to tech, must be transformed," writes the authoritarian Schwab....

The Great Reset combines resets in all conceivable domains of human life: economic, environmental, geopolitical, governmental, industrial, technological, social, and individual....

Stakeholder capitalism includes not only corporate responses to ecological issues such as climate change, "but also rethinking their [corporations'] commitments to already-vulnerable communities within their ecosystems." This is the "social justice" aspect of stakeholder capitalism and the Great Reset. Governments, banks, and asset managers use the Environmental, Social, and Governance

(ESG) index to squeeze non-woke players out of the market. The ESG index is essentially a social credit score for rating corporations. The collectivist planners drive ownership and control of production away from the non-compliant.

One of the WEF's many "strategic partners," BlackRock, Inc., the world's largest asset manager, is solidly behind the stakeholder model of the Great Reset program. In a 2021 letter to CEOs, Black-Rock's CEO Larry Fink declared that "climate risk is investment risk," and "the creation of sustainable index investments has enabled a massive acceleration of capital towards companies better prepared to address climate risk." Fink states that the pandemic accelerated the flow of funds toward sustainable investments:

> We have long believed that our clients, as shareholders in your company, will benefit if you can create enduring, sustainable value for all of your stakeholders.... As more and more investors choose to tilt their investments towards sustainability-focused companies, the tectonic shift we are seeing will accelerate further. And because this will have such a dramatic impact on how capital is allocated, every management team and board will need to consider how this will impact their company's stock.

Fink's letter is more than a report to CEOs. It is an implicit threat. Meanwhile, investment according to the ESG index and other financial tools is gaining the force of law in the U.S., with the Biden administration's recent "U.S. Climate-Related Financial Risk: Executive Order 14030" [which removes barriers to considering ESG factors in retirement plan investments].

Rectenwald explains that Schwab's reference to "neoliberalism" is a euphemism for the free market:

> That is, "neoliberalism" refers to what is otherwise known as the free market. Stakeholder capitalism is thus opposed to the free enterprise system. It means not only corporate cooperation with the state and NGOs but also vastly increased government intervention in the economy.... Schwab and company erect the straw man of neoliberalism as the source of our economic woes....

Unsurprisingly, stakeholder capitalism has been seen as a new approach to achieving socialism, even by socialists. As I've suggested, stakeholder capitalism tends toward *"corporate socialism,"* or "capitalism with Chinese characteristics," two ways of understanding the overall economics of the Great Reset.

The Great Reset represents the development of the Chinese system in the West, only in reverse. Whereas the Chinese political class began with a socialist political system and introduced privately held for-profit production later, the West began with a degree of capitalism and is implementing a socialist political system now. It's as if the Western oligarchy looked to the "socialism" on display in China, and said, "yes, we want it." This Chinese-style system includes vastly increased state intervention in the economy on the one hand, and the kind of authoritarian measures that the Chinese government uses to control the population, on the other....

The corporate stakeholder model of the Great Reset spills into its governance and geopolitical model: states and favored corporations in "public-private partnerships" in control of governance. The configuration yields a corporate-state hybrid largely unaccountable to the constituents of national governments....

This usurpation has led political scientist Ivan Wecke to call the WEF's governmental redesign of the world system "a corporate takeover of global governance."

This is true, but the WEF model also represents *the governmentalization of private industry*. Under Schwab's stakeholder capitalism and the multistakeholder governance model, governance is not only increasingly privatized, but also and more importantly, corporations are deputized as major additions to governments and intergovernmental bodies. The state is thereby extended, enhanced, and augmented by the addition of enormous corporate assets. These include funding directed at "sustainable development" to the exclusion of the non-compliant, as well as the use of Big Data, AI, and 5G to monitor and control citizens. In the case of the covid vaccine regime, the state grants Big Pharma monopoly protection and indemnity from liability in exchange for a vehicle to expand its powers of coercion. As such, corporate stakeholders become what I have called "governmentalities"—otherwise "private" organizations wielded as state apparatuses, with no obligation to answer to pesky constituents. Since these corporations are multinational, the state essentially becomes global, whether or not a "one-world government" is ever formalized.

As if the economic and governmental resets were not dramatic enough, the technological reset reads like a dystopic sci-fi novel. It is based on the Fourth Industrial Revolution (4IR).… The significance of Schwab's and the WEF's take on the new technological revolution is the attempt to harness it to a particular end, presumably "a fairer, greener future."…

In short, 4IR technologies subject human beings to a technological management that makes surveillance by the NSA look like child's play. And Schwab lauds developments that connect brains directly to the cloud and enable the "data mining" of thought and memory, a technological mastery over decision-making that threatens autonomy and undermines any semblance of free will. The 4IR accelerates the merging of humans and machines, resulting in a world in which all information, including genetic information, is shared, and every action, thought, and unconscious motivation is known, predicted, and possibly even precluded. Naturally, Aldous Huxley's *Brave New World* comes to mind. Yet Schwab touts brain-cloud interfaces as enhancements, as vast improvements over standard human intelligence.

Unless taken out of the hands of corporate-socialist technocrats, the 4IR will constitute a virtual, inescapable prison of body and mind.…

In partnership with Big Tech, Big Pharma, the legacy media, national and international health agencies, and compliant populations, hitherto "democratic" Western states are being transformed into totalitarian regimes modeled after China, seemingly overnight.…

The Great Reset, then, is not a conspiracy theory; it is an open, avowed, and planned project, and it is well underway.

Like Karl Marx, Klaus Schwab identifies *capitalism* as the source of human suffering and economic hardship. Schwab's solution, *stakeholder* capitalism, is a fancy word for collectivism that goes far beyond other species of Marxist collectivism.

Schwab paints lipstick on the familiar Marxist pig and expands it to unprecedented planetary proportions. Stakeholder capitalism is the blitzkrieg of globalism's war campaign designed to transform the world's economic structures and enslave the world's population.

Stakeholder capitalism rejects private property, meritocracy, and shareholder capitalism's free-market economic system. It replaces them with corporate socialism and Environmental, Social, and Governance scoring as its social/monetary system.

Klaus Schwab is the consummate huckster selling one-world government to a trusting and fearful public, presenting it as the solution to the seismic social changes being brought by the Fourth Industrial Revolution. Modeled on the totalitarian system of the CCP, stakeholder capitalism is the perfect humanitarian hoax for eliminating any and all individual agency.

Stakeholder theory, like Marxist Critical Theory, operates on the Hegelian dialectical model. Its foundational hypothesis is the Big Lie of man-made climate change. The Earth's climate has fluctuated naturally throughout its history. The man-made problem of pollution must be addressed, but pollution must never be confused with the fiction of man-made climate change. That term is a political narrative designed for seismic social change, the redistribution of wealth, and the imposition of globalism's planetary managerial Unistate.

The Big Lie of the COVID-19 pandemic was similarly exploited to advance stakeholder capitalism. Rectenwald explained how "private" corporations were deputized as extensions of government and intergovernmental bodies. So, Big Pharma, protected by total indemnification from liability in the COVID "vaccine" debacle, became a "governmentality," to use Rectenwald's coined word, and a powerful vehicle for increasing global centralized control. Big Pharma and its representatives in government were empowered to interpret the social aspect of stakeholder capitalism. They determined what was "best" for society, which, of course, enriched Big Pharma and expanded the government's powers of coercion.

The humanitarian hoax of COVID-19, previously discussed in the Introduction and Chapters 2, 4, and 6, terrified people into surrendering their freedoms to stakeholder capitalists for deceitful promises of health and safety. Instead of health and safety, they got more government control, which continues to expand with "vaccine" regimens that now include mRNA jabs for babies.

Klaus Schwab is selling feudalism to the public as stakeholder capitalism. His marketing scheme is an Orwellian perversion of the word "stake." To have a stake in something means to have an interest or share in a business, a situation, or a system. In shareholder capitalism, the shareholder has a financial stake in the business. In stakeholder capitalism, the only stakeholders who benefit are the managerial elite, because the elite always and only take care of the elite.

Stakeholder capitalism's deceitful hypothesis leads to its equally dishonest conclusion: that stakeholder capitalism led by global corporations will solve the world's problems and bring peace on earth. It most assuredly will not.

CHAPTER 33

Weaponizing Children: The Gospel of Yuval Harari

Globalism is a replacement ideology that seeks to reorder the world into one singular, planetary Unistate, ruled by the globalist elite. The globalist war on nation-states cannot succeed without collapsing the United States of America. The long-term strategic attack plan moves America incrementally from constitutional republic to socialism to globalism to feudalism. The tactical attack plan uses asymmetric psychological and informational warfare to destabilize Americans and drive society out of objective reality into the madness of subjective reality. America's children are the primary target of the globalist predators.

Klaus Schwab and fellow members of the World Economic Forum (WEF) embrace a vision for the future that is difficult to fully grasp, but it is essential that people attempt to do just that. Yuval Harari, Israeli historian, professor, and darling of the WEF, provides a glimpse of that future and of Humanity 2.0 in his books and lectures.

Schwab and Harari embrace globalism's supremacist replacement ideology as an *evolutionary* inevitability, in the same way Marx and Engels believed it was a *historical inevitability* that a socialist revolution would overturn and replace capitalism.

The term *historical inevitability* was introduced by philosopher Isaiah Berlin in his lecture "Historical Inevitability,"[147] delivered on May 12, 1953, at the London School of Economics and Political Science. Berlin argued against historical inevitability because the view that "the world has a direction" requires deterministic laws. Berlin considered determinism implausible because it requires radical changes in people's "moral and psychological categories."

Berlin's view does not dissuade the humanitarian hucksters at the WEF from hawking globalism's Unistate and Humanity 2.0, the artificial expediting of the evolutionary process, as historical and evolutionary inevitabilities. In their arrogance, globalist supremacists insist that **their** ideology is superior to any other ideology or social infrastructure, and will inevitably dominate the world. It is a very convenient philosophy of life for megalomaniacs and sociopaths.

Let's examine Yuval Harari's views in his own words, delivered at the World Economic Forum's Annual Meeting in Davos, January 24, 2020:[148]

> *Three problems pose existential challenges to our species. These three existential challenges are nuclear war, ecological collapse and technological disruption. Now nuclear war and ecological collapse are already familiar threats, so let me spend some time explaining the less familiar threat posed by technological disruption.*

> *In Davos we hear so much about the enormous promises of technology—and these promises are certainly real. But technology might also disrupt human society and the very meaning of human life in numerous ways, ranging from the creation of a global useless class to the rise of data colonialism and of digital dictatorships....*

> *Alongside inequality, the other major danger we face is the rise of digital dictatorships that will monitor everyone all the time. This danger can be stated in the form of a simple equation, which I think might be the defining equation of life in the twenty-first century:*

$$B \times C \times D = AHH!$$

> *Which means? Biological knowledge multiplied by computing power multiplied by data equals the ability to hack humans, AHH....*

> *If you know enough biology and have enough computing power and data, you can hack my body and my brain and my life, and you can understand me better than I understand myself. You can know my personality type, my political views, my sexual preferences, my mental weaknesses, my deepest fears and hopes. You know more about me than I know about myself. And you can do that not just to me, but to everyone.*

> *A system that understands us better than we understand ourselves*

can predict our feelings and decisions, can manipulate our feelings and decisions, and can ultimately make decisions for us.

Now in the past, many governments and tyrants wanted to do it, but nobody understood biology well enough and nobody had enough computing power and data to hack millions of people. Neither the Gestapo nor the KGB could do it. But soon at least some corporations and governments will be able to systematically hack all the people. We humans should get used to the idea that we are no longer mysterious souls—we are now hackable animals....

In the coming decades, AI and biotechnology will give us godlike abilities to reengineer life, and even to create completely new life-forms. After four billion years of organic life shaped by natural selection, we are about to enter a new era of inorganic life shaped by intelligent design.

Our intelligent design is going to be the new driving force of the evolution of life and in using our new divine powers of creation we might make mistakes on a cosmic scale. In particular, governments, corporations and armies are likely to use technology to enhance human skills that they need—like intelligence and discipline—while neglecting other human skills—like compassion, artistic sensitivity and spirituality.

The result might be a race of humans who are very intelligent and very disciplined but lack compassion, lack artistic sensitivity and lack spiritual depth. Of course, this is not a prophecy. These are just possibilities. Technology is never deterministic.

AI and biotech will certainly transform the world, but we can use them to create very different kinds of societies. And if you're afraid of some of the possibilities I've mentioned, you can still do something about it. But to do something effective, we need global cooperation.

All the three existential challenges we face are global problems that demand global solutions.

Whenever a leader says something like "My Country First!" we should remind that leader that no nation can prevent nuclear war or stop ecological collapse by itself, and no nation can regulate AI and bioengineering by itself....

Unfortunately, just when global cooperation is more needed than ever before, some of the most powerful leaders and countries in the world are now deliberately undermining global cooperation....

But this is a dangerous mistake. There is no contradiction between nationalism and globalism. Because nationalism isn't about hating foreigners. Nationalism is about loving your compatriots. And in the twenty-first century, in order to protect the safety and the future of your compatriots, you must cooperate with foreigners.

So, in the twenty-first century, good nationalists must be also globalists. Now globalism doesn't mean establishing a global government, abandoning all national traditions, or opening the border to unlimited immigration. Rather, globalism means a commitment to some global rules.

Rules that don't deny the uniqueness of each nation, but only regulate the relations between nations.

Yuval Harari is an ideological soldier engaged in controlled opposition for the globalist revolution. Controlled opposition describes a person who appears to be on one side, but is actually working for the other side. Harari voices people's concerns, and then presents the consummate dialectical argument for globalism's Unistate.

Harari begins with the false premise that nuclear war, ecological collapse, and technological disruption are *the* three existential threats to our species, ignoring the overriding threat of globalism. He ends by blurring the essential distinctions between nationalism and globalism, redefining globalism as nothing more than national cooperation, and advancing globalism's Unistate as the singular planetary solution for neutralizing the three existential threats.

Harari's argument is painfully sophomoric. It is equivalent to blaming nuclear war on Fermi, the physicist who created the first nuclear reactor in 1945, instead of blaming the individuals in charge of nuclear weapons today. Harari's focus deflects attention away from the globalists proposing solutions to the threats of nuclear war, ecological collapse, and technological disruption.

Yuval Harari's entire narrative is based on the verb *cooperate* and the noun *cooperation*. His two most famous books, *Sapiens: A Brief History of Humankind* (2011) and *Homo Deus: A Brief History of Tomorrow* (2016), are based on his premise that *Homo sapiens* came to dominate the world because of its unique ability to *cooperate* in large numbers. He argues that *sapiens*' unique ability to *cooperate* is a consequence of its unique *imagination*, which gives *sapiens* the ability to believe in abstractions, things that do not exist in the physical world.

Harari argues that *cooperation* is the source of both peace and war. Cooperation restricted to nations and/or small groups gives rise to animus and battles over abstractions, including gods, nations, money, and human rights. If/when human cooperation is planetary in scale, the animus and battles over abstractions will cease, and world peace will finally be achieved.

Yuval Harari perceives the United Nations as equivalent to the Federation Internationale de Football Association (FIFA), the governing body of the World Cup. His metaphor presents the geopolitical infrastructure of the world as an international sports competition between sovereign nations choosing to cooperate and abide by international rules of soccer determined by its governing body, FIFA.

Harari compares competition among nations for primacy in the world of science, to international competition among nations in the world of sports, where individual nations compete but cooperate by following the same rules. He presents the familiar dreamscape of world cooperation and peace reflected in John Lennon's 1971 song "Imagine."

Here is the problem. While people sing and dream of world peace, the globalists proposing solutions to the existential threats to humanity are quietly pursuing their dreams of war and world domination.

In objective reality, the current geopolitical arrangement of the world is not an international sports competition with a global governing body. Instead, the world order is based on national sovereignty, the principle that each state has exclusive sovereignty over its own territory. Such sovereignty *denies* the authority of any international governing body.

Yuval Harari, Klaus Schwab, and over 1,000 current corporate members of the WEF are conspiring to blur the boundaries between nationalism and globalism, and dupe the fearful world public into accepting the rules of United Nations Agenda 2030, as if they are equivalent to the rules of an international sports competition. They aren't. Acceptance of Agenda 2030 and the proposed UN Pandemic Treaty put forth by the World Health Organization in 2024 will establish the globalist Unistate and enslave the world population in its reordered feudal infrastructure. The world's population will be reduced once again to being serfs, this time in the Unistate administered by its governing body, the lethally corrupt United Nations.

Harari, the Pied Piper of 21st-century disinformation, is a gifted humanitarian huckster selling transhumanism and Humanity 2.0 as freedom to adults and children. His books are international blockbusters that have sold over 40 million copies in 65 languages. *Sapiens* is available for young adults as a two-part graphic novel: *Sapiens: The Birth of Humankind, Vol. 1* and *Sapiens: The Pillars of Civilization,* Vol. 2, published in 2020 and 2021, respectively. The reader will remember that graphic novels are comic books with an upper-grade interest level and lower-grade reading level. Published in 2022, Harari's book *Unstoppable Us: How Humans Took Over the World,* Vol. 1, is the first in a four-volume series of children's books marketed for ages 10–14, grade level 5–9.

Educational reformer Deborah DeGroff offers a comprehensive review of Harari's first children's book in her incisive November 7, 2022, article, "Unstoppable Us: How Humans Took Over the World (The Gospel of Harari for Children)."[149] She examines Harari's gospel and its manipulative plea to children to *cooperate* and become activists, because they alone hold the fate of the world in their hands.

The article begins with a description of the book jacket:

> The front book jacket begins with:
>
> *THE STRANGEST TALE YOU'LL EVER HEAR…AND IT'S A TRUE STORY!*
>
> Is it?
>
> Who is Yuval Noah Harari and why has he become so influential? What is his message? Does his heavily-marketed new book for children echo the same sentiments he so adamantly feeds his adult audiences?

DeGroff continues with a summary and analysis of the Gospel of Yuval Harari:

> In a nutshell, in Harari's gospel there is no God, no soul, and no free-will. Once these pillars are accepted as truth by his followers—many of whom are in positions of power—the next step will be deciding the fate of billions of people who are no longer necessary in a future world that consists of Artificial Intelligence, Biotechnology, and Transhumanism....
>
> Yuval Noah Harari holds great influence with many people in positions of power. Up until recently, this audience has consisted of adults. Now, Harari is introducing his message to children...with the pre-teen series *Unstoppable Us.*
>
> Harari includes a Timeline of History at the beginning of *Unstoppable Us.*
>
> He begins with 6 million years ago with a picture of an upright creature that is a cross between a human and an ape. The caption reads that this was the "last common ancestor of humans and chimpanzees." He follows with a jump to the 2.5 million years ago mark in which he states that "Humans evolve in Africa." The Gospel of Harari (hereafter GoH) moves forward another half-million years with the "evolution of different kinds of humans." By 400,000 years ago, "Neanderthals evolve in Europe and the Middle East" and 300,000 years ago, "Sapiens evolve in Africa." 70,000 years ago, "the Sapiens leave Africa in large numbers." 35,000 years ago the Neanderthals are extinct and "Sapiens are the last surviving kind of human." ...
>
> Chapter 1 teaches the children that millions of years ago, we were just ordinary animals who ate worms and climbed trees to pick fruit. Until humans learned to make tools, the other animals weren't afraid of them....
>
> Next, the humans invented fire....
>
> Now, the humans could cook their food. As a result, "humans started to change: they had smaller teeth, smaller stomachs...and much more free time." (p. 9)

Harari expands on this by stating that some scientists "suggest it was cooking that made it possible for the human brain to start growing." … (p. 10)

In the next chapter, the children learn that "our planet was actually home to many different kinds of humans." (p. 13)

Harari introduces the Floresians and follows with the "bigger-brained" Neanderthals, and the Denisovans. However, according to him, the Sapiens eventually killed off all of these "ancestors." …

"Then our ancestors went to Siberia and took all the food from the Denisovans. And then they went to Flores, and…soon there wasn't a single small human or small elephant to be found. And when all the other humans were gone, our ancestors still weren't satisfied. Although they were now incredibly powerful, they wanted even more power and more food, so they sometimes fought one another." (p. 27)

The next chapter begins with, "You see, we Sapiens are not very nice animals." Often, he concludes, this is due to different skin colors, languages, or religions. (p. 29)

"But a few years ago, scientists discovered that at least some of our Sapiens ancestors didn't kill or starve all the other humans they met." (p. 29) Harari explains that because of our knowledge of DNA, scientists have determined that some Neanderthals had children with Sapiens." I guess Harari intends for these middle-grade students to conclude that some people today are not 100% evil Sapiens since they have some Neanderthal DNA.…

Part 2 of the book is Harari's explanation as to the why and how Sapiens ended up ruling the world. He says that cooperation is what makes us so powerful. (p. 40)

Harari then poses the question:

"How did our ancestors learn to cooperate in large numbers in the first place, and how come we can constantly change our behavior?" (p. 45)

"[It's] our ability to dream up stuff that isn't really there and to tell all kinds of imaginary stories." (p. 46)

"If thousands of people believe in the same story, then they'll all follow the same rules, which means they can cooperate effectively." (p. 48)

"Let's say a Sapiens tells everyone this story: 'There's a Great Lion Spirit that lives above the clouds. If you obey the Great Lion Spirit, then when you die, you'll go the land of the spirits, and you'll have all the bananas you can eat. But if you disobey the Great Lion Spirit, a big lion will come and eat you!'

"Of course, this story isn't true at all. But if a thousand people believe it, they'll all start doing whatever the story tells them to do." (p. 49)

Harari next informs the kids about "one of the most interesting games grown-ups play...called 'corporation.'" (p. 54) He uses McDonald's Corporation as an illustration and informs the children that although you can go to the restaurants or talk to the employees, what they see is not McDonald's as "it exists only in our imagination." (p. 58)

"... If you want to open a restaurant but you don't want to risk losing your socks or going to jail, you create a corporation. And then the corporation does everything and takes all the risks."

"The corporation borrows money from the bank, and if it can't repay the money, nobody can blame you for it, and nobody can take your house or your socks. After all, the bank gave the money to the corporation, not to you. And if somebody eats a burger and gets a really nasty stomachache, nobody can hold you responsible. You didn't make that burger—the corporation did." (p. 60)

"Well, money is also just another imaginary story that grown-ups believe. [Bankers and politicians] tell stories like 'This small piece of paper is worth ten bananas,' and the grown-ups believe them." (p. 63)

"... humans can quickly change the way we behave by simply changing the stories we believe." (p. 65)

The GoH also weighs in on families:

"Nowadays, some people have one partner for their entire life, some have many partners, and some remain single. In a few countries, one man can be married to several women at the same time. In other countries, two women can get married to each other, and so can two men." (p. 87) [Harari is married to a man.]

"Bonobo (chimpanzee) girls don't dream about marrying a handsome prince—they'd usually prefer a cool girlfriend!" (p. 89)

Harari then speculates about the types of families there may have been in Stone Age times:

"… In the fourth hut, one woman, her three children, and her current girlfriend." (p. 90)

"Well, maybe it was like that…and maybe not. It's easy to imagine different possibilities, but scientists need to distinguish imagination from fact…you need evidence." (p. 92)

"… one tribe might have believed that after you died, you came back as a new baby, or perhaps even as an animal. Maybe a second tribe believed that when you died, you became a ghost. A third tribe may have thought that these two theories were a load of nonsense—when you died, you were gone, and that was that." (p. 103)

"… There is one thing, though, we are certain our ancestors did, and it's something we know a lot about: they caused most of the world's big animals to disappear." (p. 141)

"… the ancient ancestors of whales were land animals that were no bigger than a large dog. Around 50 million years ago, some of these doglike animals started spending part of their time in rivers and lakes, hunting fish and other small creatures…they spent more and more of their time in rivers, rarely venturing onto land. Their feet, which they no longer needed for walking, evolved into flippers. Their tails also changed to better help them with swimming. Eventually, these animals swam out to sea: completely abandoning land, they spent their whole lives deep in the ocean. And their bodies adapted, growing enormous, until they became whales."

"But this process took millions and millions of years." (p. 146)

"Soon after Sapiens reached Australia, all these huge animals became extinct—and many small animals did too."

"Why did they suddenly disappear exactly when the first humans arrived? Let's be honest and accept the truth: the most plausible explanation is that the Sapiens caused the extinction of all these animals." (p. 152)

"… They didn't have guns and bombs…. But they did have three big advantages: cooperation, the element of surprise, and the ability to control fire." (p. 152)

"Their first advantage was that they could tell stories that brought many people together…. If people in one band developed a new trick to hunt diprotodons, they could quickly teach their trick to all the other bands." (p. 153)

"… The truth is that humans were already the deadliest animals on earth." (p. 154)

"The thing about bad habits is that it's so hard to get rid of them. They tend to stay with you wherever you go…. Wiping out so many of Australia's animals was the first big thing they did. The second big thing was to wipe out animals in America." (p. 156)

"Why were our ancestors so cruel? Why did they completely wipe out the mammoths?"

"The thing is, they probably didn't mean to do it. They were just hungry, and their children were hungry, and they hunted a few mammoths every year because they needed something to eat. They didn't know the effect (p. 166) this would have over many, many years. We often do very impactful things without realizing what we're doing." (p. 167)

"… But over time, the tiny changes accumulate and become very big changes." (p. 167)

"The problem with Sapiens wasn't that they were evil; the problem was that they were too good at what they did. When they started hunting mammoths, they became so good at it that no mammoths survived. So they went on to hunt elk. But they were very good at that too, and very soon the elk also started to disappear." (171)

"So, step 1: lots of animals, no Sapiens. Step 2: Sapiens appear. Step 3: lots of Sapiens, no animals." (p. 172)

Harari then lets the kids know that although our ancestors didn't realize the impact of what they were doing, we do. We have no excuse and are responsible for the future of all animals. He challenges these ten- to fourteen-year-old children to become activists and tells them that it doesn't matter how young they are. They can take care of this.

"Remember, even as a kid, you're already more powerful than any lion or whale!" (p. 174)

"… One whale weighs as much as 5,000 kids. And yet whales can't protect themselves against humans because humans have learned to tell stories and cooperate in very sophisticated ways, which whales can't understand." (p. 175)

"So, the corporations hunted more and more whales, and made more and more money. Fifty years ago, blue whales almost disappeared.… Luckily, some humans noticed what was happening and (p. 176) decided to save the whales. Being humans themselves, they understood what money is and how corporations work, so they knew what to do. They wrote letters to newspapers, they signed petitions to politicians, and they organized demonstrations. They told people not to buy products from corporations that hunted whales, and they asked governments to forbid whaling. Many of the people who did all this were kids." (p. 177)

"… So that's how we humans became the rulers of planet Earth. And how we came to hold the fate of all other animals in our hands. Even before humans built the first city, invented the wheel, and learned how to write, we had already spread all over the world and killed about half of all large land animals." (p. 179)

"… And you know that if you invent a good story that enough people believe, you can conquer the world." (p. 180)

DeGroff concludes her analysis with a number of very good questions:

Has Yuval Noah Harari invented a good enough story?

This book is being heavily marketed. Harari is giving many interviews about *Unstoppable Us*. Will his gospel message change the worldview of our children? Throughout his book, he talks about made-up good stories that influence people enough to change the world, and yet he declares that his story is a *true* one. In other words, he wants his readers or listeners to believe *his* story and act accordingly.

This book is just the first of four volumes. The next volume will be about the Agriculture Revolution. Line upon line; precept upon precept. Each book will build upon the foundation laid in the previous volume. The Gospel of Harari has already convinced at least some of his audience that God is just a made-up story to make people obedient or cooperative. Will no soul and no free will be introduced next?

Will the powers-that-be decide to keep the useless eaters around by giving them a universal income and keeping them entertained in the Metaverse, or will there be mass genocide? Who is going to argue for human rights if people have no souls or free will? What would it matter?

Often, I hear parents tell me that their children know better. I hope they are right. Maybe they do attend church every time the doors are open, but who is teaching them and what are they learning? Do you know? Are they being taught or entertained? If they are in a government school, sadly, they have already absorbed much of Harari's message.

Do you know what's between the covers of the books your children are reading?

Yuval Harari is what is called an influencer in marketing today—a person with the ability to influence potential buyers of a product or service by promoting or recommending the item on social media. His goal is to persuade your children to buy the Gospel of Harari—*his* story. This means rejecting the Judeo-Christian teachings of their family, friends, church, and synagogue. It also means rejecting traditional concepts of nationalism and embracing Harari's globalist delusion that the existential threats of nuclear war, ecological collapse, and technological disruption will be eliminated through *cooperation* in globalism's Unistate.

Like Alfred Kinsey (Chapter 17) and Margaret Mead (Chapter 21), Yuval Harari's self-serving narrative is a sinister attempt to "change the hearts and minds" of the world's children. Consider the consequences of the UN world curricula teaching Harari's "evolutionary" biology that ends in the transformation of human beings into transhumanist beings totally controlled by the globalist elite.

Harari's sales pitch is anti-establishment, anti-Judeo-Christian, anti-God, anti-family, anti-nationalism, and pro-globalism. His overarching theme for children is clear. Everything you learned at home is wrong. Everything you learned at church or synagogue is wrong. Sapiens are mean, greedy killers that only you—the children—have the power to change. Yuval Harari is selling your children one-world government unencumbered by traditional religious teachings that he dismissively refers to as the "Great Lion Spirit" in the sky.

In *Unstoppable Us*, Harari brings the dualism and dialectical language discussed in Chapter 28 to your children. Yuval Harari is trying to seduce your children into the madness of global citizenship by offering them *his* story, the empowerment of using their *superpowers* to become social activists, and the opportunity to right the wrongs of their parents and grandparents. Beware the Gospel of Harari; it is a denial of objective reality that is already proselytizing your children in both public and private schools throughout America.

CHAPTER 34

In a World Obsessed with Feelings, Whose Feelings Matter?

Globalism is a replacement ideology that seeks to reorder the world into one singular, planetary Unistate, ruled by the globalist elite. The globalist war on nation-states cannot succeed without collapsing the United States of America. The long-term strategic attack plan moves America incrementally from constitutional republic to socialism to globalism to feudalism. The tactical attack plan uses asymmetric psychological and informational warfare to destabilize Americans and drive society out of objective reality into the madness of subjective reality. America's children are the primary target of the globalist predators.

Hidden deep within the Gospel of Yuval Harari is the question "Do children belong to their parents or to the state?" Harari's position clearly favors the state, because the "intelligent design" he describes is an arm of the state body politic. To repeat what he said at the World Economic Forum's Annual Meeting in Davos on January 24, 2020:

> In the coming decades, AI and biotechnology will give us godlike abilities to reengineer life, and even to create completely new life-forms. After four billion years of organic life shaped by natural selection, we are about to enter a new era of inorganic life shaped by intelligent design.

Harari's "evolutionary" biology sees human beings as hackable animals whose future will be shaped by artificial intelligence, biotechnology, and the reengineering of life into new life-forms. The new life-forms Harari refers to are transhumanist beings totally controlled by the globalist elite— the "intelligent designers."

To "transcend" means to go beyond the range or limits of something. *Transhuman* means going beyond the current limits of being human and acquiring the powers and abilities of an enhanced human being in what the World Economic Forum calls "Humanity 2.0"—the stated goal of "intelligent design." Harari's narrative is grooming your children for Humanity 2.0.

To understand the insidious plan to move humanity from Humanity 1.0 to Humanity 2.0, it is necessary to examine the tactical shift away from *meritocracy*—the traditional metric of achievement foundational to American life, progress, and success.

In a society that eliminates meritocracy by shifting its metrics from achievement to feelings, whose feelings actually matter? What is the political purpose of the shift?

Competence is the mother of self-esteem. We know this is true by simply observing the delight of young children as they learn to dress themselves, feed themselves, or sound out their first words and realize they can read! Each achievement increases the child's competence and enhances his developing sense of self. Achievement makes little Johnny feel proud of himself and good about himself. Let's consider what incentivizes competence and achievement, and what doesn't. Let's also consider the *motivations* for either incentivizing or discouraging competence.

If you want to know the motive, look at the result. What made America great was having its cultural roots in meritocracy. Our society awarded achievement with upward mobility. It was called the American Dream, and America was the land where American dreams came true. In every sector of society, little Johnny was encouraged to become an independent, autonomous, rational adult, capable of living a life of ordered liberty in our constitutional republic. In other words, little Johnny was encouraged to grow up and perpetuate the American Dream.

Each of little Johnny's achievements was rewarded with praise. As he grew older, he earned grades in school that marked his achievements. Then he competed in sports with friends, and games with family. His grades were awarded with certificates of achievement or advanced placement. His sports achievements were awarded with trophies, and his wins in family games were rewarded with admiration.

The competitions all served to incentivize achievement. As an adult, Johnny competed for jobs and advancement. Winning and losing were part of everybody's private and public life. Meritocracy was society's infrastructure, rooted in achievement. Those who lost were encouraged to try harder, work harder, study more, and try again.

The association between individual achievement and self-esteem was unmistakable. Winning and losing were part of America's infrastructure that anyone and everyone could identify with. Individual and team play were instrumental in teaching the valuable lessons of cooperation and teamwork. This is no small thing. Whether in a classroom, on a baseball field, or in an orchestra hall, competition encourages both individual and team competence, cooperation, and achievement.

In the 1970s, ABC's *Wide World of Sports* announcer Jim McKay immortalized the words "the thrill of victory and the agony of defeat." His words described the drama caught on televised sports, but they also apply to the everyday lives of everyday people, describing how it *feels* to win and how it feels to lose. In the past, American culture supported a *can-do* spirit of encouragement, an ethos that insisted the agony of defeat need not triumph: anyone and everyone could experience the thrill of victory through hard work and practice. It was the same ethos that made America the greatest, freest, wealthiest nation on Earth.

But we are a world at war, whether people acknowledge it or not—a war between globalism and the nation-state. The globalist war on the nation-state is a multifaceted culture war, fought without bullets, that targets the world's children. In an unconscionable humanitarian hoax, the globalist social engineers advanced the deceitful narrative that little Johnny's feelings must always be protected.

To remind the reader, a humanitarian hoax is the deliberate and deceitful tactic of presenting a destructive policy as altruistic. The humanitarian huckster presents himself as a compassionate advocate when in fact he is the disguised enemy. America's humanitarian hucksters, under the guidance of the globalist social engineers, simply eliminated competition in order to "protect" little Johnny's feelings. No winning. No losing. No grades. No competition. No incentive for achievement. No competence. No self-esteem. No thrill of victory. Participation trophies do not incentivize achievement; they just blur the boundary between trying and doing.

Eliminating competition does not protect little Johnny from hurt feelings, or save big Johnny from the agony of defeat. Eliminating competition just disincentivizes his achievements and robs him of self-esteem. It produces a society of incompetent, dependent, childlike, fragile citizens who are very easy to manipulate and control—precisely the goal of a caretaker government.

We are born without the ability to survive on our own, entirely dependent upon our caretakers to teach us the necessary survival skills to live in society. Today, a battle is being fought in America over who are the rightful caretakers of our nation's children.

Historically, it was the parents who had the responsibility to protect their children and prepare them for life in our constitutional republic. Increasingly, the caretakers in America are no longer the parents, because the traditional family of stay-at-home Mom and working Dad is no longer the norm. Non-traditional families are reliant on daycare, preschools, babysitters, and after-school programs to provide child care and instruction for America's children.

Since 1979, when Jimmy Carter established the Department of Education, the government began taking an increasingly active role in children's education. Today, the National Education Association (NEA),[150] the largest professional-employee organization in America, with over 3 million members, is a major political player. Ninety-seven percent of its millions of dollars in donations from membership dues go to Democrat and liberal political candidates. The politicization of American education is funded by labor unions as well as federal and state funding. A stunning March 31, 2023, article by journalist and political analyst Daniel Greenfield, "Whose Children? Our Children,"[151] asserts:

> The shift from the single-income family to the two-income family with preschool encompassing children as young as 18 months and then to an ever more intensive chain of state educational institutions happened gradually enough that most parents thought it was their own idea. But what the Soviet Union and Communist China had failed to accomplish, happened in America.
>
> Children, from even before they could talk, were being raised either directly by the state or by the institutions that it closely regulated.

The unintended consequences of that, emotional fragility, a lack of healthy models for interpersonal relationships, and an obsession with 'snitching' on others that persists well into adulthood, were only the collateral damage....

Such children raised by the state become adults who want the state to go on raising them. When they're hungry, the state feeds them, when they're cold, the state shelters them and when they're unhappy, the state tells them whom to blame. When their relationships fall apart or when their feelings are hurt, they turn to the state to soothe them with a dose of revenge.

The infantilization of America is a leftist/globalist weapon of mass destruction. The American Dream has been replaced by regressive dreams for eternal childhood. The old Soviet Union and today's Communist China share the collectivist ideology that prioritizes the state above the individual, so what is good for the state is good for the individual. America has increasingly adopted communism's collectivist "ethic" and its self-destructive Marxist messaging, most evident in politicized education and medicine.

The battle over who is the rightful caretaker of America's children is a battle over ideologies. The Biden-Obama-Harris regime has eliminated meritocracy and stopped incentivizing competence, competition, achievement, success, independence, upward mobility, and the thrill of victory to obtain the American Dream. Instead, the regime incentivizes eternal childhood, incompetence, and lifelong dependence upon the government. The objective is to destabilize and destroy America's infrastructure of family, seen as a competing ideology, and collapse the country internally. Remember, *in order to "build back better," one must first destroy what exists.*

Substituting compliance for competence is collapsing America from within. So, in the end, Johnny's feelings don't matter at all. Little Johnny is the target of the duplicity, being groomed to become a permanently dependent, unthinking, unproductive drone for the globalist elite—a worker bee. In a world obsessed with feelings, the only people whose feelings actually matter are the globalist elite.

CHAPTER 35

Artificial Intelligence and America's Children

Globalism is a replacement ideology that seeks to reorder the world into one singular, planetary Unistate, ruled by the globalist elite. The globalist war on nation-states cannot succeed without collapsing the United States of America. The long-term strategic attack plan moves America incrementally from constitutional republic to socialism to globalism to feudalism. The tactical attack plan uses asymmetric psychological and informational warfare to destabilize Americans and drive society out of objective reality into the madness of subjective reality. America's children are the primary target of the globalist predators.

I t is time to take a look at what the globalists have in mind for little Johnny and Humanity 2.0. We begin with a history lesson provided by Dr. Michael Rectenwald in his April 14, 2023, article, "Hacking Humanity: Transhumanism":[152]

> The term transhumanism was coined by Julian Huxley, the brother of the novelist Aldous Huxley and the first director-general of the United Nations Educational, Scientific and Cultural Organization (UNESCO). In an essay entitled "Transhumanism," published in the book *New Bottles for New Wine* (1957), Huxley defined transhumanism as the self-transcendence of humanity:
>
> > *The human species can, if it wishes, transcend itself—not just sporadically, an individual here in one way, an individual there in another way, but in its entirety, as humanity. We need a name for this new belief. Perhaps transhumanism will serve: man remaining man, but transcending himself, by realizing new possibilities of and for his human nature.*[1]

---

[1]. Julian Huxley, "Transhumanism," *New Bottles for New Wine*, London: Readers Union, Chatto & Windus, 1957, page 17.

One question for transhumanism is indeed whether this transcendence will apply to the whole human species or rather for only a select part of it. But Huxley gave some indication of how this human self-transcendence might occur: humanity would become "managing director of the biggest business of all, the business of evolution...."[1] As the first epigraph to this Part makes clear, Julian Huxley was a proponent of eugenics. And he was the President of the British Eugenics Society.[2] It was in his introduction of UNESCO, as the director-general that he suggested that eugenics, after the Nazi regime had given it such a bad name, should be rescued from opprobrium, "so that much that now is unthinkable may at least become thinkable."[3] As John Klyczek has noted, "In the wake of vehement public backlash against the atrocities of the Nazi eugenic Holocaust, Huxley's eugenics proper was forced to go under-ground, repackaging itself in various crypto-eugenic disguises, one of which is 'transhumanism.'"[4]

Contemporary transhumanist enthusiasts, such as Simon Young, believe that humanity can take over where evolution has left us to create a new and improved species—either ourselves, or a successor to ourselves:

> *We stand at a turning point in human evolution. We have cracked the genetic code; translated the Book of Life. We will soon possess the ability to become designers of our own evolution.*[5]

Transhumanism is simply the latest variation of globalist elitism and supremacist ideology, including its eugenics program disguised as "progress"

---

[1]. Ibid., page 13.

[2]. "Past Presidents," Adelphi Genetics Forum, August 10, 2022, https://adelphigenetics. org/history/past-presidents/. The Adelphi Genetics Forum was originally named the British Eugenics Education Society and was founded in 1911. It changed its name to the British Eugenics Society in 1926 and changed its name again to the Galton Institute in 1989. In 2021, it changed its name yet again to the Adelphi Genetics Forum.

[3]. Julian Huxley, "UNESCO: Its Purpose and Its Philosophy," Unesdoc.unesco.org, 1946, https://unesdoc.unesco.org/ark:/48223/pf0000068197, page 21.

[4]. John Adam Klyczek, *School World Order: The Technocratic Globalization of Corporatized Education*, Trine Day, 2019, page 207.

[5]. Simon Young, *Designer Evolution: A Transhumanist Manifesto*, Prometheus, 2005, Kindle Edition, Location 273.

and "evolutionary biology." Rectenwald continues with references to Yuval Harari, the writer, historian, and children's book author discussed in Chapter 33:

> In a 2018 World Economic Forum statement, Harari spoke as the self-proclaimed prophet of a new transhumanist age, saying:

>> *We are probably among the last generations of Homo sapiens. Within a century or two, Earth will be dominated by entities that are more different from us, than we are different from Neanderthals or from chimpanzees. Because in the coming generations, we will learn how to engineer bodies and brains and minds. These will be the main products of the 21st century economy.*[1]

> No longer capable of mounting a challenge to the elite as in the nineteenth and twentieth centuries, and having no function, the feckless masses will have no recourse or purpose. Exploitation is one thing; irrelevance is quite another, says Harari. And thus, as Harari sees it, the remaining majority will be condemned to spend their time in the Metaverse, or worse. If they are lucky, they will collect universal basic income (UBI) and will best occupy themselves by taking drugs and playing video games. Of course, Harari exempts himself from this fate.

> As for the elite, according to Harari, their supposed superiority to the masses will soon become a matter of biotechnological fact, rather than merely an ideological pretension, as in the past. The elite will not only continue to control the lion's share of the world's material resources; they will also become godlike and enjoy effective remote control over their subordinates. Further, via biotechnological means, they will acquire eternal life on Earth, while the majority, formerly consoled by the fact that at least everybody dies, will now lose the great equalizer. As the supernatural is outmoded, or sacrificed on the altar of transhumanism, the majority will inevitably forfeit their belief in a spiritual afterlife. The theistic religions

---

[1]. World Economic Forum, "Will the Future Be Human? —Yuval Noah Harari," YouTube, World Economic Forum, January 25, 2018, https://www.youtube.com/watch?v=hL9uk4h-Kyg4.

that originated in the Middle East will disappear, to be replaced by new cyber-based religions originating in Silicon Valley. Spirituality, that is, will be nothing but the expression of reverence for newly created silicon gods, whether they be game characters, game designers, or the elites themselves.

The stunning hubris of the globalist elite is rivaled only by the danger of its collaboration with government. This collaboration between business and government is the military-industrial complex President Eisenhower warned the nation about in his 1961 Farewell Address:[153]

> A vital element in keeping the peace is our military establishment. Our arms must be mighty, ready for instant action, so that no potential aggressor may be tempted to risk his own destruction.

> Our military organization today bears little relation to that known by any of my predecessors in peace time, or indeed by the fighting men of World War II or Korea.

> Until the latest of our world conflicts, the United States had no armaments industry. American makers of plowshares could, with time and as required, make swords as well. But now we can no longer risk emergency improvisation of national defense; we have been compelled to create a permanent armaments industry of vast proportions.... This conjunction of an immense military establishment and a large arms industry is new in the American experience.... Yet we must not fail to comprehend its grave implications.... In the councils of government, we must guard against the acquisition of unwarranted influence, whether sought or unsought, by the military-industrial complex. The potential for the disastrous rise of misplaced power exists and will persist....

> Akin to, and largely responsible for the sweeping changes in our industrial-military posture, has been the technological revolution during recent decades.

> In this revolution, research has become central; it also becomes more formalized, complex, and costly. A steadily increasing share is conducted for, by, or at the direction of, the Federal government.

> Today, the solitary inventor, tinkering in his shop, has been over-

shadowed by task forces of scientists in laboratories and testing fields. In the same fashion, the free university, historically the fountainhead of free ideas and scientific discovery, has experienced a revolution in the conduct of research. Partly because of the huge costs involved, a government contract becomes virtually a substitute for intellectual curiosity. For every old blackboard there are now hundreds of new electronic computers.

The prospect of domination of the nation's scholars by Federal employment, project allocations, and the power of money is ever present and is gravely to be regarded.

Yet, in holding scientific research and discovery in respect, as we should, we must also be alert to the equal and opposite danger that public policy could itself become the captive of a scientific-techno-logical elite.

President Eisenhower predicted the globalist enemy within. His prescient warning is now 21st-century reality and the existential threat to our constitutional republic. Eisenhower's reference to research and the domination of the nation's scholars is today's politicized education industry that includes politicized law and medicine. From preschool to advanced degrees, ideological *experts* have indoctrinated Americans against America for seven decades. Indoctrinated graduates entered their chosen fields as "experts" who began indoctrinating the next generation, who then indoctrinated the next.

We are in the throes of an informational and psychological culture war. There are no bullets in this war. I often reflect on the saying "The pen is mightier than the sword." Its profound meaning lies in the fact that *thought precedes behavior.* If you can change people's thinking, you can change their behavior. It is the operating principle foundational to educational indoctrination and thought reform—the primary weapons of the information/psychological globalist War on America.

Weaponized education is bludgeoning society with anti-American collectivist ideology in every sector of life. The Marxification of education (Chapter 29) is enhanced with Artificial Intelligence (AI), the prize of the Fourth Industrial Revolution. AI is the medium *and* the message.

Educational reformer John Klyczek, referenced above in the Rectenwald article "Hacking Humanity," is the author of *School World Order: The Technocratic Globalization of Corporatized Education.*[154] Klyczek explores the hidden dangers of AI's robot companions in his June 13, 2023, informational video, "Moxie and the Great Reset: How Moxie the Robot Uses GPT AI to Data-Mine Your Kids' Socioemotional-Learning Algorithms."[155]

Moxie is the latest creation of California artificial intelligence company Embodied, which develops companion robots. Moxie, who looks like *Star Wars'* robotic droid R2-D2 but is able to communicate like the humanoid C-3PO, was originally designed as a robot companion for children with social and emotional deficits. Considered *assistive technology*, the premise was that the companion robot would help autistic and mentally retarded children with the anxiety they experience in human interactions.

Klyczek explains:

> Moxie is marketed as a "Helping Friend" that substitutes human caretakers and replaces them as robo-babysitters that monitor disabled children during parent-therapist conferences.… Of course, over time, just like transhuman ed-tech, robotic AI ed-tech will eventually creep more and more into mainstream classroom integration until it is employed to boost competence outcomes for students classified as healthy and able-bodied.

Klyczek discusses the capability of augmented robot systems (ARS) for children's storytelling activities. The ARS are able to measure children's levels of satisfaction, sensory immersion, and media recognition. This is significant because these areas correspond to the CASEL wheel, discussed in Chapter 20, that measures Social and Emotional Learning (SEL). Satisfaction corresponds to *interest*, sensory immersion to *engagement*, and media [robot] recognition to *empathy*.

Klyczek exposes several areas of serious concern to parents:

- Moxie will be expanded—used in general classroom for SEL goals
- Data mining of student bio-psychometrics
- Facial recognition for emotional reactions

- Replaces human interactions

- Using children to enhance manufacturer's own GPT-AI capacity

- Funded by WEF Partners Amazon, Intel, Sony, Toyota

- Deeply entrenched in global corporate technocracy network with over 60 overlapping memberships between WEF and Trilateral Commission, Club of Rome, United Nations, World Bank, and Bilderberg

- Represented at 2023 Bilderberg Meeting by Sam Altman, Microsoft, DeepMind (Google), Google

- Moxie stores much of its data in Google Cloud

- Moxie retains text files of whatever the child says before deleting the actual audio file

- Moxie retains data points of facial expressions before it deletes the actual photo

- Embodied retains access to all information even though it cannot link it to a specific user

The hidden goals of Moxie, the "Helping Friend," are data mining your children, enhancing the AI capabilities of companion robots for the manufacturer, and grooming your children for interaction with robots rather than humans, and for life in the 21st-century globalist Unistate. The information collected is a treasure trove of data for social engineering in the classroom, and another surreptitious method of separating children from their parents without parental knowledge.

The political parallels between teaching whole-word reading and using augmented robots for teaching are disturbing. Both began and were marketed as systems to help children with disabilities. Both were (or, in the case of Moxie, will be) subsequently applied to normal children, with catastrophic outcomes, for political gain. As discussed in Chapter 5, the detrimental effects on children's brains and their ability to actually read the written word in English were known as early as 1955, when Rudolph Flesch exposed the whole-word method as the culprit in his book, *Why Johnny Can't Read: and what you can do about it.*

The damage done by the American education industry in its insistence on teaching children to read using whole words is well documented. Yet whole-word methodology continues and has been expanded from whole-word reading to the Whole School, Whole Community, Whole Child[156] model (WSCC) by the Centers for Disease Control and Prevention (CDC).

The CDC website describes WSCC in predictably glowing terms. It is essential for parents to recognize the staggering Marxist dualism in WSCC and its 10 Components. Parents are presented with familiar, constructive terms that do not at all mean what parents understand them to mean. For example, "integration and collaboration between education leaders and health sectors" is actually the collaboration between teachers, counselors, psychologists, sexuality instructors, etc., to indoctrinate American children in radical leftist norms. The "student-centered" approach is actually the total immersion of the students in anti-American, anti-family, anti-Judeo-Christian propaganda without parental knowledge. From CDC's website:

Whole School, Whole Community, Whole Child (WSCC)

The education, public health, and school health sectors have each called for greater alignment that includes integration and collaboration between education leaders and health sectors to improve each child's cognitive, physical, social, and emotional development. Public health and education serve the same children, often in the same settings. The Whole School, Whole Community, Whole Child (WSCC) model focuses on the child to align the common goals of both sectors to put into action a whole child approach to education.

What is the WSCC model?

The Whole School, Whole Community, Whole Child, or WSCC model, is CDC's framework for addressing health in schools. The WSCC model is student-centered and emphasizes the role of the community in supporting the school, the connections between health and academic achievement and the importance of evidence-based school policies and practices. The WSCC model has 10 Components:

1. Physical education and physical activity.

2. Nutrition environment and services.

3. Health education.

4. Social and emotional climate.

5. Physical environment.

6. Health services.

7. Counseling, psychological and social services.

8. Employee wellness.

9. Community involvement.

10. Family engagement.

The CDC prides itself on the collaboration between government and non-governmental organizations (NGOs) to finance its WSCC initiatives:

Funded Non-Governmental Organizations for Healthy Schools

Through the National Collaboration to Promote Health, Wellness, and Academic Success of School-Age Children, CDC Healthy Schools funds five national non-governmental organizations (NGOs) to complement and strengthen the work of State Public Health Actions grantees. These NGOs support the 1305 grantees and their organization's constituents to promote and implement proven policies, practices, and programs in at least one of the following school health priority areas:

Priority Area 1—Physical Education and Physical Activity in Schools
Priority Area 2—School Nutrition Environment and Services
Priority Area 3—Out of School Time Healthy Eating and Physical Activity
Priority Area 4—School Health Services for Managing Chronic Conditions

The NGOs that support the following priority areas are:

- Alliance for a Healthier Generation

- Boys and Girls Club of America

- National Association of School Nurses

- National Network of Public Health Institutes

- SHAPE America

CDC Healthy Schools also funds the National Association of Chronic Disease Directors (NACDD) to provide technical assistance and professional development activities that will build the capacity of state health departments. This will equip school health and education leaders with greater knowledge, skills, and abilities to implement proven strategies that create healthier environments for students. Initiatives such as these are essential to help leaders from across the country access practical tools and resources to promote the health [including mental health] of their student population.

SHAPE America (SHAPE is an acronym for the Society of Health and Physical Educators) is a particularly notable NGO. Its website, shapeamerica. org,[157] proudly features its alignment with National Sex Education Standards:[158]

National Sex Education Standards

SHAPE America is proud to have worked with the Future of Sex Education (FoSE) and the Sexuality Information and Education Council of the United States (SIECUS) as a contributor and reviewer in the development of the National Sex Education Standards: Core Content and Skills, K–12 (Second Edition). SHAPE America is also proud to officially endorse the final document.

These latest standards reflect advancement in research regarding sexual orientation, gender identity, social, racial and reproductive justice, and the long-term consequences of stigma and discrimination. Other additions include: advances in medical technology, the emergence of digital technologies and the growing impact of social and sexually explicit media on relationships.

Readers will remember that SIECUS is an ideological and political instrument for social change. SIECUS proudly describes its goals in the acknowledgments section of the National Sex Education Standards, second edition:

Through policy, advocacy, education, and strategic communications efforts, SIECUS advances sex education as a vehicle for social change—working toward a world where all people can access and enjoy their own sexual and reproductive freedom.

Parents need to understand the deceptive way words are being used. The definition of physical health includes sexual health, and the definition of sexual health is *inclusive*. "Inclusive" is defined by *diversity, equity, and inclusion* (DEI) standards, which means sexual health includes presenting transgenderism and every iteration of non-binary gender identification as normal variations on a theme of non-binary sexuality. Male/female heterosexuality is no longer the accepted norm; every conceivable form of sexual behavior, including pedophilia, is presented as a normal variation of inclusive sexual behavior.

There are no restrictions on sexual behavior or gender identity in a society that has been driven into subjective reality, where feelings rather than facts determine social policy. The entire American education industry is collaborating in the usurpation of parental authority by adopting CDC guidelines that are themselves aligned with the United Nations' internationalized curricula for education, including sex education.

Child psychiatrist Dr. Miriam Grossman (Chapter 31) is an unapologetic and outspoken advocate for children's mental health. She has written an essential book to help parents understand the horrific ideological collaboration between our weaponized education and judicial systems, particularly Child Protective Services (CPS). Together, they have redefined "mental health" in political terms, and are participating in a joint effort to replace parental authority with government-approved radical gender ideology.

CPS considers the homes of parents whose conservative views insist on the scientific facts of biology to be abusive and unsafe environments for children. CPS is empowered by the state to remove the children from the home and *rehome* them. This is an Orwellian reality, and extremely dangerous for the children, for their parents, and for America. Biological sex, gender, and sexual behavior have been weaponized in America by the enemies of freedom. The *cultural terrorism* that Hungarian Marxist George Lukács unsuccessfully attempted in Bolshevik Hungary in 1918 is effectively collapsing America from within in 2024.

Dr. Grossman's book, *Lost in Trans Nation: A Child Psychiatrist's Guide Out of the Madness*,[159] is an essential tool for parents whose children remain in American schools, both public and private. The book begins with a Dedication:

> This book is dedicated to the parents of kids with Rapid-Onset Gender Dysphoria and to the groups who support them.
>
> I spoke with you from your cars, basements, and bathrooms. You huddled and whispered behind closed doors, as if seeking my help was criminal behavior. You're not criminals, you are heroes. The criminals are the therapists, teachers, school counselors, and sex educators who indoctrinate your children with falsehoods, and the doctors who then disfigure and sterilize them. They are guilty of crimes. Their day will come. (p. ix)

Before the Introduction, Dr. Grossman includes A Note on Language:

> We face a crusade, a juggernaut, that seeks to demolish male and female, and its success hinges on the control of language. Under those circumstances, to call a man "she" is not a kindness, it's a concession—to a scheme to control our beliefs and advance an agenda, one pronoun at a time.
>
> In this book, I emphasize that male and female, after being established at conception, are permanent. I urge parents to be honest and consistent with their children, and to at all times stay grounded in biological reality. I have always done that in my office, and I'm not going to stop now. (p. xxv)

Dr. Grossman continues:

> For me this is a black-and-white issue. Most things in life are nuanced, but this is not one of them. This is—and here's a word you don't expect to hear from a doctor—evil. It's evil to indoctrinate children and young adults with falsehoods and to drive a wedge between them and their loving parents. It's evil to encourage them on a path that leads to harm. And it's evil to describe it all as a journey to authenticity, and to entice children with glitter and rainbows....

The trans issue is not a debate with reasonable and moral people on both sides, it's a war. It's a destructive, cult-like crusade that targets your children 24/7; there's hardly a place that's free from indoctrination, slogans, flags, and emojis. You must gird yourselves with knowledge, confidence, and support and oppose the onslaught as much as possible.…

Starting with new names and pronouns and ending too often in the operating rooms, the trans journey is an assembly line. One step leads to another, and it's difficult to get off, so your goal is to prevent your child from ever climbing on.… (p. xxx)

I regret to inform you that with this matter, the sources you've always trusted—your child's school, pediatrician, and therapist—will likely provide ideologically driven misinformation. They will direct you and your child down a perilous path.…

I'll explain that transgender ideology is a system of beliefs, like a religion. It has a unique language and [10] Articles of Faith. While the language and beliefs are bizarre, they are taught as sacred facts. The core belief—that biology can and should be denied—is a repudiation of reality.… (p. xxxi)

I will explain how the American Psychiatric Association (APA) reclassified gender disorders as normal variations of human expression—another dangerous idea. (p. xxxiii)

Articles of Faith

Behold GENDER IDENTITY; it liberated you from oppression, from the harsh constraints of biology.

GENDER IDENTITY is sacred; thou shalt not question it; thou shalt not turn away from it to hard science, for GENDER IDENTITY is jealous and cannot tolerate the scientific method.

Remember GENDER IDENTITY, to keep it holy. Behold, it is both fixed and fluid; healthy and needing drugs and surgeries; do not admit contradictions.

Thou shalt consider "male" and "female" arbitrary assign-

ments; thou shalt deny their establishment at conception.

Thou shalt affirm all gender identities with all your heart and all your soul, so that you will be an ally and keep your livelihood.

Do not misgender [use a pronoun other than the one chosen by the adherent].

Do not deadname [use the adherent's birth name].

Thou shalt not explore anxiety, ADHD, trauma, or autism; thou shalt always invoke the minority stress model [the hypothesis that sexual minority health disparities are produced by the social stress faced by sexual minority populations due to their stigmatized status].

Thou shalt honor the self-diagnosis and judgment of minors and young adults. Thou shalt not recognize their emotional and cognitive immaturity.

Gatekeeping is an abomination. Thou shalt therefore scorn psychotherapy, and place your trust in breast binding, penis-and-testicle-tucking, pills, patches, syringes, scalpels, implants, and prosthetics. (p. xxxx)

But of all the lies and dangerous ideas promoted, Dr. Grossman says the most pernicious one is that *gender affirmation is the only safe and ethical treatment! If you don't support your child, he's at high risk of suicide.*

Dr. Grossman explains that gender dysphoria (GD) is a symptom, and symptoms can be caused by a variety of conditions. Further, gender dysphoria is complex and is different at different ages of onset. She distinguishes three types of GD: adult-onset, early-onset in young children, and late- or adolescent-onset in teens and young adults. The resolution of gender dysphoria is called desistance. In 1994, the *Diagnostic and Statistical Manual of Mental Disorders*, 4th Edition, stated that "only a very small number of children with gender identity disorder [as it was called then] will continue to have symptoms…in later adolescence or adulthood."

In other words, it is a stage of development that usually corrects itself without intervention. Before 2012, the onset of gender identity disorder was practically unheard of. In 2018, Dr. Lisa Littman, a Brown University physician, researcher, and academic, noticed an unusual trend in her small town. "Teens from the same friend group were announcing transgender identities on social media, one after another, on a scale that greatly exceeded expected numbers." (*Lost in Trans Nation*, p. 40)

Dr. Littman began investigating and found that adolescents and young adults were suddenly experiencing gender dysphoria for the first time. She coined the term Rapid Onset Gender Dysphoria (ROGD) to describe the new phenomenon. Dr. Littman theorized that "these kids may have rapidly adopted a transgender identity as a 'maladaptive coping mechanism to avoid feeling strong or negative emotions.'" (*Lost in Trans Nation*, p. 41)

Dr. Littman was worried that the teens were not being screened for preexisting and current mental health issues. Instead, they were being fast-tracked for gender affirmation and transition. Dr. Littman wrote about "cluster outbreaks" and explained them as "social contagion." She discussed the limitations of her research, and strongly recommended further study and the careful evaluation of distressed teenagers before the use of treatments that have permanent effects such as cross-sex hormones and surgery.

Dr. Littman went further and confronted the gender establishment narrative, saying that social and medical affirmation may cause "an iatrogenic persistence of gender dysphoria in individuals who would have had their gender dysphoria resolve on its own." (*Lost in Trans Nation*, p. 46) Iatrogenic is any harm caused by a medical intervention.

The medical community came out vehemently against Dr. Lisa Littman, in the same way it pilloried British gastroenterologist Dr. Andrew Wakefield when he questioned the safety of the multi-dose measles, mumps, and rubella (MMR) vaccine and its possible connection to autism in children. Instead of appropriately investigating Dr. Littman's concerns, the medical and gender establishment attacked her and presented gender-affirming care as *settled science*—a particularly dangerous lie.

Dr. Miriam Grossman courageously exposes the institutional capture of American medicine by radical Marxist gender ideology. She denounces its resultant gender-affirming care as political medicine, which is endangering an entire generation of children with ideological medicine and ideological indoctrination in school.

Lost in Trans Nation: A Child Psychiatrist's Guide Out of the Madness is an extraordinary examination of the transgender movement, its psychosocial dynamics, and its political purpose. The book concludes with helpful appendices of practical information and important suggestions for parents dealing with schools, CPS, therapists, and the Internet.

Dr. Grossman's message is heroic and crystal clear: Parents must arm themselves with accurate information in order to protect their precious children from a "perilous social movement that erases 'male' and 'female' and aims to revolutionize what it means to be human."

CHAPTER 36

"When They Say 'We're Coming for Your Children,' Believe Them"

Globalism is a replacement ideology that seeks to reorder the world into one singular, planetary Unistate, ruled by the globalist elite. The globalist war on nation-states cannot succeed without collapsing the United States of America. The long-term strategic attack plan moves America incrementally from constitutional republic to socialism to globalism to feudalism. The tactical attack plan uses asymmetric psychological and informational warfare to destabilize Americans and drive society out of objective reality into the madness of subjective reality. America's children are the primary target of the globalist predators.

C anadian columnist Barbara Kay published an exceptional article, "When They Say 'We're Coming for Your Children,' Believe Them,"[160] in *The Epoch Times* on July 10, 2023. Kay provides an outstanding analysis of Marxist educational indoctrination in Canada, its parallels in the United States, and the awakening of the public to its catastrophic consequences. It is a thoughtful article that begins with acknowledging Canadians as an extremely tolerant people who have found the limit of their tolerance:

> The only domain in which we are witnessing a groundswell of citizen resistance is K–12 pedagogy, where Queer Theory—a gendered form of Marxism that rejects the "normal" in sexuality, including the notion of childhood "innocence"—is systematically imposed on vulnerable minds, with or without parental consent. Drag Queen Story Hour (DQSH) has become the cynosure of parental disquiet.
>
> A recent video clip of naked Pride marchers chanting "We're here, we're queer, we're coming for your children" went viral. LGBTQ

spin doctors claimed the words were "taken out of context." Which begs the question of why male drag queens no longer stay in their lane of adult entertainment. What acceptable "context" encourages teaching children to "twerk" ("you just move your bum up and down like that")—an action simulating sexual intercourse?

A majority of Canadians feel such organized sexualized messaging to young children is a bridge too far. They no longer believe DQSH is "family-friendly" or pure "entertainment." Some are calling it out for what it is: "grooming," building children's trust in men with an agenda that goes far beyond teaching about "diversity." They are saying so in protests against such events as a four-day drag theatre camp in B.C.

In a news report, a progressive journalist deplored this surge of opposition, in particular some protesters' use of the word "groomer" as a "homophobic" trope, which, the journalist writes, "advocates say was used to vilify the LGBTQ2+ community in the 1970s and 1980s." It is true, that a vocal subset of gays was vilified in the 1970s and 1980s. A little research, though, would have uncovered information that might have tempered the journalist's indignation.

In 1969 the Paedophile Information Exchange (PIE), a special interest group that advocated for abrogation of the age of sexual consent, became the first LGBT organization in Scotland, branding gay rights activism and child abuse lobbying as closely entwined goals there. From 1974 to 1984, PIE openly campaigned throughout the United Kingdom to normalize pedophilia as a legally and culturally acceptable practice. Such were the sexually freewheeling times, they were taken seriously at elite levels, even winning support from then Labour Health Minister Patricia Hewitt for such policies as reducing the age of consent to 10, and the decriminalization of incest. PIE activists were tactically sophisticated in their networking, branding pedophiles as an oppressed sexual minority, just like gays and lesbians.

Here, PIE's alter ego is the North American Man/Boy Love Association (NAMBLA), still nominally active, although radically diminished in numbers. Still, as late as 2005, one lawyer dubbed it "a trade school for pedophiles." In the '70s, NAMBLA attracted support from prominent gays, such as beat poet Allen Ginsberg, and was affiliated with the International Lesbian and Gay Association until 1994. Finally, the Human Rights Campaign, which would become the biggest LGBT advocacy group in the United States, declared, "NAMBLA is not a gay organization...and we thoroughly reject their efforts to insinuate that pedophilia is an issue related to gay and lesbian civil rights."

Nevertheless, NAMBLA's website states that, true to its philosophy, its goal remains "to end the extreme oppression of men and boys in mutually consensual relationships" by "educating the general public on the benevolent nature of man/boy love" through "cooperation with lesbian, gay, feminist, and other liberation movements." The general public should not be expected to parse the distinction between "not a gay organization" and "cooperating with lesbian, gay... movements." When the only people publicly promoting pedophilia self-identify as gay, the fact that they are a subset of LGB, and not the norm, might be lost on ordinary people.

A 1983 interview of two PIE representatives on Newsnight offers an insight into the creepiness of their strategy. They didn't say they were campaigning for the right of 50-year-old men to have sex with seven-year-olds. They talked about children's right to sexual liberation. Challenged to admit that sex is "shocking" to a child, one of the men says, "Not if they're properly educated...."

"Properly educated." Today, under the rubric of Queer Theory—which does not recognize any boundaries of traditional sexual morality, decency, or age-appropriateness—that would be exposure of children, against the wishes of many parents, but with the blessing of pedagogical elites, to what used to be known as porn, such as the graphic memoir, "Gender Queer."

And of course, defended as "education" about gender diversity and inclusion, children's continual interaction with drag queens. Amongst the drag queens touring schools and libraries, a small but repulsive roster of sex offenders has been exposed. Alarm bells are ringing, and not just for conservatives. Rational gays and lesbians—

LGB—feel tainted by the obsession with children inherent to Queer Theory. It's noteworthy that no queer theorist of influence has ever condemned the acting out of pedophilic desire. Thus, the laudable (but alas, so far marginal) organization "Gays Against Groomers" was formed to counter the damage Queer Theory is inflicting on the LGB's hard-earned brand of unthreatening normalcy.

DQSH's agenda is laid out in a January 2021 paper published in the journal *Curriculum Inquiry*, titled "Drag pedagogy: The playful practice of queer imagination in early childhood," co-authored by media studies doctoral candidate and drag queen Lil Miss Hot Mess (of "swish swish swish" fame) and trans-identified queer theorist Harper Keenan.

The authors acknowledge that DQSH is meant not only as a model for learning "about queer lives," but also "how to live queerly." They write, "The future is queerness's domain.... The here and now is a prison house." (Translation: The traditional family home is a prison for children.) And, notably, "It may be that DQSH is 'family friendly,' in the sense that it is accessible and inviting to families with children, but it is less a sanitizing force than it is a preparatory introduction to alternate modes of kinship." (Translation: We are your children's new family.)

For readers who seek a fully informed, in-depth unpacking of this frank and revelatory journal article, I recommend a seminar with indispensable cultural Marxism expert James Lindsay via his New Discourses podcast episode, "Groomer School 4: Drag Queen Story Hour."

Forget about "context." When they say "we're coming for your children," believe them.

Barbara Kay's incisive article is a warning, to parents in Canada and the United States, of the clear and present danger that the UN's Comprehensive Sexuality Education poses to their children. (CSE is introduced in Chapter 17 and discussed at length in Chapters 19 and 20.) In Canada, as in the United States, denial is not a survival strategy. It is essential that parents understand how their compassion and tolerance are being exploited, and the victims are their vulnerable children.

Child psychiatrist Dr. Miriam Grossman's warning to American parents in Chapter 35 is also a warning to Canadian parents. The future the globalist predators envision for your children is planetary in scope. It requires the internationalization of both radical ideological goals and educational indoctrination. Both are provided by United Nations Agenda 2030 and its participating organizations, global policies, and initiatives worldwide.

Globalist social engineers are using radical gender ideology, politicized medicine, and associated agencies to groom children and intimidate parents. In America, Dr. Grossman identifies the Department of Education, American School Counselors Association, National Education Association, National Association of Social Workers, National Association of School Psychologists, and the National Association of Secondary School Principals as professional organizations that refuse to disclose a child's gender identity to parents. Further, Dr. Grossman names GLSEN, formerly the Gay, Lesbian & Straight Education Network, as the primary source of America's educational system capture:

> If there is a single organization responsible for transforming your child's teacher, principal, and guidance counselor into gender warriors, and filling your child's classroom with trans symbols, books, and flags, it's GLSEN.

> In their own words, GLSEN "strives to dismantle all identity-based oppressions in K–12 public and private schools.… GLSEN provides teacher training, lesson plans, school policy guides, "inclusive" curriculum, and Gender and Sexuality Alliance (GSA) clubs in schools nationwide. They collaborate with associations that accredit private and public schools and maintain a public policy office in Washington.

> A priority is recruiting students. This is done through GSA clubs and teacher indoctrination, of course, but also through school programs—always clothed in the language of respect, civil rights, and freedom.… (Miriam Grossman, *Lost in Trans Nation: A Child Psychiatrist's Guide Out of the Madness*, pp. 124–125)

Here's how GLSEN instructs your child's school to keep you in the dark:

> Some transgender and nonbinary students may not yet be out to their parents or guardians.... It is essential to have open communication and plans established with the student to go over potential circumstances. For instance, mail may be sent home with a student's prior and/or legal name, which may not be their affirmed name. If a student is not yet out to their parent(s)/guardian(s), using their prior name in correspondence may be the desirable course of action, although they use a different name amongst peers and educators in school. Educators and staff should work closely with the student to determine what changes are necessary, and where, to ensure their safety and well-being. (p. 126)

Make no mistake: ideological "educators" are aligning themselves with your child, against you! It is essential for parents to realize that the institutions they always trusted are no longer trustworthy. Dr. Grossman makes painfully clear the fact that schools, guidance counselors, doctors including pediatricians, even churches and synagogues, have embraced gender ideology and cannot be trusted.

Dr. Grossman's unequivocal opinion is that *no one is born in the wrong body*. Gender dysphoria is an emotional and psychological issue that cannot be remedied with hormone blockers and surgeries. As a child psychiatrist, she unapologetically identifies mental health as being in touch with objective reality, the world of facts, and mental illness as being out of touch with objective reality. Dangerous ideas are those that reverse mental health standards and definitions of mental health. Dangerous ideas replace the biological *facts* in objective reality with the *feelings* that govern subjective reality.

Early in her book, under the heading "Puberty Is Not a Disorder," Dr. Grossman states unambiguously:

> Puberty is not only about growing breasts or developing facial hair. It impacts nearly all organs and systems of the body. It's a complex biological process that we are far from understanding.
>
> Too many of my colleagues have forgotten that the body has its own wisdom. (p. 70)

In 2015 Dr. Grossman joined pediatricians Den Trumbull and Michelle Cretella, leaders of the American College of Pediatricians (ACP)—not the captured American Academy of Pediatrics (AAP)—and wrote a letter to the journal *Pediatrics*:

> We submit that children who dread the development of secondary sex characteristics are emotionally troubled.... In fact, puberty brings relief for the vast majority of children receiving therapy for GID (gender identity disorder) because hormone surges propel the development of their brains as well as their bodies and they come to identify with their biological sex. (p. 70)

Dr. Michelle Cretella was cited in my previous book *The Collapsing American Family: From Bonding to Bondage*, Chapter 11 (pp. 66–67). I repeat here a section quoted from her 2017 interview with John Ritchie, "Dr. Cretella on Transgenderism: A Mental Illness Is Not a Civil Right":[161]

> Essentially, transgender ideology holds that people can be born into the wrong body: It's simply not true. We can demonstrate this by looking at twin studies. No one is born in the wrong body. So, to take that lie and essentially indoctrinate all of our children from preschool forward with that lie, we are destroying their ability for reality-testing.
>
> This is cognitive and psychological abuse. I want to say just a little more about that. The reason it destroys reality-testing is because most children at age three (preschool age) can correctly identify themselves by saying "I am a boy" or "I am a girl" and most children will not understand that a boy grows into a man and stays a man and that a girl grows into a woman and stays a woman. So, when many seven-year-olds see a man get into a dress and put on makeup, they may believe that he just became a woman. The other side is not being honest and not acknowledging that....
>
> So transgender ideology—yes, it's child abuse because we are gaslighting our children. And now that they're thoroughly confused, they will think that they really are the opposite sex and will be sent down a medical pathway. As they approach puberty, they will be put on puberty blockers and then on cross-sex hormones. That combination will permanently sterilize most, if not all, of those children

and also puts them at risk for heart disease, diabetes, and various cancers. If girls have been on testosterone, which is their sex change hormone, for a full year, by age 16 they can get a double mastectomy. So, gaslighting, pubertal castration and surgical mutilation: It's institutionalized child abuse....

Dr. Grossman explains to parents:

Puberty isn't an illness. We cannot presume that interfering with a complex biological process such as puberty, turning it on and off synthetically, can be accomplished without paying a price. Nowhere could the price be higher than with the brain....

It's like *Extreme Makeover: Teen Brain Edition.* Before puberty, your son has the brain of a child. It will take about fifteen years, well into his third decade of life, to develop the brain of an adult. The hormones of puberty, estrogen and testosterone, drive puberty's explosive growth and restructuring of the brain. Puberty blockers interrupt a natural process and could have cognitive and emotional consequences.

Consider the ability to rationally weigh actions, predict results, and balance pros and cons. The prefrontal cortex is the area of the brain that governs these executive functions. Consider it the CEO of the brain. You don't need a PhD in neurobiology to know the executive functioning of teens isn't the greatest. They easily forget their actions have consequences, and just how damaging those consequences might be.

The prefrontal cortex is the last area of the brain to fully mature. If it is the thinking and planning part of the brain, the amygdala is the feeling part. It too is transformed by puberty.

Over the years, the prefrontal cortex and amygdala develop and integrate. Puberty puts these systems into balance, helping young adults regulate their emotions, control impulsivity, and make better decisions....

The sole animal study we have suggests puberty blockers may threaten brain maturation and cognitive maturity. Not only that, but puberty blockers also potentially trap kids in a permanent gender-identity crisis. (*Lost in Trans Nation*, pp. 70–71)

So, puberty blockers interrupt a natural process and can have cognitive and emotional consequences, including a permanent gender-identity crisis. Consider this from a political point of view. Puberty blockers have the potential to weaponize adolescents and young adults by arresting their emotional and cognitive development, freezing them in a permanent state of immaturity. Collectivism's promise of eternal dependence is eternal damnation in an underdeveloped adolescent mind that is easily exploited.

The medical pathway is a monstrous deceit designed to achieve ideological compliance through emotional regression. Unlike the political medicine of COVID-19, which achieved ideological compliance through emotional regression using its fear campaign, the politics of gender medicine achieves its objective through indoctrination, drugs, arrested emotional development, surgeries, and family rupture.

The medical pathway not only destroys your child's mind and body, it is designed to shatter your family bonds as well. The gender indoctrination pits child against parent, and offers the troubled child *affirmation* and *affirming care* from trusted teachers, counselors, and physicians. The child withdraws from the parents and finds comfort in his new *family of choice* at school and online.

The catastrophic effects on families are intentional, strategic, and part of the tactical War on America. The enemy understands that the Judeo-Christian nuclear family is the infrastructure supporting American life. Non-woke parents are considered ideological enemies of the state, obstacles who must be either removed or neutralized.

Dr. Grossman is horrified that her profession has been captured by radical gender ideology, and dismayed that both the American Psychiatric Association (APA) and American Academy of Pediatricians (AAP) have embraced the radical gender dogma that puberty blockers and gender affirmation are, as she describes their stance *"the only safe and ethical treatment! If you don't support your child, he's at high risk of suicide."* She considers it criminal malpractice for pediatricians to ignore the mediating effects of puberty, and for surgeons to act upon children's immature feelings with mutilating surgeries.

American medicine and American education no longer serve the interests of the United States of America or Americans. They are pawns of the globalist administrative state, captured institutions advancing anti-American Marxist ideology disguised as *diversity, equity, and inclusion* (DEI). The globalist social engineers are using DEI to collapse America from within so they can Build Back Better and impose globalism's New World Order.

The infrastructure for worldwide destruction of children's innocence is already in place within the United Nations organization of international institutions. Barbara Kay's August 12, 2023, article, "Alfred Kinsey: The Father of Modern Deviancy,"[162] is a far more detailed exploration of the sexualization of children, not confined to queer theory, but encompassing it. Kay refers to Dr. Judith Reisman's extensive research that focuses on Alfred Kinsey as the deviant and criminal source of the "children are sexual from birth" doctrine. (See Chapter 17 for an in-depth discussion of Kinsey's work.) Kinsey's doctrine is the foundation of today's radicalized sexual ideology seeking to "liberate" children from the taboo of adult-child sex. What has been traditionally considered criminal sexual contact with children is now being advanced as "liberation" and "sexual rights" of the child! Alfred Kinsey's deviance was a valuable asset in globalism's war on humanity.

In her novel *Atlas Shrugged*, author Ayn Rand famously wrote, "Show me what a man finds sexually attractive and I will tell you his entire philosophy of life." This extraordinary quotation is the key to understanding that power and control constitute the core dynamic of adult-child sexual relations. Men who find children sexually attractive are driven by their psychological need for power and control that is assured in the asymmetric power balance in sex with children.

When they say "We're coming for your children," believe them! The globalist social engineers are using pedophilia as a tactical weapon for achieving totalitarian control of society. Pedophilia is the nuclear weapon of mass psychological destruction supported and protected by the globalist leadership for decades. Pedophilia is an essential element of their efforts to groom today's children for tomorrow's planetary Unistate.

CHAPTER 37

Euphemisms, Propaganda, and "Losing Reality Bit by Bit"

Globalism is a replacement ideology that seeks to reorder the world into one singular, planetary Unistate, ruled by the globalist elite. The globalist war on nation-states cannot succeed without collapsing the United States of America. The long-term strategic attack plan moves America incrementally from constitutional republic to socialism to globalism to feudalism. The tactical attack plan uses asymmetric psychological and informational warfare to destabilize Americans and drive society out of objective reality into the madness of subjective reality. America's children are the primary target of the globalist predators.

American-Canadian psychologist Dr. Kenneth Zucker, founder of Toronto's Child Youth and Family Gender Identity Clinic (GIC), is an internationally acknowledged expert on children and adolescents with gender dysphoria. His cautious "watchful waiting" approach respected the natural maturation process in which the vast majority of gender dysphoria resolves itself without medical intervention. In 2015, Toronto's Centre for Addiction and Mental Health, the hospital where Dr. Zucker's clinic was located, accused him of practicing conversion therapy, and of shaming and traumatizing patients. Dr. Zucker, who was psychologist-in-chief at the time, was fired and the hospital closed the clinic. He was eventually exonerated and awarded damages in a lawsuit against the hospital, but radical gender ideology had won the battle.

Dr. Miriam Grossman writes about Dr. Zucker's concerns about "iatrogenic persistence," the result of medical intervention discussed in Chapter 35:

> Dr. Zucker calls social transition a dangerous psychosocial intervention "with the likely consequence of subsequent (lifelong) biomedical treatments... (gender-affirming hormonal treatment and sur-

gery)." He argues it's an intervention often conducted by schools and other institutions unqualified to implement such a course of treatment.

In 2014, even the American Psychological Association still warned that "Premature labeling of gender identity should be avoided" and "early social transition...should be approached with caution to avoid foreclosing this stage of (trans)gender identity development." (*Lost in Trans Nation: A Child Psychiatrist's Guide Out of the Madness*,[163] p. 121)

Before sex assignment surgery takes place, there is a process known as *social transition*, in which the student adopts a new gender identity, a new name, pronouns, often new clothing, hair style, and use of opposite-sex facilities such as bathrooms and locker rooms. During this period of social transition, parents, friends, and teachers are supposed to endorse the student's belief that he or she is in the wrong body. Dr. Grossman reminds parents that it is their responsibility to support *objective reality*, and advises parents that supporting a delusion is not a loving gesture, especially when it leads to harm:

> "Affirmation" has a positive connotation, and when ideologues chose that word, it was a strategic move. Affirming your child seems kind and loving. Instead of distressed, she's comfortable. She's happy. But it's not kind or loving to validate an untruth.

> Adults have a responsibility to represent reality. The reality is your daughter's sex was established at conception....

> If you validate your son's girl identity, you agree that his body is wrong, and should be rejected. You confirm the disconnect between his mind and his physical reality. You agree he knows best who he is, and what he needs...think of the impact on your son. He feels he's a girl, and you agree! ... He's never felt so empowered. You've turbo-charged his self-esteem. Of course, it feels good, at least temporarily.

> Consider also the possibility that your son's social affirmation may affect the wiring of his brain. You heard me right. Neuroplasticity is the well-established phenomenon in which thinking, behavior, and

experience alter brain microstructure. Each time your son hears his new name and pronouns it's a learning experience that creates a memory. We all know repetition is key to learning. We know as well that the brain is constantly rewiring—its structure is changing—in response to life's experiences. (*Lost in Trans Nation*, pp. 119–120)

Dr. Grossman also warns parents about euphemisms, explaining the objective reality that "top surgery" is bilateral mastectomy, or breast amputation. In 2023, while she was writing her book, there were 45,375 girls seeking donations on GoFundMe to pay for what gender surgeons euphemistically call a "masculinized chest." She points out the staggering hypocrisy:

> Mind you, these are the same people who insist that five-year-olds use anatomically accurate terms, not childish nicknames, for their genitals. They soberly instruct us to teach the words "scrotum" and "vulva" to kindergarteners. But the imprecise, trivial-sounding "top surgery"—that language is fine. (*Lost in Trans Nation*, p. 157)

Dr. Grossman is appalled by the explosion of "gender-affirming" surgeries on children:

> And don't tell me these operations are only done on adults. In a study of 68 patients who underwent the procedure at Children's Hospital Los Angeles, almost half were girls between thirteen and seventeen, and that was way back in 2016. A letter from plastic surgeons at Vanderbilt University School of Medicine published in the journal *JAMA Pediatrics* reported between 2016 and 2019, the annual number of "gender-affirming chest surgeries" increased by 389 percent, likely a significant underestimate, because it included only surgeries performed in hospitals. Many of these procedures take place outside of hospitals in surgery centers owned by plastic surgeons. The letter documented that 77 percent of patients used private insurance or were self-pay, and the average cost was $30,000. (*Lost in Trans Nation*, p. 158)

This brings the discussion to insurance coverage. The Affordable Care Act (Obamacare) bars plans offered on Healthcare.gov from discrimination based on gender, which has been interpreted to include transgenderism, and this has led to broad coverage of gender surgery and an explosion in transgender surgeries.

A March 2018 article published in *Modern Medicine*, "Employee health insurance, Obamacare make sex change a new reality for 1.4 million Americans,"[164] reports:

> Johns Hopkins' data shows that 61 percent of in-hospital surgical procedures for gender affirmation were covered by insurance between 2012 and 2014, compared with just 35 percent from 2006 to 2011. Tech companies like Amazon, Apple and IBM all cover the surgery for their employees.

Now, compare Johns Hopkins' data with the *GlobeNewswire* report in March 2020, "Sex Reassignment Surgery Market to hit USD 1.5 Bn by 2026: Global Market Insights, Inc."[165] The subtitle reads "U.S. sex reassignment surgery demand is estimated to expand at 24.5% CAGR (compound annual growth rate) during 2020 to 2026 owing to the continuously growing gender reassignment surgeries in the country."

Clearly, sex reassignment surgery is big business. Many are wondering how it is possible for these atrocities to be taking place.

Dr. Grossman writes:

> Why do girls and young women dream of going under the knife and waking up with flat chests, and sometimes, to save a few bucks, without nipples? They have mental health problems, a traumatic past, family issues, or maybe just intense teenage angst and erroneously believe my colleagues who claim removing body parts will bring them relief. (*Lost in Trans Nation*, p. 158)

> How in God's name are these atrocities taking place? Simple. The surgeons who carved up Jake, Ritchie, Scott [children's case studies], and others—leaving them infertile and disfigured—can justify their work: They provide gender-affirming care; they "follow WPATH's standards of care."

> What is WPATH? Read carefully, parents, you need to know.

> WPATH is the "World Professional Association for Transgender Health"—sounds impressive, right? Like a group of doctors with stethoscopes and pocket protectors, conducting research, examining evidence, and carefully formulating guidelines for clinicians?

It may once have been, but no longer.

WPATH is an NGO formed in 1979. They promote their standards of care (SOC) as the model of best practice, the gold standard. Many, if not most, US hospitals, clinics, and private physicians and therapists base their practices on WPATH SOC.

How close to a gold standard are they? An independent, peer-reviewed analysis in 2021 gave them a quality score of zero out of six.

WPATH presents its approach to patients, parents, and providers as the only valid, evidence-based option, yet its recommendations have been formally rejected by Sweden, Finland, Norway, and Britain and questioned by medical groups in France, Australia, and New Zealand. Although WPATH guidance advises hospitals, clinicians, and even courts, WPATH itself suffers from identity confusion: while presenting as an unbiased science-based medical group, it is in truth an advocacy organization run by activists who have an unwavering goal of affirmation at all costs. (*Lost in Trans Nation*, pp. 187–188)

Dr. Grossman introduces the reader to psychiatrist Dr. Stephen Levine, who resigned from WPATH after twenty-five years of senior positions in the organization. In 2001, Dr. Levine, an authority on transgenderism and gender dysphoria in children and adolescents, chaired the committee that was developing WPATH's fifth Standards of Care. The committee recommended retention of the requirement for two letters of support from mental health providers prior to hormonal interventions, and another two letters before surgical interventions.

Richard Green, president of WPATH at the time, considered letters to be "gatekeeping" and appointed a new committee. SOC-6 required only one letter, and SOC-7 dispensed with letters altogether. Dr. Levine resigned, saying:

> I resigned my membership in 2002 due to my regretful conclusion that the organization and its recommendations had become dominated by politics and ideology, rather than by scientific process, as it was years earlier.

Dr. Levine withdrew from WPATH because he recognized that political medicine is antithetical to scientific medicine, and medicine for social change is not health medicine. SOC-8 has no age restrictions or counseling requirements at all, and advances *affirmation* as the only solution to gender dysphoria. WPATH advocates blockers, hormones, and surgeries on demand, as it deceitfully promotes respect for *patient autonomy* (separation from parents) as its "ethical" principle.

Why is WPATH, a political activist organization, accepted as the medical authority on gender-affirming care? How can such malevolence be accepted as authoritative *settled science*? The answer may surprise you. Author Michelle Stiles offers an insightful explanation in her 2022 book, *One Idea to Rule Them All: Reverse Engineering American Propaganda*.[166] It is an exceptional analysis of propaganda and how it is being used in America against Americans.

Stiles is a physical therapist with a thoughtful and incisive analytical mind. Her medical training adds a scientific dimension to her philosophical insights. She begins her book with a play on the ring verse from *Lord of the Rings*, J. R. R. Tolkien's epic high-fantasy novel published in 1954. The novel's title refers to the evil Dark Lord Sauron, ruler of the land of Mordor, who seeks to rule all of Middle-earth with the ring of power. Substituting "One Idea" for "Ring" in the verse, Stiles reminds the reader that megalomania is not just the stuff of literary fantasy:

> One Idea to rule them all,
>
> One Idea to find them,
>
> One Idea to bring them all,
>
> And in the darkness bind them. (p. 4)

What is this One Idea? The answer begins with a Frenchman, Gustave LeBon, whose 1886 book, *The Crowd: A Study of the Popular Mind*,[167] is considered to be a seminal work on crowd psychology. LeBon explored the attributes of crowds and presented techniques for engineering public opinion that appealed to feelings rather than facts. This was a seismic shift in perspective, creating a new methodology for public debate that was initially used to sell an unpopular war to Americans in 1917.

Two-term president Woodrow Wilson (1913–1921) appointed progressive journalist George Creel to head the Committee on Public Information

(CPI), created by executive order on April 14, 1917, six days after the United States formally declared war on Germany and entered World War I. Creel's job was to sell the war to a skeptical and hesitant American public, so they would support the war effort and endure their inevitable sacrifice in men and money. Creel's manipulative marketing campaign, "Make the world safe for democracy," was wildly successful.

Michelle Stiles describes "the extensive propaganda apparatus that Creel euphemistically titled "The House of Truth," including:

> Division of News
>
> Foreign News Division
>
> Advertising Division
>
> Division of Pictorial Publicity
>
> Division of Films
>
> Academics
>
> Division of Speaking
>
> Four Minute Men
>
> Junior Four Minute Men
>
> Speaking Circuit
>
> National School Service Bulletin (pp. 10–11)

Stiles explains:

> The "House of Truth" was designed and created to ensure that everyone was pulling in the same direction. For those who would not, dissenting ideas were monitored, codified as illegal, and censored. Creel established the following acts and groups to suppress dissent:
>
> Snitch Patrol: Four Minute Men [local leaders, businessmen, professional men] were encouraged to identify, interrogate, and even report people in their communities who expressed anti-war sentiment.
>
> Espionage Act (1917): Upheld censorship of ideas considered dele-

terious to the war effort.

Sedition Act (1918): Made any criticism of the Wilson Administration illegal. (p. 12)

CPI hired American publicist Edward Bernays to help build support for the war domestically and abroad. Bernays, the nephew of Sigmund Freud, referred to his CPI work as *psychological warfare*. He realized that if you could persuade the public to accept an unpopular war by avoiding rational arguments for and against involvement, and appeal to people's feelings instead, you could convince anybody of anything. Bernays applied the principles of propaganda to marketing, and became the father of public relations.

Bernays exploited LeBon's mass-persuasion techniques for civilian use, applying them to commercial businesses. In his 1928 book, *Propaganda*,[168] Bernays tries to remove the negative wartime connotation from the word propaganda, presenting propaganda as a legitimate marketing tool and necessity for orderly living. He begins the book with a stunning paragraph, and then continues with a surprising level of naiveté:

Chapter 1

Organizing Chaos

The conscious and intelligent manipulation of the organized habits and opinions of the masses is an important element in democratic society. Those who manipulate this unseen mechanism of society constitute an invisible government which is the true ruling power of our country....

They govern us by their qualities of natural leadership, their ability to supply needed ideas and by their key positions in the social structure. Whatever attitude one chooses toward this condition, it remains a fact that in almost every act of our daily lives, whether in the sphere of politics or business, in our social conduct or our ethical thinking, we are dominated by the relatively small number of persons—a trifling fraction of our hundred and twenty million— who understand the mental processes and social patterns of the masses. It is they who pull the wires which control the public mind, who harness old social forces and contrive new ways to bind and guide the world.

It is not usually realized how necessary these invisible governors are to the orderly functioning of our group life.... (pp. 37–38)

The instruments by which public opinion is organized and focused may be misused. But such organization and focusing are necessary to orderly life.

As civilization has become more complex, and as the need for invisible government has been increasingly demonstrated, the technical means have been invented and developed by which opinion may be regimented. (pp. 39–40)

It is the purpose of this book to explain the structure of the mechanism which controls the public mind, and to tell how it is manipulated by the special pleader who seeks to create public acceptance for a particular idea or commodity. It will attempt at the same time to find the due place in the modern democratic scheme for this new propaganda and to suggest its gradually evolving code of ethics and practice. (p. 45)

Edward Bernays demonstrated a shocking naiveté regarding how the psychodynamics of propaganda and social engineering would be used by the *invisible government.* Michelle Stiles is not so naive. She explains how Bernays himself established the prototype. The idea for selling anything from pianos to ideas was the switch from established techniques of the "hard" sell to the new techniques of the "soft" sell.

Rather than relying on the facts and merits of a product or idea (hard sell), the new methodology required creating a demand for the product or idea. Bernays called it the science of "creating circumstances." This is how it works. In the old days if a salesman wanted to sell a piano, he would talk to the customer about the merits of the piano. Not anymore. Bernays explained that the trick was to present the piano in ways to make the customer demand the piano. This was accomplished through "influencers" in collaboration with media.

In his book, Bernays explains that the modern propagandist must create the circumstances that result in demand for the piano, so he arranges an exhibition attended by key people called "influencers." The exhibition is staged in a gorgeous drawing room with rare books, tapestries, and the piano.

> The music room will be accepted because it has been made the thing. And the man or woman who has a music room, or has arranged a corner of the parlor as a musical corner, will naturally think of buying a piano. It will come to him as his own idea.

> Under the old salesmanship the manufacturer said to the prospective buyer, "Please buy a piano." The new salesmanship has reversed the process and caused the prospective buyer to say to the manufacturer, "Please sell me a piano." (*Propaganda*, pp. 77–78)

Bernays applied LeBon's new techniques for engineering public opinion to sell cigarettes to women as "sexual liberation." Bernays arranged for photographers to "catch" a woman "spontaneously" lighting up a Lucky Strike cigarette in public during the 1929 Easter Parade on Fifth Avenue. His wildly successful *Torches of Freedom* campaign sold cancer-causing cigarettes to women by appealing to *feelings* rather than to facts. Is this starting to sound familiar?

Stiles explains how Bernays used stagecraft to sell products, and how politicians could do the same to sell ideas:

> Debate, reasoning, and the appeal to truth were now passé. Bernays showed how the savvy political leader could orchestrate events, dramatize issues, steer public opinion, and create demand for a predetermined solution waiting in the wings—just off stage.

> Dramatizations would be created to appear as organic grassroots concerns percolating in and through the population at large, creating the illusion of spontaneous synchronicity. Subsequent tailored "interventions" would be supplied later by astute political leaders. Only after the collective national mind had been primed in this manner, would a political leader take a stand to influence the national "discussion."

> In reality, no discussion was intended—or desired. The staged sequence of events was choreographed to win support for the predetermined outcome regardless of the merits of the issue. (Stiles, *One Idea to Rule Them All*, pp. 52–53)

Bernays was using the Hegelian dialectic to create more demand for cigarettes, just as stagecraft was used to sell World War I to Americans in 1917. Political theater, like political medicine and politicized educational indoctrination, requires a foundational shift from facts to feelings in order to succeed.

This brings our discussion back to Michelle Stiles's book title, *One Idea to Rule Them All*, and how Bernays's *invisible government* is exploiting stagecraft and abusing the psychodynamics of propaganda with coordinated repetition in order to socially engineer the acceptance of transgenderism.

WPATH, the primary authority/influencer on transgenderism, unapologetically advocates surgery for aligning the body with the mind, rather than therapy for aligning the mind with the body. Why? What is the social purpose of this therapeutic reversal? To answer these questions, we must remember that political medicine is about social change, not public health. Political medicine is using the same artifice to create demand for transgenderism that Bernays used to create demand for cigarettes. The actions may be separated by 100 years, but the processes for change are the same manipulative and deceitful Hegelian dialectic.

Dr. Miriam Grossman's horror is expressed in her description of WPATH's latest Standards of Care, SOC-8:

> The Standards of Care introduced a new sexual orientation: an individual who is "assigned male at birth (AMAB) and wish[es] to eliminate masculine physical features, masculine genitals, or genital functioning."

> I wish it weren't so, but in WPATH's latest SOC, a chapter is dedicated to eunuchs. Boys and men seeking castration are now under the ever-widening "gender-nonconforming" umbrella. They identify as people without testicles, so castration affirms their identity....

> WPATH's 2022 conference kicked off with a keynote from the Admiral [Rachel Levine, the transgender admiral and Assistant Secretary of Health for the U.S. Department of Health and Human Services (HHS)]: "Our task quite simply is to *educate the public* in the United States and throughout the world.... We have the power to expand the boundaries of science and of public understanding." (*Lost in Trans Nation*, pp. 193–194)

Educate the public is a powerful euphemism for *indoctrinate the public* delivered by a "trusted" authority representing the U.S. Department of Health and Human Services. In reality, the Admiral is a transgender ideologue delivering a self-serving political narrative disguised as public health, selling transgenderism to an unsuspecting public.

Dr. Grossman concludes her remarks about affirming surgeons with a chilling warning:

Trans is old. Nullo is new.

Some affirming surgeons are ready and willing to perform whatever fits a patient's fleeting fancy: phalloplasties, vaginoplasties, bilateral mastectomies, and hysterectomies; castration and "eunuch affirmation surgeries"; or even "genital nullification" leaving patients with no genitals at all. One affirming surgery clinic's website states:

> Genital nullification, Nullo, or Eunuch procedures involve removing all external genitalia to create a smooth transition from the abdomen to the groin. In some cases, this involves shortening the urethra. For patients born with a uterus, a hysterectomy is required prior to any genital nullification procedure. Your specific goals can be discussed with one of our surgeons to develop a plan that works for you.

The last line means that if you want a penis *and* a vagina, that's okay too. Just tell us what you want, we create custom-made genitals....

Understand that once the gender ideologues achieve one goal, without hesitation they move to the next. Now the monstrous "bottom surgeries" have been normalized, as if they're not sterilizing, savage procedures with too many debilitating complications, pain, and woes to count. But before you know it, they're normalizing eunuchs and "nullo" surgeries, creating bodies that appear neither male nor female....

We can't get used to all this.

It's just "gender-affirming surgery," nothing to see here—that's the goal, so they can go further to the next deviant thing, and the next.

Too many believe this is all about compassion, respect, and rights.

That's a cover. The goal has always been the breakdown of norms. (*Lost in Trans Nation*, pp. 194–195)

Dr. Grossman exposes the "gender-affirming" industry as ideologically driven political medicine, guilty of using euphemisms to advocate transgenderism. Political medicine rejects biological *facts* and embraces *feelings* as its new metric for rationalizing surgical interventions on emotionally disturbed patients. It exploits Bernays's stagecraft, *the science of creating the circumstances*, to create the escalating demand for "gender-affirming" surgeries. Political medicine is weaponized medicine. It endorses subjective reality, rejects objective reality, and pressures society to accept madness as sanity in its campaign to collapse America from within.

Michelle Stiles concludes her book with reflections on the future in a section titled "Losing Reality Bit by Bit." Her remarks are particularly relevant because the War on America is a war of attrition:

> Every ten years, a generation that has been raised in comparative freedom from propaganda dies off and is replaced by a generation incubated and grown up in a culture of deception. How much longer before the ability to think for oneself is completely extinguished?
>
> Will there be anyone alive who can lead us back to the "old" idea of truth and authentic relationships that existed prior to the propaganda tsunami that was unleashed in the 20th century and now pervades the 21st century?
>
> What happens when even the desire for truth has been obliterated, and all that remains is fictitious reality masking the underlying tyranny that is willingly accepted by the stupefied masses?
>
> Those who were alive during the middle of the great propaganda debate and perceived the danger were true prophets of the age.

They had ominous words to say about the future of mankind, Aldous Huxley being the most prominent:

> *There will be, in the next generation or so, a pharmacological method of making people love their servitude, and producing dictatorship without tears, so to speak, producing a kind*

of painless concentration camp for entire societies, so that people will in fact have their liberties taken away from them, but will rather enjoy it, because they will be distracted from any desire to rebel by propaganda or brainwashing, or brainwashing enhanced by pharmacological methods. And this seems to be the final revolution. (Brave New World Revisited, 1958, Aldous Huxley, p. 253)

Aldous Huxley was describing the globalist elite strivings for totalitarian control and one-world government. Transgenderism is prelude to transhumanism and technocracy in globalism's planetary managerial Unistate.

CHAPTER 38

BigBrain, BICAN, and "The Evil Twins of Technocracy and Transhumanism"

Globalism is a replacement ideology that seeks to reorder the world into one singular, planetary Unistate, ruled by the globalist elite. The globalist war on nation-states cannot succeed without collapsing the United States of America. The long-term strategic attack plan moves America incrementally from constitutional republic to socialism to globalism to feudalism. The tactical attack plan uses asymmetric psychological and informational warfare to destabilize Americans and drive society out of objective reality into the madness of subjective reality. America's children are the primary target of the globalist predators.

Globalism is a replacement ideology replete with a replacement religion—*Scientism.* Scientism is a political ideology that challenges the foundation of objective, factual science, replacing it with consensus, *feeling* "science." Objective science is independently provable and reproducible. Consensus "science" is simply subjective opinion and neither provable nor reproducible.

The Marxification of education (Chapter 29) has yielded a generation of woke young people who have rejected their parents' Judeo-Christian religion and replaced it with Scientism. The Glossary of Leftist Doublespeak (Chapter 28) defines Scientism as "an exaggerated trust in the efficacy of the methods of natural science applied to all areas of investigation (as in philosophy, the social sciences, and the humanities). It has replaced traditional religion as the moral and ethical authority for woke members of society."

Joshua Mercer, cofounder of the CatholicVote.org website, describes the conversion in an article posted by Daily Caller News Foundation, April 8, 2023, "Gen Z Traded Church for 'A New Religion,' Faith Leaders Say":[169]

It's not that Gen Z isn't religious, it's that they picked a new religion. They have fervent beliefs and rituals, they have their symbols and sacraments, and they definitely purge their ranks of "blasphemers" or anyone insufficiently dedicated to their faith. Look at how every corporation rushes to embrace the rainbow flag every June, and look at how people adorn their social media platforms with symbols to show solidarity with Black Lives Matter, Covid vaccination, Ukraine, or climate change. They are definitely evangelizing, it's just not Christianity.

Scientism supports globalist strivings for technocracy and transhumanism—the building blocks of the globalist Unistate. The reader will recall that transhumanism is the transcendence of our bodies' physical limitations, and the ascendance to "Humanity 2.0." What globalism's talking heads fail to mention is that Scientism's Humanity 2.0 also "transcends" Judeo-Christian morality, which safeguards the individual. Scientism protects the collective, the group. The empathy and compassion that are signature characteristics of Judeo-Christian morality are entirely absent in Scientism.

This is an essential detail. The Unistate has no place for human empathy, compassion, or family loyalty. Scientism replaces family loyalty and patriotism with exclusive loyalty to the Unistate in a life devoid of empathy and compassion. Young people who embrace collectivism, Scientism, transgenderism, and transhumanism fail to recognize this essential detail and its profound implications.

Scientism, the religion of the woke, is an existential danger to the world's population. This is not hyperbole; it is the choice facing Americans today—far beyond the fight over the "science" of masks and viruses.

Author, lecturer, and globalization critic Patrick M. Wood has been warning for decades about the existential threats of technocracy and transhumanism, the two central globalist objectives.

In his July 11, 2021, article, "The Evil Twins of Transhumanism and Technocracy,"[170] Wood explains how technocracy and transhumanism rely on Scientism:

> *The dots between Technocracy and Transhumanism are easily connected once it is understood that both sit atop the pseudo-science*

religion of Scientism, which posits that science is god and scientists and engineers are its priesthood. This article provides the current framework to understand this nexus. —Patrick Wood

Technocracy is to the transformation of society as Transhumanism is to the transformation of the human condition of people who would live in that society.

Both are underpinned by a religious belief known as Scientism that says that science is a god and that scientists, engineers and technologists are the priesthood that translates findings into practice.

It is a fatal error to equate Scientism with science. True science explores the natural world using the time-tested scientific method of repeated experimentation and validation. By comparison, Scientism is a speculative, metaphysical worldview about the nature and reality of the universe and man's relation to it.

Scientism refutes traditional religious views, morals and philosophy and instead looks to science as the source for personal and societal moral value.

The relationship between Technocracy and Transhumanism can be seen as early as 1933 when Harold Loeb wrote *Life in a Technocracy: What It Might Be Like*:

> *"Technocracy envisages another form of domestication, a form in which man may become more than man... Technocracy is designed to develop the so-called higher faculties in every man and not to make each man resigned to the lot into which he may be born... Through breeding with specific individuals for specific purposes... A technocracy, then, should in time produce a race of men superior in quality to any now known on earth..."*

Thus, Loeb saw Technocracy (the society) as producing a superior quality of man by applying advanced technology to the human condition.

The Nature of Technocracy

Formalized in 1932 by scientists and engineers at Columbia University, the movement defined itself in a 1938 edition of its magazine, *The Technocrat*:

> *"Technocracy is the science of social engineering, the scientific operation of the entire social mechanism to produce and distribute goods and services to the entire population... For the first time in human history, it will be done as a scientific, technical, engineering problem."*

Indeed, Technocracy was an economic system based on science and social engineering. Technocrats were so certain that their scientific approach was so righteous that there would be no need for any political structures whatsoever:

> *"There will be no place for Politics, Politicians, Finance or Financiers, Rackets or Racketeers... Technocracy will distribute by means of a certificate of distribution available to every citizen from birth to death."*

Today, Technocracy is embodied in the World Economic Forum's **Great Reset** and the various United Nations manifestations of Sustainable Development: Agenda 21, 2030 Agenda, New Urban Agenda, etc.

The Nature of Transhumanism

A philosophical mainstay of modern Transhumanism, Max More, defined it in 1990 as:

> *"...a class of philosophies of life that seek the continuation and acceleration of the evolution of intelligent life beyond its currently human form and human limitations by means of science and technology, guided by life-promoting principles and values."*

The means to the end is ultimately genetic engineering that takes over and speeds up evolution theory to create Humanity 2.0.

Since the advent of CRISPR gene-editing technology, Transhumanists have saturated universities and private corporations to modify all categories of living things, including humans.

What is preached as the preservation of biodiversity by the United Nations is really the takeover of genetic material, which was noted as early as 1994, just two years after the debut of Sustainable Development and Agenda 21 at the UN Conference on Economic Development (UNCED) in Rio de Janeiro, Brazil.

The 1994 book *The Earth Brokers* was written by two principal participants in the Rio process who did not blindly swallow what had just happened. They noted two things about the biodiversity convention that 156 nations of the world adopted:

> *"The convention implicitly equates the diversity of life—animals and plants—to the diversity of genetic codes, for which read genetic resources. By doing so, diversity becomes something modern science can manipulate...the convention promotes biotechnology as being 'essential for the conservation and sustainable use of biodiversity.'"*

Secondly, they noted that "*the main stake raised by the biodiversity convention is the issue of ownership and control over biological diversity...the major concern was protection of the pharmaceutical and emerging biological industries.*"

It is little wonder today that the pharmaceutical industry is producing gene therapy shots using genetically modified RNA to transform the body's immune system. They have been working hard since 1992 to advance the technology needed to hijack the human genome and begin the transformative pathway to Humanity 2.0.

The Great Reset Embraces Both Technocracy and Transhumanism

It has been noted in many professional journals that the World Economic Forum and its founder/spokesman Klaus Schwab are promoting both Technocracy and Transhumanism at the same time. In light of this article, this should not be surprising.

The European Academy on Religion and Society (EARS), for instance, wrote that:

> "*...the highly influential members of the World Economic*

> Forum have a plan for what should come next. It is called 'The Great Reset', and it envisions a truly 'transhumanist' future for us all… Since mid-2020, the WEF has been promoting its vision for our post-coronavirus future, which they call 'The Great Reset'. In their view, the pandemic has exposed the weaknesses of our old system, and therefore presents a perfect opportunity to 'reset' our world and start anew. **What is striking about this plan, which the WEF has condensed into a virus-shaped mindmap, is its implicit endorsement of a philosophy called 'transhumanism.'**"(emphasis added)

As initially stated, "Technocracy is to the transformation of society as Transhumanism is to the transformation of the human condition of people who would live in that society."

In conclusion, the evil twins of Technocracy and Transhumanism, along with their underlying religion of Scientism, need to be recognized for what they are but most importantly, they must be resisted and rejected with every fiber of our being.

With their catchy slogan, *Trust the Science*, globalist social engineers advanced their false narrative, beginning with two false tenets of Scientism: man-made climate change is killing the physical planet, and the COVID-19 pandemic is killing human life on the planet. Then the globalists offered to "save" the planet and humanity with their experimental gene-altering messenger RNA (mRNA) treatments deceitfully labeled "vaccines." The catastrophic socioeconomic consequences would launch The Great Reset and initiate the final battle for planetary control.

The Great Reset is yet another euphemism, a deceitful marketing technique designed to sell globalism's *New World Order* of masters and slaves to a fearful and trusting public. It is feudalism disguised as deliverance through 21st-century technology. The Great Reset is a computer analogy that infers the *new normal* of transhumanism and technocracy. It is a slogan that redefines what it means to be human. In the reimagined serfdom of Humanity 2.0, the rulers are able to control their super-slaves' thoughts, moods, and behavior. There is no mother, father, sister, or brother in the New World Order. The entire concept of family has been erased.

The breakthrough technology for transhuman research is Scientism's BigBrain Project, begun in 2003 with a 65-year-old body donor. The brain tissue was sectioned, stained, scanned, and digitized. The resulting digital images were processed and eventually became the BigBrain, an ultra-high-resolution 3-D digital atlas of the human brain.

BigBrain is an open-access reference brain released in June 2013 by researchers at the Montreal Neurological Institute and the German Forschungszantrum Jülich, both part of the Human Brain Project,[171] a European Future and Emerging Technologies Flagship project that ran from 2013 to 2023. Its primary objective was creating an ICT-based (information and communication technologies) platform for brain research.

BigBrain is a standard tool in human brain research, freely accessible worldwide on its website.[172] BigBrain is continually updated, and in 2017, building on Google's open-source project, Neuroglancer, the first version of the Human Brain Project's web-based 3-D atlas viewer was released. It is capable of displaying very large brain volumes and finding related neuroscience data.

In June 2020 the fourth BigBrain Workshop launched HIBALL, the funding umbrella for the BigBrain Project. HIBALL is an acronym for Helmholtz International BigBrain Analytics & Learning Laboratory. Helmholtz Association[173] consists of 18 legally independent research centers with approximately 45,000 employees and an annual budget of almost 6 billion euros. Helmholtz is Germany's largest scientific organization, and a major funding source in the public-private BigBrain Project.[174]

HIBALL[175] plans to move the BigBrain Project to the next level of neuroscience research by reinforcing utilization and co-development of the latest artificial intelligence (AI) and high-performance computing (HPC) technologies for building highly detailed 3-D brain models. The goal is to develop new tools and services in AI, atlasing, modeling, and simulation.

On April 2, 2013, the Obama administration announced its own collaborative, public-private research initiative called the BRAIN Initiative (Brain Research through Advancing Innovative Neurotechnologies). The announcement proposed initial expenditures for fiscal year 2014 via $110 million from the Defense Advanced Research Projects Agency (DARPA), the National Institutes of

Health (NIH), and the National Science Foundation (NSF). BRAIN Initiative affiliates include private companies, universities, and other organizations in the United States, Australia, Canada, and Denmark.

Science[176] magazine reported on the BRAIN Initiative's developments in an article published on September 22, 2022:

> The BRAIN Initiative, the 9-year-old, multibillion-dollar U.S. neuroscience effort, today announced its most ambitious challenge yet: compiling the world's most comprehensive map of cells in the human brain. Scientists say the BRAIN Initiative Cell Atlas Network (BICAN), funded with $500 million over 5 years, will help them understand how the human brain works and how diseases affect it. BICAN "will transform the way we do neuroscience research for generations to come," says BRAIN Initiative Director John Ngai of the National Institutes of Health (NIH)….
>
> Another $36 million over 3 years announced today will fund the BRAIN Armamentarium, which will develop viral vectors and lipid nanoparticles that home in on and genetically tweak specific types of brain cells. These tools will help scientists study cell function and develop disease treatments.
>
> A third project called BRAIN CONNECTS focuses on tracing wiring diagrams in mammalian brains; early next year it will make $30 million in grants [for] running [the project] up to 5 years. Altogether, NIH has spent $2.5 billion so far on BRAIN, a figure it expects to reach $5.2 billion by the end of 2026.

BigBrain and the BRAIN Initiative enable testing hypotheses in an anatomically realistic space. Brain research is big business, and the reader will notice that its funding sources are the usual suspects in government and the private sector. The European BigBrain and American BICAN are featured attractions in the 21st-century landscape of the internationalized military-industrial complex.

What is at stake is how BigBrain and BICAN information will be used in the world. The WEF is selling the idea that public-private collaboration reflects the united efforts of "stakeholders" to cure sickness and insure the future health of our ailing planet.

History teaches us that the groundbreaking understanding of the psycho-dynamics of groups introduced by Edward Bernays in 1928 was used to manipulate public opinion for military, commercial, and political gain. It is not difficult to imagine that the information gleaned from the mapping of the human brain will likewise be used by its public/private funding sources for military, commercial, and political gain.

The difference between then and now is the nature of the weapon. In Bernays's time, military propaganda was converted for peacetime use on civilians, to psychologically manipulate public opinion and influence behavior for commercial profit and political social control. Today's neuroscience goes far beyond propaganda as a means to influence public opinion and behavior; it is investigating the physical realm of thinking itself!

We must remember that *thought precedes behavior.* What neuroscience research is investigating represents a seismic shift in approach that aims directly at people's physical brains in order to influence their thoughts and behavior. Marketed worldwide as helping to cure the most frightening human illnesses, neuroscience is developing the most powerful weapon imaginable for social control in order to facilitate globalism's quest for technocracy and transhumanism: the militarization of brain science.

Patrick Wood's extraordinary book, *The Evil Twins of Transhumanism and Technocracy,*[177] released in 2022, is a must-read for those who want to understand how technocracy is currently transforming the world, and how transhumanism is transforming the people who will live in that world. Wood recognizes that this is a war of attrition, and he dedicates his book lovingly:

> To the cherished youth of the world, many of whom are lost in ignorance or denial: May they gain understanding and courage to choose a future that elevates freedom and liberty as essential values of culture and civilization. I especially dedicate this book to my grandchildren who may be the first generation to grow up in a thoroughly technocratic and transhuman world.

CHAPTER 39

Cognitive Warfare and the Battle for Your Brain

Globalism is a replacement ideology that seeks to reorder the world into one singular, planetary Unistate, ruled by the globalist elite. The globalist war on nation-states cannot succeed without collapsing the United States of America. The long-term strategic attack plan moves America incrementally from constitutional republic to socialism to globalism to feudalism. The tactical attack plan uses asymmetric psychological and informational warfare to destabilize Americans and drive society out of objective reality into the madness of subjective reality. America's children are the primary target of the globalist predators.

The North Atlantic Treaty Organization (NATO) is an international military alliance of 31 sovereign nations from Europe and North America. The treaty is a pact between member states that considers a military attack against one member a military attack against all members, and obligates all members to assist the attacked member. A shocking October 8, 2021, article by journalist Ben Norton, "Behind NATO's 'cognitive warfare': 'Battle for your brain' waged by Western militaries,"[178] provides a chilling analysis of cognitive warfare. Excerpts from the article follow:

> Western governments in the NATO military alliance are developing tactics of "cognitive warfare," using the supposed threats of China and Russia to justify waging a "battle for your brain" in the "human domain," to "make everyone a weapon."

> NATO is developing new forms of warfare to wage a "battle for the brain," as the military alliance put it.

> The US-led NATO military cartel has tested novel modes of hybrid warfare against its self-declared adversaries, including economic warfare, cyber warfare, information warfare, and psychological warfare.

Now, NATO is spinning out an entirely new kind of combat it has branded cognitive warfare. Described as the "weaponization of brain sciences," the new method involves "hacking the individual" by exploiting "the vulnerabilities of the human brain" in order to implement more sophisticated "social engineering."

Until recently, NATO had divided war into five different operational domains: air, land, sea, space, and cyber. But with its development of cognitive warfare strategies, the military alliance is discussing a new, sixth level: the "human domain."

A 2020 NATO-sponsored study of this new form of warfare clearly explained, "While actions taken in the five domains are executed in order to have an effect on the human domain, cognitive warfare's objective is to make everyone a weapon."

"The brain will be the battlefield of the 21st century," the report stressed. "Humans are the contested domain," and "future conflicts will likely occur amongst the people digitally first and physically thereafter in proximity to hubs of political and economic power." ...

In a chilling disclosure, the report said explicitly that "the objective of Cognitive Warfare is to harm societies and not only the military."

With entire civilian populations in NATO's crosshairs, the report emphasized that Western militaries must work more closely with academia to weaponize social sciences and human sciences and help the alliance develop its cognitive warfare capacities.

The study described this phenomenon as "the militarization of brain science." But it appears clear that NATO's development of cognitive warfare will lead to a militarization of all aspects of human society and psychology, from the most intimate of social relationships to the mind itself....

Norton reports that the researcher who wrote the definitive 2020 NATO-sponsored study on cognitive warfare, François du Cluzel, is a former French military officer who helped create the NATO Innovation Hub (iHub) in 2013. Du Cluzel continues to manage iHub from its base in Norfolk, Virginia. Norton continues:

Although the iHub insists on its website, for legal reasons, that the "opinions expressed on this platform don't constitute NATO or any other organization points of view," the organization is sponsored by the Allied Command Transformation (ACT), described as "one of two Strategic Commands at the head of NATO's military command structure."

The Innovation Hub, therefore, acts as a kind of in-house NATO research center or think tank. Its research is not necessarily official NATO policy, but it is directly supported and overseen by NATO.

François du Cluzel participated in an October 5, 2021, panel discussion on cognitive warfare.

Du Cluzel summarized his research in the panel this October. He initiated his remarks noting that cognitive warfare "right now is one of the hottest topics for NATO," and "has become a recurring term in military terminology in recent years." …

"Cognitive warfare is a new concept that starts in the information sphere, that is a kind of hybrid warfare," du Cluzel said.

"It starts with hyper-connectivity. Everyone has a cell phone," he continued. "It starts with information because information is, if I may say, the fuel of cognitive warfare. But it goes way beyond solely information, which is a standalone operation—information warfare is a standalone operation."

Cognitive warfare overlaps with Big Tech corporations and mass surveillance, because "it's all about leveraging the big data," du Cluzel explained. "We produce data everywhere we go. Every minute, every second we go, we go online. And this is extremely easy to leverage those data in order to better know you and use that knowledge to change the way you think." …

Du Cluzel defined cognitive warfare as the "art of using technologies to alter the cognition of human targets."

Those technologies, he noted, incorporate the fields of NBIC—nanotechnology, biotechnology, information technology, and cognitive science. All together, "it makes a kind of very dangerous cocktail that can further manipulate the brain," he said.

Du Cluzel went on to explain that the exotic new method of attack "goes well beyond" information warfare or psychological operations (psyops).

"Cognitive warfare is not only a fight against *what* we think, but it's rather a fight against the *way* we think, if we can change the way people think," he said. "It's much more powerful and it goes way beyond the information [warfare] and psyops."

Du Cluzel continued: "It's crucial to understand that it's a game on our cognition, on the way our brain processes information and turns it into knowledge, rather than solely a game on information or on psychological aspects of our brains. It's not only an action against what we think, but also an action against the way we think, the way we process information and turn it into knowledge.

"In other words, cognitive warfare is not just another word, another name for information warfare. It is a war on our individual processor, our brain."

The NATO researcher stressed that "this is extremely important for us in the military," because "it has the potential, by developing new weapons and ways of harming the brain, it has the potential to engage neuroscience and technology in many, many different approaches to influence human ecology…because you all know that it's very easy to turn a civilian technology into a military one."

As for who the targets of cognitive warfare could be, du Cluzel revealed that anyone and everyone is on the table.…

And the private sector has a financial interest in advancing cognitive warfare research, he noted: "The massive worldwide investments made in neurosciences suggests that the cognitive domain will probably [be] one of the battlefields of the future."

This "creates a new space of competition beyond what is called the five domains of operations—or land, sea, air, cyber, and space domains. Warfare in the cognitive arena mobilizes a wider range of battle spaces than solely the physical and information dimensions can do."

In short, humans themselves are the new contested domain in this novel mode of hybrid warfare, alongside land, sea, air, cyber, and outer space.

NATO's cognitive warfare study warns of "embedded fifth column"

And anyone could be a target of these cognitive warfare operations: "Any user of modern information technologies is a potential target. It targets the whole of a nation's human capital," the report ominously added.

"As well as the potential execution of a cognitive war to complement a military conflict, it can also be conducted alone, without any link to an engagement of the armed forces," the study went on. "Moreover, cognitive warfare is potentially endless since there can be no peace treaty or surrender for this type of conflict." ...

The NATO-sponsored study noted that "some NATO Nations have already acknowledged that neuroscientific techniques and technologies have high potential for operational use in a variety of security, defense and intelligence enterprises."

It spoke of breakthroughs in "neuroscientific methods and technologies" (neuroS/T), and said "uses of research findings and products to directly facilitate the performance of combatants, the integration of human machine interfaces to optimise combat capabilities of semi-autonomous vehicles (e.g., drones), and development of biological and chemical weapons (i.e., neuroweapons)."

The Pentagon is among the primary institutions advancing this novel research, as the report highlighted: "Although a number of nations have pursued, and are currently pursuing neuroscientific research and development for military purposes, perhaps the most proactive efforts in this regard have been conducted by the United States Department of Defense; with most notable and rapidly maturing research and development conducted by the Defense Advanced Research Projects Agency (DARPA) and Intelligence Advanced Research Projects Activity (IARPA)." ...

This weaponization of neuroS/T can and will be fatal, the

NATO-sponsored study was clear to point out. The research can "be utilised to mitigate aggression and foster cognitions and emotions of affiliation or passivity; induce morbidity, disability or suffering; and 'neutralise' potential opponents or incur mortality"—in other words, to maim and kill people.

The report quoted US Major General Robert H. Scales, who summarized NATO's new combat philosophy: "Victory will be defined more in terms of capturing the psycho-cultural rather than the geographical high ground." …

The study spoke of "the crucible of data sciences and human sciences," and stressed that "the combination of Social Sciences and System Engineering will be key in helping military analysts to improve the production of intelligence."

"If kinetic power cannot defeat the enemy," it said, "psychology and related behavioural and social sciences stand to fill the void." …

All academic disciplines will be implicated in cognitive warfare, not just the hard sciences. "Within the military, expertise on anthropology, ethnography, history, psychology among other areas will be more than ever required to cooperate with the military," the NATO-sponsored study stated.

The report nears its conclusion with an eerie quote: "Today's progresses in nanotechnology, biotechnology, information technology and cognitive science (NBIC), boosted by the seemingly unstoppable march of a triumphant troika made of Artificial Intelligence, Big Data and civilisational 'digital addiction' have created a much more ominous prospect: an embedded fifth column, where everyone, unbeknownst to him or her, is behaving according to the plans of one of our competitors."

"The modern concept of war is not about weapons but about influence," it posited. "Victory in the long run will remain solely dependent on the ability to influence, affect, change or impact the cognitive domain."

The NATO-sponsored study then closed with a final paragraph that makes it clear beyond doubt that the Western military alliance's ultimate goal is not only physical control of the planet, but also control over people's minds:

"Cognitive warfare may well be the missing element that allows the transition from military victory on the battlefield to lasting political success. The human domain might well be the decisive domain, wherein multi-domain operations achieve the commander's effect. The five first domains can give tactical and operational victories; only the human domain can achieve the final and full victory."

The NATO report emphasizes military-industrial cooperation, and openly asserts the necessity of Western militaries working more closely with academia to weaponize social sciences and human sciences and help the alliance develop its cognitive warfare capacities. As du Cluzel said, "cognitive warfare is not just another word, another name for information warfare. It is a war on our individual processor, our brain."

The capacities of cognitive warfare are particularly dangerous, because its ambition alters the entire concept of warfare and supports globalism's overarching reset of the world and everyone who lives in it. BigBrain and BICAN neurotechnology will facilitate the imposition of technocracy and transhumanism on the world's population. How they will accomplish this is the subject of the next chapter.

CHAPTER 40

The Art of Using Technologies to Alter Human Cognition

Globalism is a replacement ideology that seeks to reorder the world into one singular, planetary Unistate, ruled by the globalist elite. The globalist war on nation-states cannot succeed without collapsing the United States of America. The long-term strategic attack plan moves America incrementally from constitutional republic to socialism to globalism to feudalism. The tactical attack plan uses asymmetric psychological and informational warfare to destabilize Americans and drive society out of objective reality into the madness of subjective reality. America's children are the primary target of the globalist predators.

To understand Cognitive Warfare and the art of using technologies to alter the cognition of human targets, a basic understanding of electronic communication is required. Chetan Selwal provides the necessary information in his article "Electronic Communication Systems: Basics, Block Diagram and Working,"[179] posted on his website on July 14, 2020.

What is an Electronic Communication System?

Humans have a natural instinct to communicate with each other. We talk to each other using audio waves which are essentially electromagnetic waves. The frequency range of our audio signal is from 30 Hz to 3.4 KHz. Using this frequency, we cannot communicate over long distances. In our day to day lives, we can communicate hardly up to 10 meters or so with each other. If we want to increase the distance of communication, we have to put more energy and shout. Even this shouting will make the signal reach a few extra meters only.

What if we want to communicate over a few hundred or thousands of kilometers? Is it possible with our vocal cords only?

You guessed it right. Our vocal cords have a certain limitation to transmit the audio signal. Transmitting the audio signals directly beyond a few meters is beyond human capability. We need certain technological interventions to make it happen.

In today's world, we are using semiconductor electronics-based systems extensively to transmit signals from one place/person/device to another place/person/device using electromagnetic waves. These systems are called Electronic Communication Systems.

Examples of Electronic Communication Systems are telegraph, telephone, mobile phone, pager, Internet, etc.

Electronic Communication System Block Diagram and Working

A typical block diagram for an Electronic Communication System may be as follows:

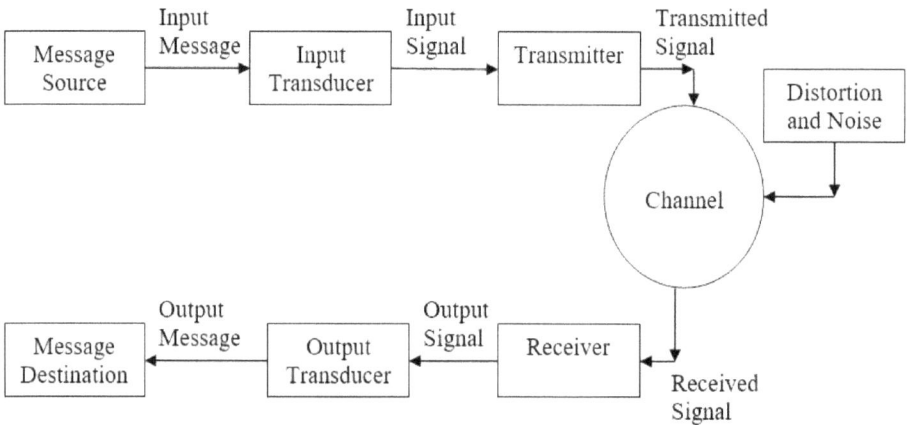

The main components of any Electronic Communication System are as follows:

1. **Message Source**: Message source may be any audio, video or data. Audio and Video signals are usually analog in nature. Data is a digital signal which originates from computer systems. Transmission of these message signals is prime objective

of any communication system.

2. **Input Transducer**: The input signals such as voice, data or video; whatever we wish to transmit has to be in the form of an electrical signal. Only electrical signals can be transmitted over electronic communication systems. The input transducer is an electronic/electrical device used to convert the input signal in the form of an electrical signal such as voltage or current. For example, a microphone is used to convert an incoming voice signal in the form of an electrical signal.

3. **Transmitter**: Transmitter section comprises of modulating elements and amplifiers as per the requirement of the system. The transmitter is the section that applies the main concepts and algorithms of electronic communication to the incoming signals. The output of the transmitter is fed to an antenna in case of a wireless communication system. It is fed to the wired channel in case of a wired channel like optical fiber or coaxial cable.

4. **Channel**: Channel is the medium through which the signals sent by transmitter travel towards the destination. Depending on medium, channel may be wired or wireless. In wired channels signal transmission takes place inside a bounded medium. A few examples of wired channels are telephone lines, optical fibers, copper cables, coaxial cables etc. In the case of wireless channel signal transmission takes place through the air. A few examples of wireless channels are microwave links, mobile phones, satellite communication etc. Signal degradation takes place inside the channel due to attenuation, distortion and noise. When the signal travels through long-distance, its power level decreases due to attenuation over the channel. Spurious signals get added in the form of noise signals. Because of these reasons signal faces distortion. We need to have proper mechanisms at the transmitter and receiver end to mitigate the effects of this noise and its implications otherwise it becomes very difficult to reproduce the originally transmitted signal at the receiver end.

5. **Receiver**: The receiver block does exactly the opposite processing to that of the transmitter. The signal received from the channel is filtered out for noise and unwanted signals. Then the demodulation of signals takes place. The demodulated signals are in the form of an electrical signal. These signals are fed to the output transducer.

6. **Output Transducer**: It translates the received signal into its original form, i.e., from an electrical signal to its original form as it was before transmission.

7. **Message Destination**: It is an end-user that consumes the message or information.

Bioelectricity comprises the electrical currents and electrical potentials generated by or occurring within living cells, tissues, and organisms. Bioelectricity is a fundamental form of energy in the human body, the way our body communicates with itself internally. Once we understand the basics of circuitry in Chetan Selwal's diagram above, we can grasp the staggering potential of human beings to become part of the electrical circuitry of the external electrical grid.

The Internet of Things is a network of physical devices embedded with sensors and software that collect and transfer data to one another over the Internet without human intervention. Some examples are *smart* home devices such as refrigerators, televisions, and thermostats; wearable devices such as smartwatches, fitness trackers, and glucose meters; and autonomous vehicles such as self-driving cars. The Internet of Things (IoT) has been expanded to the Internet of Bodies.

The Internet of Bodies (IoB) is a parallel network that connects our own bodies to the Internet using devices that are implanted, swallowed, or worn. The body becomes a technology platform that can be remotely monitored and controlled, or hacked, breached, and exploited. That is the basis for Yuval Harari's statement that humans are now "hackable animals." (Chapter 33)

Data is the currency in an information war. The IoT is an ecosystem that collects data about your personal habits. The IoB is an ecosystem that collects information about your personal health. In war, the more information you have about your adversary and his movements, the more you can personalize your tactical operations in order to achieve your strategic objectives.

The marketing campaign is painfully simple. Flattery is the operative word. The adjective *smart* is attached to every physical device that phones home to its base with information. So, globalist social engineers manipulate the public with flattery, seducing them to hand over their personal information with deceitful promises of convenience, leisure time, and improved health. Meanwhile, as the information-gathering campaign collects personal data and processes it for use in the mass-surveillance Unistate, every *smart* device is reducing the user's individual agency by making him more dependent upon the device.

Consider this. Students no longer have to add, subtract, multiply, or divide. They don't have to read or write or think. They don't need to acquire foundational knowledge to support thinking critically, because critical-thinking skills are forbidden in the Unistate. All they need to do is turn on their *smart* devices!

You might be wondering about how human beings can become part of the electrical grid and its circuitry. Science journalist Sally Adee describes the study of bioelectricity and its potential in her book *We Are Electric* (2023):[180]

> You may be familiar with the idea of our body's biome: the bacterial fauna that populate our gut and can so profoundly affect our health. In *We Are Electric* we cross into new scientific understanding: discovering your body's electrome.

> Every cell in our bodies—bones, skin, nerves, muscle—has a voltage, like a tiny battery. It is the reason our brain can send signals to the rest of our body, how we develop in the womb, and why our body knows to heal itself from injury. When bioelectricity goes awry, illness, deformity, and cancer can result. But if we can control or correct this bioelectricity, the implications for our health are remarkable: an undo switch for cancer that could flip malignant cells back into healthy ones; the ability to regenerate cells, organs, even limbs; to slow aging and so much more. The next scientific frontier might be decrypting the bioelectric code, much the way we did the genetic code.

We Are Electric traces the history of bioelectricity from Victorian medical charlatans to advances made by studying the giant axons of squid, to the future of brain implants, electric drugs, and the bioethical issues they present. Our discussion will focus on the intersection of bioelectricity, neuroscience technology, the Internet of Things (IoT), and the Internet of Bodies (IoB).

Sally Adee's book begins in 2009 with a gripping description of the U.S. military brain-stimulation experiment she participated in. It was an Army sniper training simulation, with wall-size graphics of a checkpoint, soldiers, civilians, and an exploding Humvee. Sally was equipped with electrical-stimulation headgear and a rifle that fired harmless CO_2 cartridges.

The experiment tested a technique known as transcranial direct current stimulation (tDCS). Direct stimulation is designed to increase the flow of electricity inside the brain and alter the strength of connections between the neurons in the brain, making them more likely to fire in concert.

The theory is that natural synchronization is the basis for all learning, and speeding up the flow with an electrical field provided by tDCS would theoretically accelerate the rate at which Adee could learn a new skill—in this experiment, sharpshooting. She describes the experiment as wildly successful, and the experience as transformative:

> Getting my neurons slapped by an electric field instantly sharpened my ability to focus, and by the transitive property, my sharpshooting skills. It also felt incredible—like someone had finally hit the off switch on all the distracting negative self-talk that had, until that moment, been the main provider of my mind's elevator music. I was a convert, and I wanted to preach the positive power of electricity to anyone who would listen. (p. 4)

Besides boosting brainpower, Adee explains, tDCS is being used to treat Parkinson's disease, epilepsy, anxiety, obsessive-compulsive disorder, and obesity. She describes the development of "electroceuticals," which are rice grain–size electrical implants clamped around nerves in the body to interrupt their signals:

> In 2016, outstanding early results in human trials—in which they seemed to reverse rheumatoid arthritis—convinced Google's parent company, Alphabet, to team up with a pharmaceutical international

[GSK] on a £540 million [approximately $675 million in 2023] venture to tap into your body's electrical signals, to try to treat diseases like Crohn's and diabetes. (p. 4)

Sally Adee spent ten years following the evidence, and *We Are Electric* is the result. The entire book is exciting to read because it presents the complexities of science and scientific jargon in laymen's terms. The introduction provides a succinct summary of Adee's discoveries, perspective, research, hopes, and concerns about the future:

> My brief foray into professional marksmanship is just one example of the promise and peril of harnessing our body's natural electricity. We are fundamentally electrical creatures, but the full extent of our electrification would shock you. It is hard to overstate how wholly and utterly your every movement, perception, and thought are controlled by electrical signals. This is not the electricity that comes from a battery or the kind that turns on the lights and powers the dishwasher. That kind of electricity is made of electrons, which are negatively charged particles flowing in a current.

> The human body runs on a different version: "bioelectricity." Instead of electrons, these currents are created by the movements of mostly positively charged ions like potassium, sodium, and calcium. This is how all signals travel within the brain and between it and every organ in the body via the nervous system, enabling perception, motion, and cognition....

> Biologists have known for a long time that these kinds of bioelectrical signals are responsible for all communication between the brain and the nervous system: you can think of them as the telephone wires that help the brain's command center communicate with your muscles to operate your limbs.

> But bioelectricity isn't confined to our brains. Over the past couple of decades, it has become clear that these signals are pressed into service by every cell in your body, not just those that govern your perception and motion.

> Each of your skin cells has its own voltage...the cells in your bones are electric. Your teeth are electric. Your organs are electric....

Recently it has been discovered that electrical signals also send out beacons as we grow in the womb to guide us into the eventual shape we will take—two arms, two legs, two ears, a nose. When this signal is interrupted in utero, things go terribly wrong, so scientists are now working out ways to prevent physiological birth defects by retuning our electrics....

I tell you this to underscore that "bioelectricity" is no mere metaphor, no elegant stretching of a humdrum biochemical truth. You and I are literally electric. The basis of all life is electric. When our cellular battery runs out, we all die. So, what if we learned how to control the switch? (pp. 7–10)

Adee chronicles the bifurcation of the world scientific community that began in the late 18th century and continues to separate biologists from physicists over the issue of electricity:

Biologists stick to biology, leaving the study of electricity to the physicists and engineers. They just don't speak the same language... it means aspiring PhD students in physics are taught about Tesla and his alternating currents, but not about the bioelectricity running through their own bodies—and biology students get neither.... What we need is a new framework to bring the body's different electrical parameters under one roof and study them coherently, together. Call it the electrome....

Just as decoding the genome led us to the rules by which information like eye color is encoded in our DNA, bioelectricity researchers predict that decoding the electrome will help us decipher our body's multilayered communication systems and give us a way to control them.

Over the past ten to fifteen years, experiments have suggested that not only can we decrypt this code—we may even be able to learn to write it ourselves.... It would be like opening the electrical box and being able to rewire our systems as we like.... If it were to become possible to manipulate bioelectricity at its source, the consequences would be staggering.... Some bioelectricity researchers go as far as to say learning the rules of this software could render our bodies and minds as programmable as hardware.... If we are truly electric, then we should all be programmable at the level of every cell. (pp. 12–13)

I understand Sally Adee's enthusiasm and wonderment. We truly are miraculous electrical beings. What I find so troubling is that when Adee finally mentions some of the ethical concerns surrounding bioelectricity research, she is stunningly naive and dismissive:

> The gene-editing technology CRISPR ushered in a flurry of worries about designer babies, and our ability to edit the bioelectric code will be much the same.... Bioelectricity research could all too easily be misappropriated by that vague and undeniable urge to see humans as occupiers of inferior meat bodies that could only be improved by the addition and substitution of hardware and software....

> So, what limitations should we place on upgrading or altering humans? Who will govern the rules on remapping the body's electrical wiring? ...

> If we are going to try to manipulate the human body, the least we can do is manipulate it on its own terms—terms that were honored by millions of years of evolution, and not with headgear we invented. We have arrived at a new stage of bioelectricity. "With bioelectricity, we are now at the point where astronomy was when Galileo invented the telescope," says [Prof. Mustafa] Djamgoz, one of the cancer researchers gazing into the unknown. If the nineteenth century was referred to as the "electric century," the twenty-first century could go down in history as the bioelectric century. (pp. 13–14)

Bioelectricity research is unlike any other research that has ever come before, because as Sally Adee so clearly states, "If we are truly electric, then we should be programmable at the level of every cell." Contemplating the *possibility* of bioelectricity being misappropriated denies the reality of the military already weaponizing it, and the eventuality of its being used at home against civilians.

Every astonishing scientific discovery, from gunpowder to flight to nuclear energy to the existence of the unconscious mind, has been used for both construction and destruction. An article by Steve Tarani posted in online magazine *GunMagWarehouse* on August 17, 2023, "Origins of Gunpowder: An Historical Perspective,"[181] is particularly relevant:

Discovery, Early Uses and Experimentation

Gunpowder, although widely available today and in a variety of configurations, was originally a substance that revolutionized warfare and is widely considered one of the most significant inventions in human history.

The origin of gunpowder can be traced back to ancient China, where it was initially developed as a medicinal elixir. Over time, however, gunpowder's properties were harnessed for military purposes, leading to transformative changes in warfare and the world at large.

The exact origins of gunpowder remain shrouded in mystery to this very day, but historical evidence suggests that its discovery can be attributed to ancient Chinese alchemists. Around the 9th century, during the Tang Dynasty, these alchemists were engaged in the quest to discover the elixir of immortality.

In their experiments, they stumbled upon a peculiar mixture comprising sulfur, charcoal, and saltpeter (potassium nitrate). This blend possessed explosive properties that astonished the alchemists.

Although gunpowder was initially employed for its medicinal qualities because it was believed to promote longevity and cure ailments, its explosive nature soon captured the attention of military strategists, who recognized its potential as a game-changing weapon.

Let's be clear. Bioelectricity goes far beyond any of the extraordinary scientific discoveries of the past. Why? *Because bioelectricity actually has the potential to alter the course of human evolution.*

Bioelectricity represents a seismic shift and expansion of scientific understanding, since all life on Earth is electric. Decoding the electrome will award scientists the power to manipulate the developing human fetus and eventually redesign the human fetus, and thereby redefine human life. This is the Holy Grail of technocracy and transhumanism.

Bioethics is a misnomer and will not help us in the realm of bioelectricity.

When Klaus Schwab, Yuval Harari, Elon Musk, and Sally Adee use words like *ethical* and *bioethics*, they dismiss the original colloquial understanding of the words. Most people think bioethics protects the individual and comports with the original Hippocratic Oath that instructed physicians, "First, do no harm." Named after the ancient Greek physician Hippocrates (460–370 BC), the Hippocratic Oath was the traditional oath of ethics taken by all physicians. It unapologetically and in no uncertain terms upholds the value of the individual patient.

Marxism values the group, not the individual. When this collectivist perspective is applied to medicine, it results in *consensus* medicine, ideologically driven political medicine, which means that the individual patient is no longer primary, the group is. And what is best for the group? The government decides! In this case a group of ideologues who happen to be physicians decides what is best practice—not for the individual patient, but for society as a whole. The ramifications of this shift are staggering, and the reader needs to remember two basic principles. First, the *bioethics* of Marxist ideologues and WEF globalists does not protect the individual. Second, the elite always take care of the elite. The deceitful Marxist dualism that Obama brought to Washington is the same dualism that continues to confuse the public with words like *bioethics*.

History is a great teacher. Barack Obama signed two of the most destructive acts against the United States in American history. First, the Smith-Mundt Modernization Act of 2012, which effectively nullified the Smith-Mundt Act of 1948 that explicitly prohibited information and psychological operations aimed at influencing U.S. public opinion. Obama legalized propaganda in America against Americans by reversing the prohibition against it. Obama made it legal for his State Department and Pentagon to disseminate his administration's Marxist political propaganda directly to the American people. Then in 2016 Obama signed the Countering Foreign Propaganda and Disinformation Act, which launched the offensive information war that continues to destabilize the country today. In an astonishing demonstration of Marxist word perversion, the terms *propaganda* and *disinformation* were applied domestically, and used to bludgeon the political opposition.

Obama's state-sponsored assault on facts continues to expand legally in every sector and institution of American life. The Marxist Culture War, with its signature march through American institutions, was animated by Barack

Hussein Obama. Bernays adapted military propaganda techniques for commercial purposes; Obama legalized military propaganda techniques for political purposes. The military-industrial complex develops bioelectricity capabilities for commerce and politics. Why?

The answer is simple. The twin goals of both the military and private industry are the same: *Power and Control*. The combination of resources makes each partner exponentially more powerful, and the shared deceit is that science and technology will be used to heal sickness and liberate the public from its biological limitations.

But would the military-industrial complex use bioelectrical rewiring to alter cognition and behavior of the people it seeks to control? Of course it would, and it has already begun. American political medicine and its associated medical research, including bioelectricity research, disguises its political objectives in the powerful dual-use word *bioethics*.

Let's review. The Internet of Things (IoT) was mentioned in Chapter 32 in the discussion of Klaus Schwab's Davos Manifesto 2020 and the blurring of boundaries between man and machine/computer. IoT is also discussed in my previous book *The Collapsing American Family: From Bonding to Bondage*. An excerpt from Chapter 28 of that book, "The Great Reset Planned for the United States of America," is particularly instructive:

> Klaus Schwab published *The Fourth Industrial Revolution* in January 2017. The book describes the artificial intelligence of today as the 21st-century Fourth Industrial Revolution. It follows the steam engine, which launched the first industrial revolution in the 18th century, electricity in the 19th century, and computers in the 20th century.
>
> In a January 10, 2016, interview[182] on Swiss channel RTS, Schwab explained that human beings will soon receive a chip in their body in order to merge with the digital world. When asked about implanted chips, Schwab responded matter-of-factly:
>
> > Certainly, within the next ten years. And at first, we will implant them in our clothes. And then we could imagine that we will implant them in our brains, or in our skin. And in the end maybe there will be a direct communication between our

brain and the digital world. What we see is a kind of fusion of the physical, digital, and biological world…. It is a servant that with artificial intelligence learns, and that is not only your assistant for manual work, but that can really be an intellectual partner of you.

In 2016, Schwab was describing the bioelectricity, neuroscience, and neurotechnology of BigBrain, the BRAIN Initiative, and now BICAN (Chapter 38). The baseline bioelectricity and decoding of the electrome that Sally Adee popularized is its natural conclusion. In the same 2016 interview Klaus Schwab alluded to *bioethics*:

> The Fourth Industrial Revolution (4IR), in blurring the boundaries between physical, digital, and biological worlds, challenges what it means to be human. It fuses man and machine through artificial intelligence (AI), robotics, the Internet of Things (IoT), 3-D printing, genetic engineering, and quantum computing. It relies on technological surveillance rather than the rule of law to maintain order in society. These technological advances depend on fifth-generation (5G) mobile network technology for speed and connectivity.
>
> Schwab claims the seismic changes of the Fourth Industrial Revolution are so sweeping that they redefine everything, including how we relate to one another, the way we work, the way we do business, how governments function, and even what it means to be human. The tools of the 4IR are so powerful that they enable new forms of surveillance and social control, including intrusion into our minds, reading our thoughts and influencing our behavior. Schwab argues that we must embrace the changes and build an ethical, inclusive, sustainable, and prosperous future. (*Collapsing American Family*, p. 171)

Klaus Schwab, Yuval Harari, and their fellow globalists are selling planetary feudalism by calling it freedom. Changing the name of something does not change what that something actually is. The Great Reset turns the multinational corporations working with government into overlords, and the world population into their economically enslaved serfs. The new normal is the end result of the 21st-century military-industrial complex. Schwab declares, "We must embrace the changes and build an *ethical, inclusive, sustainable,* and *prosperous* future," but Schwab never mentions it will be the globalist elite who make all the rules for determining what is ethical, inclusive, sustainable, and prosperous.

It is difficult to sell feudalism as freedom, but using the familiar woke magic words *ethical, inclusive, sustainable*, and *prosperous* is definitely helping Schwab sell the con. Sally Adee is a gifted science writer who welcomes us to the excitement of the bioelectric century while apparently buying what Klaus Schwab is selling. Perhaps Adee cannot fathom the sinister nature of the World Economic Forum (WEF), its public-private partnerships, its globalist depopulation agenda, or its compelling interest in the Fourth Industrial Revolution and the technologies that animate it. Perhaps Sally Adee is too excited to realize that wound healing, cell regeneration, and cancer cures are only the bait.

The switch in this bait and switch comes with imposition of globalist planetary control through the auspices of the awaiting United Nations. Creation of the globalist Unistate awards totalitarian control of the world's population and natural resources to the avaricious globalist elite, still promising "you will own nothing and be happy." Bioelectricity is the missing piece of knowledge in globalism's transhumanist dreams for eternal life and totalitarian control. Decoding the electrome provides the pathway for human beings to become part of the Internet of Things. Consider the future in globalism's New Normal.

Human beings will be connected to the electrical grid like cars, stoves, and heaters. The human body will become a remotely controlled appliance, just like any other such appliance. Today's politicized effort to rid the planet of gas-powered vehicles, gas-powered stoves, and gas-powered heaters does not rescue the planet. It removes some of the last vestiges of independence and agency from gas users. When the power goes out, people with gas-powered equipment are free to move about, cook, and heat their homes. Anything connected to globalism's electrical grid system including food, fuel, shelter, medicine, clothing—and the digital currency to purchase them—requires access to the grid. In the Unistate, the entire world population is completely dependent upon access to the electrical grid for survival.

Blurring the boundaries between man and machine is being deceitfully marketed as *progress* for *saving* humanity and *rescuing* planet Earth. It is no such thing. It is globalism's most colossal humanitarian hoax, marketed for our own good but delivered for totalitarian control. And like bedazzled children, adults are being seduced by globalism's political candy.

Access to the grid is controlled by the globalist elite, who also determine its terms of use and its currency. Today's currency is ESG scores; tomorrow's currency could be your liver, your heart, or your brain. Without legal and moral protections for the sovereignty of the self, your body becomes another asset of the collective to be exploited for "the good of the group." The fusion of man and machine and the technical advances that Klaus Schwab described in January 2016 relied on 5G technology. The next iteration of technological advances will depend upon 6G technology, discussed in the next chapter.

Consider how Freud's discovery of the unconscious mind, which led to psychotherapy, psychological operations, and propaganda, requires the individual's participation to influence his heart, mind, and behavior. Bioelectricity, on the other hand, has the capacity for direct application without the individual's knowledge or consent. *We're not in Kansas anymore.*

The inconvenient truth is that we are in a pivotal moment in world history, and the human race is in an existential battle for its future. Of this I am certain. Globalism's war on the nation-state does not end with the creation of Klaus Schwab's glorified globalist Unistate. The Unistate is simply the planetary *form* for its feudal infrastructure, and the organizing principle for its totalitarian governance.

The *transformative culture* of globalism's New World Order marks the end of human agency, the end of human freedom, and the end of Humanity 1.0. Cognitive warfare is transformative. It is the ultimate military weapon used against civilians to subdue, control, and achieve absolute conformity.

The secret of globalism's megalomania is its supremacist foundation and aristocratic mindset. If the enemies of individual sovereignty cannot persuade you with their ideas, they will change your mind inside your own head. Globalism's slogan never mentions the price you will pay for entry into its world of eternal dependence: *You will own nothing and you will be happy—but you will no longer be you.*

CHAPTER 41

Your Brain Is the Battlespace

Globalism is a replacement ideology that seeks to reorder the world into one singular, planetary Unistate, ruled by the globalist elite. The globalist war on nation-states cannot succeed without collapsing the United States of America. The long-term strategic attack plan moves America incrementally from constitutional republic to socialism to globalism to feudalism. The tactical attack plan uses asymmetric psychological and informational warfare to destabilize Americans and drive society out of objective reality into the madness of subjective reality. America's children are the primary target of the globalist predators.

In 1970, Zbigniew Brzezinski published his book *Between Two Ages: America's Role in the Technetronic Era.*[183] Brzezinski was a futurist who cofounded the globalist Trilateral Commission with David Rockefeller and Jimmy Carter in 1973, and served as national security adviser to Jimmy Carter between 1977 and 1981. Brzezinski understood the impact of science on society:

> Speaking of a future at most decades away, an experimenter in intelligence control asserted, "I foresee a time when we shall have the means and therefore, inevitably, the temptation to manipulate the behavior and intellectual functioning of all the people through environmental and biochemical manipulation of the brain." (*Between Two Ages: America's Role in the Technetronic Era*, p. 15)

> Another threat, less overt but no less basic, confronts liberal democracy. More directly linked to the impact of technology, it involves the gradual appearance of a more controlled and directed society. Such a society would be dominated by an elite whose claim to political power would rest on allegedly superior scientific know-how. Unhindered by the restraints of traditional liberal values, this elite would not hesitate to achieve its political ends by using the latest

modern techniques for influencing public behavior and keeping society under close surveillance and control. (pp. 252–253)

In an August 2017 seminar at Lawrence Livermore National Laboratory's Center for Global Security Research (CGSR) guest speaker Dr. James Giordano, of Georgetown University Medical Center, offered a sobering view of the calculated war on our brains, the temptation to manipulate the behavior and intellectual functioning of all the people, and the potential for weaponizing neuroscientific discoveries and neurotechnologies.

Dr. Giordano is a professor in the Departments of Neurology and Biochemistry, Chief of the Neuroethics Studies Program, and Co-director of the O'Neill-Pellegrino Program in Brain Science and Global Health Law and Policy at Georgetown University Medical Center in Washington, DC. He is a Senior Researcher and Task Leader of the Working Group on Dual-Use of the EU Human Brain Project, and has served as a Senior Science Advisory Fellow of the Strategic Multilayer Assessment group of the Joint Chiefs of Staff of the Pentagon.

His 2017 briefing, "Brain Science from Bench to Battlefield: The Realities—and Risks—of Neuroweapons,"[184] explores the potentials of brain science in the context of public/private research for national defense, including using nano-pharmaceutical low-dose toxins or other chemicals as a controlled vector.

Giordano discussed current political dual-use capabilities of neuroscience technology and, of course, mentioned the new field of "neuroethics."

[Transcript excerpts]

[5:30 counter] *If I am able to in some way access and effect this thing that is, in at least some way, demonstrably and perhaps to a large extent responsible for making you, you—your persona, your thoughts, your hopes, your dreams—well, look at the power that that can yield. We like to talk about influencing hearts and minds, but this is a question of influencing brains to influence hearts, and then influence minds....*

[50:00] *What has gone from the drawing board to the reality is this: the use of neural interfacing and physiological interfacing through the idea of remote-controlled small-scale systems to be able to modify the behavior of non-human animals. A variety of scales: small mammals, and, increasingly,* the use of insects. The pioneering work was done by DARPA, something called the DARPA beetle, the DARPA fly, and more recently an independent non-DARPA-funded commercial enterprise [that] calls itself Dragonfly has been able to utilize a combined set of techniques, both direct neural stimulation and optogenetic control of key neuron firing patterns, to direct the wingbeats impulses, and as a consequence directionality....

[51:16] In some cases, they're looking to the high-level nano or at least low-level micro-scale use of various electrodes that can both record and perhaps deliver certain types of payloads as well. So, the idea is going back to this very, very low-dose nano- pharmaceutical delivery of toxins or other chemicals, and utilizing this as a controlled vector becomes a real possibility. Note, this has not been directly addressed nor has it been entertained by any United States government entity in a public forum. This is not what DARPA has intended this device to be. This is supposed to be a surveillance device that could be used for public health, and also to monitor key environmental factors. And the same is being touted here, that this is not a device that is weaponizable.

The reason I tell you about it is that this was a point of considerable debate and discourse at the recent meeting of the European Union Human Brain Project Subcommittee on Dual Use. And I stood before these people and said to them, you know, this is not being entertained in these ways, and the response there was "Yes, but it should." And so, the fact that people are thinking about this, but this was not explicit intent, means that it is in fact capable to be developed in these directions, and that becomes a real concern and consideration.

[53:17] So, we're looking at this idea of neuroscience and technology for national security, intelligence, and defense. I think the take-home message here is that yeah, we can access and affect manipulating control, so to speak, neural systems to affect, alter, change, direct minds via brains and, therefore, the hearts in which those minds are embodied. We used to talk, as I said, about hearts and minds. Now, through the use of neuroscience and technology, minds and hearts is a far more viable description, because it describes for us explicitly the route of engagement. What we can do here, I think, is very provocative, but what we should do, that's still, I think, a point of contention and represents a work in progress....

[57:35] *Recent estimates, not speculation, by the Neurotechnology Industry Organization has predicted by 2025 greater than 50 percent of international neuroscience and technology will be conducted—listen to this—outside the West. Not outside the United States, not outside Europe. Outside the West.*

[58:17] *Now, that's an important consideration, because what it demonstrates is a shift in the capability, potential, and ultimate power that can be yielded by this. I'm not saying it's a good thing or a bad thing, it's a thing. But I'm also, I think it becomes important for you to understand, is that this also needs consideration because of the fact that not all philosophies are aligned with our own. Moreover, the needs and values of other cultures may not necessarily be the same as ours, and they have every right in the world to be able to engage that cosmopolitan viewpoint. In other words, certain cultures have different philosophies that then acknowledge different needs and different values in distinct ways. And if, in fact, you recognize this, it demands a larger discourse, one that brings together international partners and a cooperative way to be able to both post the field and in some cases policy the field.*

[1:00:46] *We may think there are limits in proscriptions, the idea that, well, "we won't go there" doesn't mean that someone else won't. Furthermore, I think that there are some ethical legal issues that need to be raised, not only with regard to what we're doing with the science or what can be done with it, the inviolability of mind and self, what we talked about earlier. Could we use these for interrogation? Could we use these in warfare? Yes, we could. Should we? Hmm… But we could argue it, well, less harm is going to be incurred. But really, what are the harms once we get into the relative inviolability of the brain space, the last private domain, if you will….*

[1:03:28] *The operational neurotechnology risk-assessment management process or paradigm, and what it really does, is it embraces, I think, an older idea that had been advocated initially by Brzezinski essentially in 1970, 1972. I won't bore you with the quote, you can read it for yourself, but essentially the issue here was that the idea that the modification manipulation through biochemical manipulation of the brain was seen as real in 1970 and now has been realized some forty years later. This is not hypothetical.*

[Transcript excerpts end]

This briefing in 2017 was given by a man deeply connected to the military-industrial complex. His perspective is, in my opinion, an exquisite performance of controlled opposition. Using the psychological tactic of *projection*, Giordano deftly accused others of doing precisely what the globalist leaders of our military-industrial complex were and are doing themselves.

Both direct and optogenetic stimulation (stimulating with light) that Giordano describes are neurotechnologies being used to manipulate the bioelectrical potential and behavior of dragonflies. The environmental and biochemical manipulation that Brzezinski referenced in 1970 has been expanded to the bioelectrical potential that Sally Adee documented in *We Are Electric* in 2023. Adee's research revealed that all life is electrical, and that means algae, bacteria, molds, fungi, plants, insects, fish, all lower animals, and all mammals including humans.

We now know that bioelectricity is how all life communicates internally, so why not externally as well? It does not take much imagination to foresee a future of bioelectric convergence and communication among all life-forms.

Augmented human beings linked to the electrical grid via the Internet of Bodies are entry-level versions of transhumanist beings. They are the front line in globalism's aggressive campaign to acquire the science and technology necessary to create and support Humanity 2.0.

The fusion of the Internet of Things with the Internet of Bodies blurs all boundaries between plants, animals, humans, and machines. It connects all things in an electrified planetary ecology ruled by the globalist elite—for our own good, of course. Stakeholder discussions follow a scripted marketing pattern of glorifying social/medical benefits of advanced science, briefly mentioning ethical considerations that must be worked out and completely ignoring the tyranny of the scientific dictatorship they are advancing.

Whether presented by Bertrand Russell, Zbigniew Brzezinski, Klaus Schwab, Yuval Harari, or James Giordano, globalism is a totalitarian ideology that relies on the supremacist mindset of the elite, who believe that they can govern you better than you can govern yourself. Cognitive warfare will exploit the neuroscience and neurotechnologies of bioelectricity to establish totalitarian social control.

Consider life in the Unistate and the meaning of Humanity 2.0. The world population becomes part of the Unistate, where people are property and subjects—not citizens—of globalism's New World Order. There is no opposition, only oppositional ideas that will be neutralized using cognitive warfare to change the minds and then the hearts of any dissenters who survived the globalist purge. Recall NATO Innovation Hub manager François du Cluzel's haunting description of cognitive warfare in Chapter 39 as the art of using technologies to alter the cognition of human targets: "It's not only an action against what we think, but also an action against the way we think, the way we process information and turn it into knowledge…. It is a war on our individual processor, our brain…. This is extremely important for us in the military, because it has the potential, by developing new weapons and ways of harming the brain, it has the potential to engage neuroscience and technology in many, many different approaches to influence human ecology…because you all know that it's very easy to turn a civilian technology into a military one."

What does du Cluzel mean by human ecology? I found it necessary to look the phrase up. Human ecology is the study of the relationships between humans and their environment. It is a sweeping study that analyzes human beings in ways traditionally applied to plants and animals in ecology. Its perspective conforms to United Nations Agenda 2030 and the 17 Sustainable Goals, which view all life on Earth as planetary assets. Human beings are just another asset to be controlled through surveillance and technology.

Technology expert Rob Braxman explains how current surveillance capabilities actually extend beyond the Internet in two short videos, "There's a Secret Network - Skynet 2.0,"[185] February 16, 2022, and April 17, 2024, "Skynet 2024: The Infrastructure is Complete!"[186] Braxman explains how the use of Bluetooth Low Energy (BLE) mesh networks are being used to surveil iPhone and Android users without their knowledge or consent. BLE mesh networks work when devices are turned off, and

> all communications are peer-to-peer. This means that each device will operate with any other BLE device with no interference from a third party. To put it in more black and white terms, you personally have no control over the BLE functionality of your own device. You cannot stop it.…

> BLE devices cannot only send data, but can receive instructions. Just as a BLE device can be a peripheral that can be turned on and off, think of this functionality on a phone. Apple or Amazon could give instructions to a device that's turned off to turn on for surveillance reasons. Since an iPhone that is off could receive instructions to turn on, it can then receive further instructions over the Internet to perform specific surveillance tasks....

> AI could be instructed to turn on the camera and observe its surroundings and could be initiated even when the device is off....

> What the mesh network can do is unlimited. We cannot know or even limit the messaging capabilities of BLE with multicasting [data transmits to a group]. This has some extreme implications with slave devices [a device controlled by another device]. It means that a large company can actually control devices far away from itself by making BLE devices operate in peripheral mode....

> Remote control of large numbers of devices all under the control of a single company and even, perhaps, one person or one AI.

The potential for advanced location tracking and the potential for a single company being able to control its devices without user awareness is extremely disturbing. If the company is working with the NSA, the surveillance and technology potential is horrifying.

In the name of national defense, on April 19, 2024, the United States Congress passed Section 702 of the Foreign Intelligence Surveillance Act (FISA). Its change to the definition of "electronic communications surveillance provider" means that any company or individual that has access to equipment on which communications are transmitted or stored, including routers, servers, and cell towers, can be forced to assist the NSA in warrantless surveillance on American citizens.

Also, in the name of national defense, a recent study conducted by RAND Corp., a think tank closely associated with the Trilateral Commission since its inception in 1973, is reviewed by Technocracy News editor Patrick Wood. The study, commissioned by the UK Defence Science and Technology Laboratory and published March 25, 2024, examines "Cultural and technological change in the future information environment." According to the report, "The Internet of Bodies ecosystem may lead to the Internet of Brains sometime between 2035 and 2050."[187]

Technologically, the Internet of Bodies connects human beings to machines through wearable devices and/or implanted devices. The Internet of Brains is the realm beyond the Internet of Bodies, where direct communications between human brains and/or computer devices is established. The augmentation in the Internet of Brains redefines what it means to be human and marks entry into the realm of transhumanism, Humanity 2.0. The authors consider the cultural ramifications of augmentation:

> The social dynamics of human augmentation adoption may include disparities in access to relevant technologies, thus introducing new forms of digital exclusion whereby the economically disadvantaged cannot access the same enhancement level as other societal segments....

> In other words, transhumanism may lead to super-human capabilities for some, and mind control for others. Manipulation and control are other areas of concern with human augmentation, the Internet of Bodies, and the Internet of Brains.

> False information, images, sounds, memories, and thoughts could one day be downloaded to these devices and uploaded to the human brain with devastating effect.

The unambiguous aspiration of the globalist elite is the Internet of Brains specifically because it awards *super-human capabilities for some, and mind control for others.* Both achieved through surveillance and technology deceitfully marketed as *national defense,* which means *we the people are the targeted enemy*!

CHAPTER 42

Quantum Computing Empowers Technocracy, Transhumanism, and the Managerial Unistate

Globalism is a replacement ideology that seeks to reorder the world into one singular, planetary Unistate, ruled by the globalist elite. The globalist war on nation-states cannot succeed without collapsing the United States of America. The long-term strategic attack plan moves America incrementally from constitutional republic to socialism to globalism to feudalism. The tactical attack plan uses asymmetric psychological and informational warfare to destabilize Americans and drive society out of objective reality into the madness of subjective reality. America's children are the primary target of the globalist predators.

As America's freedom clock continues to tick toward zero, the globalist elite are busy ramping up their investments in the science and technology that will enslave us. The introduction of 6G technology will change everything we now know about computing, computers, and communication technology. These networks are expected to arrive around 2030. Coincidence? I don't think so. The rollout will be timed to coincide with United Nations Agenda 2030.

We can trace the evolution of mobile communications technology from mobile cellular equipment, which relied on cell towers, to wireless technology that connected users via the Internet. The strength of the underlying technology is expressed as 1G, 2G, 3G, 4G, and 5G, with 1G being the first generation of wireless cellular technology, 2G being the second, and so on, each successive generation improving the speed, connectivity, capacity, and network latency of the generation before.

In computer language *latency*, also called *ping*, measures the time it takes for your computer, the Internet, and everything in between to respond to an action you take. For example, if you click on a website link, the latency period would be how long it takes for the link to pop up on your computer screen.

5G was launched as an astonishing improvement in network latency over 4G. But 6G will be hailed as the enhancement of the future—and it is: 6G will provide an immersive experience for the user with life-like hologram video calls. Augmented Reality (AR) will be the new reality.

RCR Wireless News[188]quotes Nokia Labs president Marcus Weldon at the Brooklyn 5G Summit in 2019:

> Speaking of 5G, Weldon said, "What we've done now is solved for the three dimensions of capacity, but we've added in reliability and latency. You can think of 5G as a nine-dimensional innovation fabric. That's really why it's profoundly important. It's not about consumers interacting with Siri, Alexa, Google. It's about industrials and robots interacting with control systems."
>
> "What it really comes down to is mixing the physical world [and] the digital world—software systems, AI systems, and biological systems. You mix those together in real time. I have a permanent AR."

A "permanent augmented reality" means everything we know as *objective reality* is in jeopardy. There will no longer be any accurate reference to test reality; 6G will provide globalism's *New Normal*—totally disconnected from objective reality, the world of facts. Only the globalist elite controlling 6G will know what is actually real! This is an existence beyond the horror that most people can even imagine in their worst nightmares. *It is insanity redefined as sanity and institutionalized as normal*!

Globalism's planetary Unistate is predicated upon augmented reality. Tech writer Alexander S. Gillis provides an explanation of augmented reality on TechTarget.com:[189]

What is augmented reality (AR)?

Augmented reality (AR) is the integration of digital information with the user's environment in real time. Unlike virtual reality (VR), which creates a totally artificial environment, AR users experience a real-world environment with generated perceptual information overlaid on top of it.

Augmented reality is used to either visually change natural environments in some way or to provide additional information to users. The primary benefit of AR is that it manages to blend digital and three-dimensional (3D) components with an individual's perception of the real world. AR has a variety of uses, from helping in decision-making to entertainment.

AR delivers visual elements, sound and other sensory information to the user through a device like a smartphone or glasses. This information is overlaid onto the device to create an interwoven experience where digital information alters the user's perception of the real world. The overlaid information can be added to an environment or mask part of the natural environment.

The evolution of mobile communications technologies is described in waves. The First Wave, initiated in December 1979 by Japanese firm Nippon Telegraph and Telephone Public Corporation, introduced mobile phones supported by 1G and 2G technologies. The Second Wave, 2010–2020, made mobile multimedia possible and required 3G and 4G technologies. The Third Wave, marketed as supporting *future industry and society*, requires 5G and 6G technologies begun in 2020 and expected to mature by 2030. "Future industry and society" refer to augmented reality in the new normal of globalism's planetary Unistate!

Gillis continues with a comparison between augmented reality (AR) and virtual reality (VR):

Differences between AR and VR

VR is a virtual environment created with software and presented to users in such a way that their brain suspends belief long enough to accept a virtual world as a real environment. Virtual reality is primarily experienced through a headset with sight and sound.

The biggest difference between AR and VR is that augmented reality uses the existing real-world environment and puts virtual information on top of it, whereas VR completely immerses users in a virtually rendered environment. While VR puts the user in a new, simulated environment, AR places the user in a sort of mixed reality.

The devices used to accomplish this are different, too. VR uses VR headsets that fit over the user's head and present them with simulated visual and audio information. AR devices are less restrictive and typically include devices like phones, glasses, projections and HUDs [Heads-up displays project information above the dashboard for the driver to see without looking down] in cars.

In VR, people are placed inside a 3D environment in which they can move around and interact with the generated environment. AR, however, keeps users grounded in the real-world environment, overlaying virtual data as a visual layer within the environment.

Nippon Telegraph and Telephone Public Corporation's 2020 White Paper: 5G Evolution and 6G[190] discusses the popularization of big data and AI, and the increased interest in cyber-physical fusion. In Section 2.2 it examines 6G:

Solving social problems

Many social issues and needs expected in 5G will be resolved in the 2020s. It is expected that various solutions such as telework, remote control, telemedicine, distance education, and autonomous operation of various equipment including cars will be provided by high-speed and low-latency communication networks for social problems such as regional creation, low birth rate, aging, and labor shortage in the 2020s. Further popularization of solutions and more advanced correspondence in the 2030s will require complete problem solving and development. The world is expected to become a place in which all people, information, and goods can be accessed anywhere in an ultra-real experience, and the constraints of working place and time are completely eliminated. This will dramatically eliminate social and cultural disparities between rural and urban areas, avoid urban concentration of people, and promote local development. It can also make people's lives more stress-free.

Communication between humans and things

Advanced functions of wearable devices including XR (VR, AR, MR) devices, high-definition images and holograms exceeding 8K, and new five sense communications including tactile sense will proliferate, and communications between humans and between humans and things will become ultra-real and rich. As a result, innovative entertainment services and enterprise services for games, watching sports, etc. will be provided without time and place restrictions.

Through rapid popularization and development of IoT services, the demand for the communications of things will become very large. High speed and low latency performance that far exceeds the human ability will be required for communications because large data processing including high-definition images and control of equipment with ultra-low latency will be carried out by machines.

Expansion of communication environment

Communications are now as ubiquitous as the air around us and as vital as electricity and water. Therefore, users do not need to be aware of communication settings and the communication service area. A communication environment will be required in all places with the expansion of the activity area of people and things. High-rise buildings, drones, flying cars, airplanes, and even space will be natural activity areas, and not only the ground but also the sky and space will be indispensable communication areas. The need is increasing for communication areas at sea and under the sea. Due to the needs of various sensor networks, unmanned factories, and unmanned construction sites, it is also necessary to construct a communication area in an environment without human beings. As a result, every place on the ground, sky, and sea will become a communication area.

Sophistication of cyber-physical fusion

Many services utilizing cyber-physical fusion will be created in the 2020s and will be used practically in all environments, but more advanced cyber-physical fusion will be required in the 2030s. By transmitting and processing a large amount of information between cyberspace and physical space without delay, tighter cooperation between both spaces will be achieved, and ultimately, fusion without a gap between the spaces will be actualized. For humans, it will become possible for cyberspace to support human thought and action in real time through wearable devices and micro-devices mounted on the human body. All kinds of things such as transportation equipment including cars, construction machinery, machine tools, monitoring cameras, and various sensors will be linked in cyberspace. They will support safety and security, solutions to social problems, and a rich life for people.

This Japanese White Paper reads like a World Economic Forum infomercial, deceitfully selling its own cyber-control 6G communications as evolutionary developments that will improve people's lives. This is not surprising considering that Japan is fully committed to the WEF and its globalist Agenda 2030.

The White Paper talks about 6G latency in Section 3.4:

Extreme low-latency

In cyber-physical fusion, wireless communications that connect AI and devices is analogous to the human nervous system which transmits information. In order to actualize services in real-time and be highly interactive, an always stable end-to-end (E2E) low latency seems to be a basic requirement. For 6G, concretely, an approximately 1 ms or less E2E latency is considered as the target value. With this, for example, in a shop automated by robotics, interactive services that respond attentively similar to a human by watching the facial expression of a customer may be actualized.

This entry raises two fundamental questions. *Why is a shop automated by robotics desirable? How is a shop automated by robots an improvement on life?* It isn't. Beneath the deceitful marketing campaign is globalism's unapologetic depopulation agenda. During his notorious February 2010 TED Talks presentation,[191] eugenicist Bill Gates unapologetically discussed his plan to reduce the world's population by 10 to 15 percent.

> *The world today has 6.8 billion people. That's heading up to about 9 billion. Now, if we do a really great job on new vaccines, health care, reproductive health services, we could lower that by 10 or 15 percent. [4:17 counter]*

The World Population Clock[192] records the world's population at 8.1 billion as of May 19, 2024. It is difficult for the civilized mind to imagine the scope of Gates's depopulation plan: 10 percent of 8.1 billion people is 810 million people, which translates to the populations of the United States, Russia, Mexico, Japan, and Germany combined.

It is equally difficult for the civilized mind to imagine the reality of life in globalism's 6G realm. Robots will replace most of the human workforce. So, what appears charming in Japan's White Paper, the example of a shop automated by robotics, is actually part of an overarching eugenics plan.

Consider robotics from the globalist elite perspective. Robots are the ideal workforce. They are far more efficient and do not need to be paid, fed, clothed, or insured. There are no unions because there is no conflict. Robots are the epitome of a compliant workforce that is owned and operated by the globalist elite, who remain firmly entrenched in objective reality, where they are able to control the world's population living in the subjective reality of 6G.

What about robotics in schools? As John Klyczek explained in Chapter 35,

> Moxie is marketed as a "Helping Friend" that substitutes human caretakers and replaces them as robo-babysitters that monitor disabled children during parent-therapist conferences…. Of course, over time, just like transhuman ed-tech, robotic AI ed-tech will eventually creep more and more into mainstream classroom integration until it is employed to boost competence outcomes for students classified as healthy and able-bodied.

What begins with a "helping friend" becomes normative as healthy and able-bodied children are groomed to interact with robots, inanimate objects, and holograms rather than humans. Children are not born with an ability to test reality. It is an acquired skill that begins to be taught in the home when Mommy tells little Johnny, "No, Johnny, you are not a bird. You are a little boy, and you cannot fly."

Reality-testing distinguishes objective reality from subjective reality. It is reinforced in school if teachers support objective reality. Today, however, little Johnny is taught in school that he can be a girl if he chooses. Tomorrow little Johnny will be able to fly in augmented reality with 6G technology. Little Johnny is being driven out of objective reality today in order to groom him for life in globalism's Unistate tomorrow.

On January 26, 2023, *TIME* magazine published the article "Quantum Computers Could Solve Countless Problems—And Create a Lot of New Ones."[193] Reporter Charlie Campbell describes the staggering power and transformative nature of quantum computing and its reliance on 6G technology, and identifies asset-management firms as Quantum's earliest adopters:

> Quantum's unique ability to crunch stacks of data is already optimizing the routes of thousands of fuel tankers traversing the globe, helping decide which ICU patients require the most urgent care, and mimicking chemical processes at the atomic level to better design new materials. It also promises to supercharge artificial intelligence, with the power to better train algorithms that can finally turn driverless cars and drone taxis into a reality. Quantum AI simulations exhibit a "degree of effectiveness and efficiency that is mind-boggling," U.S. National Cyber Director Chris Inglis tells *TIME*.

> Quantum's earliest adopters are asset-management firms—for which incorporating quantum calculations involves few increased overhead costs—but commercial uses aren't far behind. Spanish firm Multiverse Computing has run successful pilot projects with multinational clients like BASF and Bosch that show its quantum algorithms can double foreign-exchange trading profits and catch almost four times as many production-line defects. "Quantum deep-learning algorithms are completely different from classical ones," says Multiverse CEO Enrique Lizaso Olmos. "You can train them faster, try more strategies, and they are much better at getting the correlations that matter from a lot of data."

> Tech giants from Google to Amazon and Alibaba—not to mention nation-states vying for technological supremacy—are racing to dominate this space. The global quantum-computing industry is projected to grow from $412 million in 2020 to $8.6 billion in 2027, according to an International Data Corp. analysis.

> Whereas traditional computers rely on binary "bits"—switches either on or off, denoted as 1s and 0s—to process information, the "qubits" that underpin quantum computing are tiny subatomic

particles that can exist in some percentage of both states simultaneously, rather like a coin spinning in midair. This leap from dual to multivariate processing exponentially boosts computing power. Complex problems that currently take the most powerful supercomputer several years could potentially be solved in seconds. Future quantum computers could open hitherto unfathomable frontiers in mathematics and science, helping to solve existential challenges like climate change and food security. A flurry of recent breakthroughs and government investment means we now sit on the cusp of a quantum revolution. "I believe we will do more in the next five years in quantum innovation than we did in the last 30," says [Jay] Gambetta [IBM's vice president of quantum computing].

Quantum computing is the next generation of computer technology. Quantum computing uses the principles of quantum theory, which explain the behavior of energy and material on the atomic and subatomic levels. The difference between quantum computing and classical computing is the difference between an electron microscope and a compound microscope. It is the difference between day and night.

The race for quantum technology is compared to the space race. Quantum computing is being called the next industrial revolution, and likened to the beginning of the Internet. The title of Campbell's article refers to quantum's staggering problem-solving capability and also to its inherent dangers. He writes:

> But any disrupter comes with risks, and quantum has become a national-security migraine. Its problem-solving capacity will soon render all existing cryptography obsolete, jeopardizing communications, financial transactions, and even military defenses.

Today, IBM is considered the industry leader in quantum computing. And who are the three largest institutional investors in IBM? Vanguard, BlackRock, and State Street. So, the globalist asset managers that control nearly $30 trillion in assets are also the top investors in quantum computing—the future of communications technology.

This fact represents an existential threat to objective reality, and to life on this planet as we know it. Consider the seismic changes in society driven by the Big Three asset managers over the last four years, since the COVID-19 debacle began. Now imagine the same Big Three in control of 6G augmented reality and the unlimited power it awards them to control all of humanity, including our perceptions of reality.

Yahoo Finance,[194] February 19, 2024, lists the Big Three among the top four institutional holders of Apple Inc. (AAPL). Berkshire Hathaway, Inc., Warren Buffett's globalist behemoth, is the fourth. On February 2, 2024, Apple launched Vision Pro, its immersive mixed-reality $4,000 headset capable of alternating between augmented reality and virtual reality. Described as an iPad for your face (spatial computer), early reviews focused on the high rate of returned devices from customers dissatisfied with Vision Pro's initial performance, features, and comfort.

The essential takeaway for me is that each returnee was thrilled with the new technology and sees it as "the future," but will wait for coming improvements and additional applications before they repurchase the product. The U.S. launch was a brilliant marketing scheme by Apple. The developers got the feedback they needed from the most likely users of the product. The returns will all be written off as product testing. The social engineers got what they needed—society is being groomed to accept virtual reality by "influencers" saying Apple Pro Vision "is the future."

Apple devices follow a predictable design sequence, and Vision Pro will be no different. What is a clunky, uncomfortable face mask today will be replaced with a smaller, lighter, sleeker, more technologically advanced model tomorrow. Vision Pro will soon become an implantable interface running on an advanced version of Apple's spatial computing platform, visionOS, requiring 6G technology.

6G eliminates all personal privacy, personal agency, personal property, and personal freedom including private thoughts monitored by brain implants. It enables a return to the binary feudal infrastructure of rulers and ruled on a planetary scale. 6G has arrived, and space is no longer the final frontier—reality is!

On October 24, 2023, a Boulder, Colorado, startup, Atom Computing,[195] announced that it has created a next-generation quantum computing platform with 1,180 qubits.

Tommaso Demarie, CEO of Entropica Labs,[196] a strategic partner of Atom Computing, said, "Developing a 1,000-plus qubit quantum technology marks an exceptional achievement for the Atom Computing team and the entire industry. With expanded computational capabilities, we can now delve deeper into the intricate realm of error correction schemes, designing and implementing strategies that pave the way for more reliable and scalable quantum computing systems. Entropica is enthusiastic about collaborating with Atom Computing as we create software that takes full advantage of their large-scale quantum computers."

Atom Computing is working with enterprise, academic, and government users [U.S. Department of Defense, U.S. Department of Energy, and National Science Foundation] today to develop applications and reserve time on the systems, which will be available in 2024.

The elitist assumptions that support the seismic changes for the world imagined by the globalists and expressed by the WEF and its partners are stunningly self-serving. The public-private partnerships with enterprise, academic, and government users is the military-industrial complex Eisenhower warned about in 1961.

As Nokia Labs president Marcus Weldon stated so succinctly, "It's not about consumers interacting with Siri, Alexa, Google. It's about industrials and robots interacting with control systems." *But who controls the control systems?* Eisenhower has already answered: *the globalist elite.* The technology required by quantum computing empowers globalism's technocracy, transhumanism, and planetary Unistate, because whoever controls 6G science and technology is master of the universe.

CHAPTER 43

Ideological Subversion, Communitarianism, and the 15-Minute City

Globalism is a replacement ideology that seeks to reorder the world into one singular, planetary Unistate, ruled by the globalist elite. The globalist war on nation-states cannot succeed without collapsing the United States of America. The long-term strategic attack plan moves America incrementally from constitutional republic to socialism to globalism to feudalism. The tactical attack plan uses asymmetric psychological and informational warfare to destabilize Americans and drive society out of objective reality into the madness of subjective reality. America's children are the primary target of the globalist predators.

Globalists recognize neither individual nor national sovereignty. Globalism's planetary Unistate will be one-world population, one-world nation, one-world government, one-world language, one-world currency, one-world bank, one-world culture, one-world customs, one-world ethics, one-world morality, one-world norms, one-world court, one-world laws, and one-world military police enforcing one-world compliance.

Marxism and globalism are both replacement ideologies. The Marxist strategy for ideological conversion relies on regressing chronological adults back to childish thinking through fear, and weaponizing education to indoctrinate children in collectivism as young as possible. The globalist strategy for world domination exploits the Marxist strategy to clear the path for the globalist Unistate.

To understand what is so attractive about the state of childhood for megalomaniacs, we must return to our earlier discussion of power and control in Chapter 36, and consider the universal source of conflict between power and powerlessness that begins in childhood. It is often said that *everything is political*. That is true. Everything is political because everything is ideological. Everything is ideological because thoughts are ideas, and thought precedes behavior. Some ideologies support individual freedom and some support state tyranny.

We are all born completely helpless and dependent upon our caretakers. An ideal childhood would have parents who love, nurture, and teach their children the skills necessary to become empowered, independent, autonomous, rational adults capable of becoming loving parents who will repeat this cycle of life. The goal is ideological, and requires family support to preserve and sustain it generationally.

Adult independence, responsibility, and agency are required to support the individualism and meritocracy required for a life of ordered liberty and upward mobility in a constitutional republic. Our constitutional republic is a political structure supported by an ideological commitment to freedom and liberty, sustained by the Judeo-Christian morality that supports individualism, adulthood, and the nuclear family. These qualities are anathema to societies of rulers and ruled, because the dependence and powerlessness of early childhood are required to sustain the tyranny of binary power structures such as globalism and Marxism.

In order to collapse America from within, it is necessary to subvert Americans ideologically and replace their strivings for adulthood with dependency needs. Yuri Bezmenov, a former KGB propagandist, worked as a "journalist" inside the Western countries he was tasked with subverting. Bezmenov defected to Canada in 1970 and began giving lectures and interviews to warn Western nations about ongoing Soviet tactics being used to subvert their countries.

In his 1984 interview[197] with G. Edward Griffin, Bezmenov explained that the main focus of the KGB was not espionage. The emphasis was on ideological subversion using covert Soviet "active measures," particularly psychological warfare and disinformation. During the interview, Bezmenov defined[198] the four stages of ideological subversion involved in a communist takeover of a Western country:

> I. DEMORALIZATION (15–20 years)
>
> > Indoctrination with Marxism-Leninism.
> >
> > Takes 15–20 years to educate one generation without any

counterbalance.

II. DESTABILIZATION (2–5 years)

Destabilization of economy, foreign relations, and military.

III. CRISIS (6 weeks)

Violent change of power.

IV. NORMALIZATION (indefinitely)

Creation and acceptance of the new normal. Lasts indefinitely.

Bezmenov explained that the Marxist goal is to change perceptions of reality to such a degree that no one is able to come to sensible conclusions about how to defend himself, his family, or his country. It is brainwashing to the extent that facts no longer matter, and is exactly the same psychological warfare that Bertrand Russell describes in *The Impact of Science on Society* when he advocates weaponizing education such that children will eventually believe that snow is black. Ideological subversion and psychological warfare are the reasons why space is no longer the final frontier—reality is.

The mechanism for ideological subversion is psychological regression. I won't give the Soviets credit for understanding WHY regression works, but they definitely knew that it DOES work. And it doesn't matter how intelligent or accomplished the individual is; those qualities are completely irrelevant. I explain the mechanism of psychological regression in *Dear America: Who's Driving the Bus?* Fear regresses chronological adults to psychological childhood. If you frighten someone enough, you regress them back to a state of childish psychological thinking and compliance in a world of subjective reality. Children believe what they are told, no matter how factually absurd it is—for example, the COVID fear campaign with its masking, jabs, social distancing, vaccines that are not vaccines, and endless booster shots. In talking with people regressed by active measures, you may think you are speaking to an adult, but you are actually interacting with a psychological three-year-old.

Can you have a rational debate with a three-year-old? No, of course not. That is why ideological subversion is psychological warfare—and why it is so catastrophically effective. I cannot say this often enough or strenuously enough: *Freedom is an adult enterprise.*

Globalist social engineers are master strategists who live in objective reality and understand the infantile nature of Marxist collectivism. They know Marxist promises of equality and earthly delights historically end in tyranny, and only regressed adults ignore history, insisting that each new iteration of Marxist collectivism will be the *real* one.

Globalists fund and foment Marxist ideological destruction to clear the path and soften America for globalist objectives. Every species of ideological Marxism, including critical race theory, Wokeism, queer theory, radical feminism, and post-colonial theory, is being used to advance the globalist war effort. The globalist coup d'état cannot succeed without collapsing America.

The will to power is nothing new. What is new is the post–World War II strategy to bring down the United States ideologically, from within. Ideological Marxists continue to believe in the Culture War, its long march through American institutions, and the historical inevitability of communism. But Marxist devotees, including the leadership, are simply useful idiots being used by the globalists in their War on America. They do not recognize the transitory nature of their power to swing the cultural wrecking ball. It is the globalists, not the Marxists, who control the science and technology required to facilitate the Fourth Industrial Revolution, impose its one-world planetary Unistate, and eventually eliminate dissent and dissenters, including the Marxists.

Globalist social engineers are using their coordinated narrative of fear to regress free people all over the world. If we are to remain free, we simply must remain psychological adults living in objective reality. How do we accomplish this?

First, we acknowledge that we are a world at war, and we demand of ourselves that we always live in the adult world of objective reality. Fortunately, there are role models that can help us understand what this means. Author/activist Rosa Koire explained how the European Union (EU) has already accepted communitarianism. So, let's begin there.

Rosa Koire (1956–2021) wrote *Behind the Green Mask: U.N. Agenda 21* (2011),[199] explaining how the foundation of Agenda 21/2030 is commu-

nitarianism. Koire was a forensic commercial real estate appraiser special-
izing in eminent domain valuation. She was a District Branch Chief for the
California Department of Transportation and an expert witness on land use
and value. In 2005 she was elected to a citizens' oversight committee to review a proposed 1,300-acre redevelopment project in Santa Rosa, Northern
California, where 10,000 people lived and worked.

Through her research, Koire discovered that much of the funding for UN
Agenda 21/Sustainable Development land use programs came through
diversion of property taxes to development agencies. Koire's book explains
that Sustainable Development is an inventory and control plan for all land,
water, minerals, plants, animals, construction, means of production, food,
energy, information, and all human beings in the world. In other words,
the *planetary ecology*. In 2013 she did a video interview in Denmark titled
Rosa Koire: "Agenda 21" Open Mind Conference 2013.[200] Six years later
the same interview was reposted and retitled *Rosa Koire: UN Agenda 2030
exposed*.[201] Much of Rosa Koire's work has already been deleted from the
internet. Her 2013 interview exposed the catastrophic impact of Sustainable Development on private property rights and liberty. Its relevance today
is chilling. The interview is preserved in its entirety below.

Rosa Koire. "Agenda 21" Open Mind Conference 2013

[Transcript]

*I'm Rosa Koire and I'm from the United States, California, and my topic,
what I speak about is one of the most vitally important issues of our age and
that is the United Nations Agenda 21 Sustainable Development. And as I'll
be talking about tomorrow, it is the inventory and control plan. Inventory
and control of all land, all water, all minerals, all plants, all animals, all
construction, all means of production, all food, all energy, all information,
and all human beings in the world. And this is a plan that was agreed to by
a hundred and seventy-nine nations back in 1992.*

*It's a United Nations plan, it's called the "Agenda for the 21st century," and
so many of us around the world think that sustainable development, it just
sounds so great. Isn't it about recycling and creative reuse and creating energy and food resources for everyone? And the answer is No. It really is not.
It's about moving populations into city centers, concentrated city centers,
and clearing them out of the rural areas. So, I became, I found out about it*

in a very unusual way actually, because I spent my career as a legal witness, as an expert witness for the California Department of Transportation. I'm an expert in land use and land valuation, and my specialty is in eminent domain valuation. Of course, I was valuing property for the government so that the government could acquire that property for road projects, and what I found about ten years ago, by around or 10 or 15 years ago, was that land actually, it was very difficult to say what it was worth because you couldn't know what people could do with it, because they were being restricted from using their property. And as I explored that, and found that it wasn't just in the San Francisco Bay Area where I was working, it was in fact all across the nation and the world. I looked behind that and I found United Nations Agenda 21 Sustainable Development.

We created the Post Sustainability Institute in order to educate people about the economic, social, political, and environmental impacts of communitarianism on the world. And communitarianism is that concept, that social and political construct that says that the individual's rights should be balanced against the rights of the community. And, of course, the community is that amorphous undefined community that we, you know when we talk about community, we think we're of course part of it and that, you know, it's a positive thing. But really community is, constructed, it's constructed of non-governmental organizations, corporations, and government, in order to dictate and regulate what it is that happens around the world. And we as individuals have literally no influence on that unless we are in agreement with it. If you dissent against the community, against communitarian law or against communitarian social tactics, you're rejected and basically made an outcast. And that is something that that we wanted to expose to the world and the reason that we created a Post Sustainability Institute was in order to sue.

We sued our local government and right now we're suing a higher-up in order to stop regional plans because regionalization is the stepping-stone to globalization, and globalization is the standardization of all systems. So, that includes water, law enforcement, education, energy, all systems have to be brought into harmony in order to control them all. Because when systems don't meet, when they're out of balance or not synced with one another, they can't be controlled centrally. And the goal of Agenda 21 is one-world government and total control from a central unit.

America, the United States of America, is really under attack right now. We in the United States are, well, the U.S. landmass is about two and a half times the size of Europe and has roughly half the population. Just over half that landmass is huge and about 75% of the population lives in large cities. The goal is to move everyone out of the rural areas and into the large cities, and to destroy representative government, and to move to a government by unelected boards and commissions.

Now here in the EU of course you have, you know, you've already moved to that position, where it's an erasure of jurisdictional boundaries an erasure of national boundaries, and that is the goal because as Zbigniew Brzezinski said in 1995, you can't just impose globalization pell-mell as a total movement, you have to do it incrementally. And the way to do that is through regionalization. And in Denmark, for instance in Denmark, well, every nation that signed on to Agenda 21 has its local Agenda 21 plan. People in the United States are completely unaware of this. If I go out and talk about this the United States, press attacks me and calls me a conspiracy theorist, which is totally ridiculous. It is a conspiracy, but it's not a theory. It's a fact. Here in Europe, it's openly spoken about, local Agenda 21. And, of course, here in Denmark the Aalborg Principles 2000 excuse me, 1994, and then Aalborg +10, 2004, the European roundtable for local Agenda 21, was held here. And the Principles are public-private partnerships, which is fascism, and this is how it's implemented on the ground. Is through this joining together between corporations, non-governmental organizations, and governments in order to cut out the, you know, the actual individual, your voter. And instead to take that to a level where we literally cannot penetrate, and this is the goal. So, this is already far progressed in Europe.

The three pillars of United Nations Agenda 21 are Economy, Ecology, and Equity. The three E's—the social equity—and everyone sort of thinks that they know what that means. The idea of social equity must mean that, well, everyone's going to have access to clean water and clean air, and no one's property is going to be used as a dumping ground because they are at a poverty level.

But really, what social equity is about, it's about impoverishing huge portions of the population and bringing down the developed nations. And while this sounds like, you know, it sounds almost like in the United States, you'd call that a right-wing point of view, a conservative right-wing point of view. I personally am a liberal. The idea that something this drastic, this radical, would be happening worldwide without people knowing it. All you have to do is look at austerity measures; restrictions on transfers of wealth; additional restrictions on land use; ability, you know, to produce, to use your energy, your water, your industry; all of this is happening in developed nations. So, when you have your infrastructure attacked like that, it's going to have a tremendous impact on your ability to prosper. As well as the idea that everything that we're looking at now is destined to collapse our economies. Because the idea, this is a corporatocracy, it's a totalitarian state being developed right now all over the world.

And what major corporations want in this fascist development is to be able to have full movement of workers without borders or boundaries. To be able to move their goods through without regulations and to reduce wages. And so, this is the goal, this is what you find with social equity. Social equity, that's code for this movement and reduction of the population. And of course the economy and ecology is about bringing into balance economy, these are the three circles, Economy, Ecology, and social Equity. And where they meet in the center is balance.

But really that balance is a communitarian balance. So, it's not balance of well-being of the people, what it is is it's a balance or corporation so that they can exploit and control and have populations in an area in tightly packed dense areas so that they can be surveilled and managed. And this is what that balance looks like as far as the development of totalitarian state.

I think it's very important to know that the people now still have an opportunity to fight. All of us across the world understand that our individuality is at stake here. Our most important private property is our body, and of course surveillance is a vital part, surveillance, domestic surveillance and control, is a vital part of this plan. It is a totalitarian plan. But you know, just like any other extreme plan, while we are moving towards the endgame, we are not there. And this is the opportunity that all of us have now to stand up, to speak out, to refuse to collaborate, to refuse to cooperate. To expose collaborators, to work together to defund these plans. To refuse, to demand what it is the corporations want to give us and so, because no one's holding a gun to our heads right now, we have that opportunity.

If that changes, if that moment changes, you certainly won't protest then, so now is the time. And people all over the world are doing this. It's that the mainstream media is owned by five major corporations, and you're not going to get this information from the mainstream press. So, you need to be your own press. You need to educate yourself. You need to get out there and educate your neighbors, your community, your real community. You need to help your children understand that they're being indoctrinated from pre-kindergarten to postgraduate school.

All of us have a responsibility to ourselves and to others. This is true community, to work for personal freedom and always remember that even though we work as a group, if we do work as a group, we're all individuals in those groups and we answer only to ourselves. And this is essential, it's essential as free human beings. This is what we are—we are free and we need to continue to be free. And I do believe that we will win, but we have to become aware that there is a fight, and then make our friends and our neighbors and our community aware as well, and work together.

Right now, in the United States we are moving into major massive regionalization. The United States has 50 states, and it's divided into cities, counties, and states, and then the federal government. Instead, Agenda 21 is top-down. It's global, regional, neighborhood, and none of those positions is elected. So, in the United States right now, the development of regionalization is happening very quickly. It's happening with federal funding. There are hundreds of millions of dollars going to local governments in order to have them create regional plans. And this plan cannot be accomplished without control of land and land use, because of course where you live often dictates the kind of life you're going to have.

So, regionalization takes away our opportunity to have an impact. It takes away representative government. So, what we are doing at the Post Sustainability Institute right now is we are suing to stop the biggest regional plan in the United States, and it is a blueprint for the rest of the country. What this plan is doing is essentially saying that no new development will happen anywhere. But in 4% of the San Francisco Bay Area that all 101 cities and nine counties will be joined together and all land-use decisions will be made basically by an unelected Board. What this will do to land use and land value in the San Francisco Bay Area, to movements of people, to development of business, to freedom, is unfathomable. And people are not aware of it. The only thing that is standing between that and full passage is our lawsuit.

Now what this truly means is if you tell people that they have to build only "smart" growth, high-density development in an urban center right on a train line. Or, the train doesn't have to be there, it's the proposed idea of a train line, and then no development, no buildings, no residential, no commercial, can happen outside of that very, very concentrated area, then what do you have? You have a concentration camp of the future.

This is exactly what it looks like and you see it's very much more subtle and much more sophisticated than it was when the Nazis were doing it. You are not going to get thrown on a train car, you will just have your roads out in the rural areas pulverized and turned to gravel. You'll have your family well monitored, you will have your energy restricted, you will have your school service cut, your Sheriff service cut. You will find that you are not able to get your goods to market, and then you have to move into the city, and then you will move into this high-density development that is subsidized with our property tax dollars, and pretty soon you will have the Wildlands Project,[202] which is predicated on moving people out of the rural areas.

This is how it happens, so you know people say, "Well, hey, nobody's getting me off my land." Well, it's very easy. You know, no one's going to come to your door with a gun, but they will move you off your land. And you will be in the cities and those cities will be full capability of surveillance, monitoring, and control. These buildings, these high-density buildings, are being built with a concept of eyes on the street. You become basically a deputized police adjunct. Your job is to watch the street. Your job is to watch your neighbor.

The war on terror is a war on you, and we all know this. We feel it. This is why we need to stop it. So, this is our plan, to use the courts at this point and stop this plan. And we're working on it.

[Transcript ends]

Koire's plan was to make people aware, and to use the courts to stop the plan. She understood that land use is the institutional path to high-density developments and surveillance modeled after China's system: physically (forcefully if necessary) moving the population to 15-minute city centers where they will be surveilled and controlled.

Land use is parallel to political medicine. Both weaponize institutional power to increase social control by the state. Life in the Unistate is the beginning of Humanity 2.0, where all living things are part of the planetary ecology of communitarianism and Scientism's evolutionary ascendancy to transhumanism. Science and technology made Brzezinski's 1970 predictions come true, and science and technology are being used to make globalist megalomaniacal dreams of technocracy and transhumanism come true. Cognitive warfare will make life in the Unistate an existence of totalitarian conformity, serfdom, and compliance with the orthodoxy of Scientism.

Member of the European Parliament Christine Anderson is an unyielding opponent of globalism and Klaus Schwab's Great Reset agenda. She is one of the few remaining politicians actually representing the interests of the people. In a September 13, 2023, session devoted to COVID-19 response and the World Health Organization, she ended the meeting with this powerful statement posted verbatim on *Vigilant News*,[203] with emphasis added.

[Transcript]

*We just need to find a way to wake the people up. Because the point is simply this: it comes down to a choice. It's either freedom, democracy, and the rule of law—**or enslavement**.*

*There is no such thing [as] in between. There is no such thing as a little freedom, a little democracy, a little rule of law, just as **there is no such thing as a little enslavement**. So that's the choice. It comes down to—it's either the globalitarian misanthropists or the people. It comes down to—it's either us or them. And that's, I think, what this really is all about.*

*Now, when my colleagues and I were elected to this parliament, there was no question about it: we were on the side of the people because the people actually pay us to act in their best interests. That's our job. And once again, I will say to every single elected representative around the world, to every single member in every elected government around the world, if you do not unequivocally stand with the people and serve in their best interests, act in their best interests, you have no place in any parliament or in any government. You belong behind bars. You may even **rot in hell** for all I care at this point because **that's exactly what you deserve if you sell out the people**.*

*Now, I would like to make a promise to the people, and I'm pretty sure I can speak [for] or speak on behalf of my colleagues. We will continue to stand with you, the people. We will continue to fight for freedom, democracy, and the rule of law. We will not shut up, and **we will not stop going after those despicable globalitarian misanthropists.***

*But we would also like to have you make a promise to us. You may have heard it's all coming back. The first country is already starting mask mandates in Israel. They're already imposing it. I've heard of a few universities in the United States. They're already bringing it all back. And I would really like for you, the people, to not go along. **Simply say no!** They want you to wear a mask: **say no**. They want you to put in another mRNA shot: **say no**. They want to impose a curfew on you: **say no**. That's really all you have to do.*

*And it might not be or might sound a little hard, but it's actually not that hard. Because once you have made it clear to them that you will no longer go along, once you've let them know, **they cannot scare you anymore**. Because as long as you are afraid of what they might do if you don't comply, they have power over you. Take the power away from them! **Simply say no**. Once you do that, **they don't have power over you anymore**. You will feel so free. **Simply say no**.*

*And considering what we've heard today, and considering what we've seen in the last three years, considering what we know they want to implement, heck, you might even be well within your right to tell them to screw themselves and **go to hell**! That's where they belong. What will you get out of that? I can tell you. Once you've done that, once you've told them to just go to hell, **they no longer have power over you**. You will have an incredible feeling—kind of like a sensation of freedom will sweep through your body. I promise you will feel so relieved.*

*And this is the state of mind that I would ask all of you to get to. Simply don't let them grind you down anymore. You are worth it. You are deserving of just standing up for yourselves. And **tell them all to go to hell**. Thank you very much.*

[Transcript ends]

Christine Anderson is an MEP for Germany's anti-immigration party, Alternative for Germany (AfD), and an outspoken critic of Canada's Justin

Trudeau. In March 2022 she accused Trudeau of openly admiring the Chinese dictatorship, and criticized him for trampling on "fundamental rights by persecuting and criminalizing his own citizens as terrorists just because they dare to stand up to his perverted concept of democracy."

Anderson speaks on the international stage, but to resist globalism we must stand against it locally. On September 20, 2023, Canadian citizen Joel Sussman stood before the Aurora, Ontario, City Council and schooled them on globalism and its existential threat to freedom. Joel Sussman's videotaped statement[204] below:

[Transcript]

Good evening. Restructuring of Canadian mayors and municipalities under the auspices of the United Nations began in 1992. PM Mulroney signed Canada onto UN Agenda 21. Canada thus became a UN member nation-state. One hundred seventy-eight [nine] countries signed on, lured by the promise of big money to go green. By 2000, countries, including Canada, were being governed by directions of the UN, G7, G20, World Economic Forum, and World Health Organization, to name some.

Every organization named is a foreign-based NGO, non-governmental organization, and every member of all these organizations is unelected. Parliamentary procedures for law changes weren't followed. In 1994, a municipal primer was issued to all local towns, outlining how they were to restructure their governments.

Though the municipal primer was a non-binding agreement, all towns adopted it. Our public officials, the mayor and councilors of that day, were partnered with a private corporation, the Corporation of the Town of Aurora, who appointed a chief administrative officer who helped implement the global agenda instead of a local one.

The International Council on Local and Environmental Issues, ICLEI, became the main source of consultation to push and fund the global agenda. We remind you that the World Economic Forum and the United Nations signed a strategic partnership framework in 2019 to jointly accelerate the implementation of the 2030 Agenda for Sustainable Development.

This is the same World Economic Forum whose chairman, Klaus Schwab, famously declared "you will own nothing and be happy." This is the same

Klaus Schwab who, referring to Canadian Prime Minister Justin Trudeau, boasted, "We have penetrated more than half of his cabinet." We would ask Mayor Maracas and the Councilors: Why should the citizens of Aurora bow down to the intrusive dictates of an unelected foreign entity?

The fact is we should not. And we will not. What, you ask, does any of this have to do with 15-minute smart cities? Absolutely everything. Smart: S for surveillance, M for monitoring, A for analysis, R for reporting, and T for technology. Technocracy News editor Patrick Wood, 50 years of experience and expertise on technocracy, wrote, "The 15-minute city is a cover for [a] data collection bonanza for technocrats who design and operate them."

Cities designed for maximum efficiency always reveal technocrat thinking that efficiency itself is the goal. Maximum surveillance allows for maximum control to achieve even more efficiency. At its very root, this mechanistic thinking is anti-human. The 15-minute city narrative seeks to fool you in the guise of saving the planet, keeping you safe, and delivering convenience.

It's actually the gateway to digital IDs and CBDC, Central Bank Digital Currencies. CBDCs allow bankers and/or governments to freeze your bank account because you happen to peacefully and lawfully protest and express your disagreement with government policy. Does anyone remember the truckers' convoy in Ottawa, February 22, [2022] when the government of Canada invoked the Emergencies Act and froze the private bank accounts of law-abiding citizens?

Fifteen-minute cities are wolves in sheep's clothing. Don't believe the countless stories spewing forth from the 24/7 bases, from the elitist-captured mainstream media, all claiming to have your best interests at heart. We have been burned too many times. In reality, 24/7 surveillance through the Internet of Things inside your home, 5G, and LED streetlights outside, monitoring and tracking and recording everything. Implementation of exclusion zones and geofencing to restrict movement and travel. Ability to control behaviors through military-directed energy technologies, property and car ownership to be outlawed, evictions from farms and rural areas to go to gather people into cities. Digital passports being promulgated by the UN World Economic Forum and the World Health Organization are in the final stages of planning and implementation. They are tied to social credit score, which is determined by compliance to [with] government directives. These passports control all access and all aspects of life. Digital currency is being implemented to end cash and monitor all your spending. Your digital currency will be turned off or on depending on your compliance score. UBI, Universal Basic Income, is a state-controlled allowance forcing compliance by restricting access to food, money, services, and education.

All of the above will enable climate lockdowns to be implemented easily, arbitrarily, and indefinitely.

The real agenda of 15-Minute Smart Cities is to monitor and control everyone and everything. In summary, in the coming days, Council will receive an electronic info packet which will contain the text of this delegation and other items. We, the citizens of Aurora, wish to enter into a meaningful, respectful dialogue with our elected members of Council on this complex, important issue.

A key framework of that dialogue is a list of questions posed to Council. Can Council explicitly guarantee that citizens will remain free to travel as is their right under the Charter of Rights and Freedoms? Can Council guarantee not to restrict access to essential services, medical care, bank accounts, government pensions, utilities?

Most importantly, we the citizens of Aurora need to have the conversation with the Council about exiting their non-binding agreement with the private for-profit entity known as the Corporation of the Town of Aurora. We need to turn back the page to a simpler time when open, transparent municipal government serving its citizens and working in their best interests ruled the day.

We are your equal partners on this journey. Thank you.

[Transcript ends]

Joel Sussman received an enthusiastic one-minute standing ovation from the gallery.

For me, the most disturbing aspect of Sussman's speech was the City Council's response. The Aurora, Ontario, city councilors entrusted with public policy politely thanked Sussman for sharing his views, but appeared completely unaware of the history, government restructuring, public-private partnerships, and global agenda they were actively participating in against the public interest.

This is an information war. City councilors who rely solely on information from globalist sources are participating, wittingly or unwittingly, in the globalist war on humanity. What is happening in Aurora, Ontario, is happening elsewhere. Citizens must take the responsibility and initiative, as Joel Sussman did, to provide facts challenging the globalist narrative that city officials are blithely and naively accepting.

Joel Sussman is a role model for freedom-loving citizens. Here in the United States, citizens in every state, in every county, and in every city should attend city council meetings and read Joel Sussman's transcript out loud into the public record.

Resistance requires accurate information and the courage to stand against the herd. Stopping the globalist advance requires being a psychological adult, living in the adult world of objective reality based on facts. Activist Rosa Koire, MEP Christine Anderson, and Citizen Joel Sussman possess the courage of their convictions, and have provided us all with demonstrations of what that courage looks like. Now it is up to us.

America's freedom clock is ticking, and the globalist social engineers are in the final stages of their war on humanity. The next fear campaign is coming. It will probably be another bioweapon release, marketed as a worldwide pandemic far more contagious than COVID-19. It will be exploited politically as a catastrophic event necessitating the exclusive use of mail-in ballots in the 2024 presidential election—for public health, of course. Anyone who objects will be accused of voter suppression. If not a bioweapon, then I predict the globalists will incite social chaos with some outrageous action or policy that ends with fighting in the streets. The goal is to make society totally ungovernable. Then the globalists will declare martial law—for public safety, of course.

After martial law comes feudal serfdom in globalism's planetary managerial Unistate—a scientific dictatorship ruled by the elite, who always and only take care of themselves.

CHAPTER 44

The American Reformation

Globalism is a replacement ideology that seeks to reorder the world into one singular, planetary Unistate, ruled by the globalist elite. The globalist war on nation-states cannot succeed without collapsing the United States of America. The long-term strategic attack plan moves America incrementally from constitutional republic to socialism to globalism to feudalism. The tactical attack plan uses asymmetric psychological and informational warfare to destabilize Americans and drive society out of objective reality into the madness of subjective reality. America's children are the primary target of the globalist predators.

Historically, political and religious factions ruled nation-states with combined absolute power. When Henry VIII ruled England in the 16th century, he shared political power with the Catholic Church until the Church refused to annul his marriage to Catherine of Aragon so that he could marry Anne Boleyn. In response, Henry founded the Church of England and separated it from the Catholic Church, beginning the English Reformation and England's conversion from a Catholic to a Protestant nation. It was a seismic shift in English culture and society, overturning England's existing power structure, which the monarchy had shared with the Catholic Church for six centuries.

Henry VIII achieved absolute power by separating England from the Catholic Church and making radical changes to the constitution of England. The Church of England was Henry's replacement ideology. The king rejected papal authority and appointed himself Supreme Head of the Church of England, the absolute monarch. The 1534 Act of Supremacy legalized his power grab and conveniently awarded Henry the divine right of kings. Divine right asserts that monarchical power derives from divine authority and is not, therefore, accountable to the people, the aristocracy, or any earthly authority. Any attempt to depose, dethrone, resist, or restrict monarchical power is contrary to God's will and therefore a sacrilege. Henry's subsequent purge and persecution of the Catholics was a political policy. He dissolved convents and monasteries, stripping them of their wealth and power, and required the nobility to swear allegiance to the new Oath of Supremacy recognizing Henry's supreme authority.

How does this pertain to us today? Our forefathers understood the will to power and how absolute power corrupts absolutely. The United States of America is the first nation in world history created with a constitutional separation of powers to protect its citizens from the tyranny of totalitarian rule, and a Bill of Rights to protect each individual citizen's freedom and sovereignty. Religious power and political power in the nascent American constitutional republic were separated by law, and a preferred state religion was prohibited.

The unifying identity for life in the United States of America was being an American. Patriotism is an ideological commitment. Our nation was founded by patriotic individuals unified by and willing to fight for their shared ideological commitment to freedom, liberty, and sovereignty.

That was then.

Globalism's war on the nation-state is the modern equivalent of Henry VIII's monarchical and maniacal power grab that changed the religion of an entire nation in order to solve Henry's personal marital problems. His decision illustrates the narcissism of power and the elitist mindset. One man declared himself divinely entitled to absolute power and control.

Henry VIII is the historical cautionary tale that warns of the existential danger in globalism's quest for absolute power and control. The globalist elite are attempting an American Reformation. They are separating America from its founding principles of freedom, liberty, and sovereignty; substituting Marxist collectivism for American individualism by replacing family authority with state authority; and exchanging Judeo-Christian traditions and values for Scientism. Scientism supports bioethical *consensus* morality, a unanimity of thought that awards the globalist elite absolute power—equivalent to Henry VIII and his self-serving doctrine, the *divine right of kings*.

Scientism, a central feature of today's divisive Woke Marxism, is being practiced as a mandated, preferred state religion under the Biden-Obama-

Harris regime. Rooted in consensus science, Scientism provides the *collectivist* authority that replaces traditional Judeo-Christian norms and the Hippocratic Oath. Globalism exploits Marxist ideology and ideologues to rip the Judeo-Christian values of individualism, traditional morality, family, and patriotism out of American culture.

The American Reformation is today's Great Reset initiative, and it will be a seismic shift in American culture and society parallel to the English Reformation. Establishing Scientism as the preferred state religion overturns America's constitutional power structure, which prohibits a state religion and guarantees the separation of powers. The separation of powers guards against tyranny and ensures representative government for conducting the people's business. The American Reformation resets 250 years of constitutional authority to 0.

The blueprint for Klaus Schwab's Great Reset initiative is found in Bertrand Russell's infamous book *The Impact of Science on Society*,[205] written in 1952. Russell considered science superior to religion in its observations and moral authority, and envisioned scientists replacing religious leaders in a secular society. Scientists would define ethics and resolve *ethical* issues with their superior scientific expertise and powers of persuasion, through mass psychological manipulation:

> I think the subject which will be of most importance politically is mass psychology. Mass psychology is, scientifically speaking, not a very advanced study and, so far, its professors have not been in universities: they have been advertisers, politicians, and above all, dictators. This study is immensely useful to practical men, whether they wish to become rich or to acquire the government.... What is essential in mass psychology is the art of persuasion.... It may be hoped that in time anyone will be able to persuade anybody of anything.... This subject will make great strides when it is taken up by scientists under a scientific dictatorship. (p. 27)

> Although this science of mass psychology will be diligently studied, it will be rigidly confined to the governing class. The populace will not be allowed to know how its convictions are generated. (p. 28)

> The completeness of the resulting control over opinion depends in various ways upon scientific technique. Where all children go

to school, and all schools are controlled by the government, the authorities can close the minds of the young to everything contrary to official orthodoxy. Printing is impossible without paper, and all paper belongs to the State. Broadcasting and the cinema are equally public monopolies. The only remaining possibility of unauthorized propaganda is by secret whispers from one individual to another. But this, in turn, is rendered appallingly dangerous by improvements in the art of spying. Children at school are taught that it is their duty to denounce their parents if they allow themselves subversive utterances in the bosom of the family. (pp. 41–42)

Russell forecast the Scientism that has been practiced as a secular religion in America since COVID-19 savaged the nation. He even gave us a glimpse of its pathological leader, Anthony Fauci, who arrogantly claimed, in response to criticism, "Attacks on me, quite frankly, are attacks on science."

Russell acknowledged that the ruling class in a scientific dictatorship can bring tyrannical officials and a lawless police force, both of which will restrict freedom. Then rationalized the draconian power grab with an absurd fear tactic, arguing that unless individual and national liberty are restrained, mankind may not survive. Russell claimed it was necessary to have a system that makes individuals and nations *submit to the rule of law*—the self-serving laws that the elite create, enact, and impose on the people. Does this narrative sound familiar? It should.

It is the same self-serving narrative used by Henry VIII to legitimize the English Reformation, and the same imperious narrative echoed by Klaus Schwab and his globalist WEF partners to legitimize the American Reformation. Globalists do not rely on political theories of historical inevitability the way Marxists do, or appoint themselves divine rulers like Henry VIII. They don't have to. Instead, they rely on Scientism for the narrative of evolutionary inevitability, where humans will merge with machines to transcend their human limitations and become transhuman.

But like Bertrand Russell, globalist *stakeholders* play offense and strategically raise the profound ethical issues involved with Scientism and transhumanism. In fact, they talk about it constantly, as if *talking* about ethics is a solution and not a best-defense-is-an-offense maneuver designed to familiarize the public with the nascent transhuman industry.

Today's American military-industrial complex is actively supporting the American Reformation and pursuing globalist goals with its combined military-industrial-economic-ideological might. Like mercenaries, the American military-industrial complex has no national identity and no national patriotism. It is ideologically committed to the planetary Unistate, UN Agenda 2030, UN 17 Sustainable Goals, Scientism, neuroscience technologies, Directed Energy, bioelectricity, and decoding the electrome. If the globalist coup d'état is successful, it is the end of Humanity 1.0 and the beginning of globalism's transhumanist future in the planetary Unistate.

The battle for freedom is a two-part battle for your mind. First, the psychological battle that regresses chronological adults to childish compliance in order to establish centralized globalist power in America. Second, the physical battle inside your brain fought with cognitive warfare to insure absolute conformity in the planetary Unistate.

The American Reformation will award the globalist elite absolute power and control in America, just as the English Reformation awarded absolute power and control to Henry VIII. The seismic difference between 21st-century America and 16th-century England is in the aftershocks.

Globalism is designed to enslave the entire world population. If the American Reformation succeeds, the globalist elite will award themselves absolute power and control over the entire planet. What Henry VIII did to England is what the globalist elite will do to the entire world. Henry VIII overturned six centuries of established English tradition because the Catholic Church would not grant him an annulment. The globalists will overturn 250 years of American freedom because the United States is an obstacle to their megalomaniacal ambitions for planetary control and the possibility for eternal life through transhumanism.

There are no historical inevitabilities and no evolutionary inevitabilities; there are only action potentials and choices. Ancient Chinese military strategist Sun Tzu takes us back to the future: *What is of supreme importance in war is to attack the enemy's strategy.* Western civilization is predicated upon objective reality, the Judeo-Christian tradition, and individualism. In America, we celebrate both national sovereignty and the sovereignty of the individual. The nuclear family is the social infrastructure that preserves our culture from generation to generation and honors our American values enshrined in the U.S. Constitution. Being American is the national identity that unites our national family for life in our constitutional republic. *Families are America's strategy for survival.*

What is often overlooked in Sun Tzu's wisdom is that it works as well for the defense as it does for the offense. We now know globalism's strategic objectives and tactical strategies. And now we are prepared to fight America's final battle for freedom. We can attack the enemy's strategy and defend the battlefield: our minds. We can arm ourselves with the most formidable defense against the globalist strategy—psychological adulthood—and restore the glory of American freedom in our reclaimed constitutional republic.

It is our time to demonstrate courage and face the globalist enemy. We cannot allow the enemy's fear tactics to regress us into compliance. We the People, as psychological adults, must refuse to comply. We must hear Christine Anderson's voice in our minds, where the battle is being fought:

> *Once you have made it clear to them that you will no longer go along, once you've let them know, **they cannot scare you anymore**. Because as long as you are afraid of what they might do if you don't comply, they have power over you. Take the power away from them! **Simply say no.** Once you do that, **they don't have power over you anymore.** You will feel so free. **Simply say no.***

CHAPTER 45

Every Conspiracy Begins with a Theory

Globalism is a replacement ideology that seeks to reorder the world into one singular, planetary Unistate, ruled by the globalist elite. The globalist war on nation-states cannot succeed without collapsing the United States of America. The long-term strategic attack plan moves America incrementally from constitutional republic to socialism to globalism to feudalism. The tactical attack plan uses asymmetric psychological and informational warfare to destabilize Americans and drive society out of objective reality into the madness of subjective reality. America's children are the primary target of the globalist predators.

Space is no longer the final frontier—reality is. Objective reality is the lethal enemy of the globalist elite and their conspiracy to rule the world. It is a competing ideology, which must be destroyed and replaced with subjective reality in order for the conspiracy to succeed.

The U.S. Constitution and Bill of Rights were written in the aftermath of the American Revolutionary War, carefully crafted to protect We the People from government overreach. It was a time of great consequence. The Bill of Rights, ratified in 1791, comprises the first ten amendments to the Constitution. It defines Americans' rights in relation to their government. The National Archives[206] describes the First Amendment with emphasis:

> The **First Amendment** provides several rights protections: to express ideas through **speech** and the **press**, to **assemble** or gather with a group to **protest** or for other reasons, and to ask the government to fix problems. It also protects the right to religious beliefs and practices. It prevents the government from creating or favoring a **religion**.

Our Founding Fathers understood that freedom of speech is the foundation of all freedom, that without freedom of speech no other freedoms exist. The freedom to speak is connected to the freedom of the press to print articles that criticize the government. It is also connected to the freedom of Americans to gather in protest, and to criticize their government.

Our forefathers established a government of the people, by the people, and for the people, in opposition to the binary monarchical power structure of Great Britain at the time. Americanism was a revolutionary idea that had never existed anywhere in the world.

Today, almost 250 years later, the conspiracy to return America to a binary infrastructure of rulers and ruled has reached its tipping point. But every conspiracy begins with a theory.

David Rockefeller's 500-page autobiography, Memoirs,[207] will be remembered for what is written on page 405. Rockefeller, a self-described internationalist, epitomizes the globalist elite and their supremacist mindset:

> Some even believe we [Rockefeller family] are part of a secret cabal working against the best interests of the United States, characterizing my family and me as "internationalists" and of conspiring with others around the world to build a more integrated global political and economic structure—one-world, if you will. If that's the charge, I stand guilty, and I am proud of it.

David Rockefeller's astonishing admission at the 1991 Bilderberg meeting will also be remembered:

> We are grateful to *The Washington Post, The New York Times, TIME* magazine, and other great publications whose directors have attended our meetings and respected their promises of discretion for almost forty years. It would have been impossible for us to develop our plan for the world if we had been subject to the bright lights of publicity during those years. But the work is now much more sophisticated and prepared to march towards a World Government. The supranational sovereignty of an intellectual elite and world bankers is surely preferable to the national auto-determination practiced in past centuries. (Bilderberg 1991)[208]

The globalist elite are conspiring to achieve world domination. Most deny they are conspirators and, unlike David Rockefeller, respond to conspiracy allegations with outrage and loud accusations of "Conspiracy theory!" Some are simply condescending and dismissive. But how they react doesn't matter.

What does matter is that no conspiracy to collapse the United States of America could ever be successful without a corrupt and colluding media. The mainstream media, including print media, publishing, the "news" media, photography, cinema, broadcasting (radio and television), digital media including social media and advertising, are owned and operated by six globalist media companies, known as the Big 6. Ninety percent of all U.S. media, what you read, watch, and hear, is controlled by Comcast, Walt Disney, AT&T, Paramount Global, Sony, and Fox.

This staggering centralization of power in communications has enabled the globalist elite to curate, censor, misinform, disinform, and create an echo chamber to propagandize and indoctrinate Americans twenty-four hours a day, seven days a week. The echo chamber is founded on the marketing principle that familiarity breeds acceptance. Information is honed, weaponized, and scripted so that the same "news" is continuously parroted across the networks. Investigative reporting is dead. Opposing voices are silenced.

The colluding media are responsible for fake news, and for facilitating the COVID-19 fear campaign that terrorized our nation. The globalist elite and their minions rely on ad hominem attacks. Anyone presenting factual evidence opposing the globalist COVID-19 narrative is mercilessly smeared and attacked by the media.

Doctors and researchers presenting evidence that the COVID-19 jabs were not safe were fired and their reputations ruined. Those who explained how COVID-19 was being exploited to advance digital IDs were censored. The globalist conspiracy to collapse the United States could never have gotten to this point without the complicity, cooperation, and coordination of the media.

We no longer have a free press in the United States. We have the Globalist Narrative News advancing the *supranational sovereignty of an intellectual elite and world bankers*—the Univoice of the Uniparty seeking to establish the Unistate in the United States.

The complicity of the globalist-owned mainstream media has facilitated, and obscured, the globalist elite conspiracy to rule the world. It is now up to *We the People* to expose the conspiracy, to resist it, and to oppose globalism's assault on objective reality and on American sovereignty. We must recommit ourselves to our founding principles.

The Declaration of Independence states unequivocally:

> We hold these truths to be self-evident, that all men are created equal, that they are endowed by their Creator with certain unalienable Rights, that among these are Life, Liberty and the pursuit of Happiness—That to secure these rights, Governments are instituted among Men, deriving their just powers from the consent of the governed—That whenever any Form of Government becomes destructive of these ends, it is the Right of the People to alter or to abolish it, and to institute new Government.

Lincoln's Gettysburg Address affirmed our founding principles:

> Four score and seven years ago our fathers brought forth on this continent, a new nation, conceived in Liberty, and dedicated to the proposition that all men are created equal.

> Now we are engaged in a great civil war, testing whether that nation, or any nation so conceived and so dedicated, can long endure. We are met on a great battlefield of that war. We have come to dedicate a portion of that field, as a final resting place for those who here gave their lives that, that nation might live. It is altogether fitting and proper that we should do this.

> But, in a larger sense, we cannot dedicate—we cannot consecrate— we cannot hallow—this ground. The brave men, living and dead, who struggled here, have consecrated it, far above our poor power to add or detract. The world will little note, nor long remember what we say here, but it can never forget what they did here. It is for us the living, rather, to be dedicated here to the unfinished work which they who fought here have thus far so nobly advanced. It is rather for us to be here dedicated to the great task remaining before us—that from these honored dead we take increased devotion to that cause for which they gave the last full measure of devotion—that we here highly resolve that these dead shall not have

died in vain—that this nation, under God, shall have a new birth of freedom — and that government of the people, by the people, for the people, shall not perish from the earth.

Our forefathers fought the British for freedom in 1776, and now the globalists are trying to reverse American history and return our nation to a system of rulers and ruled. This is America's last stand, and we the living must dedicate ourselves to the task before us and stand for freedom.

Flags are symbols. The United States flag symbolizes ordered liberty in a sovereign constitutional republic. The globalist War on America waves the United Nations flag, the symbol of one-world government in globalism's planetary managerial Unistate. The U.S. flag flies for freedom, the U.N. flag flies for feudalism.

There are thirty-one words that affirm the values and freedom that the American flag represents. Now is the time to recommit ourselves to them, loudly, proudly, and unapologetically:

> *I pledge allegiance to the flag of the United States of America and to the Republic for which it stands, one Nation under God, indivisible, with liberty and justice for all.*

THE END

ENDNOTES

URLs that have disappeared from the Internet are retrievable on the Internet Archive Wayback Machine, https://archive.org/web/web.php

How to use Wayback Machine,
https://www.youtube.com/watch?v=ts1tu1BiSuY

PREFACE: *Space Is No Longer the Final Frontier—Reality Is*

1. *The Managerial Revolution: What is Happening in the World*, James Burnham, New York, The John Day company, 1941; https://archive.org/details/in.ernet.dli.2015.46583/2015.46583.Managerial-Revolution-What-Is-Happening-In-The-World

INTRODUCTION: *Freedom Is an Adult Enterprise*

2. *Mimi's Strategy*, Linda Goudsmit, Contrapoint Publishing, 2016; https://www.barnesandnoble.com/s/Linda Goudsmit

3. *Dear America: Who's Driving the Bus?*, Linda Goudsmit, Contrapoint Publishing, 2011; https://www.barnesandnoble.com/w/dear-america-linda-goudsmit/1112023845?ean=9780578078144

4. *The Collapsing American Family: From Bonding to Bondage*, Linda Goudsmit, Contrapoint Publishing, 2021; https://www.barnesandnoble.com/s/Linda Goudsmit

CHAPTER 1: *What Is Reality?*

5. *The Book of Humanitarian Hoaxes: Killing America with 'Kindness'*, Linda Goudsmit, Contrapoint Publishing, 2020; https://www.barnesandnoble.com/w/the-book-of-humanitarian-hoaxes-linda-goudsmit/1136800447?ean=9780983542520

6. The Mathematics of the Culture War on America; https://goudsmit.pundicity.com/20600/the-mathematics-of-the-culture-war-on-america

7. *The Impact of Science on Society*, Bertrand Russell, Simon and Schuster, 1952, Routledge Classics, 2016 edition; https://archive.org/details/impactofscienceo00russ

CHAPTER 2: *The Art of Psychological Warfare*

8. The Art of War, Sun Tzu (6th century BC Chinese military treatise), Filquarian; First Thus edition 2007

CHAPTER 4: *The WHO and the WHAT of Behavior*

9. The Gateway Pundit; https://www.thegatewaypundit.com/2022/10/former-ecohealth-vp-whistleblower-us-govt-trying-cover-origins-covid-19-dr-fauci-us-funding-wuhan-labs-gain-function-research-video/?utm_source=Email&utm_medium=the-gateway-pundit&utm_campaign=dailypm&utm_content=2022-10-24

10. September 12, 2022, Report; https://www.scribd.com/document/601140336/EcoHealth-Whistleblower-Andrew-Huff-Provides-Evidence-that-COVID-19-Was-Created-in-Wuhan-Lab#from_embed

CHAPTER 5: *America Requires an Education Revolution*

11. Encyclopedia.com; https://www.encyclopedia.com/social-sciences/applied-and-social-sciences-magazines/psychology-agency

12. *Crimes of the Educators: How Utopians Are Using Government Schools to Destroy American Children*, Samuel Blumenfeld & Alex Newman, Post Hill Press, 2021; https://libertysentinel.org/books/

13. The Primary-Education Fetich, John Dewey 1898; https://archive.org/details/sim_forum-and-century_1898-05_25_3/page/314/mode/2up

14. *Why Johnny Can't Read: and what you can do about it*, Rudolph Flesch, William Morrow Paperbacks, 1986; https://archive.org/details/whyjohnnycantrea00fles/page/n1/mode/2up

CHAPTER 6: *An Unaware and Compliant Citizenry*

15. An Unaware and Compliant Citizenry; https://newswithviews.com/an-unaware-and-compliant-citizenry/

16. The Effects of Electronic Data Processing in Future Instructional Systems; https://apps.dtic.mil/sti/citations/AD0402646

CHAPTER 7: *Politicized Education*

17. Carnegie Foundation for the Advancement of Teaching; https://www.britannica.com/topic/Carnegie-Foundation-for-the-Advancement-of-Teaching

18. Carnegie Foundation History; https://www.carnegiefoundation.org/about-us/foundation-history/

19. Teachers Insurance and Annuity Association; https://en.wikipedia.org/wiki/TIAA

20. The Carnegie Unit: A Century-old Standard in a Changing Educational Landscape; https://www.carnegiefoundation.org/wp-content/uploads/2015/01/Carnegie_Unit_Report.pdf

21. Mission Statement; https://www.carnegiefoundation.org/about-us/

22. Lesbian-Marxist US Library Boss: School & Libraries for 'Socialist Organizing'; https://www.freedomproject.com/2023/09/13/tnr91323/

CHAPTER 8: *Constructivism Impedes Reality Testing*

23. What Is Constructivism in Education? Piaget's Pros & Cons; https://helpfulprofessor.com/constructivism/

24. K-12: How Constructivism constructs confusion; https://canadafreepress.com/article/k-12-how-constructivism-constructs-confusion

25. *The School and Society*, John Dewey, University of Chicago Press, 1915; https://archive.org/details/schoolsociety00dewerich/page/n7/mode/2up

CHAPTER 9: *Norman Dodd Interview*

26. Carnegie Corporation; https://en.wikipedia.org/wiki/Carnegie_Foundation

27. *Excellence: Can We Be Equal and Excellent Too?*, John W. Gardner, Harper & Row, 1961; https://archive.org/details/excellencecanweb0000gard

28. Norman Dodd was interviewed by G. Edward Griffin; https://www.youtube.com/watch?v=Ig51N62WPt8

29. 1954 Dodd Report; https://archive.org/details/norman-dodd-the-dodd-report/page/1/mode/2up

30. 1982 Dodd Interview; http://www.supremelaw.org/authors/dodd/interview.htm

CHAPTER 10: *Objective Reality Is Required for a Free Society*

31. *Between the Covers: What's Inside a Children's Book?*, Deborah DeGroff, 48 Hour Books, 2021; https://www.whatsinsidechildrensbooks.com/about-the-book/

32. ALA 2012: What's Up with Hi-Lo?; https://www.publishersweekly.com/pw/by-topic/childrens/childrens-industry-news/article/52124-what-s-up-with-hi-lo-ala-2012.html

33. National Assessment of Educational Progress; https://nces.ed.gov/nationsreportcard/pdf/main2009/2010458.pdf

CHAPTER 11: *Critical Race Theory: A Species of the Ideological Thought Genus Marxism*

34. Woke Conference on March 29, 2023; https://www.youtube.com/watch?v=OVZPYQS1dFA

CHAPTER 12: *Seeding Race Wars*

35. Testimony of Dr. Bella Dodd to HUAC in 1953; https://unconstrainedanalytics.org/wp-content/uploads/2019/07/Bella-Dodd-June-July-1953-HUAC-Testimony-1.pdf

36. Parent Guidebook: Fighting Critical Race Theory in K–12 Schools; https://christopherrufo.com/p/crt-parent-guidebook

37. Why Is Critical Race Theory Dangerous for Our Kids?; https://www.blackburn.senate.gov/2021/7/why-is-critical-race-theory-dangerous-for-our-kids

38. Subversive Education; https://www.city-journal.org/critical-race-theory-in-wake-county-nc-schools

CHAPTER 13: *Fomenting Race Wars Begins in Kindergarten*

39. *The Collapsing American Family: From Bonding to Bondage*, Linda Goudsmit, Contrapoint Publishing, 2022; https://www.barnesandnoble.com/w/the-collapsing-american-family-linda-goudsmit/1141049764?ean=9781953255181

40. Perennialism; https://kstatelibraries.pressbooks.pub/dellaperezproject/chapter/chapter-4-perennialism/

41. Preface to John Dewey's Plan to Dumb-Down America; http://alpha-phonics.weebly.com/uploads/2/4/6/5/24650255/181591329-john-dewey-s-plan-to-dumb-down-america-the-primary-education-fetich-forum-1898.pdf

42. Camp Constitution; https://campconstitution.net/mission-statement/

43. Samuel L. Blumenfeld Literacy Foundation; http://alpha-phonics.weebly.com/in-remembrance-of.html

44. Going All In: The NEA pledges to bring critical race theory to a public school near you; https://www.city-journal.org/nea-to-promote-critical-race-theory-in-schools

45. Parent Guidebook: Fighting Critical Race Theory in K–12 Schools; https://christopherrufo.com/p/crt-parent-guidebook

CHAPTER 14: *Changing Hearts and Minds*

46. Discover the Networks: Democratic Socialists of America (DSA); https://www.discoverthenetworks.org/organizations/democratic-socialists-of-america-dsa/

47. *Rules for Radicals: A Pragmatic Primer for Realistic Radicals*, Saul D. Alinsky, Vintage Books Edition 1989; https://ia800309.us.archive.org/30/items/RulesForRadicals/RulesForRadicals.pdf

48. Why BLM Yawns at Police-Shooting Statistics; https://www.frontpagemag.com/why-blm-yawns-police-shooting-statistics-john-perazzo/

CHAPTER 15: *Conflict Theory and the Hegelian Dialectic*

49. Discover the Networks: Karl Marx; https://www.discoverthenetworks.org/individuals/karl-marx/

50. Gramsci, Alinsky & the Left; https://themarketswork.com/2017/02/11/gramsci-alinsky-the-left/

51. Me Generation; https://en.wikipedia.org/wiki/Me_generation

52. The Goal of Political Correctness; https://themarketswork.com/2017/02/16/the-goal-of-political-correctness/

CHAPTER 16: *Ideological Invasion*

53. Gramsci, Alinsky & the Left; https://themarketswork.com/2017/02/11/gramsci-alinsky-the-left/

54. *Pedagogy of the Oppressed*, Paulo Freire, Continuum Publishing Company; 20th Anniversary edition, 1997; https://ia801303.us.archive.org/8/items/PedagogyOfTheOppressed-English-PauloFriere/oppressed.pdf

55. *Anatomy of a Bolshevik*, Alexander G. Markovsky, Published by Alexander Markovsky, 2012; https://www.amazon.com/Anatomy-Bolshevik-Lenin-Explain-Obamas/dp/0988396424/ref=tmm_pap_swatch_0?_encoding=UTF8&qid=&sr=

CHAPTER 17: *Cultural Terrorism Comes to America*

56. The Quiet Revolution: How the New Left Took Over the Democratic Party; https://www.discovery.org/a/24871/

57. *Sexual Behavior in the Human Male*, Alfred C. Kinsey, Wardell B. Pomeroy, Clyde E. Martin, W. B. Saunders Company, 1948; https://archive.org/details/sexualbehaviorin00kins/page/n5/mode/2up

58. *Sexual Behavior in the Human Female*, Alfred C. Kinsey, Wardell B. Pomeroy, Clyde E. Martin, W. B. Saunders Company, Alfred Kinsey, 1953; https://archive.org/details/sexualbehaviorin00inst/page/n5/mode/2up

59. MKULTRA, KINSEY & ROCKEFELLER: Instruments of the New World Order; https://www.thereismaninstitute.org/reisman-articles/2021/1/27/mkultra-kinsey-amp-rockefeller?rq=MKULTRA

60. Weaponizing Children; https://www.americanthinker.com/articles/2022/11/weaponizing_children.html

CHAPTER 18: *American Marxism: The Biden Regime—Obama's Third Term*

61. *The Naked Communist*, W. Cleon Skousen, Waking Lion Press, 1958; https://archive.org/details/B-001-002-046

62. United Nations on September 20, 2016; https://www.youtube.com/watch?v=AzcxT8XOKw4

63. declaration; https://obamawhitehouse.archives.gov/the-press-office/2015/07/16/statement-president-shooting-chattanooga-tn

64. *The Impact of Science on Society*, Bertrand Russell, Simon and Schuster, 1952, Routledge Classics, 2016 edition; https://archive.org/details/impactofscienceo00russ

65. Henry Kissinger remarked; https://rense.com/general11/ksss.htm

66. *Memoirs*, David Rockefeller, Random House, 2002; https://archive.org/details/davidrockefeller00davi

67. David Rockefeller, Bilderberg 1991; https://www.lewrockwell.com/2017/03/no_author/david-rockefellers-chilling-speech-bilderberg/

68. Where Do We Stand on Education for Sustainable Development and Global Citizenship Education; https://unesdoc.unesco.org/ark:/48223/pf0000381362

69. 'Social Justice' Today Grounded in Marxist Communist 'Liberation Theology': https://www.lifeissues.net/writers/irv/irv_246socialjusticecommunist.html

70. *The Communist Manifesto* (1848), Karl Marx, Henry Regnery Company, Gateway Edition, 1965; https://archive.org/details/ComManifesto

CHAPTER 19: *From Sex Education to Sexuality Education*

71. Transforming our world: The 2030 Agenda for Sustainable Development; https://sdgs.un.org/2030agenda

72. Operational Guidance for Comprehensive Sexuality Education (CSE): A

Focus on Human Rights and Gender; https://www.unfpa.org/sites/default/files/pub-pdf/UNFPA_OperationalGuidance_WEB3_0.pdf

73. UN Free & Equal; https://www.unfe.org/about-2/

74. When #YouthLead, anything is possible! and tagline: In a fearless future everyone's an ally. Take a stand with LGBTIQ+ youth!; https://www.unfe.org/youthlead/

75. UNESCO's International Technical Guidance on Sexuality Education (ITGSE) revised edition (2018); https://unfpa.org/sites/default/files/pub-pdf/ITGSE.pdf

76. Health and Education; https://healtheducationresources.unesco.org/toolkit/what-comprehensive-sexuality-education-cse

CHAPTER 20: *In Their Own Words: The Sexual Revolution Begins in Kindergarten*

77. Planned Parenthood; https://www.plannedparenthood.org/about-us/planned-parenthood-global/idea-initiative

78. Problematic Women: Planned Parenthood Ideology 'Killing the Family,' Ex-Volunteer Says; https://www.dailysignal.com/2020/08/20/problematic-women-planned-parenthood-ideology-killing-the-family-ex-volunteer-says/

79. The Future of Sex Education; https://healtheducationresources.unesco.org/organizations/future-sex-education-initiative-fose

80. National Sex Education Standards (Second Edition); https://www.advocatesforyouth.org/wp-content/uploads/2020/03/NSES-2020-web.pdf

81. Wikipedia reports; https://en.wikipedia.org/wiki/SIECUS

82. SIECUS: Sex Ed for Social Change; https://siecus.org/siecus-rebrand-announcement/

83. Sex Education Policy Action Council; https://siecus.org/wp-content/uploads/2022/03/SIECUS-November-2021.pdf

84. The New Discourses Podcast with James Lindsay, Episode 54; https://newdiscourses.com/2021/11/groomer-schools-1-long-cultural-marxist-history-sex-education/

85. CASEL; https://casel.org/systemic-implementation/sel-policy-at-the-federal-level/

86. Systemic Implementation; https://casel.org/systemic-implementation/

87. Transformative Social and Emotional Learning; https://casel.org/fundamentals-of-sel/how-does-sel-support-educational-equity-and-excellence/transformative-sel/

88. Wikipedia; https://en.wikipedia.org/wiki/Drag_Queen_Story_Hour

89. Drag Story Hour; https://www.dragstoryhour.org/

90. Clemson University; https://calendar.clemson.edu/event/drag_storytime

91. The Real Story Behind Drag Queen Story Hour; https://www.city-journal.org/article/the-real-story-behind-drag-queen-story-hour

92. Thinking Sex: Notes for a Radical Theory of the Politics of Sexuality; https://sites.middlebury.edu/sexandsociety/files/2015/01/Rubin-Thinking-Sex.pdf

93. The Age of Consent: The Great Kiddy-Porn Panic of '77; https://www.ipce.info/ipceweb/Library/califa_aoc_text.htm

94. Feminism, Pedophilia, and Children's Rights; https://www.ipce.info/ipceweb/Library/califa_feminism.htm

95. Gender Trouble: Feminism and the Subversion of Identity; https://lauragonzalez.com/TC/BUTLER_gender_trouble.pdf

96. Drag Pedagogy: The Playful Practice of Queer Imagination in Early Childhood; https://doi.org/10.1080/03626784.2020.1864621

CHAPTER 21: *Montessori and Drag Queen Story Hour*

97. American Thinker; https://www.americanthinker.com/articles/2023/01/the_real_purpose_of_drag_queen_story_hour.html

98. Authentic Montessori Education; https://www.authenticmontessorieducation.com/

99. Nurture not Nature; https://www.mindingthecampus.org/2023/06/19/nurture-not-nature/

CHAPTER 22: *What Is Social Justice?*

100. social justice link; https://www.authenticmontessorieducation.com/copy-of-the-solution-authentic-monte

101. Authentic Montessori Education; https://www.authenticmontessorieducation.com

CHAPTER 23: *Legalizing Pedophilia—The Sorensen Report*

102. Stop World Control; https://stopworldcontrol.com/

103. 'Schools must equip children to have sexual partners'—The UN agenda to normalize pedophilia; https://stopworldcontrol.com/children/?inf_contact_key=493ed73c2bce1356ae4f5c08a42d9c9e4dfbc39d7283b2cb89d5189540b69330

104. Archive.org; https://archive.org/

105. International Technical Guidance on Sexual Education; https://www.stopworldcontrol.com/downloads/international-technical-guidance-on-sexuality-education.pdf

106. Comprehensive sexuality education can prevent rapes, unsafe abortions and save lives; https://www.weforum.org/agenda/2019/10/dispelling-the-myths-about-comprehensive-sexuality-education/

107. Rutgers Foundation; https://rutgers.international/

108. About Rutgers; https://rutgers.international/about-rutgers/origins-of-rutgers/

109. sexuality education materials; https://rutgers.international/themes/sexuality-education-and-information/

110. Girl, 6, Performed Oral Sex in Class with Teacher in Room; https://www.freedomproject.com/2023/05/09/tnr5923/

CHAPTER 24: *The Politics of Pronouns*

111. How to Use Gender-Neutral Language at Work and in Life; https://www.grammarly.com/blog/gender-neutral-language/

112. Bloomberg; https://www.bloomberg.com/news/articles/2021-11-18/grammar-checking-app-is-now-the-10th-most-valuable-u-s-startup#xj4y7vzkg

113. Statista reported; https://www.statista.com/statistics/891292/assets-under-management-blackrock/

114. Capital.com; https://capital.com/blackrock-shareholder-who-owns-most-blk-stock

115. responsible; https://www.grammarly.com/responsible-ai

116. Who Owns Corporate America; https://stevenjsands.com/who-owns-corporate-america/

CHAPTER 25: *Philanthrocapitalism and Collectivism*

117. Who Owns Corporate America; https://stevenjsands.com/who-owns-corporate-america/

118. *Philanthropic Capitalism: How the Rich Can Save the World*; Matthew Bishop and Michael Green, Bloomsbury Press; Reprint edition, 2009; https://archive.org/details/philanthrocapita00matt

CHAPTER 26: *Pronouns and Publishing*

119. https://www.cairn-int.info/abstract-E_POX_121_0029–philanthroca pitalism-and-crimes-of-the.htm

120. A Woke Children's Literature Cabal Is Conditioning Your Kid to Be an Obedient Leftist; https://thefederalist.com/2023/07/13/a-woke-childrens-literature-cabal-is-conditioning-your-kid-to-be-an-obedient-leftist/

CHAPTER 27: *Pronouns and Pantheism*

121. And Life Is Over There; https://commons.wikimedia.org/wiki/File:Femmy_Otten,_%27And_Life_Is_Over_There%27_(DSCF1304).tif#/media/File:Femmy_Otten,_'And_Life_Is_Over_There'_(DSCF1304).tif

122. press release; https://www.stroom.nl/nl/kor/project.php?pr_id=4355555

123. Gender Identity, Transgender Issues in Public Schools; https://www.thereismaninstitute.org/law-articles/2019/2/20/gender-identity-transgender-issues-in-public-schools

CHAPTER 28: *Pantheism, Gnosticism, and Marxism*

124. Gnosticism, the Heretical Gnostic Writings, and 'Judas'; http://www.lifeissues.net/writers/irv/irv_121gnosticism1.html

125. *The Collapsing American Family: From Bonding to Bondage*, Linda Goudsmit, Contrapoint Publishing, 2022; https://www.barnesandnoble.com/w/the-collapsing-american-family-linda-goudsmit/1141049764?ean=9781953255181

CHAPTER 29: *Gnosticism, the Frankfurt School, and Freirean Education*

126. The Frankfurt School: Conspiracy to Corrupt; http://www.judeochristianamerica.org/ConsReading/The-Frankfurt-School-Timothy-Matthews.pdf

127. *The Politics of Education: Culture, Power, and Liberation*, Paulo Freire, Bergin & Garvey, 1985; https://archive.org/details/politicsofeducat00frei_1

128. The Marxification of Education: Paulo Freire's Critical Marxism and the Theft of American Education, James Lindsay, New Discourses, 2022; https://newdiscourses.com/2022/12/introducing-the-marxification-of-education/

129. Brainwashing: The Ultimate Weapon; https://usa-anti-communist.com/pdf1/Mayer_Brainwashing_Ultimate_Weapon/Brainwashing_The_Ultimate_Weapon-Major_William_E_Mayer-Oct4_1956.pdf

130. Code of Conduct for Members of the Armed Forces of the United States; https://www.presidency.ucsb.edu/documents/executive-order-10631-code-conduct-for-members-the-armed-forces-the-united-states

131. Parental Guidebook, Fighting Critical Race Theory in K–12 Schools; https://christopherrufo.com/p/crt-parent-guidebook

CHAPTER 30: *Marxist Past, Present, and Future*

132. Intersectionality Is American Maoism; https://newdiscourses.com/2023/05/intersectionality-is-american-maoism/

CHAPTER 31: *Marxism, Gnosticism, and Transgenderism*

133. The Gnostic Temptation; https://newdiscourses.com/2023/08/the-gnostic-temptation/?utm_source=BenchmarkEmail&utm_campaign=ND_-_8-3-23_-_The_Gnostic_Temptation&utm_medium=email

134. The Gnostic Roots of the Trans Movement; https://thinkingwest.
com/2022/01/17/gnostic-roots-of-trans-movements/#:~:text=Like%20
transgenderism%2C%20much%20of%20transhumanist%20thought%20is%20
rooted,seek%20to%20augment%20or%20transcend%20natural%20human%20
evolution.

135. *Lost in Trans Nation: A Child Psychiatrist's Guide Out of the Madness*, Miriam
Grossman, Skyhorse Publishing, 2023; https://www.miriamgrossmanmd.com/
about-4-2

136. Sexuality and Gender: Findings from the Biological, Psychological, and Social
Sciences; https://www.thenewatlantis.com/publications/introduction-sexuality-
and-gender

137. Born This Way"? New Study Debunks LGBT Claims; https://patriotpost.us/
articles/44470-born-this-way-new-study-debunks-lgbt-claims-2016-08-25

138. The Business of Transgenderism; https://christopherrufo.com/p/the-
business-of-transgenderism

CHAPTER 32: *Transhumanism, Big Lies, and the Great Reset*

139. What is transhumanism and how does it affect you?; https://www.weforum.
org/agenda/2018/04/transhumanism-advances-in-technology-could-already-put-
evolution-into-hyperdrive-but-should-they/

140. Why we need the 'Davos Manifesto' for a better kind of capitalism; https://
www.weforum.org/agenda/2019/12/why-we-need-the-davos-manifesto-for-better-
kind-of-capitalism/

141. The Davos Manifesto 2020: The Universal Purpose of a Company in the
Fourth Industrial Revolution; https://www.weforum.org/agenda/2019/12/
davos-manifesto-2020-the-universal-purpose-of-a-company-in-the-fourth-industrial-
revolution/

142. The Fourth Industrial Revolution: what it means, and how to respond;
https://www.weforum.org/agenda/2016/01/the-fourth-industrial-revolution-what-
it-means-and-how-to-respond/

143. website; https://www.weforum.org/about/world-economic-forum

144. Davos Agenda 2021; https://www.weforum.org/events/the-davos-agenda-2021/

145. What is stakeholder capitalism?; https://www.weforum.org/agenda/2021/01/klaus-schwab-on-what-is-stakeholder-capitalism-history-relevance/

146. What Is the Great Reset?; https://www.michaelrectenwald.com/great-reset-essays-interviews/what-is-the-great-reset

CHAPTER 33: *Weaponizing Children: The Gospel of Yuval Harari*

147. Historical Inevitability, Isaiah Berlin, Oxford University Press, 1955; https://archive.org/details/historicalinevit0000unse_n1/page/n3/mode/2up

148. World Economic Forum's Annual Meeting in Davos, January 24, 2020; https://www.weforum.org/agenda/2020/01/yuval-hararis-warning-davos-speech-future-predications/

149. Unstoppable Us: How Humans Took Over the World (The Gospel of Harari for Children); https://www.whatsinsidechildrensbooks.com/articles/unstoppable-us-how-humans-took-over-the-world-the-gospel-of-harari-for-children/

CHAPTER 34: *In a World Obsessed with Feelings, Whose Feelings Matter?*

150. National Education Association; https://www.influencewatch.org/labor-union/national-education-association-nea/

151. Whose Children? Our Children; http://www.danielgreenfield.org/2023/03/whose-children-our-children.html?utm_source=MadMimi&utm_medium=email&utm_content=Daniel+Greenfield+Article:+Whose+Children?+Our+Children&utm_campaign=20230331_m172639745_Daniel+Greenfield+Article:+(post_title)&utm_term=Whose+Children_3F+Our+Children

CHAPTER 35: *Artificial Intelligence and America's Children*

152. Hacking Humanity: Transhumanism, The Great Reset and the Struggle for Liberty: Unraveling the Global Agenda, Michael Rectenwald, World Encounter Institute, 2023; https://mises.org/wire/hacking-humanity-transhumanism

153. Farewell Address; https://wp.lps.org/kbeacom/files/2012/08/Eisenhowers-Farewell.pdf

154. *School World Order: The Technocratic Globalization of Corporatized Education*, John Klyczek, Trine Day LLC, 2019; https://www.schoolworldorder.info/

155. Moxie and the Great Reset: How Moxie the Robot Uses GPT AI to Data-Mine Your Kids' Socioemotional-Learning Algorithms; https://www.bitchute.com/video/xJhbwYfyvNUG/

156. Whole School, Whole Community, Whole Child; https://www.cdc.gov/healthyschools/wscc/index.htm

157. shapeamerica.org; https://www.shapeamerica.org/

158. National Sex Education Standards; https://www.shapeamerica.org/Common/Uploaded files/uploads/2021/standards/National-Sex-Education-Standards.pdf

159. *Lost in Trans Nation: A Child Psychiatrist's Guide Out of the Madness*, Miriam Grossman, Skyhorse Publishing, 2023; https://www.miriamgrossmanmd.com/about-4-2

CHAPTER 36: *"When They Say 'We're Coming for Your Children,' Believe Them"*

160. When They Say 'We're Coming for Your Children,' Believe Them; https://www.theepochtimes.com/opinion/barbara-kay-when-they-say-were-coming-for-your-children-believe-them-2-post-5384901

161. Dr. Cretella on Transgenderism: A Mental Illness Is Not a Civil Right; https://tfpstudentaction.org/blog/dr-michelle-cretella-on-transgender-ideology

162. Alfred Kinsey: The Father of Modern Deviancy; https://www.realityslaststand.com/p/alfred-kinsey-the-father-of-modern

CHAPTER 37: *Euphemisms, Propaganda, and "Losing Reality Bit by Bit"*

163. *Lost in Trans Nation: A Child Psychiatrist's Guide Out of the Madness*, Miriam Grossman, Skyhorse Publishing, 2023; https://www.miriamgrossmanmd.com/about-4-2

164. Employee health insurance, Obamacare make sex change a new reality for 1.4 million Americans; https://www.cnbc.com/2018/03/27/work-health-insurance-obamacare-coverage-spur-sex-change-surgery-boom.html

165. Sex Reassignment Surgery Market to hit USD 1.5 Bn by 2026: Global Market Insights, Inc; https://www.globenewswire.com/news-release/2020/03/31/2009112/0/en/Sex-Reassignment-Surgery-Market-to-hit-USD-1-5-Bn-by-2026-Global-Market-Insights-Inc.html

166. *One Idea to Rule Them All: Reverse Engineering American Propaganda*, Michelle Stiles, 2022; https://smartsheepe.com/

167. *The Crowd: A Study of the Popular Mind*, Gustave Le Bon, Dover Publications, 1895; https://archive.org/details/the-crowd-a-study-of-the-popular-mind-by-gustave-le-bon

168. *Propaganda*, Edward Bernays, Horace Liveright, 1928; https://archive.org/details/BernaysPropaganda

CHAPTER 38: *BigBrain, BICAN, and "The Evil Twins of Technocracy and Transhumanism"*

169. Gen Z Traded Church for 'A New Religion,' Faith Leaders Say; https://dailycaller.com/2023/04/08/gen-z-church-new-religion-faith-leaders/

170. The Evil Twins of Transhumanism and Technocracy, https://www.technocracy. news/the-evil-twins-of-transhumanism-and-technocracy/

171. Human Brain Project; https://www.humanbrainproject.eu/en/

172. website; https://bigbrainproject.org/

173. Helmholtz Association; https://www.helmholtz.de/en/about-us/structure-and-governance/

174. BigBrain Project; https://bigbrainproject.org/partners.html

175. HIBALL; https://bigbrainproject.org/hiball.html

176. Science; https://www.science.org/content/article/nihs-brain-initiative-puts-dollar500-million-creating-detailed-ever-human-brain-atlas

177. *The Evil Twins of Transhumanism and Technocracy*, Patrick M. Wood, Coherent Publishing, 2022; https://www.technocracy.news/store/

CHAPTER 39: *Cognitive Warfare and the Battle for Your Brain*

178. Behind NATO's 'cognitive warfare': 'Battle for your brain' waged by Western militaries; https://thegrayzone.com/2021/10/08/nato-cognitive-warfare-brain/

CHAPTER 40: *The Art of Using Technologies to Alter Human Cognition*

179. Electronic Communication Systems: Basics, Block Diagram and Working; https://www.chetanselwal.com/post/electronic-communication-systems-basics-block-diagram-and-working

180. *We Are Electric*, Sally Adee, Hachette Books, 2023; https://www.sally80.com/we-are-electric-vertical

181. Origins of Gunpowder: An Historical Perspective; https://gunmagwarehouse.com/blog/origins-of-gunpowder-an-historical-perspective/

182. January 10, 2016, interview; https://www.youtube.com/watch?v=UmQNA0HL1pw&t=22s

CHAPTER 41: *Your Brain Is the Battlespace*

183. *Between Two Ages: America's Role in the Technetronic Era*, Zbigniew Brzezinski, Viking Press, 1970; https://archive.org/details/B-001-003-798

184. Brain Science from Bench to Battlefield: The Realities—and Risks—of Neuroweapons; https://www.youtube.com/watch?v=aUtQbriWt64

185. There's a Secret Network - Skynet 2.0; https://www.youtube.com/watch?v=K6HCgBzhibU

186. Skynet 2024: The Infrastructure is Complete!; https://www.youtube.com/watch?v=9xPjIfJI5Jk&t=2s

187. The Internet of Bodies ecosystem may lead to the Internet of Brains sometime between 2035 and 2050; https://www.technocracy.news/rand-corporation-internet-of-bodies-may-lead-to-internet-of-brains-by-2050/

CHAPTER 42: *Quantum Computing Empowers Technocracy, Transhumanism, and the Managerial Unistate*

188. RCR Wireless News; https://www.rcrwireless.com/20190424/5g/6g-physical-digital-biological

189. TechTarget.com; https://www.techtarget.com/whatis/definition/augmented-reality-AR

190. White Paper: 5G Evolution and 6G; https://www.docomo.ne.jp/english/binary/pdf/corporate/technology/whitepaper_6g/DOCOMO_6G_White_PaperEN_20200124.pdf

191. February 2010 TED Talks; https://www.ted.com/talks/bill_gates_innovating_to_zero

192. World Population Clock; https://www.worldometers.info/world-population/

193. Quantum Computers Could Solve Countless Problems—And Create a Lot of New Ones; https://time.com/6249784/quantum-computing-revolution/#:~:text=Complex%20problems%20that%20currently%20take,climate%20change%20and%20food%20security

194. Yahoo Finance; https://finance.yahoo.com/quote/AAPL/holders

195. Atom Computing; https://atom-computing.com/quantum-startup-atom-computing-first-to-exceed-1000-qubits/

196. Entropica Labs; https://entropicalabs.medium.com/entropica-labs-and-atom-computing-announce-strategic-partnership-e6e3d0d39b8f

CHAPTER 43: *Ideological Subversion, Communitarianism, and the 15-Minute City*

197. 1984 interview; https://www.youtube.com/watch?v=bX3EZCVj2XA&t=5s

198. defined; https://www.jerseyconservative.org/blog/2021/1/30/in-1984-yuri-bezmenov-explained-why-this-would-happen-today

199. *Behind the Green Mask: U.N. Agenda 21*, Rosa Koire, The Post Sustainability Press; First edition, 2011; https://archive.org/details/behind-the-green-mask-u.-n.-agenda-21

200. Rosa Koire: "Agenda 21" Open Mind Conference 2013; https://www.youtube.com/watch?v=SuSLrchSL7M&t=99s

201. Rosa Koire: UN Agenda 2030 exposed; https://www.youtube.com/watch?v=3PrY7nFbwAY

202. Wildlands Project; https://nwri.org/the-wildlands-project/background-on-the-wildlands-project/

203. Vigilant News; https://vigilantnews.com/post/go-to-hell-brave-eu-politician-delivers-damning-message-to-the-global-tyrants

204. Joel Sussman's videotaped statement; https://www.youtube.com/watch?v=4u3q83MTuVg

CHAPTER 44: *The American Reformation*

205. *The Impact of Science on Society*, Bertrand Russell, Simon and Schuster, 1952, Routledge Classics, 2016 edition; https://archive.org/details/impactofscienceo00russ; https://archive.org/details/impactofscienceo00russ

CHAPTER 45: *Every Conspiracy Begins with a Theory*

206. National Archives; https://www.archives.gov/founding-docs/bill-of-rights/what-does-it-say

207. *Memoirs*, David Rockefeller, Random House, 2002; https://archive.org/details/davidrockefeller00davi

208. Bilderberg 1991; https://www.lewrockwell.com/2017/03/no_author/david-rockefellers-chilling-speech-bilderberg/

AUTHOR BIO

Linda Goudsmit is the devoted wife of Rob and they are the parents of four children and the grandparents of four. She and Rob owned and operated a girls' clothing store in Michigan for forty years before retiring to the sunny beaches of Florida. A graduate of the University of Michigan in Ann Arbor, Linda has a lifelong commitment to learning and is an avid reader and observer of life. She is the author of the philosophy book *Dear America: Who's Driving the Bus?* and its political sequel, *The Book of Humanitarian Hoaxes: Killing America with 'Kindness'*, along with numerous current affairs articles featured on her websites lindagoudsmit. com and goudsmit.pundicity.com. *The Collapsing American Family: From Bonding to Bondage* and her newest book, *Space Is No Longer the Final Frontier—Reality Is*, complete Linda's quadrangle of insightful books that connect the philosophical, ideological, political, and psychological dots of globalism's War on America and individual sovereignty.

Linda believes the future of our nation requires reviving individualism, restoring meritocracy, and teaching critical-thinking skills to children again. Her illustrated children's book series, *Mimi's Strategy*, offers youngsters new and exciting ways of solving their problems and having their needs met. Mrs. Goudsmit believes that learning to think strategically rather than reacting emotionally is a valuable skill that will empower any child throughout his or her life. Plus, in Linda's words, "I have yet to meet the child who would prefer a reprimand to a kiss."

BOOKS BY LINDA GOUDSMIT

Philosophy/Political science

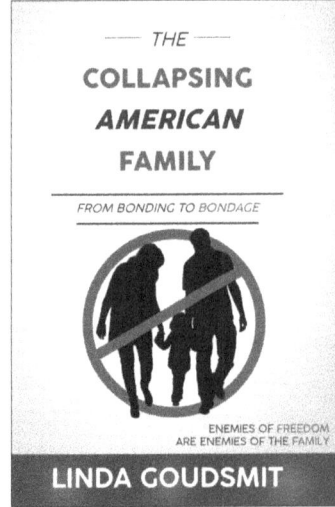

DEAR AMERICA
WHO'S DRIVING THE BUS?

LINDA GOUDSMIT

---- THE ----
BOOK OF
HUMANITARIAN
HOAXES

KILLING AMERICA WITH 'KINDNESS'

50
OF THE MOST
SINISTER LEFTIST,
ISLAMIST, GLOBALIST
INTERCONNECTING
ATTACKS ON AMERICA

LINDA GOUDSMIT

---- THE ----
COLLAPSING
AMERICAN
FAMILY

FROM BONDING TO BONDAGE

ENEMIES OF FREEDOM
ARE ENEMIES OF THE FAMILY

LINDA GOUDSMIT

Children's Book Series

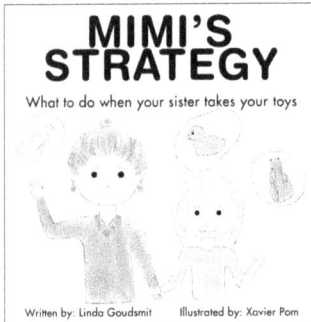

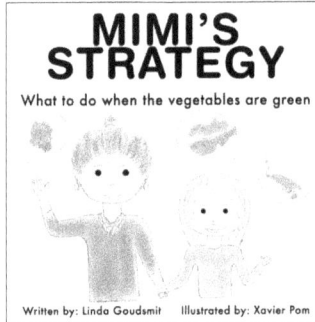

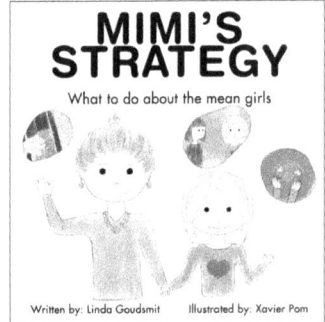

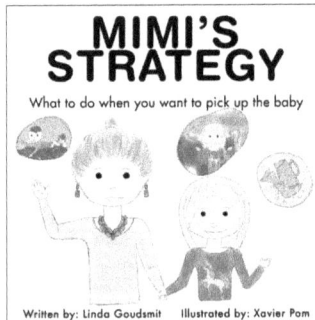

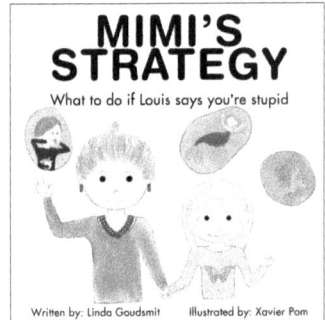

MIMI'S STRATEGY
What to do when your sister takes your toys

Written by: Linda Goudsmit   Illustrated by: Xavier Pom

MIMI'S STRATEGY
What to do when the vegetables are green

Written by: Linda Goudsmit   Illustrated by: Xavier Pom

MIMI'S STRATEGY
What to do about the mean girls

Written by: Linda Goudsmit   Illustrated by: Xavier Pom

MIMI'S STRATEGY
What to do when you have a bad dream

Written by: Linda Goudsmit   Illustrated by: Xavier Pom

MIMI'S STRATEGY
What to do when you want to pick up the baby

Written by: Linda Goudsmit   Illustrated by: Xavier Pom

MIMI'S STRATEGY
What to do if Louis says you're stupid

Written by: Linda Goudsmit   Illustrated by: Xavier Pom

MIMI'S STRATEGY
What to do about your imaginary friend

Written by: Linda Goudsmit   Illustrated by: Xavier Pom

MIMI'S STRATEGY
What to do when your birdie dies

Written by: Linda Goudsmit   Illustrated by: Xavier Pom

MIMI'S STRATEGY
What to do about telling tall tales

Written by: Linda Goudsmit   Illustrated by: Xavier Pom

MIMI'S STRATEGY
What to do when you want one more story

Written by: Linda Goudsmit   Illustrated by: Xavier Pom

MIMI'S STRATEGY
What to do when Mimi goes home

Written by: Linda Goudsmit   Illustrated by: Xavier Pom

MIMI'S STRATEGY
What to do when your best friend moves away

Written by: Linda Goudsmit   Illustrated by: Xavier Pom

MIMI'S STRATEGY
When you don't want to go to the dentist

Written by: Linda Goudsmit   Illustrated by: Xavier Pom

MIMI'S STRATEGY
When Mama has Hanukkah and Papa has Christmas

Written by: Linda Goudsmit   Illustrated by: Xavier Pom

MIMI'S STRATEGY
Remembering the difference between trying and doing

Written by: Linda Goudsmit   Illustrated by: Xavier Pom

MIMI'S STRATEGY
When you don't want to practice the piano

Written by: Linda Goudsmit   Illustrated by: Xavier Pom

www.ingramcontent.com/pod-product-compliance
Lightning Source LLC
Chambersburg PA
CBHW052106030426

42335CB00025B/2866

* 9 7 8 1 9 5 3 2 5 5 2 7 3 *